Representing Reality

£18. 50

REPRESENTING REALITY

Issues and Concepts in Documentary

BILL NICHOLS

INDIANA UNIVERSITY PRESS

Bloomington and Indianapolis

The paper used in this publication meets the minimum requirements of American
National Standard for Information Sciences—Permanence of Paper for Printed
Library Materials, ANSI Z39.48–1984.

Manufactured in the United States of America

Library of Congress Cataloging-in-Publication Data

Nichols, Bill.
 Representing reality : issues and concepts in documentary / Bill Nichols.
  p. cm.
 Includes bibliographical references and index.
 ISBN 0–253–34060–8 (alk. paper). — ISBN 0–253–20681–2 (pbk. :
alk. paper).
 1. Documentary films—History and criticism. I. Title.
PN1995.9.D6N54 1991
070.1'8—dc20   91–2637

4 5 6 7   99 98 97 96

Dedicated to the memory of
Emile de Antonio (1920–1989)
and Joris Ivens (1898–1989)

CONTENTS

Axes of Orientation

Documentary: A Fiction (Un)Like Any Other

Documentary Representation and the Historical World

PREFACE

The pleasure and appeal of documentary film lies in its ability to make us see timely issues in need of attention, literally. We see views of the world, and what they put before us are social issues and cultural values, current problems and possible solutions, actual situations and specific ways of representing them. The linkage between documentary and the historical world is the most distinctive feature of this tradition. Utilizing the capacities of sound recording and cinematography to reproduce the physical appearance of things, documentary film contributes to the formation of popular memory. It proposes perspectives on and interpretations of historic issues, processes, and events.

Representing Reality examines the styles, strategies, and structures of documentary film. It does not offer a general survey of documentary film history so much as a conceptual overview of the form itself: what qualities of cinema underpin it, what institutional structures sustain it, what rhetorical operations inform it, what interpretive perspectives encompass it. How these questions arrange themselves into recurrent patterns and preoccupations will be the central focus. A comparable work does not yet exist in the field of documentary film although there are many such works for fiction film. I have drawn heavily from work done on narrative, rhetoric, and realism, and on ideology, power, and knowledge as it applies to documentary film.

Remarkably, the last wave of single-author books on documentary film occurred fifteen years ago.[1] Films made since the early 1970s address new issues and adopt new approaches in form. Observational styles of filmmaking no longer dominate. Interview-based histories, reflexive, experimental, and personal documentaries, often with strong elements of narrative structure, have established themselves as viable subgenres. New topics and issues such as the women's movement; gay and lesbian rights; the environment; ethnicity, race, class, and nationality; multinational corporations; AIDS; homelessness; and conflicts in Central America, southern Africa, and the Middle East are the subject of numerous documentaries and special television reports. The documentary representation of these issues deserves critical attention as well. The absence of a book-length study of documentary film form remains a glaring omission in the fields of journalism, film, media, and cultural studies.

The status of documentary film as *evidence from* the world legitimates its usage as a source of knowledge. The visible evidence it provides underpins its value for social advocacy and news reporting. Documentaries show us situations and events that are recognizably part of a realm of shared experience: the historical world as we know and encounter it, or as we believe others to encounter it. Documentaries provoke or encourage response, shape attitudes and assumptions. When documentary films are at their best, a sense of urgency brushes aside our efforts to contemplate form or analyze rhetoric. Such films and their derivatives (television news and advertising, political campaign messages, propaganda and pornography) have a powerful, pervasive impact.

The status of documentary as *discourse about* the world draws less widespread attention. Documentaries offer pleasure and appeal while their own structure remains virtually invisible, their own rhetorical strategies and stylistic choices largely unnoticed. "A good documentary stimulates discussion about its subject, not itself." This serves as many a documentarist's motto, but it neglects to indicate how crucial rhetoric and form are to the realization of this goal. Despite such a motto, documentary films raise a rich array of historiographic, legal, philosophic, ethical, political, and aesthetic issues. It is the patterns and preoccupations surrounding these issues that *Representing Reality* addresses.

Questions of structure and style alter and evolve, shift and adapt to changing social conditions, to the quasi-autonomous history of the documentary film genre, as well as to the immediate contingencies posed during the act of filming itself. It is the choices available for representing any given situation or event—choices involving commentary and interviews, observation and editing, the contextualization and juxtaposition of scenes—that raise historiographic, ethical, and aesthetic issues in forms that are distinct to documentary. What relationship between knowledge and pleasure does documentary film propose that differs from narrative fiction? How shall oral histories or expert testimony be used? What criteria should be brought to bear to govern objectivity, the selection and arrangement of facts, voices of authentication, and interpretive procedure? What are the responsibilities of filmmakers to their audience and their subjects? How should they account for their own presence and effect, not only behind the camera but also in front of other people, as they build confidences that might be subsequently betrayed?

The absence of a substantial body of work engaged with these issues strikes me as remarkable. Despite the significant degree of commitment to a cinema of political contestation and social transformation among both filmmakers and critics since the late 1960s, the most explicitly political film form, documentary, has received negligible attention compared to the enormous outpouring of work on narrative fiction. The rise of academic film studies within the context of literature and the humanities rather than sociology and the social sciences has considerable bearing, but so does the popular disposition to associate movies with feature fiction films and to associate feature fiction with questions of art, entertainment, and its effects. (A moment in Robert Aldrich's *The Legend of Lylah Claire* when the producer played by Ernest Borgnine rails against a reference to the "films" he has made captures this disposition perfectly: "Films! Films! Whatever the hell happened to movies!? . . . Remember I make *movies, not films!*")

This leaves the study of contemporary documentary film something of a *terra incognita* in film criticism, especially in conceptual or theoretical terms. (Several have helped begin charting this terrain in recent articles and anthologies, among them Julianne Burton, Stuart Cunningham, E. Ann Kaplan, Julia Lesage, Eileen McGarry, David MacDougall, Peter Morris, Joyce Nelson, Michael Renov, Alan Rosenthal, Jay Ruby, Vivian Sobchack, Tom Waugh, and Brian Winston.[2] Far too often we assume that documentary is simply a disguised fiction, a form of narrative, like written histories, that makes special claims for its authority by minimizing its fictive aspects. All too frequently, the categories and criteria adopted for narrative film analysis are assumed to be readily transferable to documentary, with, perhaps, some minor adjustments. The pathologies of scopophilia (voyeurism, fetishism, narcissism, etc.) may not organize the representation of women quite so relentlessly as in the work of Hitchcock, but the camera's gaze can still be treated as gendered and fully implicated in questions of desire as well as control. Little, though, has been done to spell out how this might be so or in what ways a documentary gaze may raise questions quite distinct from those of a fictional one.

For this reason *Representing Reality* does not go as far as I originally planned in discussing specific films, in examining the full range of issues taken up by recent, more reflexive documentaries, in comparing and contrasting documentary work from different countries and regions of the globe, or in tracing the development of particular filmmakers, styles, techniques, or rhetorical strategies. What loomed as more urgent, and fundamental, was gaining purchase on documentary filmmaking as a distinct form of cinema (or the movies), with problems and pleasures of its own. Terms and tools of analysis did not lie readily at hand. Truth; reality; objectivity; uncontrolled cinema; living cinema; direct cinema; cinema verité; categorical, rhetorical, abstract, and associational formal systems (the last four come from an introductory film textbook, Bordwell and Thompson's *Film Art*) : such terms raise as many problems as they solve.

The impulse to pursue the path toward a theory of documentary film practice is frequently cut off at the knees by the reflex reaction that documentary is a fiction like any other—it's just more ashamed of the company it keeps and tries to hide it—or that documentary is a genre like any other and we have all the concepts needed to categorize, analyze, historicize, or contextualize it (even though the concept of film genre itself remains ill-defined). A major goal of this book is to suggest that truisms such as these mask as much as they reveal, that *differences*—if not distinctions—from fictional narrative are as crucial to documentary as to the experimental film tradition, and that we may have quite a long way to go before these differences can be put in the form of comprehensive, coherent propositions with sufficient explanatory power to leave the inquiring mind content. Such propositions would form the basis for a documentary film theory, and my hope is that this book helps formulate at least some of them as well as some of the terms and concepts needed for analyzing individual documentary films.

Representing Reality, then, could be called an attempt to establish a theory of documentary film, but I am somewhat uncomfortable with how the word "theory" is commonly used in film study. *Representing Reality* is not the importation of a previously existing body of theoretical (often nonfalsifiable) concepts, priorities, and procedures which are then applied to film. This exercise serves to demonstrate (1) the power of the preexisting theory (it can tell us things about cinema), (2) the validity of the application (the analysis conforms to the guiding presuppositions of the theory), and (3) the theoretical credentials of the author (the ability to mobilize and apply a preexisting theory promotes one to the ranks of cinematic theoretician).

This somewhat tautological exercise has become the standard form of film theory today. Its time has passed.[3] The early application of semiotics, structuralism, poststructuralism, contemporary Marxist theory, psychoanalysis, deconstruction, formalism, phenomenology, and feminist theory had great value. It provided an enormous arsenal of interpretive tools and conceptual models. It galvanized an entire generation of film scholars. It opened up new levels of formal complexity in cinema and helped us better understand film in social, sexual, and political terms. It made theory an indispensable part of the film study enterprise. But it has also tended to lump films together under the rubric of pervasive "effects" or to treat specific works as symptomatic examples of larger issues.[4] These applications have had an enormous impact, but they have not contributed quite as much to a *film* theory as we might wish. They have not significantly increased the number of concepts available to critics and filmmakers alike beyond what we had in the early 1960s. And many areas or issues—documentary but also experimental film; cross-cultural representation (versus the old chestnut of "national cinemas"); viewer response; and historical analysis—stand neglected or undertheorized. Psychoanalysis, for example, though a boon to feminist film theory and criticism, has proven generally unhelpful in addressing issues of historical placement and questions posed by women of color; semiotics has not contributed useful tools for exploring cross-cultural representation or viewer response.

For these reasons my goal is not to import a theory and show that it will work for documentary (by aiming at those aspects of documentary pertinent to the strengths and emphases of the theory), but neither is it to coin interpretive tools (concepts like modes of documentary production, typologies of interview forms and indexical anchorage, or three axes of bodily representation) in a theoretical vacuum. Documentary film theory should be capable of addressing the full range of documentary film practice, the entire structure and all the elements of a given work, both recent and antecedent films and the relations between them. It may, as narrative theory has, concentrate on certain pertinent features or symptomatic conditions, but if it can only address instances where the gaze, the fetish, or problems of expository closure come to the fore documentary theory will be incomplete. Explicit argument on behalf of a set of overarching propositions that have extensiveness (they cover the subject of study, possibly more, but not less), internal consistency (including not only logical consistency but also categories and distinctions that have analytic value and explanatory power), historical awareness, and a clear sense of purpose make a theory more than a critical method (which can be put into practice without formulating the underlying theoretical presuppositions). Few works of film study are theoretical in this sense.

Of course, I am loath to withdraw this book from nomination to the ranks of theory just because it does not do what many works of film theory do. The perception that one is "doing theory" has considerable symbolic and perhaps even economic exchange value in the academic marketplace. (Ironically, it seems to carry inverse exchange value in the larger market of the general reading public and nonacademic reviewing.) When asked by friends and acquaintances to describe this book, I avoid calling it a work of cultural theory ("Oh, you mean something like Einstein's relativity theory?"), or a poetics ("Oh, I didn't know you could write a whole book in verse"), or an anatomy of documentary criticism ("Oh . . . ?"). Most often I say it is about issues and concepts in documentary: different ways of making documentaries, the kinds of claims they make about society, the effects they have, and so on. Though "theory" or "poetics" would be helpful labels in other contexts, I do not intend a poetics of the neoformalist sort nor a theory that remains out of reach or unhelpful to filmmakers and nonspecialists in film theory as it is conventionally practiced.

To theorize is to generalize and yet documentary, like the individual work of fiction, holds theory at bay. We cannot generalize about "all documentary" and say anything that is not subject to modification, subversion, or overthrow in a given text. We cannot speak generally, ignoring the specific, material effects of individual texts, and say anything that will address the heart of the matter. Film in general and documentary in particular does not even have that convenient level of abstraction available to spoken and written language where words ("hope," "umbrella," "garden") leave the provision of a specific referent to the imagination. Film signifiers come with images attached. They *are* images, and sounds, and they are always concrete, material, and specific. What films have to say about the enduring human condition or about the pressing issues of the day can never be separated from *how* they say it, how this saying moves and affects us, how we engage with a work, not with a theory of it. Most contemporary theory is quite deficient in addressing this level of affect—though not its ideological or symptomatic effects.

Representing Reality deals with meanings and values, interpretations and purposes, not simply with signs and systems. That material practices like

documentary film production and consumption are self-perpetuating domains caught up in the very webs of signification they also address may
disqualify them as objects of scientific study (in the Popperian sense where
we formulate falsifiable hypotheses about external processes), but it hardly
spares us from their affective consequences. The values we uphold, the
meanings we assign, the interpretations we offer, and the purposes we
pursue have consequences. They make things happen. Being unaware of
underlying presuppositions, being unable to formulate them in theoretical
terms, makes little difference to their efficacy.

If this book be theory, it is so in the sense of seeking to make more
conscious and explicit what documentary is and does. It is *not* an attempt
to subsume all documentary films to governing rules, laws, or formulas. It
is not an attempt to corral all individual films as examples of what they
"merely" embody, nor an attempt to prescribe what ought to be done or
proscribe what ought not. It is an attempt to locate and identify the ways
and means by which specific films have an effect and to propose categories,
concepts, and issues that help us see how they do so more clearly. Films do
not answer to theory, but theory must answer to film—if it is to be more
than idle speculation.

In overview, *Representing Reality* has a three-part structure, arranged in an
ascending order of complexity. Early chapters establish some of the concepts and terms that should prove useful to more advanced work. The latter
chapters, more contentious, try to assess problems and tendencies within a
broadly political perspective.

Part 1, "Axes of Orientation," attempts to give the field of documentary
film production a greater sense of definition. It addresses the following
topics.

Chapter 1, "The Domain of Documentary," takes up the problems of
defining a form of filmmaking that makes distinct claims about its relationship to the historical world but cannot be cleanly separated from the
strategies of narrative or the fascination of fiction. Institutional, textual,
and audience-based definitions are examined.

In chapter 2, "Documentary Modes of Representation," four major
modes of representation receive consideration: expository (classic "voice-
of-God" commentaries, for example); observational (which minimizes the
filmmaker's presence); interactive (where the filmmaker and social actors
acknowledge one another overtly in conversation, participatory actions, or
interviews), and reflexive (where the filmmaker draws the viewer's attention to the form of the work itself). Some of the philosophic, social, and
aesthetic implications of each mode are drawn out.

Chapter 3, "Axiographics: Ethical Space in Documentary Film," examines how each of these modes of representation establishes a different set
of ethical challenges and constraints. The representation of social actors
involves the use of people (rather than professional actors) whose lives may
be permanently altered by the process. The filmmaker's presence—or

feigned absence—carries significant implications. The organization of cinematic space (the placement of the filmmaker, the camera's proximity to subjects, the exclusion or inclusion of contextual information) becomes the principal means by which ethical issues concretely manifest themselves in documentary filmmaking. Historical place becomes ethical space. Specific films such as *Model, Streetwise, Hotel Terminus: The Life and Times of Klaus Barbie, Shoah, First Contact,* and *Numero Deux* provide source material for this exploration of the politics and ethics of documentary filmmaking.

Part 2, "A Fiction (Un)Like Any Other," examines the differences between representing an imaginary world and the historical world, between telling a story and making an argument, between establishing subjective character identification and establishing an impression of objectivity or responsibility toward a historical subject. The extended nature of part 2 is due in large part to the ambivalent, closely intertwined relationships between documentary and fiction, narrative, and exposition and the lack of previous study of them. Formal strategies overlap but their context and implications often differ significantly.

Part 3, "Documentary Representation and the Historical World," carries the discussion into more affective and propositionally complex realms of investigation. Can documentary film continue to operate under the banner of liberal humanism particularly in its ethnographic manifestations? How does the documentary representation of the body respond to the fundamental question of "What to do with people?" These are the two questions most central to this final section. Chapter 7, "Pornography, Ethnography, and the Discourses of Power" (based on a coauthored article as described in the Acknowledgments) asks how representations of the strange and exotic support specific forms of desire, pleasure, and knowledge. The function of distance (the organization of space as an index of power) and the clinical gaze (the camera's view as stand-in for an institutional purview) epitomize the parallels between the two social practices, pornography and ethnography. The chapter summarizes recurring themes of ethics, politics, style, rhetoric, representation, and the body as they figure in contemporary Western discourse, reexamining the prevailing modes of documentary representation in light of challenges and alternatives to the Western tradition evidenced by such films as Raul Ruiz's *Of Great Events and Ordinary People,* Marilu Mallet's *Unfinished Diary,* Tisuka Tamasaki's *Patriamada,* and Trinh Minh-ha's *Surname Viet Given Name Nam.*

Chapter 8, "Representing the Body: Questions of Meaning and Magnitude," offers a consideration of how the human, gendered body can be represented in documentary as (1) a social agent, (2) a fictional character, and (3) a mythical figure. Films like *Roses in December, Hard Metal's Disease, The Act of Seeing with one's own eyes, Our Marilyn, Speak Body,* and *Rosie the Riveter* suggest ways of situating the historical person in recognizable tension with myths and stereotypes which evade the claims of historical contingency and human mortality. Some documentaries open onto orders of magnitude they cannot contain. Historical contingency and human mortality carry us beyond the realm of textual representation. The representation of the human body plays a crucial role in questions of magnitude. This concluding chapter explores how the documentary film experience can both be a force unto itself and move us beyond itself, toward that historical arena of which it is a part.

ACKNOWLEDGMENTS

Several grants helped provide the time needed for the completion of this book. I am indebted to the National Endowment for the Humanities for a summer stipend in 1988 and a Fellowship for College Teachers and Independent Scholars in 1990–91, and to San Francisco State University for a summer stipend in 1989. Without this support this book would have been far longer in gestation.

Some of the material in this book appeared in article form but all of it has been substantially rearranged and rewritten. Portions of chapter 2 first appeared as "The Voice of Documentary," *Film Quarterly* 36, no. 3 (Spring 1983). Portions of chapter 8 appeared as "Questions of Magnitude" in John Corner, ed., *The Documentary and Mass Media* (London: Edward Arnold Publishers, 1986) and as "History, Myth and Narrative in Documentary," *Film Quarterly* 41, no. 1 (Fall 1987). Chapter 7 originated as a term paper by Catherine Needham and Christian Hansen in my Fall 1986 seminar on ethnographic film at Queen's University. The parallelism between pornography and ethnography struck me as a fundamental insight with more significant implications than the parallelism of pornography and narrative film, most notably the musical as described in Paul Willemen's "Letter to John," *Screen* 21, no. 2 (Summer 1980): 53–65. The three of us subsequently revised the paper, collaboratively, as an article, "Skinflicks: Ethnography/ Pornography and the Discourses of Power," published in a special issue of *Discourse*, "(Un)Naming Cultures," ed. Trinh T. Minh-ha (*Discourse* 11, no. 2 [Spring 1989]: 65–79). I have revised the published version for inclusion here. I have tried to retain the insights and arguments of the article while adapting it, but I must bear full responsibility for any distortions and diminutions of Catherine and Chris's contribution while acknowledging the indispensable part they have played in shaping the argument. In particular, I have rewritten and expanded the opening few pages of the article into the first three subsections of the chapter. I have also introduced a few reconsiderations, several of them prompted by reading Linda Williams's *Hard Core: Power, Pleasure, and the "Frenzy of the Visible."*

I also wish to express my appreciation to several groups and individuals who provided opportunities for me to refine my ideas and present them in a public forum. Peter Steven, of Development Education Centre, Toronto, invited me to talk on "Art, Politics, and the New Documentary" at an all-day gathering of independent film and video makers in May 1987. Mary Louise Pratt extended an invitation to deliver "Documentary Dilemmas: Theorizing the Untheorized" to an interdisciplinary graduate seminar at Stanford University in April 1989. The questions and comments by students and faculty at the seminar were particularly helpful in rethinking some of my assumptions about observational styles in documentary.

The Humanities Research Centre at the Australian National University invited Julianne Burton and me to organize a film festival on contemporary documentary, June 30–July 3, 1989. The unstinting efforts of Professors Leslie Devereaux and Roger Hillman at the HRC and of Bruce Hodgson at the Film Studies Unit, National Library of Australia, made it possible to select films from around the world that were not yet available in Australia. The opportunity to assemble such an extensive and well-supported film program and to offer public lectures on the selected films was an enormous help in advancing my own thought about the documentary film. The conference that followed the film series, "Coming to Terms with the Photographic Image," added yet another opportunity to engage in meaningful dialogue on issues of considerable importance to the final form of the book. I am especially thankful for the stimulation and advice offered by David and Judith MacDougall during my stay in Australia, and to Director Ian Donaldson and Deputy Director Graeme Clarke of the HRC whose remarkable flair has created a humanities center where dialogue and debate flows freely and profitably.

Paul Sandro, at Miami University (Oxford, Ohio), invited me to give a public lecture entitled "Documentary Desire" in February 1990. This occasion was of great help in developing some of the ideas that involved subjectivity in documentary. In June 1990 I had the opportunity to present a program on contemporary documentary in North America and Europe at the Short Film Festival in Grimstad, Norway. Malte Wadman, Director of the National Center for Screen Studies, Oslo, extended the invitation that made my visit possible. A comparable presentation at the same conference by Peter Mostovoi, head of RISK, the documentary film studio in Moscow, offered a rare opportunity to view recent, innovative work from the Soviet Union, while the Short Film Festival and the Nordic Film Festival, which immediately followed it, allowed me to see a wide array of contemporary work from the Nordic countries.

Most instrumental in advancing my thought about documentary film have been the students who have participated in the courses I have offered on ethnographic and documentary film over the last twelve years. These students, at both Queen's University in Kingston, Ontario and San Francisco State University, often served more like colleagues than novices. The freshness of their insights and the boldness of their conjectures, their willingness to challenge and rethink what had come before, and their own inventiveness as filmmakers and critics have been a continual source of inspiration. If this book contains some small fraction of the total wisdom possessed by those whom I have been privileged to teach, I will feel truly justified. I want to acknowledge the remarkable esprit of the individuals who made up my ethnographic film seminar at Queen's University in the fall of 1986 and with whom I attended the Grierson Film Seminar where lively discussions and great camaraderie provided incentive for this project. Among this group were Chris Hansen and Catherine Needham whose term paper on ethnography and pornography subsequently became a collaboratively authored article and then a chapter in this book.

David Neice and George Lovell, in the sociology and geography departments, respectively, at Queen's University, participated in two of the seminars I gave in ethnographic film—David as a coinstructor and George as a colleague. The ability to exchange views in a structured teaching environment with them was of considerable value. The seminar offered with David Neice, in 1979, was supported by a Development Grant for interdisciplinary instruction from Queen's University which allowed us to purchase a substantial number of important ethnographic films and to bring ethnographic filmmaker David MacDougall to Queen's for a period of four weeks. This support was of immense value in launching the research and dialogue that eventually led to this book. I am also grateful to Colin Leys of the Political Studies Department, Queen's University, for including me in a reading course on ideology organized by an exceptionally gifted graduate student in his department, Radika Desai. Work done in this context was instrumental to my thoughts on ideology and documentary film.

E. Ann Kaplan, Michael Renov, Vivian Sobchack, and Tom Waugh have all provided much needed encouragement and assistance during the process of planning the structure of the book and seeking funding support for its completion. Their own research and writing on documentary have set a standard to which I hope I have done justice.

During the course of preparing this book, I have gained a far deeper respect for the extraordinary knowledge and skill of those who program the festivals that often bring new documentary into public view. The extensiveness and currency of knowledge possessed by these individuals exceeds that of most of us who teach the subject, and their ability to leaven our exposure to the texts with direct encounters between filmmakers and viewers often leads to insights that could not have occurred otherwise. I am particularly grateful for the work of Laura Thielen and Peter Scarlett at the San Francisco International Film Festival and to Brian Gordon, for his administration of the Golden Gate Award juries at the San Francisco Festival; he has given me the opportunity to see a remarkable array of contemporary work that I would not have otherwise seen. I am also immensely appreciative of the exceptionally fine work done by Helga Stephenson, Piers Handling, and Kay Armatage at Toronto's Festival of Festivals. I have considered it a semi-well-kept secret, until the last few years, that they spearhead what is probably the best single film festival in the world. They have certainly afforded me countless opportunities to see films and meet filmmakers that have proven to be an integral part of this book. Connie Fitzsimmons, at the Long Beach Museum of Art, and Geoffrey Gilmore, Head of Programming at the UCLA Film and Television Archive, have also afforded me access to valuable work not easily available.

Bob Rosen, Director of the UCLA Film and Television Archives, has also proven an indispensable colleague and friend. I have benefited from innumerable discussions on documentary and fiction film with him as we have crossed paths everywhere from Beijing to Havana and from Los Angeles to Moscow. His skepticism about the tendency of academics to contemplate the world in isolation from it has been an entirely salutary one for me.

During the period of writing, from 1987–90, I benefited in more ways than I can acknowledge from the support, insights, encouragement, and criticism of Julianne Burton. It was her substantial revision of my original efforts to distinguish between direct and indirect address in documentary that led to the elaboration of four modes of documentary representation in the present volume. Her own work on the Latin American documentary (see her anthology, *The Social Documentary in Latin America*, University of Pittsburgh Press, 1990) broadened my frame of reference considerably; she introduced me to many films from Latin America that helped me contextualize and rethink received wisdom regarding North American and European documentary. The structures and mechanisms for the international distribution of documentary film remain as underdeveloped as the concepts and categories for cross-cultural theorization of the documentary form. I am grateful to Julianne for the ways in which she has made this apparent to me as a continuing problem. And I am immensely thankful for her formidable skills as an editorial advisor and consultant. Lisa Kernan also offered valuable suggestions for improving the manuscript.

Part I

Axes of Orientation

I

THE DOMAIN OF DOCUMENTARY

Documentary Dimensions

Can we love the cinema and Plato, too? If our love is for the feature fiction film, the answer would surely be, "No." Movies as reflections, though an imprecise analogy and one that denies all the *work* of the cinema as apparatus, institution, and textual structure, does capture both the fascination and the taint of cinema. In fact, the fascination with reflections is part of the taint, at least in the Platonic tradition. The reflection is a diversion. It draws us away from something we ought to behold more directly. Distortions impinge in ways that cannot be ascertained. Prestidigitations occur just beyond our line of sight, deceiving us with trompe l'oeil effects.

As Plato himself put it, "When the mind's eye is fixed on objects illuminated by truth and reality [the sun], it understands and knows them, and its possession of intelligence is evident; but when it is fixed on the twilight world of change and decay, it can only form opinions, its vision is confused and its opinions shifting, and it seems to lack intelligence."[1] Cinema presents us with the images of things. Images are mimetic distractions and counterfeitings; they cannot engage our reason nor nourish our hunger for Truth.

If our love is for documentary film, the answer may be less obvious, but, finally, it is still "No." Nonnarrative is but another part of cinema, perhaps all the more devious for claiming to be above the deceptive means with which it makes its point (moving images). Images are mysterious imitations of the very things that written language can demystify, make into an object of knowledge, and render available for productive purposes. At best images may *illustrate* a point that must finally return to words for its meaning or implications.

Documentary film has a kinship with those other nonfictional systems that together make up what we may call the discourses of sobriety. Science, economics, politics, foreign policy, education, religion, welfare—these systems assume they have instrumental power; they can and should alter the world itself, they can effect action and entail consequences. Their discourse has an air of sobriety since it is seldom receptive to "make-believe" characters, events, or entire worlds (unless they serve as pragmatically useful simulations of the "real" one). Discourses of sobriety are sobering because they regard their relation to the real as direct, immediate, transparent. Through them power exerts itself. Through them, things are made to happen. They are the vehicles of domination and conscience, power and knowledge, desire and will. Documentary, despite its kinship, has never been accepted as a full equal.

This is a little odd inasmuch as documentary film often builds itself around the spoken word. Works from Frank Capra's Why We Fight series (1942–45) on the reasons for United States involvement in World War II to Ken Burns's *The Civil War* (1990) would be subject to endless interpretation if we had nothing but their extraordinarily diverse and historically intriguing images to guide us. Commentary points us toward the light, the truth. In a more modern way of discussing reason and its own shadow-realm of the irrational, fiction attends to unconscious desires and latent meanings. It operates where the id lives. Documentary, on the other hand, attends to social issues of which we are consciously aware. It operates where the reality-attentive ego and superego live. Fiction harbors echoes of dreams and daydreams, sharing structures of fantasy with them, whereas documentary mimics the canons of expository argument, the making of a case, and the call to public rather than private response. It clearly is the fiction film that should be designated as marginal, deviant, and perhaps perverse, at least in relation to the historically prevalent ideologies of our culture. Why, then, is documentary not spared the same opprobrium?

Essentially, documentary films appear as pale reflections of the dominant, instrumental discourses in our society. If movies (fiction) "reflect" our culture, and if this mirror image is the fundamental, determining definition of cinema, then documentaries, too, must pass through this "defile" of a reflection. Instead of directly confronting an issue or problem, the discourse must ricochet off this image-based, illusionistic medium of entertainment. Documentary's alliance with the discourses of sobriety falls under attack due to the imagistic company it keeps.

A deep-rooted response in documentary filmmaking has been vigorous dissociation from the distracting shadow-play of fiction. Early documentarists were particularly vehement in their judgments of the fiction film. Soviet filmmaker Dziga Vertov and British documentarists like John Grierson, Paul Rotha, Humphrey Jennings, and Basil Wright drew harsh and unflattering comparisons between the fiction film industry and both the formal potential of cinema and the social purpose of documentary. They lambasted Hollywood as a symbol for escapist, meretricious spectacles. If documentary also depended on images they were at least grounded in more formally innovative and socially responsible motives and intentions.

But such attacks did not win the documentary equal footing with the written essay or book, the scientific survey or report. This higher level of factual, pragmatic discourse about real-life issues remains controlling. It conforms to the preoccupation with production in all its guises that dominates our culture. The preference for nonfiction, nonnarrative, instrumental knowledge and "hard" science complements the engine of progress and capitalism's productive power as a socioeconomic system. This is so commonsensical that it goes without saying. Our weekly magazines subscribe to the discourses of sobriety, beginning with politics and economics and devolving, in the hintermost pages, to movies, books, art, and obituaries. And to prove the point by the exception, late-night talk shows—where a steady stream of celebrities and stars replace the politicians, issues, and dilemmas—feature such individuals precisely because the talk is understood to be inconsequential and diverting. Talk shows market "good conversation" as entertainment. Serious pronouncements are not welcome.

The hierarchy of topics in news magazines, the organization of television news, the nature of talk show conversation all confirm the persistence of the biases that early documentarists sought to overcome. Images may fascinate but they also distract. Productive and interpretive power resides in words. Documentary may also rely on words but these function partly to distract us from the images to which they are companions.

But what of the bond between image and reality? There is, indeed, a distinctive bond between a photographic image and that of which it is a record.[2] Something of reality itself seems to pass through the lens and remain embedded in the photographic emulsion. If we consider the imaginary realm of fiction as having a metaphoric relation to history and lived experience—as a kind of carefully shaped, translucent cloud that displays contours and shapes, patterns and practices that closely resemble the ones we encounter in our own lives, we might think of documentary as a mode where this fictive cloud has settled back to earth. The elevation provided by metaphor, the sense of remove, is drained away as special properties of photographic film and magnetic tape hold the documentary image to the exact shapes and contours, patterns and practices, of the historical world. We expect to apply a distinct form of literalism (or realism) to documentary. We are less engaged by fictional characters and their destiny than by social actors and destiny itself (or social praxis). We prepare ourselves not to comprehend a story but to grasp an argument. We do so in relation to sounds and images that retain a distinct bond to the world we all share.

But the ability of photographic images (and magnetically recorded sound) to replicate what it records has not elevated documentary to the ranks of the other discourses of sobriety. For one thing, all photographic and motion picture images made according to the prevailing conventions that allow light reflected from physical objects to be registered on photosensitive film or videotape will exhibit a distinctive bond between image and object. (Digital sampling techniques destroy this claim; this study is limited to nondigitized imagery.) The bond of image to object will not, therefore, certify the historical status of the object nor the credibility of an argument; later, we will pursue these points in greater detail. Most documentary films also adopt many of the strategies and structures of narrative (though not necessarily those of the popular entertainment film). Compounding the difficulty, many "social problem" fiction films are made with as civic-minded and socially responsible a purpose as many documentaries. Thus documentary fails to identify any structure or purpose of its own entirely absent from fiction or narrative. The terms become a little like our everyday, but unrigorous, distinction between fruits and vegetables.

In the Shadow of Plato

Narrative as a mechanism for storytelling seems quite different from documentary as a mechanism for addressing nonimaginary, real-life issues. But not all narratives are fictions. Exposition can incorporate large elements of narrative, as historical writing vividly demonstrates. Documentary can depend on narrative structure for its basic organization, as American cinema verité demonstrated by taking shape around a crisis. (This shape provides a beginning from which an unstable state of affairs emerges, a middle in which a problem gains in force and complexity, and an ending in which some form of resolution occurs.) Documentary form may also incorporate concepts of character development and subjectivity, continuity or montage editing, and the invocation of off-screen space. Like fiction, documentary can also suggest that its perceptions and values belong to its characters, or adhere to the historical world itself: the film merely reveals what we could have seen around us had we, too, looked with a patient, discerning eye. Just as the looks, speech, and gestures of characters can seem to propel a story along all by themselves, so the eye of the documentary camera in the hands of a Robert Flaherty or Fred Wiseman can seem to reveal qualities of the historical world that were there all along.[3]

No, documentary cannot be loved if we seek (Platonic) truth. Nor can it be loved if we reject the Platonic ideal forms but swing instead to a condemnation of simulations and simulacra. Jean Baudrillard chooses this latter tack, reviving Platonism for a postmodern world. In *The Evil Demon of Images* Baudrillard has this to say:

> The secret of the image . . . must not be sought in its differentiation from reality, and hence in its representative value (aesthetic, critical or dialectical), but on the contrary in its "telescoping" into reality, its short-circuit with reality, and finally, in the implosion of image and reality. For us there is an increasingly definitive lack of differentiation between image and reality which no longer leaves room for representation as such. . . .
> There is a kind of primal pleasure, of anthropological joy in images, a kind of brute fascination unencumbered by aesthetic, moral, social or political judgments. It is because of this that I suggest they are immoral, and that their fundamental power lies in this immorality.[4]

Baudrillard no longer perceives a reality out there but only images that simulate something that is no longer accessible except through these simulations. It is as though the entrance to Plato's cave were sealed off and all we can see behind us, casting shadows on the wall, are the figures on the parapet. These figures, though, are not the world of historical reality. They are themselves there in order to cast shadows; that is their function and reality. Nothing else exists behind or beyond them; the only other thing are the shadows that make up a circular implosion of image and reality, signs and what they refer to. Reality has been constituted by and for the shadow-play it entertains. We can no longer say that there is some structure or concept for which the figures on the parapet are an imitation and the images on the wall but copies of this copy. All metaphors of depth and abstraction, of "higher" or "deeper" levels of meaning and reality collapse into the endless surface of simulations and simulations of simulations.

Intriguing as these assertions are, I do not accept them. This book is devoted to another set of propositions, ones in which the separation between an image and what it refers to continues to be a difference that makes a difference. Our access to historical reality may only be by means of representations, and these representations may sometimes seem to be more eager to chase their own tails than able to guarantee the authenticity of what they refer to. Neither of these conditions, however, precludes the persistence of history as a reality with which we must contend. Baudrillard, like Plato, carries things to an extreme; in his case it is an extreme of nihilism rather than idealism. It is quite possible, however, to accept the grain of truth about the immorality of images in Baudrillard's argument without jumping into a nihilist sandbox with him. Lives continue to be lost in events such as the invasion of Grenada even if such a "war" is reported and perceived far more as a simulation of war than war itself. The reality of pain and loss that is not part of any simulation, in fact, is what makes the difference between representation and historical reality of crucial import-ance. It is not beyond the power of documentary to make this difference available for consideration.

There is one other little problem with Plato's critique of the image, if not Baudrillard's: we are not a bit closer to the society envisioned in Plato's *Republic* than socialist states have been to the communitarianism envi-sioned by Marx. The idealism that informs Plato's utopian Republic ex-tends beyond the notion that images are but copies from which we must, however reluctantly, free ourselves. His conception of knowledge and his philosopher as ruler are uncontaminated not only by the dross of worldly distractions but also by ideology and desire.

"The true philosopher," Plato reminds us, "has no time to look at the affairs of men, or to take part in their quarrels with all the jealousy and bitterness they involve. His eyes are turned to contemplate fixed and immutable realities, a realm where there is no injustice done or suffered, but all is reason and order, and which is the model which he imitates and to which he assimilates himself as far as he can."[5] And, Plato continues, the

Guardians or Rulers "must be told that they have no need of mortal and material gold and silver, because they have in their hearts the heavenly gold and silver given them by the gods as a permanent possession, and it would be wicked to pollute the heavenly gold in their possession by mixing it with earthly, for theirs is without impurity, while that in currency among men is a common source of wickedness. They alone, therefore, of all the citizens are forbidden to touch or handle silver or gold. . . . Upon this their safety and that of the state depends."[6]

Plato does away not only with greed but also jealousy and possessiveness since desire in all its forms is a manifestation of the contrary of reason—the irrational. The family and all of its neuroses and perversions dissolve as sex becomes an exercise in genetics rather than libidinous cathexes: "our men and women Guardians should be forbidden by law to live together in separate households, and all the women should be common to all the men: similarly, children should be held in common, and no parent should know its child, or child its parent."[7]

The quest for the reasoned life takes its toll, but more to the point, the uses of reason are far more diverse, complexly layered, and potentially nefarious than Plato would tolerate. The impurity of images is not the final impediment to truth but part and parcel of a culture in which Plato's Republic remains an (impossible) ideal. Our Guardians and their "auxiliaries" (the professional, managerial class) sit comfortably at the table of "irrational" desires. They freely touch the forbidden fruits of monetary reward and capital accumulation, and they, like us, arise from and, in their turn, give rise to that succession of family affairs Freud did so much to begin to unravel. In short, reason stands in service to the society that deploys it but not disinterestedly. There is the matter of ideology to consider when we speak of reason and justice. Ideology, which Plato might have understood as opinion and belief, if at all, is far harder to expunge from the pages of history than from a utopia.

The Image and Ideology

The dependence of ideology on images and the imaginary (a psychic realm of significant images around which our sense of identity forms) makes the image, copy, representation, and likeness a far more central and dynamic category than Plato would have admitted. Ideologies, beginning with those of gender, will attach themselves to this imaginary sense of self. (Our identity begins with our likeness to and difference from our mothering and fathering parents.) Ideologies will also offer representations in the form of images, concepts, cognitive maps, worldviews, and the like to propose frames and punctuation to our experience. Such ideologies and images are inescapable. No outside exists to the conceptual envelope they establish. Images are at the heart of our construction as subjects and perhaps for that reason images are also impugned as imprecise, unscientific, *unmanageable* things in need of subordination and control.

And yet images are not quite as unmanageable as they appear. They can be joined together with words or other images into systems of signs, and hence, meaning. They can be framed and organized into a text. Semiology addresses this broad domain of signification, and one of the favorite objects of semiotic scrutiny in the 1970s was the cinema, especially that dominant-but-marginal cinema of the narrative film that banishes the rest of film with the catch-all phrase of "nonnarrative." Semiotics and, after it, psychoanalysis, turn attention to fiction films where they analyze the work of the unconscious and its affinities with ideology. The fiction film presents a cornucopia of symptoms of social and male disease; of real contradictions resolved by sleight of hand or not at all; of projections working to represent women as an imaginary figure, Woman, in her various (stereotypical) guises; of desires sparked and circulated as part of an economy working—at some risk to itself, to be sure—to manage contradiction and propose utopian ideals immune from the very ideologies that underwrote their construction.

If documentary remained marginal in all of this it was because it was not marginal enough. It did not seem to betray with the same intensity, once decoded or its internal gaps and fissures detected, the same central contradictions of gender, race, class, or nationality. It might well address these issues and be susceptible to analyses that would reveal blind spots, hidden assumptions, and faulty conclusions, but the deep structure of the unconscious would slip away, undetected and unconfronted. Ideology would remain at large.

This assumption of documentary's complicity with the dominant discourses of sobriety and, so situated, its lack of a royal road to the unconscious and the secret underbelly of society relegated it to subordinate status in critical theory, a position mirroring its subordination to those primary discourses whose servant documentary was presumed to be: cultural geography for the nature film; history for the historical documentary; sociology and political science for the social issue film; symbolic interactionism for American cinema verité (a more covert referent than some of the others); anthropology and written ethnography for the ethnographic film; "real" science for the "scientific" or educational film; the vanguard party, radical left, or the conservative alliances and reactionary right for the films of political contestation. Dr. Helen Caldicott's antinuclear speech can be a moving experience for an audience, but why attend or scrutinize a film of it (*If You Love This Planet*) when there is a wealth of printed information from experts to be examined? Why dwell on films that are merely imitations of concepts and images generated elsewhere when the controlling discourse is itself available for scrutiny?

This, however, is to neglect the extent to which image, ideology, and utopia are fundamentally joined. Images help constitute the ideologies that determine our own subjectivity; images make incarnate those alternative subjectivities and patterns of social relation that provide our cultural ideals or utopian visions. The critique of the image made eminent sense within the frame of nineteenth-century liberal thought where the word reigned supreme. Now the word has troubles of its own. Language can seem a prison-house confining us to a fixed range of predetermined possibilities and barring any more direct access to the real beyond its bounds. To the extent language speaks us rather than we it, we find that the critique of the copy now applies to language itself (it fabricates a world after its own image) although the hope of retrieving or attaining that lost object of the real has also faded.

Documentary film may not provide as direct or scenic a route to the unconscious as most fiction does. Documentary films, though, are part and parcel of the discursive formations, the language games, and rhetorical stratagems by and through which pleasure and power, ideologies and utopias, subjects and subjectivities receive tangible representation. In the beginning was the Word but now there is television—and photographs, movie theaters, the political campaigns of press conferences and photo opportunities, choreographed debates and paid advertisements, the spectacles of space shuttles, Olympic contests, and living room wars.[8] Dimensions of documentary contribute to all of this. The goal of documenting reality, the hope of arriving at a final resting point where "reason and order," truth and justice prevail, of achieving freedom and diversity within a frame of perfect symmetry, recedes.

Historical reality is under siege. Imperfect utopias and diverse affinities propose themselves as alternatives to the ordered lives constructed by the master narratives of Christian salvation, capitalist progress, or Marxist revolution. Less tainted by its reliance on an image that has become ubiquitous and formative, documentary's alliance with the dominant discourses of the day returns as the fundamental concern but no longer in terms of a supporting or ancillary role. Instead the propagation of images is all about us. The disparagement of images and movies, marking both a dominant feature film industry and a marginal nonnarrative cinema, draws on both idealist and pragmatic traditions to promote the illusion that that which affects us most—images—matters least.

Documentary, like other discourses of the real, retains a vestigial responsibility to describe and interpret the world of collective experience, a responsibility that is no small matter at all. But even more, it joins these other discourses (of law, family, education, economics, politics, state, and nation) in the actual *construction* of social reality. Dziga Vertov advocated in his writings and his films an active process of social construction, including the construction of the viewer's historical-materialist consciousness, and Walter Benjamin, in his seminal essay, "The Work of Art in the Age of Mechanical Reproduction," foresaw the degree to which the image would be placed in the service of the dominant ideology as spectacle and distraction but would also retain the explosive potential to reassemble time and space into whatever order one desired: "Our taverns and our metropolitan streets, our offices and furnished rooms, our railroad stations and our factories appeared to have us locked up hopelessly. Then came the film and burst this prison-world asunder by the dynamite of the tenth of a second, so that now, in the midst of its far-flung ruins and debris, we calmly and adventurously go travelling."[9]

John Berger, in his provocative series of four films, *Ways of Seeing*, carries Benjamin's declaration forward into the latter half of the twentieth century. Berger demonstrates, with sound and images of his own, how the oil painting tradition has passed on many of its functions to photography and, in particular, to advertising. Advertising constructs a view of the world that is at once "mad" and yet irresistible. It constructs mystique-laden objects that threaten to occupy our future, to provide the target for our desire. Advertising constructs the subjectivity that sustains such desires inside of us. This is no mere documentation but an active process of fabrication, if not of physical objects then of a production of meanings and values, concepts and orientations to surround them. Such fabrications propose specific forms of social relation with distinctive places for men and women, rich and poor, First and Third World, black and white. The connotations and assumptions that result occupy our imagination and become a fundamental part of our mental landscape even as we retain the potential to qualify, contest, subvert, or overthrow this particular regime of the visible. "Reality" is ours for the making.

Maryknoll World Video has produced, and distributes by mail, an extraordinary three-part series, *Consuming Hunger*, that addresses the issue of famine in Africa in terms similar to John Berger's approach to painting and advertising. Like the commodity, famine is made and cut to measure. A social reality is produced, in images, by discourses of the real, not by the discourse of fiction. We look past this act of production to the "fact" of famine at our own peril. In this case the organizing agent for our image of famine is television news and the first two parts of the series unravel the narrative braid with which this "story" has been told. What does it take for a historical event to gain entry into the circulatory system of prime time news, especially if there are no publicists to make a case for it? When does the "ordinary" matter of individual death and the occasional misfortune of starvation reach an order of magnitude that requires comment? What evidence must be provided, aurally or visually, before the event can be brought before our attention as a "tragedy" and why, despite the simultaneity of this tragedy with its representation, does the newscast keep its distance, asking nothing more of us than that we lend an ear?

Such representations play on and derive from longstanding assumptions about the Third World, Africa, the iconography of plagues and disasters, and the mythologies that address the causation of "natural" events like famine. So did the organized response that arose in 1985, aimed at a mass level by means of such events as the Live-Aid concert heard round the world. As *Consuming Hunger* argues, such events construct their own representation of disaster, offer their own image of (charitable) response, provide a modus for self-congratulation similar to that ascribed to the purchase of a commodity ("Oh, what a feeling!" "Reach out, reach out and touch someone") and transferred to the joy of offering a helping hand, painlessly, with a simple phone call and a modest pledge, and erase from sight questions of economics, self-help, and Third World assistance, or even more, Third World perspectives.

The last thing such mega-events need is to hear from those who have been nominated to stand as victims. It suffices to see them, nameless but not faceless, desperate and without dignity, aware but silenced. For a great many people, these images and these representations will be, if not the sum total of their knowledge, a dominating factor in their awareness. Such representations actively construct a historical reality we may not otherwise see—cobbling much of it together from shards of myth and fact, from the tissue of sometimes contradictory ideologies already circulating within the culture.

Films like *Ways of Seeing* and *Consuming Hunger* enter the fray, putting another construction on things, qualifying and contesting those that prevail. Across the spectrum of issues and values that throb with the urgency of unresolved contradiction, representations are made, images and subjectivities proposed. The subordination of the image was Plato's folly, its equation with reality Baudrillard's. In an age of mechanical production/photographic reproduction, electronic dissemination/cybernetic simulation we dare not repeat such follies. Our lives and our destiny rest in the balance.

Defining Documentary

Documentary as a concept or practice occupies no fixed territory. It mobilizes no finite inventory of techniques, addresses no set number of issues, and adopts no completely known taxonomy of forms, styles, or modes. The term *documentary* must itself be constructed in much the same manner as the world we know and share. Documentary film practice is the site of contestation and change. Of greater importance than the ontological finality of a definition—how well it captures the "thingness" of the documentary—is the purpose to which a definition is put and the facility with which it locates and addresses important questions, those that remain unsettled from the past and those posed by the present.

Rather than one, three definitions of documentary suggest themselves since each definition contributes something distinctive and helps identify different sets of concerns. Let us consider documentary from the point of view of the filmmaker, the text, and the viewer. Each starting point leads to a different yet not contradictory definition. As an ensemble these definitions help demonstrate how we constitute our objects of study and how that very process then determines much of the work that will follow.

One common but misleading way of defining documentary from the point of view of the filmmaker is in terms of control: documentary filmmakers exercise less control over their subject than their fictional counterparts do. Douglas Gomery and Robert Allen adopt this definition in their discussion of cinema verité in *Film History: Theory and Practice*.[10] Gomery and Allen base their definition on one given by an introductory textbook that does not even have a chapter on documentary film (it is subsumed into that great Other of "Nonnarrative Formal Systems"). In *Film Art: An Introduction*, Bordwell and Thompson claim, "We often distinguish a documentary film from a fiction film on the basis of production. Typically, the documentary filmmaker controls only certain variables of preparation, shooting, and assembly; some variables (e.g., script, rehearsal) may be omitted, whereas others (e.g., setting, lighting, behavior of the figures) are present but often uncontrolled."[11]

Apart from all the qualifiers ("often," "typically," "certain variables," "some," "may"), the definition assumes that the "basis of production" is self-evident, unfalsifiable, and therefore a consistently reliable guide. They ignore the extent to which fiction films can mimic these very qualities or the high degree of control exercised over setting, lighting, and behavior in poetic or classic expository documentaries as well as in more recent works like *The Thin Blue Line* or *Far from Poland*. To define documentary strictly in terms of the filmmaker's control over the variables offered by the definition also sidesteps all the social (versus strictly formal) issues that a consideration of "control" invites: what relations (of power, hierarchy, knowledge) pertain between filmmaker and subject; what forms of sponsorship or consent pertain; who will own and distribute the film and to what end?

In addition, even within the very restricted confines of American cinema verité of the sort practiced by Leacock and Pennebaker or by Fred Wiseman, where the filmmakers went to great lengths to minimize the effect of their own presence during shooting and tried to let events unfold as if they were not there at all, control over the production phase of the filmmaking was hardly absent.[12] None of these individuals nor other observational filmmakers pretended to forfeit control over what occurred. Their directorial strategy sought to elicit highly naturalistic performances that conveyed the vivid impression of people "being themselves." This required a sophisticated form of nonintervention which, like the techniques of participatory observation or sociological and anthropological field work generally, placed considerable demands on the filmmaker to exercise a type of control that was largely unnoticeable.

Dziga Vertov called for montage before, during, and after shooting a film and the observational filmmakers with their strongly narrative-structured films certainly retained tight control of the before and after. It is also clearly possible to argue that nonintervention may forfeit control over what occurs in one sense but that it requires considerable control over what occurs in another sense: when people behave "as if the camera were not there," which is often described as something that "just happens," this occurs only under controlled conditions where other forms of behavior are skillfully discouraged. And the crew (often just one or two people) must exercise a high degree of self-control, disciplining themselves in how they cohabit a space from which they also absent themselves. The discipline and control of mise-en-scène that would have been directed toward what occurs in front of the camera gets turned on those behind it. They must move and position themselves to record actions without altering or distorting those actions at the same time. This requires a great deal of control and helps explain why so much critical discussion of observational film styles dwells, not at all paradoxically, on that very aspect of filmmaking where control is presumably least: the moment of filming and the work of the camera.

This is so because "control" does define, in a backhanded way, a key element of documentary. What the documentarist cannot fully control is his or her basic subject: history. By addressing the historical domain, the documentarist joins the company of other practitioners who "lack control" over what they do: social scientists, physicians, politicians, entrepreneurs, engineers, and revolutionaries. If the reader detects a small measure of derision in this rebuttal, it is because the notion of control as a defining criterion perpetuates a muddleheadedness about documentary film-making scarcely less egregious than claims for the truth of documentary representation or for the self-evidence of facts.

A Community of Practitioners

What does characterize documentary filmmaking generally is its status as an institutional formation. Without taking on the firm outline of those institutions that pursue socially defined goals with specific budgetary commitments, legislative mandates, and criteria for membership such as academia, the priesthood, or the military, documentary filmmaking still displays most of the signs of institutional status. Members are defined, somewhat tautologically but nonetheless meaningfully, as those who make or otherwise engage in the circulation of documentary films; members share a common, self-chosen mandate to represent the historical world rather than imaginary ones: they share similar problems and speak a common language regarding the peculiar nature of this mandate—ranging from questions of the suitability of different film stocks for low levels of available light to the relative importance of voice-over commentary in the structure of a text to the difficulties of reaching their intended audience.

A distinct circuit of distributors and exhibition sites function to close the loop between production and consumption. It operates in a tangential or marginal manner to the dominant loop of commercial, theatrical distribution, sometimes duplicating it (as happened with *Nanook of the North* or, more recently, *The Thin Blue Line*), more often operating in a parallel but decidedly less commercial vein (ranging in venue from union halls to art galleries). Specialized distributors add density to the institutional nature of the field as do professional organizations like the International Documentary Association, the Film Arts Foundation, and the Foundation for Independent Film and Video (the latter two stressing independent [non-studio based] production generally). Funding sources ranging from individual contributors and special interest groups to national agencies like the National Endowment for the Arts, the Corporation for Public Broadcasting, the British Film Institute, or the Canada Council establish definite guidelines and criteria for the support of documentary or independent work. Magazines like *The Independent*, various newsletters from *RAIN* (Royal Anthropological Institute News) to *Release Print*, and specialized conferences, seminars, and festivals such as the Mannheim Documentary Festival, the Flaherty and the Grierson seminars contribute to the sense of institutional and community identity. All these characteristics also have a historical dimension as groups and organizations arise and disband, split or transform, with considerable variation in the intensity and extent of activity by region or nation.

What an institutional definition does is begin to hint at the importance, for the filmmaker, of a shared sense of common purpose. Documentary filmmakers may shape and transform the traditions they inherit, but they do so precisely in dialogue with that tradition and with their cohorts. Such dialogue may be oblique—through the films they make and the innovations these works suggest to others—as well as direct, through conversation, written criticism, or manifestos. At one level we might say documentary is what those who regard themselves as documentarists produce. This begs the question of who defines the documentarists, or, perhaps better, acknowledges that this group is largely self-defining. Rather than proposing any ground or center outside the practices of documentary, such a definition stresses how the field operates by allowing itself to be historically conditioned, unfolding, variable, and perpetually provisional, based on what documentarists themselves consider admissible, what they regard as limits, boundaries, and test cases, how boundaries come to exert the force of a definition, however loosely, and how the qualification, contestation, or subversion of these same boundaries moves from inconsequential anomaly to transformative innovation to accepted practice.

An Institutional Practice

In this light documentary film can be considered as an institutional practice with a discourse of its own. Guided by a fundamental preoccupation with the representation of the historical world, various organizational principles, patterns of distribution and exhibition, styles, structures, techniques, and modes will arise and contend. As Jean-François Lyotard notes, this process is similar to ordinary conversation but with added constraints:

> An institution differs from a conversation in that it always requires supplementary constraints for statements to be declared admissible within its bounds. The constraints function to filter discursive potentials, interrupting possible connections in the communication networks: there are things that should not be said. They also privilege certain classes of statements (sometimes only one) whose predominance characterizes the discourse of the particular institution: these are things that should be said, and there are ways of saying them. Thus, orders in the army, prayer in church, denotation in the schools, narration in families, questions in philosophy, performativity in business [representation in documentary—BN]. Bureaucratization is the outer limit of this tendency.[13]

Documentary filmmaking is a long way from this outer limit of bureaucracy and the rigidification of what can and cannot be said. Still, there are material supports for the discourse that occurs and this apparatus of groups, organizations, festivals and conferences, companies, film, media and journalism schools, funding and sponsoring agencies, and news networks provides for a measure of regulation in the discursive traffic that takes place. The normal process of qualification, contestation, and transformation in the rules of the game proceeds apace in the discourse of documentary, just as they do in the feature fiction film industry where the aesthetic and economic constraints on what can be said and done remain open to change. How things may get said and done—possible patterns of ownership, economic power and artistic control, technical and technological innovation, the development of new stories—works itself out around a different class of characteristic statements often coded under the rubric of "entertainment." As a governing concept, entertainment may, in fact, come closer to policing the limits of what can be said and the ways of saying it than representation has done for documentary, but, even here, considerable variation can be noted over time and across national boundaries.

Michel Foucault captures something of the fluid nature of an institution, apparatus, or discourse when he describes how the apparently disparate discourses on madness across the centuries need to be organized in relation to their incommensurateness. We need to substitute documentary for madness in reading his comments and to regard his commentary not as the antithesis of Lyotard's emphasis on regulation but as an insistence on avoiding the production of a static essence that neglects the regulation of diversity itself:

> The unity of discourses on madness would not be based upon the existence of the object "madness," or the constitution of a single horizon of objectiv-

ity; it would be the interplay of the rules that make possible the appearances of objects during a given period of time; objects that are shaped by measures of discrimination and religious casuistry, in medical diagnosis, objects that are manifested in pathological descriptions, objects that are circumscribed by medical codes, practices, treatments and care. Moreover, the unity of the discourses on madness would be the interplay of the rules that define the transformations of these different objects, their non-identity through time, the break produced in them, the internal discontinuity that suspends their permanence. Paradoxically, to define a group of statements in terms of its individuality would be to define the dispersion of these objects, to grasp all the interstices that separate them, to measure the distances that reign between them—in other words, to formulate their law of division.[14]

We will take up Foucault's invitation to define the dispersion of the object of study further in a discussion of documentary modes.[15]

What Foucault's orientation invites us to recognize is the extent to which our object of study is constructed, and reconstructed, by an array of discursive participants or interpretive communities. For example, a common but no longer inviolate continuity through much of the discourse on and practice of documentary centers on the presumption that it is more important to talk about something than to talk about how we talk about something. In other words, discursive operations themselves tend to occupy an unproblematic position as tool or vehicle for gaining access to something else, which is, most often, the historical world. Documentary may talk about anything in the historical world except itself (until we consider reflexive documentaries where this very presupposition becomes the object of scrutiny). It is hard to be reflexive if you have something urgent to say about a pressing issue, and for most documentarists the urgency of the said takes far higher precedence than the self-consciousness of the saying. This defines one of the classic traits of documentary at the same time that it helps explain why the "discursive formation" it establishes (in Foucault's terms) remains somewhat underdeveloped and unexamined.

Documentary as an institutional practice raises questions of the constraints brought to bear by the various discourses that are in play. These constraints may gain the density of codes, ethical dicta, and ritual practices such as, in observational documentary, continuity editing with synchronous sound, the responsibility of the filmmaker to the institution of documentary above responsibility to the film's subjects (the right of "final cut" remains with the filmmaker not his or her subjects), and a practice of nonintervention in what occurs before the camera. In classic expository documentary these constraints include evidentiary editing (cutting to bring together the best possible evidence in support of a point), the filmmaker's responsibility to make his or her argument as accurately and convincingly as possible even if it requires recontextualizing the points of individual witnesses or experts, and a practice of intervening in what occurs before the camera by means of the interview but without showing the filmmaker or even including the filmmaker's voice. Individuals will both adhere to and inflect these constraints through their filmmaking practice, insuring that the films we call documentary retain a relative autonomy from any final or determining definition for them.

A Corpus of Texts

Another, perhaps even more familiar, way to define documentary is in terms of the texts directly. We might consider documentary a film genre like any other. Films included in the genre would share certain characteristics. Various norms, codes, or conventions display a prominence missing from other genres. Each film establishes internal norms or structures of its own but these frequently share common traits with the textual system or organizing pattern of other documentaries. Many of these distinguishing features of the documentary film are the subject of the following chapters. A few of the most salient can serve here as examples.

Documentaries take shape around an informing logic. The economy of this logic requires a representation, case, or argument about the historical world. The economy is basically instrumental or pragmatic: it operates in terms of problem-solving. A paradigmatic structure for documentary would involve the establishment of an issue or problem, the presentation of the background to the problem, followed by an examination of its current extent or complexity, often including more than one perspective or point of view. This would lead to a concluding section where a solution or path toward a solution is introduced.

Downwind, Downstream, for example, begins with images of the splendor and beauty of the Rocky Mountain high country only to show and inform us how the streams, lakes, and snowpacks are contaminated by heavy metals across much of the Rockies. The film explains how this came to be, going back to the early gold rush days when numerous mines were dug only to be subsequently abandoned. The mineshafts then filled with water which came into contact with heavy metal deposits well below the earth's surface. This contaminated water then leached out or spilled out during the spring run-off. The present-day problem extends still further since mining operations have expanded; this is compounded by smelters that spew acid and metal-laden smoke into the atmosphere that returns to the mountain range as rain. Because of the altitude, plant and animal life is even more susceptible to contamination than surface level ecologies. The quality of drinking water for much of the western United States and the survival of the Rocky Mountain environment are both in jeopardy. The film concludes by returning to individuals who have appeared earlier, giving testimony about the extent of the problem. Now we hear them speaking about organizations and committees, grass-roots activities and governmental lobbying, individual efforts and legislative reforms that, in aggregate, suggest how the problem may be addressed and, eventually, resolved.

Such a structure occurs in a great many documentaries, although some of the most interesting ones approach this paradigmatic pattern mischievously (for example, *Poto and Cabengo, Demon Lover Diary, British Sounds*, and *Sans Soleil* all thwart our expectations of finding a well-defined problem and readily available solution). Documentaries that are primarily observational exhibit structures closer to those of narrative fiction: an economy of character-based conflict, complications, and resolution replaces that of problem/solution and documentary logic. Still, the problem/solution structure exerts considerable influence and shapes the organization of scenes as well as full films. A typical scene in narrative fiction establishes time and place; presents characters advancing in their attempts to address the conflict, lack, or disequilibrium, and terminates with suggestions of further actions or response required in another time and place (a new scene). In documentary, a typical scene establishes time and place and a logical tie to previous scenes; it presents the evidential nature of some portion of a larger argument (such as an illustration, example, interview with witness or expert, visual metaphor or sound/image counterpoint), and it terminates with suggestions of how the search for a solution might lead to another scene, in another time or place.

To describe a typical scene is to offer broad generalizations. Many scenes will confound this sketch by appearing to terminate on either the sound or image track but not the other (we jump to another mine site visually in *Downwind, Downstream*, for example, but the same point about heavy metals leaching into ground water continues on the sound track). In fact, documentary scenes are more heavily organized around the principle of sound, or spoken commentary, than fiction scenes. In the *Downwind* example, a visual jump to a municipal swimming pool while someone continued to discuss heavy metal contamination would not necessarily violate the logic of the scene: it may imply that the water in such pools is no longer as safe as we assume. The visual, geographic leap is bridged by a logic of implication. In other words, a documentary film can sustain far more gaps, fissures, cracks, and jumps in the visual appearance of its world even though it represents the familiar, historical world. People and places can appear in a manner that would be disturbingly intermittent in fiction. An intermittent representation of people and places, based on the requirements of a logic, can, in fact, serve as a distinguishing characteristic for documentary.

Documentary film structure generally depends on evidentiary editing in which the classic narrative techniques of continuity editing undergo significant modification. Instead of organizing cuts within a scene to present a sense of a single, unified time and space in which we can quickly locate the relative position of central characters, documentary organizes cuts within a scene to present the impression of a single, convincing argument in which we can locate a logic. Leaps in time or space and the placement of characters become relatively unimportant compared to the sense of the flow of evidence in the service of this controlling logic. Classic narrative fiction achieves spatial and temporal continuity even if the advance of the plot occurs in the face of leaps in logic. Classic documentary will tolerate gaps or leaps in space and time as long as there is continuity in advancing the argument.

Evidentiary editing achieves a different kind of "match" continuity from that of fiction films. In narrative fiction, two pieces of space are joined together to give the impression of one continuous world that spills beyond the frame in every direction uniformly through such devices as "match action" where an action begun in one shot is completed in the next, or through point-of-view shots which shuttle between views of a character and what the character sees. In documentary, two pieces of space are joined together to give the impression of one continuous argument that can draw on disparate elements of the historical world for evidence. This is a form of control fiction film directors seldom have available outside of classic "montage" sequences connoting a general process.

A "match action" edit may occur in documentary but will be less likely to involve the movements of a character than the "movement" of a logic. A typical example would be the sight of a tree falling matched to a log being fed into a sawmill; the match is still between actions but the emphasis is less on spatial continuity than on the concept of a process: logging. The causality that might in fiction film have been attributed to a character (a man moves toward a chair/cut/he sits down), shifts to the social domain beyond the film (in logging, trees are felled/cut/they are sawn into lumber). In each case the edit is motivated, but in one case the motivation is relayed through an imaginary story, in the other it is relayed through an argument about a social or historical process.

Implicit in this text-centered definition of documentary is the assumption that sounds and images stand as evidence and are treated as such, rather than as elements of a plot. This, in turn, gives priority to the structuring elements of an argument concerned with something external to the text rather than to the structuring elements of a story internal to it. Though shaping a plot and making a case may involve similar forms and strategies, they are also distinct. Stories occur in an imaginary universe however closely based on actual events or characters. Arguments occupy an imaginary space (they are abstract), but, in documentary film, they address or represent issues that arise in the lived, historical world. Stories characteristically depend on plot; arguments, on rhetoric. Stories must be plausible; arguments must, in addition, be persuasive. If we understand the argument, we should be ready to explain it; if we comprehend a story, we should be able to interpret it.

The centrality of argument gives the sound track particular importance in documentary. This is in keeping with the relation between documentary film and those social discourses of sobriety that circulate through the Word. Arguments require a logic that words are able to bear far more easily than images. As one major example, images do not allow for negation. A picture of a pipe is *a picture* of a pipe. (Magritte's *La condition humaine*, with its inscription, "Ceci n'est pas une pipe," brings this very quality into the foreground.) Images are concrete. They are always of a particular time and place. Words allow for abstractions like "love" and for designations like "umbrella" that clearly signal the class of objects known as umbrellas without having to refer to any one member of that class. Combinations of images—through editing or montage, intertitles, and the juxtaposition of images with sounds—can overcome some of these obstacles, but most documentaries still turn to the sound track to carry much of the general import of their abstract argument.

Documentary relies heavily on the spoken word. Commentary by voice-over narrators, reporters, interviewees, and other social actors figure strongly in most documentary. Although we may well be able to infer the story of many fiction films by watching the succession of images alone (watching a movie on an airplane without headphones will bear this out), we would be hard pressed to infer the argument of a documentary without access to the sound track. In this spirit, the recounting of a situation or event by a character or commentator in documentary frequently has the aura of truthfulness about it. Documentaries usually invite us to take as true what subjects recount about something that happened even if we also see how more than one perspective is possible. (Each recounting conveys a *situated* truth, akin to the varying points of view of characters toward the same event in fiction.) Fiction, though, often invites us to take what characters say about what happened as suspect, more tightly circumscribed or restricted to the knowledge and perspective of a character; other information must also be incorporated. (This is particularly evident in detective films.) In documentary, an event recounted is history reclaimed. Qualification and subjectivity infrequently intrude as complicating factors.

Conversely, documentaries run some risk of credibility in reenacting an event: the special indexical bond between image and historical referent is ruptured. In a reenactment, the bond is still between the image and something that occurred in front of the camera but what occurred occurred *for* the camera. It has the status of an imaginary event, however tightly based on historical fact. Fictions, on the other hand, frequently place greater credibility in reenactments than recountings. We can see and hear what is reputed to have occurred; the reenactment is presented as a (fictional) confirmation of what had merely been alleged. After hearing several verbal accounts of a rape in *The Accused*, we are asked to believe the one account (by a male eyewitness) that is presented as a reenactment. And in *Citizen Kane* we are asked to believe the validity of each of several flashback/reenactments even as the film proposes that the story of Mr.

Kane exceeds them all. (Interestingly, written nonfiction such as *Indecent Exposure, Final Cut*, and *All The President's Men* has taken to attaching actual dialogue to accounts of past events. Not burdened with the problem of an actual actor who would approximate without being the historical personage, such dialogue provides a credibility to written accounts that visual reenactments still lack. Written dialogue heightens the sense of authenticity; spoken dialogue the sense of a fiction.)

The structure of the documentary text will also display parallels with other texts. These parallels can be on several different levels. They may pertain to a movement, period, national cinema, style, or mode. Like the concept of genre, these are all ways of characterizing films by their likenesses to rather than their differences from one another. If documentary itself is considered a genre (as well as an institution), subdivisions within documentary may go by other names. A movement is a group of films made by individuals who share a common outlook or objective. Neorealism is a prime example in fiction and American cinema verité is one in documentary. A period is a historical unit of time within which the similarities and differences among films take on special importance in reference to the times. The period of the 1930s, for example, saw most documentary work take on a newsreel quality as part of a Depression-era sensibility and a political perspective that stressed social and economic action. The category of national cinema is sometimes useful for identifying characteristics common to work from a given country, usually during a specific period as well. The work of Unit B at the National Film Board of Canada during the late 1950s and 1960s, with its emphasis on marginal groups and unusual practices seen with an ironic or detached but not sensationalistic eye, constitutes one vivid example (in films like *The Back-Breaking Leaf*; *Lonely Boy*; *Quebec, USA*; *Rouli-roulant*; *Blood and Fire*; *I Was a Ninety Pound Weakling*; and *The Universe*).

Style refers to the distinctive way an individual filmmaker has of putting things but also to the common way of putting things shared by a collectivity. Style in this second sense becomes similar to an institutional discourse, with rules and constraints governing its operations, rules which are themselves subject to change. Style supports the unfolding of a plot to constitute a story and style supports the unfolding of evidence to make an argument. If there is one style that has characterized documentary most forcefully, it is realism. Realism has been such a widespread and pervasive influence that it fails to offer a particularly distinctive foothold for documentary analysis. The concept itself requires clarification and focus given its pervasiveness in our culture generally. Subcategories of national and historical variation, associated with different forms of technology and distinct articulations of purpose, need to be established. The similarities and differences between realism in the fiction and documentary films (again differentiated into related subcategories such as the Free Cinema in 1950s England and the "kitchen sink" realism of British fiction films at that time, or the American observational or cinema verité documentary and the Italian neorealist cinema) also require extended discussion. These are challenges well worth considering, and are deferred for chapter 6 in order to introduce other subcategories of documentary production here.

Modes of documentary production, for example, identify major historical and formal divisions within the institutional and discursive base in a way that complements studies of style but also grounds them in material practices. Four modes of documentary film practice are discussed in chapter 2: expository (the "classic" mode of documentary), observational, interactive, and reflexive. Each mode establishes a hierarchy of specific conventions or norms that remain flexible enough to incorporate a great deal of stylistic, national, and individual variation without loosing the force of an organizing principle. (In observational documentaries noninterference during shooting is more important than maximum-fidelity sound recording; in most interactive documentaries, the filmmaker or interviewer may be seen and heard but the words and gestures of interviewees take precedence over the interviewer's own. In expository documentaries the logic of the argument takes priority over the spatial and temporal continuity between shots.)

Practitioners of one mode have much less in common with practitioners of another mode than with each other. They establish a community of their own within the overall institution of documentary film. Modes can carry across different periods and national cinemas. They may begin as a movement (the expository mode seems to have begun with John Grierson; the reflexive with Dziga Vertov; observational with Flaherty, and interactive with Jean Rouch and the National Film Board of Canada), but the mode persists beyond a particular time and place, adding new variations in structure and content.

Modes are something like genres, but instead of coexisting as different types of imaginary worlds (science fiction, westerns, melodrama), modes represent different concepts of historical representation. They may coexist at any moment in time (synchronically) but the appearance of a new mode results from challenge and contestation in relation to a previous mode. (We might say that reflexive documentaries call into question assumptions common to all three of the other modes; that interactive documentaries break out of the present tense limitations of an observational mode; that observational documentaries reject the argumentative pitch of the expository mode; and that expository documentaries seek to challenge the invitation to escape from the social world implicit in much fiction.) An orderly succession, however, does not in fact follow since established modes are not rendered inoperative or incapable of producing results by newer ones. Also, some challenges remain anomalous; their potential to stimulate alternative forms of practice lies dormant for a period. And a new mode may attempt to serve a different purpose from that of a previous mode or it may seek to address a deficiency or problem. Almost certainly it will simultaneously create new ones as well.

A Constituency of Viewers

Finally, we may define documentary not in institutional (discursive) nor textual terms but in relation to its viewers. Taking a text in isolation, there is nothing that absolutely or infallibly distinguishes documentary from fiction. The paradigmatic form; the invocation of a documentary logic; reliance on evidence, evidentiary editing, and the construction of an argument; the primacy of the sound track generally, commentary, testimony, and recountings specifically; and the historical nature and function of the different modes of documentary production can all be simulated within a narrative/fictional framework. Films like *No Lies, David Holzman's Diary,* and *Daughter Rite* help make this clear. The distinguishing mark of documentary may be less intrinsic to the text than a function of the assumptions and expectations brought to the process of viewing the text.

fiction can do the the same thing as doc

What are the assumptions and expectations that characterize the viewing of a documentary? To the extent that they can be generalized, they will be the product of previous experience rather than predispositions conjured on the spot. Their latent presence is what a narrative fiction film can capitalize upon and what a documentary will modify within limits but also reinforce as a basically correct form of punctuation within the domain of the cinema at large.

Most basically, viewers will develop procedural skills of comprehension and interpretation that will allow them to make sense of a documentary.[16] These procedures are a form of recipe knowledge derived from an active process of making inferences based on prior knowledge and the text itself. (This knowledge would encompass such things as recognizing a picture of Martin Luther King, Jr. as the likeness of a historical figure, understanding that spatial dislocations can be unified by an argument, assuming that social actors do not conduct themselves solely at the behest of the filmmaker, and hypothesizing the presentation of a solution once a problem begins to be described.) The text provides cues while the viewer proposes hypotheses which are either confirmed or abandoned. Such skilled, learned activity becomes, at its basic levels, habitual; it seldom intrudes upon consciousness proper since the process seldom confronts problems it cannot handle. (Consciousness can be regarded as a mode of awareness directed toward problems; we are always conscious *of* something that engages us precisely because it is problematic.)

These procedures, then, are also intimately tied to matters of ideology. They govern many of our assumptions about the nature of the world—what is in it, what appropriate action consists of, and what alternatives can be legitimately entertained. Procedural skills of viewing, like habits and the Freudian unconscious generally, orient us toward the world, or a text, in specific ways that are open to change but also quite capable of coping with setbacks and refutations (the process we call "exploration" is not abandoned if it leads us into a cul-de-sac; the basic procedure remains intact while the specific application undergoes modification). Previous experience with documentary and cinema, narrative and exposition, will establish procedures that no one text is likely to overthrow. In time, however, the inferences we form and the hypotheses we test can change considerably based on the accumulation of experience and transformations of style, structure, and mode in texts we encounter.

The most fundamental difference between expectations prompted by narrative fiction and by documentary lies in the status of the text in relation to the historical world. This has two levels. Cues within the text and assumptions based on past experience prompt us to infer that the images we see (and many of the sounds we hear) had their origin in the historical world. Technically, this means that the projected sequence of images, what occurred in front of the camera (the profilmic event), and the historical referent are taken to be congruent with one another. The image is the referent projected onto a screen. In documentary we often begin by assuming that the intermediary stage—that which occurred in front of the camera—remains identical to the actual event that we could have ourselves witnessed in the historical world (Hitler speaks at Nuremberg in *Triumph of the Will*, fishermen go about their work in *Drifters*, concentration camp survivors and victims are discovered in *Night and Fog*, miners go on strike in *Harlan County, U.S.A.*).

In many documentaries we may modify this assumption to take account of how the presence of the camera and filmmaker inflect events they appear to record. This necessitates speculation since what might have happened were the camera not there cannot be ascertained. Though inconclusive, the very dynamic of engaging in such conjecture distinguishes a documentary mode of engagement for the viewer. In a narrative fiction we assume that the profilmic event was itself constructed for the purpose of telling a story, that its relation to anything historical is metaphorical, that the people we see, even if they "play themselves" or are nonprofessionals, are nonetheless trained or rehearsed and that the places, though possibly authentic, may just as readily be replicas and simulations without jeopardizing the status of the narrative.

On a second, more global level we set up a pattern of inferences that helps us to determine what kind of argument the text is making about the historical world itself, or at least some small part of it. Instead of using procedural schemata to formulate a story, we use them to follow or construct an argument. Like other discourses of the real, the documentary argument pertains to the historical world itself rather than to an imaginary world more or less similar to the one we inhabit physically. Even if the images forfeit their claims of congruence, even if the documentary constructs what occurs in front of the camera as a representation of what occurs in the world, as do the films *Night Mail*, *Louisiana Story*, *Nanook of the North*, *Letter from Siberia*, and *The Thin Blue Line*, we still persist, as long as we assume it is a documentary that we are watching, in inferring an argument about the world. The documentary viewer employs "procedures of rhetorical engagement" rather than the "procedures of fictive engagement" that guide the viewing of classic narrative film.

Our procedures for viewing documentary will include ways of assigning motivation to what we see. As a formal term motivation refers to the way the presence of an object is justified in relation to the text.[17] In documentary a primary motivation is realism: the object is present in the text because of its function in the historical world. The hills and fields of the Liri Valley are present in *The Battle of San Pietro* because they were the historical location on which bloody fighting took place during World War II. They defined the shape of the battle; their visible appearance enjoys a historical mandate.

Another form of motivation is functional: the argument itself justifies or makes necessary the appearance of an object. The introductory remarks by General Mark Clark in *The Battle of San Pietro*, for example, have a functional justification: they present the official argument regarding the importance of the battle and the acceptability of its cost. Similarly, the close-ups of dead enemy soldiers can be motivated realistically (these are some of the men who actually died in the hills near San Pietro) and functionally (these faces of dead men illustrate the terrible price exacted by war—a proposition that is part of the film's overall argument).

Intertextual motivation also comes into play. Here the justification for the presence of something in the film arises from its expected or anticipated presence in films of a particular kind. In *The Battle of San Pietro* this would include the montage sequences of artillery barrages where guns fire in loud and rhythmic succession, shots of Italian villagers cheering the arrival of American troops, and the shots of foot soldiers advancing across contested terrain, under fire. Such shots are staples of the war documentary just as extended interviews with participant witnesses have become a staple of the historical documentary. They have the force of conventions and help define a genre, subgenre, or mode of documentary production.

Finally, formal motivation occurs when we justify the presence of an image by its contribution to a formal or stylistic pattern intrinsic to the text. This is the type of motivation least often attributed to documentary but it can still be an important factor. The faces of dead soldiers, for example, may receive their primary motivation realistically (these are some of the actual dead), functionally (as part of an argument about the terrible price of war), or even intertextually (as an image we expect to find in documentaries about war), but they also operate formally: the shots of these faces establish a formal pattern of composition and rhythm in which the series of dead American soldiers contrasts with another series representing the dead enemy such that the emotional overtones of battle and the etiquette of recording it calls for different renderings of American and enemy dead (we see the faces of the enemy dead but not of the American dead).[18]

Likewise, the images of the church and its chancel take on multiple motivations which we as viewers process. Realistically, we regard it as authentic images of the San Pietro church; functionally, the image serves to support the argument that the war has taken a severe toll on the normal patterns of village life (the church has been bombed). Intertextually, the images fall into the general category of examples of the devastation of war, especially of the damage caused to nonmilitary or civilian targets. (They are also motivated, ironically, by an intertextual reference to documentaries that catalogue and display noteworthy works of art.) Formally, the composition and chiaroscuro qualities of the images render the church as an object of intrinsic beauty. The juxtaposition of these visual elements with the voice-over commentary in the style of an art appreciation tour ("Note the interesting treatment of the chancel") adds another type of formal motivation: the "interesting treatment" is the result of bombing, not artistry, but the irony of this juxtaposition requires our recognition of the inappropriateness of the statement. This in turn requires that we grasp how the formal organization of the text invokes a distinct set of conventions (those of the discourse of art appreciation) in the spirit of irony—that is, not erroneously but knowingly. (Another, similar example of formal motivation is the tendency to use tighter close-ups of teachers than of students in Fred Wiseman's *High School.* The presence of these close-ups is not justified on realistic, functional, or intertextual grounds as much as formal ones: they establish an affective, poetic pattern of social representation which we grasp by aesthetic means.)

One fundamental expectation of documentary is that its sounds and images bear an indexical relation to the historical world. As viewers we expect that what occurred in front of the camera has undergone little or no modification in order to be recorded on film and magnetic tape. We are wont to assume that what we see would have occurred in essentially the same manner if the camera and tape recorder had not been there. This is a different assumption from that of minimal intervention that governs observational film. This assumption carries with it no necessary expectation that the film as a whole will subordinate itself to its subject. The kind of ironic commentary and the formal series that juxtapose American and enemy dead in *The Battle of San Pietro*, while "artificial," are acceptable, inasmuch as they do nothing to violate the assumption that the images themselves represent what any observer of these historical events could have observed: the church was not destroyed nor the men posed or murdered in order to be filmed. The camera angle and distance can be carefully chosen; we grant to the documentarist the right of composition much more readily than that of rearrangement. The specific images are not the product of mise-en-scène as they almost certainly would be in a fiction film even though the arguments made about them are clearly the product of a documentary logic and textual economy.

The literalism of documentary centers around the look of things in the world as an index of meaning. Churches and planes, rooms and fields:

these retain the appearance they present to a passer-by or onlooker. Situations and events, where a temporal dimension comes into play, usually retain the chronological arrangement of their actual occurrence (though they may be abbreviated or extended, and arguments regarding causation or motivation may be applied). Individuals will retain their everyday appearance; what's more, they will represent themselves over time, that is, perform, in a manner commensurate with their everyday presentation of self. Their persona will not change significantly (unless as a result of time itself, as in *28 Up* or *A Man Marked to Die: Twenty Years After,* or to indicate how the presence of a filmmaker disrupts their normal style of self-presentation as communicated by an apparently unnatural degree of self-consciousness—in which case this very effect is indexically documented for us to see).

These are some of the expectations and procedural operations that documentary invokes. They arise in relation to conventions that inform the documentary text, especially those associated with realism. These conventions guide our response and provide a starting point for our method of processing the information conveyed by the text. We settle into a distinct mode of engagement in which the fictional game calling for the suspension of disbelief ("I know this is a fiction, but I will believe it all the same," a continual oscillation between "Yes, this is true," and "No, it is not") transforms into the activation of belief ("This is how the world is, but still, it could be otherwise"). Our oscillation now swings between a recognition of historical reality and the recognition of an argument about it.

As we shall see, things are not quite this simple. All of these assumptions of literalness, of the denotative authenticity of an indexical bond, and of the conventions of realism, can themselves be thrown into question by documentary, especially but not exclusively by reflexive documentaries. But most of the time the viewer recognizes a documentary when assumptions or hypotheses applied to the text confirm this set of expectations rather than others. The viewer then sets out to process the film with an understanding that the metaphorical distance from historical reality established from the outset by fiction ("Once upon a time . . .") has been closed ("And that's the way it is . . ."). The text presents a metonymic representation of the world as we know it (the sounds and images bear a relation of part to whole; they partake of the same order of reality as that to which they refer) rather than a metaphorical rendering (where the images and sounds operate on a separate and distinct plane of resemblance to the historical world). Where fiction achieves a "reality effect" by sprinkling doses of authentic historical references across the realm of its creation—costumes, tools, vehicles, known places, or prominent figures—the same references within documentary serve as tangible evidence from the historical world in support of an argument.

The viewer engages documentary with less expectation that a sustained identification with well-developed characters will follow. Although grounded in a denotative literalism that comes from the optical and acoustic properties of film and magnetic tape, documentary most often draws our attention to an issue, concept, or problem that is at the center of the film's argument. Dependent on the specificity of its images for authenticity, documentary also invites us to regard the specific as an instantiation of something more general, of a way the world is in some broader frame. Even in observational films like *Primary, Jane,* or *A Married Couple,* and especially in works by Fred Wiseman like *Hospital, High School,* or *Model,* the strong sense of an indexical bond between what occurred in front of the camera and its historical referent draws us not only into the details of the everyday but also into the formulation of a perspective on these institutional domains of the real. We process the documentary not only as a series of highly authentic sounds and images that bear the palpable trace of how people act in the historical world, but also as the serial steps in the formation of a distinct, textually specific way of seeing or thinking.

Though an imaginary realm, fiction depends for its success on its ability to draw us into a highly specific situation through the psychodynamics of identification with characters and turns of plot. Documentary also begins with the concrete representation of people and places, situations and events but depends for its success far more on its ability to induce us to derive larger lessons, broader outlooks, or more overarching concepts from the detail it provides. Every edit or cut is a step forward in an argument. It may seem like a wound on the surface of the world for a Bazinian aesthetic of "respect for reality," but it is also a fundamental building block for the reality of a statement or argument about this world.[19]

The notion of the "history lesson" as a central aspect of documentary and as a manifestation of the documentary's affiliation with the discourses of sobriety—the ones that address the historical world of politics and economics, policy and action—shifts our expectations regarding subjectivity and objectivity. In most cases social actors who speak to the camera will not speak of themselves but of events, issues, or topics of which they have special knowledge. Our expectation is that even if a social actor does not speak to the camera but is instead observed by it we will view their speech and actions from the position of a third-person observer. Point-of-view shots, shot/reverse shots, over-the-shoulder shots, and other devices for aligning the camera with the perspective of a particular character in order to establish a first-person, more fully subjective rendering of time and space are rare. If nothing else, these forms of alignment require more thorough collaboration between performer and camera than is possible in the thick of an unfolding event recorded by a single camera. Stopping the action to realign the camera transforms history into mise-en-scène; it becomes a cue that we have crossed into the realm of narrative fiction. Subjectivity, rather than enhancing the impact of a documentary, may actually jeopardize its credibility and shift the focus of attention to the fictional representation of an actual person or event. Our identification with specific social actors therefore has less of the intensity common to fiction.

If our expectations of interiority diminish, our expectations of access to a shared exteriority increase. Objectivity looms as a more crucial criterion and point of engagement. The claim that "This is so," with its tacit "isn't it?"—a request for consent that draws us toward belief—makes objectivity, and the denotative, a natural ally of documentary rhetoric. At its simplest, objectivity refers to camera views that are not relayed to us through a character but seem to represent a third-person voice or to imply the presence of an author. Such views can be highly expressive or even expressionistic (much of the archival footage used in *Dear America: Letters Home from Vietnam* is both, for example, as are shots in *Berlin: Symphony of a Great City*), but when they are expressionistic these qualities seem to be prompted by the nature of the historical event represented rather than by personal choice. Expressive forms of objectivity attest to qualities of the historical world rather than to qualities of artistic vision.

A more complex notion of objectivity centers around those conventions that govern the fairness and impartiality of a representation. These conventions are allied to but distinct from the ones that govern scientific observation and experiment. In scientific investigation, the criteria of verification place the author inside a parenthesis: the author's personal presence cannot be a prerequisite for the manifestation of the phenomenon; others must also be able to produce the same result. History, though, does not allow for repetition. Objectivity enters in as a more explicit adjunct of rhetoric, as a way to convey the apparent truthfulness of what is said or claimed or to mask the partialities of the reporter. Even when reportage or documentary moves more clearly toward advocacy, effectiveness often depends on satisfying this expectation of impartiality. The advocate may have his or her reasons, but the need for one action rather than another must be logically convincing and fairly argued; opposing views should not be so readily disparaged that doubts as to their merits linger. The viewer's expectation is that the empathetic identification with characters so common in fiction will remain tenuous but that intellectual and emotional engagement with a topic, issue, or problem will gain in prominence, and be mediated by the conventions and rhetoric of objectivity.

This points toward another basic expectation held by the documentary viewer; that the desire to know will find gratification during the course of the film. Documentary invokes the desire to know when it identifies its subject and proposes its own variant on the "history lesson." How did this come to pass (*Smoke Menace*; *Hunger in America*; *Years of Lightning, Days of Drums*)? How does this institution work (*Hospital, High School, Joan Does Dynasty*)? What happens to people in a situation like this (*Soldier Girls, Obedience, Let There Be Light*)? What is the source of the problem and how bad is it (*Housing Problem*; *Downwind, Downstream*; *A Man When He Is a*

Man)? What price does war exact on those who wage it (*Dear America, The Battle of San Pietro, Nicaragua: No Pasarán*)? What kind of tensions arise in a situation like this (*Family Business, Primary, The Back-Breaking Leaf*)? How do members of another culture organize their lives (*Wedding Camels*, The Netsilik Eskimo Series, *Dead Birds*)? What happens when one culture encounters another (*Kenya Boran, First Contact, Ocamo Is My Town*)?

Documentary convention spawns an epistephilia. It posits an organizing agency that possesses information and knowledge, a text that conveys it, and a subject who will gain it. He-who-knows (the agency is usually masculine) will share that knowledge with those who wish to know; they, too, can take the place of the subject-who-knows. Knowledge, as much or more than the imaginary identification between viewer and fictional character, promises the viewer a sense of plenitude or self-sufficiency. Knowledge, like the ideal-ego figures or objects of desire suggested by the characters of narrative fiction, becomes a source of pleasure that is far from innocent. Who are we that we may know something? Of what does knowledge consist? What we know, and how we use the knowledge we have, are matters of social and ideological significance. These issues are at the center of this book's examination of the representation of reality by documentary film.

II

DOCUMENTARY MODES
OF REPRESENTATION

Modes

Situations and events, actions and issues may be represented in a variety of ways. Strategies arise, conventions take shape, constraints come into play; these factors work to establish commonality among different texts, to place them within the same discursive formation at a given historical moment. Modes of representation are basic ways of organizing texts in relation to certain recurrent features or conventions. In documentary film, four modes of representation stand out as the dominant organizational patterns around which most texts are structured: expository, observational, interactive, and reflexive.*

These categories are partly the work of the analyst or critic and partly the product of documentary filmmaking itself. The terms themselves are essentially my own, but the practices they refer to are filmmaking practices that filmmakers themselves recognize as distinctive approaches to the representation of reality. The four modes belong to a dialectic in which new forms arise from the limitations and constraints of previous forms and in which the credibility of the impression of documentary reality changes historically. New modes convey a fresh, new perspective on reality. Gradually, the conventional nature of this mode of representation becomes increasingly apparent: an awareness of norms and conventions to which a given text adheres begins to frost the window onto reality. The time for a new mode is then at hand.

A very cursory history of documentary representation might run like this: expository documentary (Grierson and Flaherty, among others) arose from a dissatisfaction with the distracting, entertainment qualities of the fiction film. Voice-of-God commentary and poetic perspectives sought to

---

* The four modes treated here began as a distinction between direct and indirect address in my *Ideology and the Image*. Julianne Burton revised and refined this distinction into an extremely useful and much more nuanced four-part typology in "Toward a History of Social Documentary in Latin America" in her anthology, *The Social Documentary in Latin America* (Pittsburgh: University of Pittsburgh Press, 1990): 3–6. This chapter is a further elaboration of Burton's typology.

disclose information about the historical world itself and to see that world afresh, even if these views came to seem romantic or didactic. Observational documentary (Leacock-Pennebaker, Fredrick Wiseman) arose from the availability of more mobile, synchronous recording equipment and a dissatisfaction with the moralizing quality of expository documentary. An observational mode of representation allowed the filmmaker to record unobtrusively what people did when they were not explicitly addressing the camera.

But the observational mode limited the filmmaker to the present moment and required a disciplined detachment from the events themselves. Interactive documentary (Rouch, de Antonio, and Connie Field) arose from the availability of the same more mobile equipment and a desire to make the filmmaker's perspective more evident. Interactive documentarists wanted to engage with individuals more directly while not reverting to classic exposition. Interview styles and interventionist tactics arose, allowing the filmmaker to participate more actively in present events. The filmmaker could also recount past events by means of witnesses and experts whom the viewer could also see. Archival footage of past events became appended to these commentaries to avoid the hazards of reenactment and the monolithic claims of voice-of-God commentary.

Reflexive documentary (Dziga Vertov, Jill Godmilow, and Raul Ruiz) arose from a desire to make the conventions of representation themselves more apparent and to challenge the impression of reality which the other three modes normally conveyed unproblematically. It is the most self-aware mode; it uses many of the same devices as other documentaries but sets them on edge so that the viewer's attention is drawn to the device as well as the effect.

Though this short summary gives the impression of a linear chronology and of an implicit evolution toward greater complexity and self-awareness, these modes have been potentially available from early in the cinema's history. Each mode has had a period of predominance in given regions or countries, but the modes also tend to be combined and altered within individual films. Older approaches do not go away; they remain part of a continuing exploration of form in relation to social purpose. What works at a given moment and what counts as a realistic representation of the historical world is not a simple matter of progress toward a final form of truth but of struggles for power and authority within the historical arena itself.

From an institutional point of view, those who operate largely in terms of one mode of representation may well define themselves as a discrete collectivity, with distinct preoccupations and criteria guiding their film practice. In this regard, a mode of representation involves issues of authority and the credibility of speech. Rather than standing as the idiosyncratic utterance of the individual filmmaker, the text demonstrates compliance with the norms and conventions governing a particular mode and, in turn, enjoys the prestige of tradition and the authority of a socially established and institutionally legitimated voice. At issue for the individual filmmaker are strategies of generalization, ways of representing the highly specific and local as matters of broader import, as issues with larger ramifications, as behavior of some lasting significance through recourse to a representational frame or mode. Attaching a particular text to a traditional mode of representation and to the discursive authority of that tradition may well strengthen its claims, lending to these claims the weight of previously established legitimacy. (Conversely, if a mode of representation comes under attack, an individual text may suffer as a result of its attachment.)

Narrative—with its ability to introduce a moral, political, or ideological perspective to what might otherwise be mere chronology—and realism— with its ability to anchor representations to both quotidian verisimilitude and subjective identification—might also be considered modes but they are of yet greater generality and frequently appear, in different forms, in each of the four modes discussed here. Elements of narrative, as a particular form of discourse, and aspects of realism, as a particular representational style, inform documentary logic and the economy of the text routinely. More precisely, each mode deploys the resources of narrative and realism differently, making from common ingredients different types of text with distinctive ethical issues, textual structures, and viewer expectations. It is to these that we shall now turn.

The Expository Mode

The expository text addresses the viewer directly, with titles or voices that advance an argument about the historical world. Films like *Night Mail*, *The City*, *The Battle of San Pietro*, and *Victory at Sea* that utilize a "voice-of-God" commentary are the most familiar examples. Network news with its anchorperson and string of reporters in the field is another. This is the mode closest to the classic expository essay or report and it has continued to be the primary means of relaying information and persuasively making a case since at least the 1920s.

If there is one overriding ethical/political/ideological question to documentary filmmaking it may be, What to do with people? How can people and issues be represented appropriately? Each mode addresses this question somewhat differently and poses distinct ethical questions for the practitioner. The expository mode, for example, raises ethical issues of voice: of how the text speaks objectively or persuasively (or as an instrument of propaganda). What does speaking for or on behalf of someone or something entail in terms of a dual responsibility to the subject of the film and to the audience whose agreement is sought?

Expository texts take shape around commentary directed toward the viewer; images serve as illustration or counterpoint. Nonsynchronous sound prevails (expository representation prevailed before location sound recording in sync became reasonably manageable around 1960). The rhetoric of the commentator's argument serves as the textual dominant, moving the text forward in service of its persuasive needs. (The "logic" of the text is a subordinated logic; as in law, persuasive effect tends to override the adherence to the strictest standards of reasoning.) Editing in the expository mode generally serves to establish and maintain rhetorical continuity more than spatial or temporal continuity. Such evidentiary editing adopts many of the same techniques as classic continuity editing but to a different end. Similarly, cuts that produce unexpected juxtapositions generally serve to establish fresh insights or new metaphors that the film-maker wishes to propose. They may, as an aggregate, introduce a level of counterpoint, irony, satire, or surrealism to the text as the strange juxtapositions in *Land without Bread* or *Blood of the Beasts* do.

The expository mode emphasizes the impression of objectivity and of well-substantiated judgment. This mode supports the impulse toward generalization handsomely since the voice-over commentary can readily extrapolate from the particular instances offered on the image track. Similarly it affords an economy of analysis, allowing points to be made succinctly and emphatically, partly by eliminating reference to the process by which knowledge is produced, organized, and regulated so that it, too, is subject to the historical and ideological processes of which the film speaks. Knowledge in expository documentary is often epistemic knowledge in Foucault's sense of those forms of transpersonal certainty that are in compliance with the categories and concepts accepted as given or true in a specific time and place, or with a dominant ideology of common sense such as the one our own discourses of sobriety support. What each text contributes to this stockpile of knowledge is new content, a new field of attention to which familiar concepts and categories can be applied. This is the great value of the expository mode since a topical issue can be addressed within a frame of reference that need not be questioned or established but simply taken for granted. The title of the National Film Board documentary centering on a speech by Dr. Helen Caldicott about nuclear holocaust, *If You Love This Planet*, illustrates the point. If you do love the planet, then the value of the film is the new content it offers in terms of information about the nuclear threat to survival.

Both strange juxtapositions and poetic modes of exposition qualify or contest the commonplaces on which exposition depends, and make what has grown familiar strange. The films of Buñuel and Franju mentioned above challenge our tendency to describe other cultures within the morally secure framework of our own (*Land without Bread*) and undercut our blasé assumption that meat on our table symbolizes our own hunting and gathering ancestry and the nobility of him who procures our food rather than the mass production techniques of the modern abattoir (*Blood of the Beasts*). Classics of poetic exposition like *Song of Ceylon* and *Listen to Britain*, like the works of Flaherty, give emphasis to the rhythmic and expressive elegance of their own form in order to celebrate the beauty of the quotidian and those values that unobtrusively sustain day-to-day endeavor (enterprise and valor, reserve and determination, compassion and civility, respect and responsibility). Flaherty, Jennings, and Wright, among others, sought to promote a social or collective subjectivity based on these often taken-for-granted cornerstones of middle-class life and a humanistic-romantic sensibility. Their efforts, though poetic, fall within the mode of expository representation. The emphasis, however, shifts from a direct argument or statement, to which illustrations attach, to an indirect evocation of a way of being in the world that derives from the formal structure of the film as a whole.

More recent films such as *Naked Spaces: Living Is Round* and *Sky* tend less to celebrate than *identify* a set of alternative values, drawn from other cultures and ways of life. They do so in an equally poetic, oblique style. *Sky* offers glimpses of an annual ritual honoring the dead among the Xingu in the Brazilian Amazon but provides minimal explanation. Built almost entirely around the type of suspense utilized by Flaherty in the famous sequence of Nanook hunting a seal where we only grasp the significance of actions retrospectively, but without the "pay-off" we get in *Nanook*, without any concluding summation or holistic frame, *Sky* leaves us with a sense of textures, colors, and rhythms, actions, gestures, and rituals that elude any one strategy for comprehension without ever suggesting that the events are incomprehensible or merely raw material for poetic expression. The linear, chronological flow of image and argument in Flaherty's work and in most expository films—driven by the diachronic march of cause/effect, premise/conclusion, problem/solution—turns into the "vertical," more musical pattern of association where scenes follow one another for their poetic resonance rather than for their fidelity to temporal and logical progression.

Naked Spaces shows us West African villages and some of their architectural details (but few of their people). It does not tell us about the history, function, economics, or cultural significance of these particular forms. Instead a trio of female voices composes the voice-over sound track, accompanied by indigenous music from the various regions. Each voice offers a different form of anecdotal commentary on questions of fact and value, meaning and interpretation. The film signals an acute awareness that we can no longer assume that our epistemic theories of knowledge provide unproblematic access to another culture. Poetic exposition no longer functions bardically, to draw us together into a social collectivity of shared values, but instead exposes, poetically, the social construction of that form of collectivity which allows for hierarchy and representation to go hand in hand. Trinh Minh-ha refuses to speak for or evoke the poetic essence of another culture, and instead renders the rhetorical strategy of empathy and transcendental unity strange and does so within the terms of a poetic exposition rather than with metacommentary such as a reflexive documentary might adopt.

Exposition can accommodate elements of interviews but these tend to be subordinated to an argument offered by the film itself, often via an unseen "voice of God" or an on-camera voice of authority who speaks on behalf of the text. Any sense of give and take between interviewer and subject is minimal. (Matters of duration, content, the limits or boundaries of what can and cannot be said are heavily determined by the expository text even though there may well be elaborate strings of question and answer, or even repartee between interviewer and subject. These matters circulate as tacit knowledge among practitioners and form part of the institutional matrix for expository documentaries, a matrix which the other three modes contest when it comes to the status of those recruited to appear in the film.) The voices of others are woven into a textual logic that subsumes and orchestrates them. They retain little responsibility for making the argument, but are used to support it or provide evidence or substantiation for what the commentary addresses. The voice of authority resides with the text itself rather than with those recruited to it.[1] From *Housing Problems* (1935) to the latest edition of the evening news, witnesses give their testimony within a frame they cannot control and may not understand. The tone and perspective are not theirs to determine. Their task is to contribute evidence to someone else's argument, and when well done (*Harvest of Shame, All My Babies, The Times of Harvey Milk, Sixteen in Webster Groves*) our attention is not on how the filmmaker *uses* witnesses to make a point but on the effectiveness of the argument itself.

The viewer of documentaries in the expository mode generally holds expectations that a commonsensical world will unfold in terms of the establishment of a logical, cause/effect linkage between sequences and events. Recurrent images or phrases function as classic refrains, underscoring thematic points or their emotional undercurrents, such as the frequent montages of artillery fire and explosions in combat documentaries that stress the progression of a battle, its physical means of implementation, and its human cost. Similarly, the refrain of images of rich farm land turned to dust in *The Plow That Broke the Plains* gives affective emphasis to the thematic argument for reclamation through federal programs of conservation. Causation tends to be direct and linear, readily identifiable, and subject to modification by planned intervention.

The authoring presence of the filmmaker is represented by the commentary and sometimes the (usually unseen) voice of authority will be that of the filmmaker him- or herself as it is in *The Battle of San Pietro*. In other cases such as the evening news, a delegate, the anchorperson, will represent a broader, institutional source of authority. (We do not assume that the structure or content of the evening news arises from the anchorperson but that he or she represents a discursive field and gives it anthropomorphic embodiment. In either case the viewer attends less to the physical presence of the commentator as a social actor engaged with the world than with the movement of the argument or statement about the world which the commentator advances. In other words, the authoring or institutional agency is represented by the logos—the word and its logic—more than by the historical body of an actual agent.)

Finally, the viewer will typically expect the expository text to take shape around the solution to a problem or puzzle: presenting the news of the day, exploring the working of the atom or the universe, addressing the consequences of nuclear waste or acid rain, tracing the history of an event or the biography of a person. This organization plays a role similar to the role of the classic unity of time in narrative where imaginary events occur within a fixed period of time and often move toward a conclusion under some form of temporal urgency or deadline. Rather than the suspense of solving a mystery or rescuing a captive, the expository documentary frequently builds a sense of dramatic involvement around the need for a solution. The felt need itself can be as much a product of expository organization as of narrative suspense, even if it does refer to a problem located in the historical world. The viewer expects entry into the text by these teleological devices and substitutes the dynamics of problem-solving for the dynamics of anticipation, retardation, feints, and enigmas that constitute the stuff of suspense.

The Observational Mode

Observational documentaries are what Erik Barnouw refers to as direct cinema and what others like Stephen Mamber describe as cinema verité. (Barnouw reserves cinema verité for the interventionist or interactive filmmaking of Jean Rouch and others.) For some practitioners and critics the terms direct cinema and cinema verité are interchangeable; for others they refer to distinct modes, but some may assign direct cinema to the more observational stance and others cinema verité. For these reasons I have chosen to sidestep both terms in favor of the more descriptive appellations, *observational* and *interactive* modes of documentary representation. The observational mode stresses the nonintervention of the filmmaker. Such films cede "control" over the events that occur in front of the camera more than any other mode. Rather than constructing a temporal framework, or rhythm, from the process of editing as in *Night Mail* or *Listen to Britain*, observational films rely on editing to enhance the impression of lived or real time. In its purest form, voice-over commentary, music external to the observed scene, intertitles, reenactments, and even interviews are completely eschewed. Barnouw summarizes the mode helpfully when he distinguishes direct cinema (observational filmmaking) from Rouch's style of cinema verité.

The direct cinema documentarist took his camera to a situation of tension and waited hopefully for a crisis; the Rouch version of cinema verité tried to precipitate one. The direct cinema artist aspired to invisibility; the Rouch cinema verité artist was often an avowed participant. The direct cinema artist played the role of uninvolved bystander; the cinema verité artist espoused that of provocateur.[2]

Observational filmmaking gives a particular inflection to ethical considerations. Since the mode hinges on the ability of the filmmaker to be unobtrusive, the issue of intrusion surfaces over and over within the institutional discourse. Has the filmmaker intruded upon people's lives in ways that will irrevocably alter them, perhaps for the worse, in order to make a film?[3] Has his or her need to make a film and build a career out of the observation of others led to representations about the nature of the project and its probable effects on participants in disingenuous forms? Has he or she not only sought the informed consent of the participants but made it possible for informed consent to be understood and given? Does the evidence of the film convey a sense of respect for the lives of others or have they simply been used as signifiers in someone else's discourse?[4] When something happens that may jeopardize or injure one of the social actors whose life is observed, does the filmmaker have a responsibility to intervene; or conversely, does he or she have the responsibility, or even the right, to continue filming? To what extent and in what ways shall the voice of people be represented? If they are observed by someone else, to what extent do their own observations on the process and results of observation deserve a place in the final film?

This last question begins to shade toward the issues of interactive filmmaking. For the moment the specific properties of observational works as texts deserve consideration. Such works are characterized by indirect address, speech overheard rather than heard since the social actors engage with one another rather than speak to the camera. Synchronous sound and relatively long takes are common. These techniques anchor speech to images of observation that locate dialogue, and sound, in a specific moment and historical place. Each scene, like that of classic narrative fiction, displays a three-dimensional fullness and unity in which the observer's location is readily determined. Each shot supports the same overall system of orientation rather than proposing unrelated or incommensurate spaces. And the space gives every indication of having been carved from the historical world rather than fabricated as a fictional mise-en-scène.

Rather than a paradigmatic organization centered around the solution to a puzzle or problem, observational films tend to take paradigmatic form around the exhaustive depiction of the everyday. *A Trial for Rape*, for example, compresses days of argumentation during two separate legal hearings into one hour of screen time, but the viewer has a vivid sense of comprehensive documentation (largely due to shots that are held longer and individual statements that continue longer than they would in a realist fiction or a typical news report). When Fred Wiseman observes the making of a thirty-second television commercial for some twenty five minutes in his film *Model,* he conveys the sense of having observed everything worth noting about the shooting. (He omits the pre- and post-production elements of the activity, which is not unusual in observational cinema: since these films tend to cover specific moments exhaustively, they avoid the type of summarization of a process that would require a montage of typical moments. Also, in this film, Wiseman's focus is on the interaction of the advertising system with its social agents, the models, rather than on the entire system: its economic structure, the decision-making process, marketing strategies, and so on.)

The sense of exhaustive (and telling) observation frequently comes not only from the ability of the filmmaker to record particularly revealing moments but also from the ability to include moments representative of lived time itself rather than what we might call "story time" (time propelled by the cause/effect logic of classical narrative where an economy of carefully justified and well-motivated actions prevails). "Dead" or "empty" time unfolds where nothing of narrative significance occurs but where the rhythms of everyday life settle in and establish themselves. In this mode of representation, each cut or edit serves mainly to sustain the spatial and temporal continuity of observation rather than the logical continuity of an argument or case. Even when the text shifts to a different scene or locale, the sense of an underlying spatial and temporal continuity prevails, one which is consonant with the moment of filming, making observational cinema a particularly vivid form of "present-tense" representation.

The presence of the camera "on the scene" testifies to its presence in the historical world; its fixity suggests a commitment or engagement with the immediate, intimate, and personal that is comparable to what an actual observer/participant might experience (without unrestricted recourse to the dynamization of time and space that cinema allows). The sounds and images used are recorded at the moment of observational filming, in contrast to the voice-over and images of illustration in the expository mode, which do not propose or require so intimate a tie to the moment of filming. This makes the expository film, and the interactive one, available for historical investigations whereas the observational film most readily addresses contemporary experience.

The absence of commentary and the reluctance to use images to illustrate generalizations encourages an emphasis on the activity of individuals within specific social formations such as the family, the local community, or a single institution or aspect of one (such as the play between an institution and those it recruits or serves that we find in so many of Fred Wiseman's films). Such observations frequently take shape around the representation of typicality—the types of exchanges and activities that are likely to occur (*High School*), process—the unfolding of a set of relationships over time (*An American Family*), or crisis—the conduct of individuals under pressure (*Primary*).

"Strange juxtapositions" often function as examples of a hybrid style in which the filmmaker chooses to turn to techniques associated with one of the other modes, as when Fred Wiseman cross-cuts in *Titicut Follies* between the forced feeding of a patient and the later preparation of the same patient for burial. These juxtapositions work to make an editorial point in the spirit of expository cinema rather than allow events to unfold according to their own rhythm. The conventions of observation make abrupt shifts of time or location less likely as ways to jar the viewer into fresh insight. More likely are abrupt, surprising, or unexpected shifts in the perspective of or self-presentation by a social actor, as when Sgt. Abing in *Soldier Girls* drops his tough drill instructor demeanor to confess how deeply wounded and emotionally crippled he has become as a result of his combat experience. Such moments serve as epiphanies and seem "real," that is, to have originated in the historical world rather than in the de-familiarizing strategies of an argument. The leaps or juxtapositions that jar and unsettle stem from the ways in which people and events take twists and turns that, as is often said, appear stranger than fiction. Matters of placement within the film, rhythm, camera position, sound quality, and intimations of the felt presence of the filmmaker may contribute to the force of the juxtaposition as much as its basis in actual behavior of people, but, to the extent that the film subscribes to an observational realism, these factors will tend to be unobtrusive and rarely commented upon.

Recurring images or situations tend to strengthen a "reality effect," anchoring the film to the historical facticity of time and place and certifying to the continuing centrality of specific locations. These refrains add affective texture to an argument; they stress the historical specificity of the observed world and the micro-changes that occur from day to day. The repeated presence of the home in *A Married Couple* and of the pizza parlor in *Family Business*, for example, locate the site of dramatic engagement. These locales take on more and more significance in terms of the emotional geography of space (the way in which specific zones of a bedroom, a kitchen, the cash register, or pizza oven become associated with specific characters and their own sense of place and identity, a sense of self often tested or put at risk through their interactions with others). Though observational films are rooted in the present, they also take time, and such recurrences heighten the impression of narrative development, of transformation over time, as opposed to the alternative impression of an atemporal slice of selected scenes from a single moment in time.

The observational mode of representation has enjoyed considerable use as an ethnographic tool, allowing filmmakers to observe the activities of others without resorting to the techniques of exposition that turn the sounds and images of others into accomplices in someone else's argument. Observational filmmaking and the social science approaches of ethnomethodology and symbolic interactionism have a number of principles in common.[5] All three stress an empathetic, nonjudgmental, participatory mode of observation that attenuates the authoritative posture of traditional exposition. Observational cinema affords the viewer an opportunity to look in on and overhear something of the lived experience of others, to gain some sense of the distinct rhythms of everyday life, to see the colors, shapes, and spatial relationships among people and their possessions, to hear the intonation, inflection, and accents that give a spoken language its "grain" and that distinguish one native speaker from another. If there is something to be gained from an affective form of learning, observational cinema provides a vital forum for such experience. Though still problematic in other ways, there are qualities here that no other mode of representation duplicates.

For the viewer, observational documentaries set up a frame of reference closely akin to that of fiction film. (The differences are pursued in detail in the following chapters.) We look in on and overhear social actors. This term stands for "individuals" or "people." Those whom we observe are seldom trained or coaxed in their behavior. I use "social actor" to stress the degree to which individuals represent themselves to others; this can be construed as a performance. The term is also meant to remind us that social actors, people, retain the capacity to act within the historical arena where they perform. The sense of aesthetic remove between an imaginary world in which actors perform and the historical world in which people live no longer obtains. The performance of social actors, though, is similar to the performance of fictional characters in many respects. Individuals present a more or less complex psychology, and we direct our attention toward their development or destiny. We identify and follow the codes of actions and enigmas that advance the narrative. We attend to those semic or behaviorally descriptive moments that fold back over characters and give further density to their behavior. We give considerable attention to the referential codes imported or "documented" by the text as the operational codes of the culture that the social actors adhere to or contest in discernible ways. We may note the play of a symbolic code that governs the economy of the text in metaphysical or psychoanalytic terms (such as the desire for the fullness of knowledge and the transcendental authority of the observing gaze or the desire for unity between observer and observed, viewer and text, without reminders of lack, deficiency, or fissure between the text and the real, representation and referent).

Through its kinship with fiction (first posited by observational filmmakers themselves in relation to Italian neorealism), these films invite the viewer to take an even more complex relation to the film's referential dimension. If fictional aesthetics involves us in relation to "nonpractical ends," a fairly conventional if not unproblematic definition, observational documentary also extends this possibility of nonpractical, aesthetic involvement.[6] Instead of the suspension of disbelief that could be put as "I know very well [that this is a fiction] but all the same . . . [I will treat it as if it were not]," the observational documentary encourages belief; "Life *is* like this, isn't it?" Though spared any requirement of practical application, the reprieve is even less clear than it is in fiction. The viewer experiences the text as a template of life as it is lived; the attitude taken toward it proposes itself as (or derives from) the attitude appropriate for the viewer were he or she "on the spot," as it were, placed in a position where the interaction from which the camera restrains itself were expected. We imagine the screen pulled away and direct encounter possible. One element of the viewer's engagement, then, is less an imaginative identification with character or situation and more a practical testing of subjective responses as an eligible participant in as well as observer of the historical world represented.

This testing depends on the work of realism and its ability to render the impression of reality, a sense of the historical world as we, in fact, experience it, usually on a quotidian basis. This, in turn, hinges on the presence of the filmmaker or authoring agency as an absence, an absent presence whose effect is noted (it provides the sounds and images before us) but whose physical presence remains not only unseen but also, for the most part, unacknowledged. When a psychiatrist filmed working with a patient in Fred Wiseman's *Hospital* looks at the camera in dismay, after an exasperating phone call to a social worker, and says, "She hung up on me," the film cuts to another scene rather than continue the shot and force the filmmaker to take responsibility for a reply. When a tribesperson in *Joe Leahy's Neighbors* speaks of the filmmaker to his companion and asks his friend if they should sing a song, the friend replies, "No, it's not that kind of film." This produces a moment of amusement for the viewer but by cutting immediately to another shot, the filmmakers also dodge the implied responsibility to explain what kind of film it is. This would require a form of presence they prefer to avoid, allowing the film to explain itself (to the viewer at least; how it was explained to the subjects remains purely speculation).

Observational cinema, therefore, conveys the sense of unmediated and unfettered access to the world. The physical body of a particular filmmaker does not seem to put a limit on what we can see. The person behind the camera, and microphone, will not draw the attention of the social actors or engage with them in any direct or extended fashion. Instead we expect to have the ability to take the position of an ideal observer, moving among people and places to find revealing views. The fact that the mise-en-scène of the film is not fabricated on a set but in the arena of historical reality imposes more constraints on the ideal observer than we find in fiction— and, by dint of the evidence of physical or technical difficulty, we may be reminded of the filmmaker's presence in the face of the real—but the expectation of transparent access remains. As in classical narrative fiction, our tendency to establish a repertoire of imaginary relationships with characters and situations prospers on condition of the filmmaker's presence as absence. Their unacknowledged, nonresponsive presence clears the way for the dynamics of empathetic identification, poetic immersion, or voyeuristic pleasure.

The Interactive Mode

What if the filmmaker does intervene and interact? What if the veil of illusory absence is shorn away? This is the possibility promoted by Dziga Vertov in the 1920s as *kino-pravda*. Filmmakers in several countries renewed this possibility in tentative, technically limited ways during the early to mid 1950s. In the late fifties this mode became technologically viable through the work of filmmakers at the National Film Board of Canada (particularly with the Candid Eye series, 1958–59, and Gilles Groulx and Michel Brault's *Les Racquetteurs* in 1958). The mode regained prominence and became the center of controversy with Jean Rouch and Edgar Morin's *Chronicle of a Summer* (1960), which they named a work of cinema verité, and with the success of *Primary* (1960) by Drew Associates in the United States.[7]

Beginning in the late 1950s the availability of very portable synchronous sound recording equipment made interaction more feasible than it had been theretofore. Speech need no longer be reserved for postproduction in a studio, far removed from the lives of those whose images grace the film. The filmmaker need not be only a cinematic, recording eye. He or she might more fully approximate the human sensorium: looking, listening, and speaking as it perceives events and allows for response. The filmmaker's voice could be heard as readily as any other, not subsequently, in an organizing voice-over commentary, but on the spot, in face-to-face encounter with others. The possibilities of serving as mentor, participant, prosecutor, or provocateur in relation to the social actors recruited to the film are far greater than the observational mode would suggest.

Interactive documentary stresses images of testimony or verbal exchange and images of demonstration (images that demonstrate the validity, or possibly, the doubtfulness, of what witnesses state). Textual authority shifts toward the social actors recruited: their comments and responses provide a central part of the film's argument. Various forms of monologue and dialogue (real or apparent) predominate. The mode introduces a sense of partialness, of *situated* presence and *local* knowledge that derives from the actual encounter of filmmaker and other. Issues of comprehension and interpretation as a function of physical encounter arise: how do filmmaker and social actor respond to each other; do they react to overtones or implications in each other's speech; do they see how power and desire flow between them? (This last question forms the core of Ross McElwee's *Sherman's March* as the filmmaker journeys through the South, recording his interactions with a variety of women to whom he is drawn.)

Editing operates to maintain a logical continuity between individual viewpoints, usually without benefit of an overarching commentary, the logic of which shifts to the relationship between the more fragmentary statements of subjects in interviews or the conversational exchange between filmmaker and social actors. (To the extent that the film may be *about* the interaction itself, as in *Sherman's March* or *Hotel Terminus*, the logic of the text leads less to an argument about the world than to a statement about the interactions themselves and what they disclose about filmmaker and social actors alike.) Spatial relations may well be noncontiguous or even incommensurate (such as the spatial leaps from the site of one interview to another and from the mise-en-scène of interviews to that of archival footage in *In the Year of the Pig* or other interactive, historical documentaries).

Unexpected juxtapositions may involve graphic intertitles (like the dictionary definition of a screw inserted after a rape victim speaks of being "screwed" in JoAnn Elam's work, *Rape*). Unusual framing, especially during an interview when we roam away from the "talking head" to explore some other aspect of the scene or person, such as the pan to a bee on the lapel of a pompous speaker in Chris Marker's *Le Joli Mai* or the emphasis given to the "empty space" between filmmaker and subject in Trinh Minh-ha's *Surname Viet Given Name Nam*, put the solemnity and authority of the interview itself into question. Incongruous or contradictory statements about the same issue, such as the reassembled remarks of Richard Nixon in Emile de Antonio's *Millhouse* or the two different interpretations presented in *First Contact* when historic photographs and film of the first encounters between whites and New Guinea Highlanders are described by the participants from each culture, also achieve the effect of a strange juxtaposition. They prompt the viewer to reassess an initial set of statements in light of a second, discrepant set. Such juxtapositions contest the flow of thought appropriate to the first frame of reference to induce surprise, insight, or possibly, laughter.[8] They become, apart from the process of interaction itself, a key tool in the filmmaker's discursive repertoire.

These possibilities pose distinct ethical issues for practitioners. How far can participation go? How are limits beyond which a filmmaker cannot go negotiated? What tactics does "prosecution" outside of a formal legal system allow? The word "prosecution" refers to the process of social or historical inquiry in which the filmmaker engages in dialogue with witnesses to carry forward an argument. Actually, the relation to witnesses may be closer to that of public defender than prosecutor: it is not commonly an adversarial relationship but one in which information is sought for an argument. The ethical issue in such a relationship pivots on the manner in which the filmmaker represents his or her witnesses, particularly when differing motives, priorities, or needs are at work. In a Public Broadcasting System interview with Bill Moyers, Errol Morris, director of *The Thin Blue Line*, differentiated his primary goal as a filmmaker from his subject's overriding desire to prove his innocence. For Morris, making a "good movie" came first. The film has also served his subject well, as it happens, but in other cases the results are not always so happy. (*The Things I Cannot Change*, an early Challenge for Change documentary from the National Film Board of Canada, for example, is a good movie but it had a negative impact on the lives of the poverty-line family on which it focuses.) The methods of ABC's "Nightline" exemplify how the interests of constructing a good program can work to the detriment of the program's subjects by depriving them of control over how they are represented. The show features newsworthy individuals with whom host Ted Koppel interacts, but they are placed in a separate studio (even when they are in the same building in Washington, D.C.); they are not provided with a monitor on which to see Koppel or themselves in dialogue, and they must rely on an ear plug to hear their interlocutor's questions and comments.[9]

These tactics are not discernible to the viewer and may seem quite mild compared to the tendentious, inflammatory harangues of Morton Downey. "The Morton Downey Show" encourages representations of excess. The appearance of fairness seems thoroughly abandoned in the midst of inflammatory harangues where the progressive or conservative quality of the views expressed matters less than emotional intensity and imperviousness to reasoned dialogue. This show goes so far beyond the bounds of normal dialogue that it may well presage the death of public service discourse, however loosely construed, or mark its return as participatory spectacle. (The show failed to garner adequate ratings after becoming available nationally; it is no longer on the air.)

Mr. Downey's proximity to the ethics of the Roman circus poses another, related questions: How far can provocation go? When a Geraldo Rivera eggs white supremacists into physical violence, what responsibility does he bear for the consequences (an issue somewhat blunted when his own nose, rather than that of one of his guests, is broken)? When Claude Lanzman urges, if not insists, in *Shoah*, that his witnesses speak of the trauma they suffered as concentration camp victims can we assume that the result is as therapeutic as Mr. Lanzman seems to believe it will be? When the actor-scientist in Stanley Milgram's film, *Obedience* (the film demonstrates Milgram's classic experiments on obedience to authority), urges unwitting subjects to administer what would be lethal shocks to faulty learners, what responsibility remains with the filmmaker for the emotional aftermath of the experience, and not just in the immediate moment but in the succeeding years? In the latter cases, the filmmakers represent themselves with a particular honesty that allows us to see the process of negotiation that leads to the result they seek. We can make our own assessment of their conduct, the procedures governing their inquiry, and the balance between information gained and its personal price, but is this a sufficient form of exoneration? What are the ethical or political standards that organize patterns of social exchange such as these? What further negotiations, particularly in the process of editing—in choices of what to show and what to omit—might there be that also deserve a place in the finished film?

Interaction often revolves around the form known as the interview. This form raises ethical questions of its own: interviews are a form of hierarchical discourse deriving from the unequal distribution of power, as in the confessional and the interrogation. How is the inherently hierarchical structure of the form handled? Does the filmed oral history (or audiovisual history) pose ethical issues distinct from those of oral histories intended for archival use as primary source material? What rights or prerogatives does the interviewee retain? Legal safeguards to privacy and protection from slander or libel provide guidelines in some cases, but not in all. The ethical principle of informed consent provides another, but many documentary filmmakers choose to disregard it, arguing that the process of social or historical inquiry benefits from the same principles of free speech and a free press that allow considerable license to journalists in their pursuit of the news.[10]

Beyond the interview and oral history as such lie other nagging questions of the filmmaker's responsibility for historical accuracy, objectivity, and even the visual complexity of source material.[11] *Who Killed Vincent Chin?* for example, about the case of a young Chinese-American beaten to death by a laid-off, white auto worker and his stepson in Detroit partly because they mistook him for Japanese, gives considerable time to the explanations by the auto worker and his son themselves, as well as to their friends. The restraint—all the more evident when put in the context of Renee Tajima and Christine Choy's status as women of color and Choy's long record of political filmmaking—does not function as an obedient bow to the canons of good journalism but as a powerful rhetorical strategy. The diversity of perspectives—combining the account by the auto workers with that of friends and family of the murdered Mr. Chin and extensive footage taken from television news reports made at the time of the incident—and the juxtapositions created by the complex interweaving of source material in the editing require the viewer to arrive at his or her own answer to the question posed by the film's title.

The interactive text takes many forms but all draw their social actors into direct encounter with the filmmaker. When heard, the voice of the filmmaker addresses the social actors on screen rather than the spectator. Some works, like Rouch's seminal *Chronicle of a Summer*, or later films like Jon Alpert's *Hard Metal's Disease*, Octavio Cortázar's *For the First Time*, and *Talking about Punto Cubano*, Jean-Pierre Gorin's *Poto and Cabengo*, Michael Rubbo's *Sad Song of Yellow Skin*, or Bonnie Klein's *Not a Love Story* (as well as Ross McElwee's *Sherman's March*) are rooted in the moment of interaction itself. The present-tense quality is strong and sense of contingency vivid. Events yet to unfold may take alternative courses based on the process of interaction that we witness. In a later, ethnographic work, *Tourou et Bitti*, for example, Rouch confides to the viewer in voice-off as he strides toward a small village square that his intention is to use the camera he carries (and which records the traveling long shot we see) to provoke a trance that has been attempted unsuccessfully on several recent occasions. The remainder of the film records the event more or less observationally, but Rouch's opening remark makes clear the interactive powers of the camera as the trance ceremony proceeds to a successful conclusion.

Other films, like Emile de Antonio's pioneering *In the Year of the Pig,* or subsequent films like *With Babies and Banners, The Wobblies, Seeing Red, Rosie the Riveter, Shoah, Solovki Power,* or *Hotel Terminus,* turn to the past or, more precisely, to the relationship between the past and the present. Some, like *Shoah,* stress the influence of the past on the present by making the interview process itself the central aspect of the film. Others, like *Are We Winning the Cold War, Mommy?* and *Rosie the Riveter,* stress the continuous process whereby the past is reconstructed in the present by moving beyond the interviews to a visual interpretation of the past from archival footage. *In the Year of the Pig,* for example, builds around a series of interviews with various observers of or participants in the American involvement in the war in Vietnam. The film helped establish the genre of historical reconstruction based on oral history or witness testimony and archival footage rather than on a voice-over commentary. De Antonio's presence is relatively oblique but constantly implied both by editorial commentary (such as the statues of Civil War soldiers with which the film opens, suggesting the internal, basically Vietnamese rather than external, "free world vs. enslaved world" nature of the conflict) and by the interview format itself. We only hear de Antonio once (in an interview with Senator Thurston Morton where he takes particular pains to stress the fact of the interview as such) and never see him on camera, but the clear historical account of the war's origins, which is obviously at odds with the United States government account, indirectly points toward de Antonio's organizing presence. The *argument* is his but it arises out of the selection and arrangement of the evidence provided by witnesses rather than from a voice-over commentary. (There is no voice-over commentary at all.)

With Babies and Banners, Union Maids, and *Seeing Red,* on the other hand, give the impression that the argument is the witnesses' and that the filmmaker merely acts to present and illustrate it. (There is still no voice-over commentary and the structuring presence of the filmmaker is also less in evidence.) The difference is quite significant, but the important point here is the shift of emphasis from an author-centered voice of authority to a witness-centered voice of testimony.[12] When interviews contribute to an expository mode of representation, they generally serve as evidence for the filmmaker's, or text's, argument. When interviews contribute to an interactive mode of representation, they generally serve as evidence for an argument presented as the product of the interaction of filmmaker and subject.

Other filmmakers interact overtly and are both seen and heard routinely.

This is the case with Jean Rouch himself, with Barbara Kopple in *Harlan County, U.S.A.*, Jon Alpert in *Hard Metal's Disease*, Bonnie Klein in *Not a Love Story*, Marilu Mallet in *Unfinished Diary*, Claude Lanzman in *Shoah*, Tony Bubba in *Lightning over Braddock*, and Marcel Ophuls in *Hotel Terminus*. The filmmaker's felt presence as a center of attention for the social actors as well as the viewer leads to an emphasis on the act of gathering information or building knowledge, the process of social and historical interpretation, and the effect of the encounter between people and filmmakers when that experience may directly alter the lives of all involved. The encounter may be formalized via interviews as it is in *Shoah* or more unstructured and spontaneous as it is in *Lightning over Braddock* but the sense of the precariousness of the present moment, as the direction of the film hangs in the balance with every exchange, distinguishes the interactive or participatory mode of representation quite sharply from the observational one.

The degree of latitude within which social actors can engage in the process of self-presentation varies considerably, from the maximal autonomy allowed by observational cinema to the highly restrictive limitations of formal interviews like those utilized by Ted Koppel on "Nightline" or CBS's "Meet the Press." When interaction occurs outside of one of the formal interview structures, as will be discussed below, the filmmaker and social actors engage one another as peers, taking up positions on the common ground of social encounter, presenting themselves as social actors who must negotiate the terms and conditions of their own interaction. (These positions, of course, are not necessarily those of full equals; the act of filming alone usually sees to that.) Parts of *Hard Metal's Disease* when Alpert becomes a full participant in events, for example, when he steps in to translate statements by American disease victims into Spanish for the Mexican workers whom the Americans have come to warn, erase the sense of the constraints of an interview structure. Alpert is not an observer but a full participant, if not instigator, in the events he films.

Likewise, the exchanges between the filmmaking team of Joel Demott and Jeff Kreines and their subjects, a group of Pittsburgh filmmakers whose attempt to make a low-budget horror film they document in *Demon Lover Diary*, are those of individuals engaged in a common project.[13] The film underscores the extent to which a participatory approach, where the interactions are themselves part of the final record and their effect significant to the outcome of events, becomes a type of metaobservational film as well. The filmmakers extend their observations to include the process of exchange between themselves and their subjects in a systematic and substantive manner. (The idea of "metaobservation" is particularly apt here because Jeff Kreines operates one camera, recording the making of the low budget film, while a different individual operates a second camera, recording Jeff and Joel's interactions with the feature filmmakers. At times, Joel DeMott records diaristic entries about the unfolding events, voice-over. We are left with the impression that the film they would have produced was observational but that to this they added a second, more "meta" set of observations and diaristic commentaries.)

A participatory dynamic is one that extends beyond the use of interview material in an expository text. Commentary made by or on behalf of the filmmaker clearly subordinates the interviews to the film's own argument. Man-in-the-street interviews tucked into *Prelude to War* or sandwiched among narrator Roger Mudd's points about military waste in *The Selling of the Pentagon* convey a minimal sense of participatory engagement. A participatory dynamic also goes further than the occasional gesture or passing acknowledgment that a film is being made. (One example occurs in *Joe Leahy's Neighbors*, discussed below, chap. 7.) An interactive text extends beyond passing acknowledgments to the point where the dynamics of social exchange between filmmaker and subject become fundamental to the film. Jon Silver's *Watsonville on Strike* establishes a vividly interactive mode in its opening scene inside the Teamster union hall in Watsonville. The room is crowded with striking cannery workers, most of whom are Chicano. A Teamster official, Fred Heim, looks toward the camera and insists that Silver leave the room. Rather than debate the point with Heim, Silver asks the workers, in Spanish, if he can stay. The camera pans away from Heim to show dozens of striking workers shout out, "Si!" The scene becomes a lively confrontation between these workers and their purported union leader. Silver continues this pattern of interactive engagement throughout the film, principally by means of interviews that make his own allegiances clear and situate him less as an observer than a metaparticipant, someone actively engaged with other participants but also engaged in constructing an argument and perspective on their struggle.

The interview is an overdetermined structure. It arises in relation to more than oral history and it serves far more than one function. Most basically, the interview testifies to a power relation in which institutional hierarchy and regulation pertain to speech itself. As such, the interview figures into most of the fundamental discourses of sobriety, as I have termed them, and into most of the dominant institutions in our culture. Michel Foucault speaks extensively of the patient-client interview in social management, particularly sexual therapy, originating in the religious practice of the confession.[14] The regulatory function of such exchanges, which appear to emancipate sexuality from a burden of silence only to place it within the disciplinary procedures of an institutional regime, draws most of Foucault's emphasis, but the interview extends well beyond its religious-psychotherapeutic use. In medicine, it goes by the name of "case history," where patient-generated narratives of symptoms and their possible source become rewritten in the discourse of medical science. In anthropology, the interview is the testimony of native informants who describe the workings of their culture to the one who will rewrite their accounts into the discourse of anthropological investigation. On television it has spawned the genre known as the talk show. In journalism, it is the press conference and interview as such, and in police work, the interrogation. (The difference is one of degree.) In law, we find depositions, hearings, testimony, and cross-examination. In education, the Socratic dialogue as well as the lecture with question/answer period represent different versions of this basic structure.

In each case, hierarchy is maintained and served while information passes from one social agent to another. In contrast to what Teresa de Lauretis has called, after Foucault, the "technologies of gender," which work, discursively, to implant a gendered, sexual subjectivity in every individual, we might use the term "technologies of knowledge" for those activities that work to implant a gendered, social subjectivity that never disrupts the linkage of knowledge (any more than sexuality) from power.[15] The interview in its various guises has a central role to play among these technologies. In cinema, this linkage of technique to power takes material form as space and time, particularly space. Like the ethical issues concerning the space between filmmaker and subject and how it is negotiated, a parallel set of political issues of hierarchy and control, power and knowledge surround the interview.

No one-to-one correlation exists between form and content with regard to the interview any more than to low-angle shots or high-key lighting. But each choice of spatio-temporal configuration between filmmaker and interviewee carries implications and a potential political charge, an ideological valence, as it were, that deserves attention. At one extreme would be "conversation," a free exchange between filmmaker and subject that seems to follow no predetermined course and to address no clearly specified agenda. (The word is in quotes since the very process of filming such a conversation makes it something other than the natural and obvious thing it appears.) Talk shows, with their hosts who serve as surrogates for the filmmaking or television apparatus and whose speech appears spontaneous and wide-ranging, come to mind, as do the informal exchanges between Ross McElwee and the women he meets or visits in his *Sherman's March*. In these cases, the filmmaker or surrogate is clearly visible or, if off screen (usually wielding the camera), still the primary center of attention for the characters on screen. Conversation is at the boundary of institutional control, as Lyotard suggests when he contrasts it with discourse inside an institutional frame. Conversations draw our attention to the byplay and maneuvering, along a gradient of power, between the filmmaker and subject. Like the oral history, case history, deposition, or court testimony, conversation within a film is also destined to be scrutinized by interested onlookers, giving these quasi-public maneuvers an added measure of complexity.

A variation on "mere" conversation, even less obviously organized by the filmmaker, is the "masked interview."[16] In this case the filmmaker is both off screen and unheard. Equally significant, the interviewee no longer addresses the filmmaker off screen but engages in conversation with another social actor. An example is the discussion between Guyo Ali and Iya Duba in *Kenya Boran* when the two men discuss birth control practices promoted by the Kenyan government. Guyo Ali introduces the topic without giving any sense that this is the result of a request by the filmmakers, who did no more than request its introduction. (David MacDougall has described his occasional use of this technique in *Kenya Boran* in private discussion.)

The impression rendered is very hard to differentiate from ordinary conversation of the sort found in observational films. The key difference, however, is that we observe an implanted conversation. What topic the social actors address and the general drift of what they say has been prearranged. Sometimes the discussion will give the impression of being more strictly focused than ordinary conversation, but there are no clear-cut guidelines for determining this, especially in a cross-cultural or ethnographic context. Rather than making the interview structure evident, the masked interview slides toward the oblique stylistics of the fiction film, and the work of a *metteur en scène*. The sense of a fissure or discrepancy between the performance we observe and the codes we expect to govern it opens up. Dialogue has an "imperfect" quality, but without further, contextual information, the viewer is left uncertain whether to construe this discrepancy as cultural difference (including speech protocol associated with rituals), camera consciousness, or self-consciousness that stems from the act of presenting an interview in the guise of conversation.

A more structured interaction between filmmaker and social actor where both are present and visible may give the impression of "dialogue," again in quotes because of the hierarchy of control that guides and directs the exchange, privileging the interviewer as the initiator and arbiter of legitimacy and framing the interviewee as primary source material, potential repository of new information or knowledge. This form of exchange might also be termed "pseudo-dialogue" since the interview format prohibits full reciprocity or equity between the participants. The interviewer's skill is often revealed by his or her ability to appear at the service of the interviewee whose speech he or she actually controls, somewhat in the manner of a ventriloquist. Michel Brault and Gilles Groulx's *Les Racquetteurs,* Jean Rouch and Edgar Morin's *Chronicle of a Summer,* Michael Rubbo's films such as *Sad Song of Yellow Skin, Waiting for Fidel,* and *Wet Earth, Warm People,* the types of discussions conducted by Barbara Walters or Bill Moyers on American television, among others, adopt this tack, heightening a sense of equity between discussants and giving the sense of an agenda that does not require a formalized, preestablished sequence of exchanges. The resulting impression of a pseudo-dialogue disguises the degree to which such exchanges are, in fact, as highly formalized here as they are in other institutional contexts.

The common interview is even more structured than conversation or dialogue. A specific agenda comes into play and the information extracted from the exchange may be placed within a larger frame of reference to which it contributes a distinct piece of factual information or affective overtone. Unlike the opening café scene in Godard's *Vivre sa vie*—when the camera moves back and forth behind the two main characters seated at a café bar trying to frame them and see their faces but apparently lacking the authority to make them turn to face this intrusive instrument—and unlike the reflexive tactics of *Surname Viet Given Name Nam* that allow subjects to move outside the frame, subverting the formality of the interview itself, the common interview normally requires subjects to provide a frontal view of themselves and generally discipline their bodies to oblige the camera's requirements regarding depth of field and angle of view. The individual identity, autobiographical background, or idiosyncratic qualities of those interviewed become secondary to an external referent: some aspect of the historical world to which they can contribute special knowledge. (Personal traits are not irrelevant; they add "grain," or texture, to knowledge and can be crucial to the rhetorical credibility of what is said. This is particularly evident in films like *Word Is Out, Before Stonewall,* or Valeria Sarmiento's *A Man When He Is a Man,* since qualities of personality are themselves aspects of the subject at hand.)

In the Year of the Pig is built entirely around common interviews, as is a great deal of *Who Killed Vincent Chin?* Each film's argument arises indirectly, from the selection and arrangement of witnesses, rather than directly from the voice-over commentary of a narrator. Although such films continue to make a case about the historical world, just as an expository documentary might, they do so in a distinctive manner. Both the specific ways and means individuals have of telling their part of a story and the filmmaker's tactics for combining each account into a larger picture draw our attention. We shuttle between these two points of authority, authorship, and rhetorical suasion. The film is joined with what it presents. *Not a Love Story,* for example, builds much of its case against the pornography industry around interviews between the filmmaker, Bonnie Klein, or her companion, ex-stripper Linda Lee Tracy, and various participants in the pornography trade. Each interview finds a place within a textual system that stresses the spiritual journey of the two interviewers into this dark corner of the human soul and their subsequent redemption. Each interview provides both factual information and an opportunity for the interviewers to mark another station on their personal passage. What narrative development there is surrounds the acquisition of knowledge about pornography and, somewhat atypically in relation to most interactive films, the moral growth of the interviewers as social actors.

In *Not a Love Story,* no doubt due to the unusual emphasis placed on the interviewers' experiences, the exchanges place the filmmaker and the subject within the frame, in shared social space. This form of spatial arrangement is more typical of television interviews, where the personality of the host-anchorperson-interviewer can itself acquire iconic status and therefore economic exchange value through repetition in program after program. In a great many instances, particularly in those films that make history their subject rather than the effect of the interview experience itself, the interview takes place across the frameline. The filmmaker/interviewer remains off screen, and, quite often, even the interviewer's voice disappears from the text. The interview structure remains self-evident because the social actors address the camera, or a location on a proximate axis (their eyeline presumably aimed at the interviewer), rather than other social actors and because not only their words but their bodies seem held in the grip of the mise-en-scène. *Seeing Red*, *In the Year of the Pig*, *Word Is Out*, *The Day after Trinity*, *Ethnic Notions*, *The Color of Honor*, *Family Gathering*, and *Rosie the Riveter* are but a few examples of films using a technique where the interview approximates the style and structure of oral history.

The visible presence of the social actor as evidentiary witness and the visible absence of the filmmaker (the filmmaker's presence as absence) gives this form of the interview the appearance of a "pseudomonologue." Like the musings directed to the audience in a soliloquy, the pseudomonologue appears to deliver the thoughts, impressions, feelings, and memories of the individual witness directly to the viewer. The filmmaker achieves a suturing effect, placing the viewer in direct relation to the interviewee, by absenting him- or herself.[17] Instead of watching and overhearing an exchange between the filmmaker and his/her subject, which then requires specific measures such as the shot/reverse shot editing pattern to place the viewer in a position of subjective engagement rather than detachment, the pseudomonologue violates the dictum, "Don't look at the camera" in order to achieve a more immediate sense of being addressed by the subject. The pseudomonologue makes the viewer *the* subject of cinematic address, erasing the very mediations of filmmaker/subject/viewer that the interactive mode accentuates.

The degree of filmmaker absence in the pseudomonologue can vary considerably. Frequently the filmmaker is neither seen nor heard, allowing witnesses "to speak for themselves." Sometimes the voice of the filmmaker is heard while the body remains unseen. This occurs in the one scene in *In the Year of the Pig* with Senator Morton, in portions of *Harlan County, U.S.A.*, and throughout *Sad Song of Yellow Skin* and other films by Michael Rubbo. The sense of an aural presence echoes the strategy of voice-over commentary in expository films but the voice is now turned toward the subjects within the frame, the interviewees, rather than the viewer, or, as in *Sherman's March* and *Demon Lover Diary*, the filmmaker's voice addresses us in a personal, diaristic tone, adding another individual point of view to what we see and hear.

Often the quality of the sound recording suggests that the filmmaker

occupies contiguous space, just off screen, but it is also possible for th
filmmaker to record the questions to which interviewees respond after the
fact, in an entirely separate space. In this case, spatial discontinuity establishes an existential discontinuity as well: the filmmaker, or the mechanism
of inquiry, operates at a remove from the historical world of the social actor
and the contingency of direct encounter. The interviewee moves "under
glass," framed, held within the space of an image from which the interviewer is not only absent but over which the filmmaker retains mastery. The
interviewer's voice occupies space of a higher logical type: it defines and
contains the messages that emanate from the historical world. It takes on
the mantle of a fuller, more complete authority. But just as the image
inevitably points to an absence (of the referent to which it refers, of the
authoring agent behind the camera and the enunciating apparatus in
toto), so, too, the disembodied voice of inquiry points to another, paradoxical absence (the absence of the interviewer from the arena of the historical
present, the placement of the voice in a transcendental, ahistorical field
that can only be a fiction of the text).

This discontinuity can be brought to a focus more overtly when the
filmmaker displaces the spoken voice with the written word. Intertitles
may provide the other half of the "dialogue" rather than a voice-off. Ron
Mann's *Comic Book Confidential*, a history of the American comic book,
mimics comic books themselves by tying interviews together with brief
intertitles that suggest the narrative line of the film (for example, "Mean-
while the superheroes battle each other," or "And then the fifties arrived,"
and so on). David and Judith MacDougall's *Wedding Camels* contains a scene
in which they interview the bride by means of a set of questions represented
by intertitles (in English; the replies are in Turkana, with subtitles, another
graphic mediation). One question is, "We asked Akai [the bride] whether
a Turkana woman chooses her husband or if her parents choose for her."
Although this tactic places the filmmaker "on screen," in the two-dimensional space of the graphic intertitles, a sense of absence remains. This
space is discontinuous from the three-dimensional space of the interview;
it stands in for or represents the filmmaker without embodying him or her.
An advantage is that the difference between the graphic and indexical
(realist) signifiers, between the written word and the image of the speaking
body, can work to acknowledge the hierarchical difference between interviewer and interviewee. The turn toward the written word serves as a trace
of an encounter that did occur and acknowledges the authority of the
filmmaker to frame and control his or her subjects without requiring the
disembodiment of the voice and the paradoxical transference of its grain,
its historical specificity, into the realm of an apparently timeless logos.
Graphic intertitles can achieve the effect of an unexpected or strange
juxtaposition, adding to our awareness of the hierarchical structure of
interaction. As such they have the potential to move us toward the reflexive

nentary representation without being sufficient to do so in
ves.

:tations are quite different for interactive films than for
expository or observational ones. Expository and observational films unlike
interactive or reflexive ones, tend to mask the work of production, the
effects of the cinematic apparatus itself, and the tangible process of enunciation, the saying of something as distinct from that which is said. When
the interactive film takes the form of oral histories strung together to
reconstruct a historical period or event, the reconstruction is clearly the
result of assembling these discrete pieces of testimony. The process is more
rooted in individual perspectives or personal recollections than a disembodied voice-of-God commentary and evidentiary editing would be. The
sense of being addressed by others who are themselves historically situated
or implanted and who speak directly to us, or to our surrogate, the
filmmaker/interviewer, shifts these texts closer to *discours* than *histoire*.
(The awareness of s/he-who-speaks, so vivid in everyday conversation, does
not evaporate into the evasive lure of a narrative that seems to issue from
nowhere, that can simply announce, through an anonymous agency,
"Once upon a time. . . .")

The viewer of the interactive text expects to be witness to the historical
world as represented by one who inhabits it and who makes that process of
habitation a distinct dimension of the text. The text, whatever else, addresses the ethics or politics of encounter. This is the encounter between
one who wields a movie camera and one who does not. The sense of bodily
presence, rather than absence, locates and holds the filmmaker to the
scene, even when masked by certain strategies for interviewing or representing encounter. Viewers expect conditional information and situated or
local knowledge. The extension of particular encounters into more generalized ones remains entirely possible, but the possibility remains, at least in
part, one that viewers must establish through their own engagement with
the text itself.

The Reflexive Mode of Representation

If the historical world is a meeting place for the processes of social
exchange and representation in the interactive mode, the representation
of the historical world becomes, itself, the topic of cinematic meditation in
the reflexive mode. Rather than hearing the filmmaker engage solely in an
interactive (participatory, conversational, or interrogative) fashion with
other social actors, we now see or hear the filmmaker also engage in
metacommentary, speaking to us less about the historical world itself, as in
the expository and poetic or interactive and diaristic modes, than about the
process of representation itself. Whereas the great preponderance of doc-

umentary production concerns itself with talking about the historical world, the reflexive mode addresses the question of *how* we talk about the historical world. As with poetic exposition, the focus of the text slides from the realm of historical reference to the properties of the text itself. Poetic exposition draws attention to the pleasures of form, reflexivity to its problems. It internalizes many of the issues and concerns that are the subject of this study, not as a secondary or subsequent mode of retrospective analysis, but as an immediate undeferrable issue in social representation itself. Reflexive texts are self-conscious not only about form and style, as poetic ones are, but also about strategy, structure, conventions, expectations, and effects.

Reflexive documentaries like *The Man with a Movie Camera, The Thin Blue Line, Daughter Rite, Reassemblage, Lorang's Way, Of Great Events and Ordinary People, Poto and Cabengo, Far from Poland,* and *Unfinished Diary* pose the ethical dilemma of how to represent people in two distinct ways. First, it is posed as an issue the text may itself address specifically (as we find in *Far from Poland* and *Daughter Rite*). Second, the text poses it as an issue for the viewer by emphasizing the degree to which people, or social actors, appear before us as signifiers, as functions of the text itself. Their representativeness in terms of the institutions and collectivities that operate beyond the frame of the film, in history, becomes more problematic as we recognize the extent to which we see a constructed image rather than a slice of reality. Interactive films may draw attention to the process of filmmaking when this process poses a problem for the participants; the reflexive mode draws attention to this process when it poses problems for the viewer. How can a representation be adequate to that which it represents? How can the struggles of the trade union Solidarity be represented in a film, especially when the filmmaker cannot travel to Poland (the subject of *Far from Poland*)? How can the emotional bonds of mother-daughter be represented when they are not readily available for documentation, having occurred in the past, out of sight of any camera (an issue in *Daughter Rite*)? How can the viewer be drawn into an awareness of this problematic so that no myth of the knowability of the world, of the power of the logos, no repression of the unseen and unrepresentable occludes the magnitude of "what every filmmaker knows": that every representation, however fully imbued with documentary significance, remains a fabrication?

People represented within a text that poses such a problem will, inevitably, not be available for assimilation by the conventions of realism. Realism provides unproblematic access to the world through traditional physical representation and the untroubled transference of psychological states from character to viewer (by means of acting style, narrative structure, and cinematic techniques such as point-of-view shots). Reflexive documentaries will employ such techniques only to interrupt and expose them. *The Thin Blue Line,* for example, relies heavily on the conventions of the interview with its affinities for the confessional, but also draws attention to the tensions that arise when statements contradict one another. Director Errol Morris so emphasizes these contradictions that the appeal to testimony as an index of "what really happened" becomes thoroughly enmeshed in the testimony's function within a liturgy of mutually contradictory statements of self-vindication.[18] This overarching pattern, however, by definition cannot be perceived or shared by any of the characters. And in the case of the protagonist, Randall Adams, who serves a life sentence for the murder of a police officer he swears he did not commit, the very notion of such a pattern threatens to entrap his own assertions of innocence within a babble of inconclusive, competing ones. Morris dramatizes the quest for evidence, and underlines the uncertainty of what evidence there is. He reminds us of how every documentary constructs the evidentiary reference points it requires by returning us, again and again, to the scene of the crime by means of a reenactment that highlights suggestive, evocative, but also completely inconclusive aspects of the event (such as a milkshake tumbling through the air in slow motion or a car taillight held in close-up while the physical identity of the killer remains resolutely indeterminate). Though realist in many respects, the film blocks the "natural," largely unquestioned assumption of a direct correspondence between realism and the truthfulness of claims about the world.

As a result, the belief systems of social actors become repositioned within the text's own metacommentary about competing belief systems and the proclivity of the judicial system to grant an authority to the narratives of "fact" generated by police and prosecutors that it denies to those cast as the accused. This is the work of the text, not the point of view of any of the witnesses we see and hear. The hazard of the many interactive texts that subordinate their own textual voice to that of their witnesses no longer threatens; if anything, we have the converse hazard of a textual voice overwhelming the discrete voices of social actors with a message of its own about the problematics of representation.

The reduction of the social actor to a slot within the textual system presents us with the issues of performance and, in several cases, the reflexive text opts for a performance as such rather than to compel others to disguise self-presentation in the form of a virtual performance. *Far from Poland, Daughter Rite, The Thin Blue Line,* and both *David Holzman's Diary* and *No Lies* (films that are reflexive interrogations of the ethics of the observational mode of representation) all rely on performances by actors to represent what documentary might have been able to convey if it conscripted social actors to represent roles and subjectivities that are not their own. Such films give reflexive emphasis to the question of "using" people while avoiding some of the ethical difficulties of using social actors for this purpose.

The same reasoning prompts many reflexive texts to present the filmmaker him- or herself—on screen, in frame—less as a participant-observer than as an authoring agent, opening this very function to examination.

Elements of this approach occur in Vertov's pioneering *The Man with a Movie Camera* and in Rouch and Morin's *Chronicle of a Summer*. They are carried to a far greater extreme in Godard's *Numero Deux* while both *Of Great Events and Ordinary People* and *Far from Poland* extend the concept. In all of these cases the filmmakers' acknowledgment of their own difference from those they represent—their function as the representative of the film and the constraints this function imposes on their ability to interact with others—positions them within the text as the occupant of a historical, discursive space paradoxically incommensurate with that of their subjects. (That which defines and frames a space cannot also occupy that space at the same time, or as Bertrand Russell put it, a class cannot be a member of itself.) *Numero Deux* begins and ends with Godard himself in an editing room, playing through the sounds and images of his actors who represent the family he has chosen to investigate. He is historically situated in this space (the space of production, textual space) and yet he is at a palpable remove from the space of the representation occupied by his "family" (the space of story, scenographic space). The possibility of direct interaction between subject and filmmaker that figures so powerfully in *Chronicle of a Summer, Hard Metal's Disease,* or the work of Michael Rubbo no longer seems tenable. Reflexive mediations have pulled the two series of images apart, into distinct, hierarchical registers of representation. And to make his point, Godard turns to professional actors rather than ordinary people, a turn that may not resolve all the ethical issues that such a text both addresses and provokes.[19]

In fact, one of the oddities of the reflexive documentary is that it rarely reflects on ethical issues as a primary concern, other than with the sigh of a detached relativism readier to criticize the choices of others than to examine its own. The preference for professional performances and the appearance of the filmmaker seldom serve to point to ethical issues directly. Actors help avoid difficulties that might arise with non-actors since their profession revolves around willingly adopting a persona and being available as a signifier in someone else's discourse. Using actors spares the filmmaker from using people to make a point about the nature of representation rather than about the nature of their own lives, but the use of actors does not solve the problem of how to combine the two issues. The desire to address the politics or aesthetics of representation requires increased attention to and organization of what occurs in front of the camera, and to the juxtaposition of individual shots or scenes. Actors help facilitate this process. Their use does not mean that the film will necessarily take up questions involving the filmmaker's ethical responsibilities either to the film's subjects or viewers. To do so would be to challenge not only the conventions but also the prerogatives on which the documentary form depends. Explorations of the difficulties or consequences of representation are more common than examinations of the *right* of representation.

A vivid exception is *No Lies*, which is explicitly about the ethics of the filmmaker/subject interaction and, by extension, the text/viewer relationship. By using actors to represent a situation in which a male "cinema verité" filmmaker relentlessly interviews a female friend about her recent rape while allowing the viewer to believe that the film *is* the documentary footage of this encounter, *No Lies* not only questions the latent voyeurism in observational or interactive filmmaking, the power of the camera to extract confessional performances, and the indifference to personal, emotional consequences that such filmmaking may encourage, it also places the viewer in the position of being manipulated, and betrayed, very much like the female friend. We only learn after the fact, from the credits, that the two characters are actors. Some feel cheated by the revelation. They have tendered belief in the reality of a representation they should have treated as a fiction, but this violation of trust is precisely the point. *No Lies* reflexively heightens our apprehension of the dynamic of trust that documentaries invite, and of the betrayals—of subjects, and of viewers—made possible by this very trust.

The reflexive mode of representation gives emphasis to the encounter between filmmaker and viewer rather than filmmaker and subject. This mode arrives last on the scene since it is itself the least naive and the most doubtful about the possibilities of communication and expression that the other modes take for granted. Realist access to the world, the ability to provide persuasive evidence, the possibility of indisputable argument, the unbreakable bond between an indexical image and that which it represents—all these notions prove suspect. As Hayden White puts it when speaking of irony as a historiographic trope:

> The trope of Irony, then, provides a linguistic paradigm of a mode of thought which is radically self-critical with respect not only to a given characterization of the world of experience but also to the very effort to capture adequately the truth of things in language. It is, in short, a model of the linguistic protocol in which skepticism in thought and relativism in ethics are conventionally expressed.[20]

In its most paradigmatic form the reflexive documentary prompts the viewer to a heightened consciousness of his or her relation to the text and of the text's problematic relationship to that which it represents. Editing often works to increase this sense of awareness, a consciousness of cinematic form rather than of the historical world on the other side of the realist window—as long takes also do when they extend beyond the duration necessary for "reading time": the time needed to take in their socially significant meaning. When an image lingers it eventually calls attention to itself, to its composition, to the *hold* it exerts over its content, to the frame surrounding it.

Unexpected juxtapositions work in the manner described by the Russian formalists who termed their effect *ostranenie,* the making strange of the familiar and the making familiar of the strange. Frames of reference collide, usually the representational and the referential, such that an initial untroubled sense of access to the world becomes troubled or problematized. Unexpected juxtapositions or stylistic departures from the norms of a text or the conventions of a genre make realism and referentiality themselves strange. They fold the viewer's consciousness back onto itself so that it comes into contact with the work of the cinematic apparatus rather than being allowed to move unimpeded toward engagement with a representation of the historical world.

The reflexive mode emphasizes epistemological doubt. It stresses the deformative intervention of the cinematic apparatus in the process of representation. Knowledge is not only localized but itself subject to question. Knowledge is hyper-situated, placed not only in relation to the filmmaker's physical presence, but also in relation to fundamental issues about the nature of the world, the structure and function of language, the authenticity of documentary sound and image, the difficulties of verification, and the status of empirical evidence in Western culture.

Jean-Pierre Gorin's *Poto and Cabengo,* for example, reflexively addresses the issue of language and signification directly. The film combines interactions between Gorin and a set of twins reputed to have evolved a private language with a reflexive critique of the very process of scientific investigation and journalistic reporting that Gorin's own film also pursues. Like Raul Ruiz in *Of Great Events and Ordinary People,* where Ruiz, a Chilean exile living in Paris and speaking a second language, questions his own function and presence, Gorin, a Frenchman living in San Diego and speaking English with a pronounced accent, questions his own relation to a pair of twins whose idiosyncratic use of language singles them out. Gorin combines a diaristic voice-over describing his relation to the twins and scenes of himself interacting with them with ironically toned reports on the results of scientific investigations (they speak a variation of English, not a unique language) and the journalistic reports (the parents hope to get an offer from Hollywood, they are ambivalent about whether to accept or discourage their children's "abnormality").

What counts as normal? What anchors signifiers to English language and speech? What influence does a German-speaking grandmother and a "word salad" of everyday conversation in the home (mixing German, English, and idiolect in one discursive bowl) have on the twins? What influence does the attention they receive exert? What language should we expect from twins who eat *gemesht* salad, use *käse* knives, and call each other Poto and Cabengo?

Gorin makes his own *gemesht* (mixed) representation of the issues, combining observational footage, interactive engagement, subtitles and intertitles that reproduce and mock the vocabulary of the linguists and reporters, the voices of his subjects over a black screen, blow-ups of news-paper clippings and Katzenjammer cartoons, and an exhaustive break-down of sixteen different ways to say "potato," including "Poto."

Gorin's interest is less in getting an "answer" to the question of the status of the twins' language, or in observing how the media affect the lives of this family (as we find in Richard Leacock's *Happy Mother's Day*, about the Dion quintuplets), than in meditating on the nature of language and represen-tation as social phenomena in general. What are the necessary and suffi-cient terms for linguistic competence? What validates the ordering of signifiers; what keeps them from sliding across one another in an endless succession? And, to complete the reflexive turn, how can this film call its own use of language, as well as the physical presence of the authoring agent (Gorin), into question at the same time that it attempts to question the social responsibility of people (parents, filmmakers) with linguistic mastery to those around them? (Gorin's apparent answer to the ethics of represen-tation and his responsibility to this particular family involves outlasting the scientists and press. Once the story has exhausted itself for them, Gorin remains to "follow up" and chronicle the state of the family after their dreams of movie contracts fall through and the husband's job collapses. As *An American Family*, with its twelve-hour length culled from three hundred hours of footage, suggests, duration has an indeterminacy of its own that may not resolve ethical questions so much as postpone or extend them.)

Viewer expectations for reflexive documentaries differ from expecta-tions for the other modes: in place of the representation of a topic or issue, with or without attention to the interactive role of the filmmaker, the viewer comes to expect the unexpected, functioning not with a surreal intent to shock and surprise so much as to return the film systematically to questions of its own status and that of documentary in general. Refrains, should they occur, no longer underline thematic concerns or authenticate the camera's and filmmaker's presence in the historical world, but refer to the construction of the text itself. (The ongoing argument between Jill Godmilow and Mark Magill, her companion, about the efficacy of her strategies in *Far from Poland* is one example; the repeated shots that frame the documentary image on a video monitor and surround it with darkness in *Numero Deux* is another.) The terms and conditions of viewing that are normally taken for granted may be subject to scrutiny, particularly as they pertain to the film being viewed at that moment. The phenomenology of filmic experience, the metaphysics of realism and the photographic image, epistemology, empiricism, the construction of the individual subject, the technologies of knowledge, rhetoric, and the visible—all of that which supports and sustains the documentary tradition is as much the focus for the viewer's consciousness as the world beyond. A thickened, denser sense of the textuality of the viewing experience is in operation. The sense of vicarious transport into the historical world doubles back on the trail of representation itself.

More than the sense of the filmmaker's presence in the historical world found in the interactive mode, the viewer experiences a sense of the text's presence in his or her interpretive field. The situation to be experienced and examined is no longer located elsewhere, marked and referred to by the documentary text; it is the viewing situation itself. A longer-standing tradition in fiction, where satire, parody, and irony all enjoy a prominent position, this reflexive move is relatively new to the documentary. This questioning of its own status, conventions, effects, and values may well represent the maturation of the genre. Further formal advance necessarily involves a return to the earlier, presumably more naive forms, but with a heightened awareness of their limitations.

The reflexive documentary arises in part from a history of formal change in which the constraints and limits of a mode of representation provide the context for its own overthrow. A new mode may also arise from a more directly political history when the efficacy of a previously accepted mode diminishes or when the stance it sanctions toward the historical world is no longer adequate. The institutional framework surrounding documentary, however, served for several decades to shelter this cinematic genre from twentieth-century tendencies toward radical doubt, uncertainty, skepticism, irony, and existential relativism that gave impetus to modernism and the even more disaffected scavenging of postmodernism.

When a reflexive mode of documentary representation did gain some degree of prominence in the 1970s and '80s (with a few notable precursors like *The Man with a Movie Camera*), it clearly derived both from formal innovation and political urgency. The poststructuralist critique of language systems as the agency that constitutes the individual subject (rather than empowering it); the argument that representation as a semiotic operation confirmed a bourgeois epistemology (and voyeuristic pathology); the assumption that radical transformation requires work on the signifier, on the construction of the subject itself rather than on the subjectivities and predispositions of an already constituted subject all converge to insist that the representation of reality has to be countered by an interrogation of the reality of representation. Only this can lead to any significant political transformation.

The problem is that the transparency and empowering capacity of language, the knowability of the visible world and the power to view it from a disinterested position of objectivity (not pathology), the assumption that transformation comes from persuasive intervention in the values and beliefs of individual subjects (not debates about the ideology of the subject as such) are the cornerstones of the documentary tradition. Having been sheltered from skepticism and radical doubt for most of its history, the institutional discourse available to documentary filmmakers had few tools at its disposal to address the issue of the reflexive or ironic, and, even less, to see it as a potentially more powerful political tool than the straightforward, persuasive presentation of an argument.

One of the first considerations of reflexivity in documentary film was Julia Lesage's "The Political Aesthetics of the Feminist Documentary Film."[21] Lesage does not treat the feminist documentaries she discusses as formally innovative. *Growing up Female, The Woman's Film, Three Lives, Joyce at Thirty-four, Woman to Woman, Self-Health, Chris and Bernie, Like a Rose, We're Alive,* and *I Am Somebody* are generally simple in narrative structure, traditional in their reliance on realist conventions, and show "little self-consciousness about the flexibility of the cinematic medium."[22] Their reflexivity emerges as a parallelism. Just as the women's movement of the 1970s stressed consciousness-raising as the cornerstone for transforming the personal into the political, for recontextualizing what had seemed purely individual or "merely" domestic experience into the shared experience of a political collectivity and feminist movement, these films also "show women in the private sphere getting together to define/redefine their experiences and to elaborate a strategy for making inroads in the public sphere."[23] As Lesage puts it:

> Film after film shows a woman telling her story to the camera. It is usually a woman struggling to deal with the public world. . . . Yet the stories that the filmed women tell are not just "slices of experience." These stories serve a function aesthetically in reorganizing women viewer's expectations derived from patriarchal narratives and in initiating a critique of those narratives. . . . The sound track of the Feminist documentary film often consists almost entirely of women's self-conscious, heightened, intellectual discussion of role and sexual politics. The film gives voice to that which had in the media been spoken for women by patriarchy. Received notions about women give way to an outpouring of real desires, contradictions, decisions, and social analyses.[24]

Reflexivity, then, need not be purely formal; it can also be pointedly political.

Unexpected juxtapositions here occur between the internal conventions, iconography, and, especially, speech of these films and the dominant (masculinist or patriarchal) ideology operating in society at large. Rather than drawing attention to the means of representation, to the process of constructing meaning, these feminist works challenge entrenched notions of sexuality and gender, empowering women who can now give a commonly shared political name (oppression, exploitation, manipulation, self-deprecation, devalorization . . .) to experience that had previously seemed personal or inconsequential. (An exception is JoAnn Elam's *Rape*, a film that does call attention to the cinematic apparatus and the process of constructing meaning at the same time that it, too, addresses the acutely personal and highly political experience of rape through the same structuring principle of consciousness-raising as the other films.)

Such films, which could be classified as predominantly expository, interactive, or observational, remind us of the "impure," hybrid nature of most films. (The four modes of representation are partly based on discursive formations, institutional practices, and conventions, and partly serve as a heuristic model, drawing out more cleanly defined alternatives than we find in practice.) Even more, the parallelism that Lesage notes—and chooses not to identify as reflexive because it does not call attention to the process of signification or of viewing as such—reminds us that reflexivity is not quite the purely formal operation we have so far made it. The affinities it has with a sensibility of exhaustion, and a relativist perspective, need to be counterbalanced with its affinity for a process of political engagement based on *ostranenie*, or, in somewhat more familiar, Brechtian terms, on the experience of an alienation effect that pleases, instructs, and alters social consciousness in precisely the manner Lesage describes.

The tools that documentary discourse lacked, feminism provided. It instigated a radical reconceptualization of subjectivity and politics that achieved through the programmatics of consciousness-raising an effect comparable to that of reflexivity. The viewer, especially the female viewer, encountered an experience that reexamined and recontextualized the ground of experience itself. Evidence from the lives of women, no longer contained within the masculinist mythologies of Woman, called for a radical, retroactive reconsideration of categories and concepts every bit as fundamental as any reflexivity could require. If the reflexive mode of representation serves to make familiar experience strange, to draw attention to the terms and conditions of viewing, including the subjective position made available to the viewer, the feminist documentaries described by Lesage, despite an apparent lack of awareness of the "flexibilities of the cinematic medium," achieve precisely this result. And they do so in relation to matters where the difference can truly be said to make a difference.

The bipolarity of reflexive strategies—calling attention to form itself or to the "other side" of ideology where we can locate a utopian dimension of alternative modes of material practice, consciousness, and action—is not unique to this mode. The other three can also align themselves for or against aspects of dominant ideology, for or against concerted change of a progressive or regressive kind. Expository films like *Blood of the Beasts* or *Land without Bread*, observational films like *High School*, *Hospital*, or *Seventeen*, interactive films like *In the Year of the Pig*, *Rosie the Riveter*, or *Hard Metal's Disease* can also challenge convention and propose alternative, heightened modes of consciousness for the viewer. In this sense they, too, might be seen as politically reflexive. The distinction is perhaps sharpest with the reflexive mode, however, since this is where the fundamental issue of whether new form, and a heightened awareness of form, is a necessary precondition for radical change takes clearest shape.

Peter Wollen describes the issue as that of two materialisms. One, regarding the materiality of the cinematic signifier, becomes the central concern of the avant-garde. The other, regarding the materiality of social practices, including that of viewing and the cinematic apparatus but extending well beyond it to the discursive formations and institutional practices that characterize a given society, becomes the central concern of a political, Brechtian cinema.[25] From an ontology concerned with the ability of the indexical image to capture something of the essence of things to an ontology addressing the essence of cinema itself, and from a materialism concerned with the ensemble of social relations to a materialism of the signifier, shorn of its semantic burden and making no reference beyond itself, between these two poles debates about political efficacy oscillate. Wollen contrasts Brakhage, the romantic visionary trying to change how we *see* in fundamental ways, with Brecht, the socialist artist trying to change how we *live* beyond the theater:

> For Brecht, of course, the point of the *Verfremdung*-effect was not simply to break the spectator's involvement and empathy in order to draw attention to the artifice of art, an art-centered model, but in order to demonstrate the workings of society, a reality obscured by habitual norms of perception, by habitual modes of identification with "human problems." . . . Film-making can be a project of meaning with horizons beyond itself, in the general arena of ideology. At the same time it can avoid the pitfalls of illusionism, of simply being a substitute for a world, parasitic on ideology, which it reproduces as reality. The imaginary must be de-realized; the material must be semiotized. We begin to see how the problem of materialism is inseparable from the problem of signification, that it begins with the problem of the material in and of signification, the way in which this material plays the dual role of substrate and signifier.[26]

Dana Polan makes a similar point in his comparison of a Daffy Duck cartoon, *Duck Amuck*, to Brechtian theater.[27] *Duck Amuck* is extraordinarily reflexive, but in a limited way: the dangers and hazards suffered by Daffy prove to be the work of his animator, but we ultimately discover this to be none other than Bugs Bunny. As Polan argues, if this reflexive loop moves beyond a heightened awareness of animation technique and the kind of self-consciousness common to comedic forms, it remains noticeably disengaged from the material conditions confronting a spectator as social actor: "The film opens up a formal space and not a political one in viewer consciousness. *Duck Amuck* closes in on itself, fiction leads to and springs from fiction, the text becomes a loop which effaces social analysis. This is the project of all non-political art, realist or self-reflexive."[28]

What *Duck Amuck* lacks is precisely what Brecht provided: a political position, not only *in* the work, but *for* the spectator. Polan states:

> For Brecht the attitudinal position of the viewing subject springs from an attitudinal position in the work—the political artwork embodies a difference between the way things are and the way they can be. . . . To avoid the new world of possibility appearing as nothing but noise, the artwork must

also make use of the old world as a standard. Meaning, and its realization in action, comes from the differences between the two world views. Political art defamiliarizes the world. But it does so by playing off our connections to that world.[29]

Reflexivity and consciousness-raising go hand in hand because it is through an awareness of form and structure and its determining effects that new forms and structures can be brought into being, not only in theory, or aesthetically, but in practice, socially. What is need not be. The unquestioned givenness of ideological constraints can be juxtaposed with alternative positions and subjectivities, affinities and relations of production, precisely as the feminist documentary has done. As a political concept, reflexivity grounds itself in the materiality of representation but turns, or returns, the viewer beyond the text, to those material practices that inform the body politic.

Like poetry, reflexive strategies remove the encrustations of habit. Political reflexivity removes the ideological encrustations that support a given social order, particularly those practices, experienced in everyday life, that revolve around signification and the discursive. Too tight a reflexive loop squeezes this crucial social element out. Instead of what can be represented through realism (lived experience) forming the focus of reflexivity, the question of realism itself, or of representation (formal structure), becomes the focus. Like the schema developed in Hayden White's *Metahistory*, such an approach is essentially formalist, proposing categories that bear a relation principally to texts rather than to the relation between texts and their readers or viewers. To seek change on any level other than that of the signifier, the materialism of form, and the construction of the bourgeois subject requires something of a dialectical or divided consciousness. We must attend to formal reflexivity since the content of the form, in Hayden White's phrase, is indeed decisive, but we must also attend to political reflexivity since the form of the content is equally critical. If credulity and skepticism mark the normal oscillation of the viewer in relation to the claims of a text, fiction or documentary, the commensurate form of critical engagement requires suspicion and revelation, attention to the workings of ideology, whatever mode of representation is at work, and attention to a utopian dimension signifying what might or ought to be.[30]

In *Women and Film: Both Sides of the Camera*, E. Ann Kaplan addresses directly the issue of realism in relation to a feminist cinema, thereby continuing the line of thought begun by Julia Lesage. She argues that the uses of realism carry as much importance as the question of realism as such. She asserts that a discussion of feminist documentary cannot even begin without considering the relation of text to ideology, that is, the politics of the text as formal construct. This, in turn, establishes the importance of assessing the effect of realist conventions on the viewer rather than of trusting to realism as an inherently appropriate style. *Joyce at Thirty-four* and *Janie's Janie* are taken as examples of films that adopt a realist, largely interview-based form and succumb to similar limitations regarding the use of narratives of optimism (the characters are on the way to better things as a result of the film's structuring principles); an innocent trust that the portraits of Joyce and Janie capture their "true" selves rather than particular constructions of the women; a reluctance to draw attention to themselves as films, allowing some customary viewing habits to go unquestioned; and the assumption that there is, at the heart of human behavior, a unified, coherent self that forms the origin of both personal and social change.[31]

This critique could apply to virtually any realist documentary, formally reflexive or not. It leaves out of consideration other issues that Kaplan argues are equally vital. By examining the two films more closely, Kaplan argues that *Janie's Janie* breaks out of the bourgeois individualism that encloses *Joyce at Thirty-four*. Janie addresses her own sense of herself as Other in relation to her father and husband, not as a purely personal issue, but as a function of the symbolic order of things under patriarchy. And, like *The Woman's Film, Growing up Female, Rosie the Riveter, A Song of Air,* and other feminist works, *Janie's Janie* also disturbs the iconographic norms of sexual representation in cinema by offering a portrait of a working-class woman who cannot be contained within strategies of condescension, charity, or victimology.[32] The familiar forms of female representation are rendered strange, not in a strictly formalist manner but one that is reflexive all the same.

At one point Kaplan, in contrast to Polan's suggestion that alternative visions need to play themselves off against dominant ones, calls for the abandonment of "prevailing realist codes . . . to challenge audiences' expectations and assumptions about life."[33] But as her argument develops, she moves to a more dialectical position in which any blanket assumption about the ideology of such generalities as realism or the cinematic apparatus requires qualification. She suggests, as her comparison of the two documentaries demonstrates, that "the same realist signifying practices can indeed be used for different ends. . . . Taken simply as a cinematic style, which can be used in different genre (i.e., documentary or fictional), realism does not insist on any special relation to the social formation."[34]

What provides the litmus test for political reflexivity is the specific form of the representation, the extent to which it does not reinforce existing categories of consciousness, structures of feeling, ways of seeing; the degree to which it rejects a narrative sense of closure and completeness. All representations distance reality and place it within a frame that, in Metz's word, "unrealizes" the real (it *is* in a frame, in a different time and space from that which is represented).[35] Some, however, seek to substitute themselves for that reality, to give the full-blown *impression* of reality. Others seek to maintain their distance, not simply to remind us of their status as text, discourse, narrative, or art, but also of the need to move beyond the text if we, too, are to engage with the world that a text can only represent.

Reflexive Strategies

Different authors mean different things by reflexivity. A primary concern here is to differentiate the formal and political dimensions of reflexivity. These are not alternatives but different ways of inflecting, and viewing, a given set of operations. In the terms described here the same device (reference to the off-screen space of the image or acknowledgment of the filmmaker's presence and power, for example) will begin as a formal operation that upsets norms, alters conventions, and draws the viewer's attention. In certain circumstances it will also be politically reflexive, drawing our attention to the relations of power and hierarchy between the text and the world. This difference and some of the best-known types of formal operation can be summarized as follows:

(1) Political Reflexivity. This form of reflexiveness operates primarily on the viewer's consciousness, "raising" it in the vernacular of progressive politics, decentering it in an Althusserian politics in order to achieve a rigorous awareness of commonality. Both the Portuguese *conscientização* and the Spanish *conscientización* stress a reference to social or collective awareness rather than the personal pilgrimage and its attendant topography of an improved or superior self that the English term "consciousness-raising" sometimes implies. It is this broader form of socially situated awareness that is meant here. Each type of formal reflexivity may have a political effect. It depends on how it works on a given viewer or audience. The effect can occur with works whose importance is primarily located at the level of content, as *The Woman's Film* and *Janie's Janie* indicate, with their affinities to the politics of agitprop, but it can also occur in relation to form, as the *Ways of Seeing* series demonstrates with its radical juxtapositions and recontextualizations of the Western tradition of oil painting.

(2) Formal Reflexivity. The techniques of reflexivity can be broken down into further categories. In discussing them we attempt to identify the formal device brought into play more than the political effect it might achieve. At the same time, it is important to note that no one political effect is assured by a given device or strategy, nor is a political effect dependent on any single type of formal procedure.

Both Alfred Hitchcock's *Rear Window* and Tomas Gutierrez Alea's *Memories of Underdevelopment* use formal devices to generate a reflexive awareness of the cinema's similarity to voyeurism (both central characters take pleasure from viewing others through binoculars; both construct narratives from what they see that involve themes of impotence and desire; both characters are isolated from their social milieu by profession or class background). *Rear Window*'s reflexivity remains essentially formal, its political dimension a repressed subtext (of male ambivalence toward women, of the latent pathology of voyeurism and fetishism) that may well pass most viewers by. *Memories of Underdevelopment*'s reflexivity operates more overtly to locate the character's remoteness in a social context. The text prompts a heightened awareness of the patriarchal and class basis for ambivalence toward women and recourse to pleasure at a distance. Nothing, though, is guaranteed. The effects of reflexivity ultimately depend on the viewer.

(a) Stylistic Reflexivity. Here we might group those strategies that break received conventions. Such texts introduce gaps, reversals, and unexpected turns that draw attention to the work of style as such and place the obsessions of illusionism within brackets. Expressionist styles are frequently of this sort. The multivoiced commentary in Trinh Minh-ha's *Naked Spaces* upsets our assumptions about the normative guidance usually offered by commentary. Departures from internal norms set up by a text also belong here. (The recurrence of surreal moments in *Blood of the Beasts*—such as tossing the heads of lambs into the corner of a room, or the long shot down a row of still-twitching carcasses—work this way, building up a contrapuntal movement to the business-as-usual tone of the commentator.)

Two extreme forms might be, first, those documentary styles that draw attention to their own patterns so consistently that they evolve into a poetic or essayist mode of representation, loosening the linkage to a historical referent in favor of more internally generated foci such as color, tonality, composition, depth of focus, rhythm, or the personalized sensibilities and perceptions of the author. (Documentaries like *The Nuer, Rain, Naked Spaces, Listen to Britain, Industrial Britain, Glass, Louisiana Story, N.Y., N.Y., Letter from Siberia, Sundays in Peking, Poto and Cabengo*, and *A Divided World* indicate something of the spectrum of work in a poetic or essayist vein.)

The other extreme would be those works that provide a metacommentary on method and procedure while remaining within a realist, as opposed to a poetic, sensibility. Raul Ruiz's *Of Great Events and Ordinary People* is of this sort, with its reference to shots that "might be" suitable to a documentary, to the heterogeneous objects swept together in classic exposition, and its attempt to situate Ruiz himself as an exile and outsider to the events he is immersed in reporting. *The Ax Fight* is another example, acknowledging the presence of the camera and the ethnographic witnesses to the violent confrontation it records, wheeling in anthropological theories and explanations to account for it, and concluding with a narrative-like reconstruction of the events they initially recorded in more haphazard, inchoate fashion. More obliquely, films like *No Lies, David Holzman's Diary*, and *Chronicle of a Summer* produce, through their structure, a critical metacommentary on the circumstances of their making, prompting us to ponder the ethics and politics of representing the lives of others in texts not of their own making.[36]

In a manner similar to interactive reflexivity (below), stylistic reflexivity depends upon the viewer's prior knowledge of documentary convention. One convention that has come in for considerable reflection is objectivity. The introduction of the subjective elements of, for example, stylistic expressivity and character development can pose basic questions about the nature of certainty, the variability of factual interpretation, and the attitudinal relation of the filmmaker to his or her material. Errol Morris's *The Thin Blue Line* is a prime example with its highly subjectivized re-creations of events and its iconically suggestive images of typewriters and guns. Like Peter Watkins and Raul Ruiz, Morris opts to present what might have been (conditional mood) rather than what was. Morris's own tone may also seem quite distant from the normally scrupulous sincerity of the investigative reporter who wants to be believed; Morris (as author, not person) might be read as someone more interested in ironic or reflexive effect than in seeing that justice is done.

The use of stylistic devices to achieve a reflexive effect runs the risk of manipulating social actors for textual effect rather than provoking a reflexive consideration of how texts are constructed. When the filmmaker moves to center stage—as in Michael Moore's *Roger and Me*, or, to a lesser extent Bonnie Klein's *Not a Love Story*—the risk is that other characters will fall into the narrative slots reserved for donors, helpers, and villains. Social actors (people) will be subordinated to the narrative trajectory of the filmmaker as protagonist. As the filmmaker moves further from a diaristic or participatory mode of self-representation as one among many, and closer to hero or protagonist of the drama—its center and propelling force—the greater the risk becomes. Bonnie Klein, for example, retains the role of investigative reporter though the film is laced with a spiritual narrative of redemption through personal trial and tribulation; whereas Michael Moore overtly, if also ironically, embraces the role of hero and champion.

Roger and Me, praised by many for its attack on General Motors's indifference to the individual suffering it causes, reduces most of the individuals it portrays to victims or dupes. In order to tell his story of coming to the rescue by confronting the elusive CEO of General Motors, Roger Smith, Michael Moore renders others as helpless, indifferent, or ignorant in contrast to his heroic and determined if also somewhat nebbish-like persona. His portrait of a deputy sheriff charged with evicting tenants for nonpayment is more vivid and engaging than his portrait of the people evicted. (Like Moore, the sheriff also acts, but in the wrong way.) Moore's use of irony and satire makes it difficult to be certain if he meant to be as critical of the unemployed as he is of General Motors, but as a character, "Michael Moore" seems as distant from the now redundant auto workers (of whom we actually meet very few) as he is from the inaccessible Roger Smith.

In *Roses in December*, Ana Carringan retains the role of mostly invisible reporter. Her stylistic reflexivity focuses more strongly around the representation of others than of filmmaker/reporter. *Roses in December* employs a great many narrative strategies, ranging from imaginative reenactments to rich, warm lighting in certain interviews (they are obviously lit to achieve this effect and not the result of filming with available light), but avoids the risk of manipulation by minimizing the narrative function of the filmmaker as character. The text stresses biographical investigation, albeit in a more fully subjective register, regarding its historical subject, Jean Donovan. The investigator recedes before the impressions that the process discovers. Individuals are not required to fulfill narrative functions in relation to a filmmaker as central protagonist.

When social actors are required to adopt such narrative functions as donor or helper, the outcome has greatest reflexive effect when subjective dimensions prevail. That is to say, individuals reveal significant qualities about themselves while ostensibly serving as helpers to the filmmaker's central role (usually involving a quest for knowledge or the righting of a wrong). In neither Marcel Ophul's *Hotel Terminus* nor in Claude Lanzman's *Shoah* does the complexity of individual lives become diminished by being restricted to narrative roles. Characters, in giving witness, give witness to their own complexity and multidimensional subjectivity. The more limited goals of Michael Moore, or Ross McElwee in *Sherman's March* (to save the community, to find a mate—classic goals for male fiction heroes) abate this sense of complexity. The structural resolution of these classic quest narratives demands a degree of subordination, and reduction, in the representation of others relative to the hero that the classic documentary quest for knowledge does not necessarily require. *Daughter Rite*, like *No Lies*, resorts entirely to fictional enactment, but structures the interactions between the two daughters who reflect on their relationship with their mother according to the conventions of documentary. This offers another way of avoiding the risks of misrepresentation, or abuse, that poetic and narrative strategies run. *Daughter Rite* also regains what it loses in historical authenticity in the reflexive attention it draws to the documentary conventions of authentication themselves.

(b) Deconstructive Reflexivity. The object here is to alter or contest dominant codes or conventions in documentary representation, thereby drawing attention to their conventionality, The stress is less on effects of style than of structure, and although stylistic strategies may come into play, the main effect is one of a heightened awareness of what had previously seemed natural or had been taken for granted. *Land without Bread* was one of the first such films, but in 1932 the power of the conventional travelogue was strong enough to prompt some reviewers and, presumably, audiences to dismiss the musical score and the oddly disjunctive commentary as the work of a tasteless distributor rather than the author, Buñuel.[37] More recent works such as Chris Marker's *Sans Soleil*, Raul Ruiz's *Of Great Events and Ordinary People*, and Trinh T. Minh-ha's *Reassemblage* successfully deconstruct many of the conventions of objectivity in documentary, bringing about a reflexive highlighting of the conditional nature of any image and the impossibility of arriving at certain truth.[38] In written anthropology, some have given preferred status to heteroglossic or dialogical forms of writing in which no one authorial point of view prevails, where native, informant, and ethnographer occupy equal status within the commentaries arranged without the usual hierarchy of ascending tory power.[39] The emergence of works of this sort in documentary is not yet evident, although films like *First Contact, Surname Viet Given Name Nam, Wedding Camels,* and *Far from Poland* all find ways of deconstructing or displacing some of the usual hierarchies of knowledge and power in cross-cultural representation.

(c) Interactivity. This entire mode of documentary representation possesses the potential to have a consciousness-raising effect, drawing attention to the oddity of filming events where the filmmaker is nowhere to be seen and encouraging us to recognize the situated nature of documentary representation. Interactivity can work reflexively to make us aware of the contingencies of the moment, the shaping force of the representational project itself, and the modifications of action and behavior that it can produce. *Hard Metal's Disease* and *Chronicle of a Summer* both achieve this effect as does *No Lies* in a somewhat different register (since the events were constructed specifically to make this very point).[40] In *Poto and Cabengo,* Jean-Pierre Gorin's diaristic asides to the viewer, in English but with a noticeable French accent, and his interaction with the twins from San Diego (Poto and Cabengo) who appear to have invented a language of their own, with Germanic overtones, generate a heightened awareness of how speech constructs subjectivity as well as expressing it.

(d) Irony. Ironic representations inevitably have the appearance of insincerity since what is overtly said is not what is actually meant. The ironist says one thing but means the opposite. A heightened awareness of tradition usually informs the ironic; it is burdened with an excess of knowledge and a deficiency of invention, especially in its postmodern phase. As a tone or attitude, irony comes after romance, tragedy, and comedy; it sets them all on edge; it undermines their solidity and sobriety.[41]

Irony raises in an acute form the question of the author's own attitudinal relation to his or her subject matter. It is still a relatively rare phenomenon in documentary, one of the few of our culture's discursive formations or institutional practices to have sidestepped much of the impetus of modernism, reflexivity, and irony generally. It does crop up, however, in *The Thin Blue Line, Of Great Events, Roger and Me, Le Joli Mai, Les maîtres fous, Les Racquetteurs,* and *Lonely Boy,* among others, but seldom as a sustained, radically reflexive operation. Often, as in *Lonely Boy* or *The Thin Blue Line,* this ironic potential seems more specifically aligned to a fairly localized tendency toward detachment or skepticism when the filmmaker wants to signal distance from specific characters but not necessarily from the representational procedures of documentary themselves.

Raul Ruiz's *Of Great Events and Ordinary People* represents as thoroughgoing an ironic point of view as any in its radical interrogation of documentary form. Ruiz, though, does not settle on a detached relativism. Instead his irony derives from his own status as Chilean exile working in Paris where the Third World functions as a structuring absence in relation to the immediate issue of French national elections.[42]

Ruiz suggests that ironic categories of perception require detachment from a local scene or restricted frame of reference. To become politically reflexive this irony must reattach itself to a larger perspective. In relation to a broader scene or larger frame irony rebounds as a reflexive self-aware-ness of the prices and penalties of distance (such as we also find in Solas's fiction film, *Lucia*).[43] As Ruiz's voice-over commentary puts it near the end of the film, as we watch very grainy, high-contrast, generic images of Third World people:

> The documentary of the future must show the poverty in countries still knowing joy and freedom. We must show the sadness of those countries with the wealth and freedom to be happy or sad. It must show attacks on freedom in countries emerging from poverty even at the price of innocence and joy. In this way the future documentary will endlessly repeat these three truths:
>   So long as poverty exists, we shall still be rich.
>   So long as sadness exists, we shall still be happy.
>   So long as prisons exist, we shall still be free.[44]

(e) Parody and Satire. Parody can provoke a heightened awareness of a previously taken-for-granted style, genre, or movement; satire is one device for sharpening consciousness of a problematic social attitude, value, or situation. These forms are somewhat underdeveloped in documentary, where the prevalence of the discourses of sobriety and a Calvinist sense of mission have attenuated their status, particularly in English-speaking coun-tries. They do have a certain standing, however, as a subgenre of social criticism. *Sixteen in Webster Groves* and *Millhouse* are satires of upper middle-class teenagers and of Richard M. (Milhous) Nixon, for example, while *Cane Toads* and *Quebec, USA* are parodies of nature and tourist films respec-tively. *Poto and Cabengo* includes moments of sharp satire directed against the behavioral scientists who study and attempt to explain the twins' language skills in a social vacuum, strictly in relation to recorded utterances and their etymological analysis. Films like *The Most* and *The Selling of the Pentagon* use their subjects (Hugh Hefner and the military-industrial com-plex, respectively) as sources of satire by incorporating activities seemingly second nature to the subjects but not the audience. Such satire tends to be limited to specific moments rather than a global viewpoint. The fear of being considered "unfair" to one's subject is a strong constraint. (Films like *Thy Kingdom Come* and George Csicery's *Where the Heart Roams*, on religious fundamentalism and women's romance literature, respectively, include such satirical moments but strain to avoid all-out satire lest it alienate rather than inform.)

Although irony can be an effective weapon for both parody and satire, it is rare to have an ironic parody or satire as such since this would call into question the very form of parody or satire rather than accept these forms as suitable and appropriate ways of criticizing the ways of others. (The ironist is self-critical in a way that the parodist or satirist is likely not.) Fredric Jameson speaks of pastiche as the postmodern form of parody, wherein a normative judgment about previous styles is avoided in favor of an affect-less borrowing, a nostalgia that neither reveres nor loathes that which it retrieves.[45] The use of clips from period fiction films to provide a historical referent for the issues taken up in *The Thin Blue Line* or *The Making of a Legend* (on the making of *Gone with the Wind*) are more in the spirit of pastiche than parody or satire (the clips are of B-gangster films and late 1930s dramas respectively): these clips introduce fictional styles associated with a bygone era to evoke that period as though the fictional style were now itself a historical fact but one which we continue to enjoy in a nostalgic frame of mind. This affords the benefits of both historical documentation and narrative pleasure without necessarily calling either into question. Political reflexivity propels parody and satire beyond pastiche with its reassuring nostalgia or comfortable iconoclasm. It brings these forms into an arena where, subject to audience reception, they do more than mock or unsettle accepted convention. Heightened awareness carries beyond the immediate experience of the text into social praxis rendered more conceivable by dint of its documentary representation.

III

AXIOGRAPHICS

ETHICAL SPACE IN DOCUMENTARY FILM

Erotics/Ethics

Laura Mulvey argues that a social science approach to cinema—be it statistical shot analysis, interviews with audience members, economic studies of the industry, or cognitive psychology—cannot fathom the affective dimension of narrative. The psychodynamics of the gaze elude such categories and concepts. Both the scopophilic pleasure of sighting an object of desire and the identificatory pleasure of watching an other who serves as model for the self demand a different form of analysis: "Both pursue aims in indifference to perceptual reality, creating the imagized, eroticized concept of the world that forms the perception of the subject and makes a mockery of empirical objectivity."[1]

Mulvey's concern with the eroticization of the gaze and the gender hierarchy that classic (Hollywood) narrative imposes does not translate directly into the terms and conditions of documentary production. (Although it is hardly alien either.) The institutional discourse of documentary does not support it, the structure of documentary texts does not reward it, and the audience expectations do not revolve around it. Voyeurism, fetishism, and narcissism are present but seldom occupy the central position they have in classic narrative.

The difference in this regard between fiction and documentary is akin to the difference between an erotics and an ethics, a difference that continues to mark out the movement of the ideological through the aesthetic. Mulvey's feminist and psychoanalytic dissection of Hollywood erotics—the cost of aesthetic pleasure within the economy of that system—could be paralleled by a dissection of documentary ethics—the cost of epistephilia, or desire for knowledge, within the economy of this system. In both cases the intersection of ideology—the ways in which propositions are made regarding the viewer's relation to the world that involve imaginary, hierarchical, and hegemonic relations—with the formal structures of the text serves as a focal point for analysis.

Consider this remark by Mulvey: "Playing on the tension between film as

controlling the dimension of time (editing, narrative) and film as controlling the dimension of space (changes in distance, editing), cinematic codes
create a gaze, a world, and an object, thereby producing an illusion cut to
the measure of desire."[2] Might we not rewrite this comment with documentary in mind?—Playing on the tension between film as controlling the
dimension of time (exposition, narrative) and film as controlling the
dimension of space (changes in distance, place, perspective), cinematic
codes create a gaze aimed at the historical world, and an object (the desire
for and promise of knowledge), thereby producing an argument cut to
ethical, political, and ideological measure.

The Place of the Filmmaker

One way to give further consideration to this shift in problematics from
narrative to documentary would be to address the specific qualities of the
documentary gaze and its object of desire: the world it brings into sight.
What we might call axiographics moves to the fore. This neologism stems
from axiology, the study of values (ethics, aesthetics, religion, and so on),
with "particular reference to the manner in which they can be known or
experienced" (*Webster's Third International*). Axiographics would address
the question of how values, particularly an ethics of representation, comes
to be known and experienced in relation to space. Instead of the fictional
space of narrative and questions of style, we confront the axiographic space
of documentary and questions of ethics. How do the visual representations
of the camera place the filmmaker in relation to the historical world?[3] The
world we see is the historical world of which the filmmaker is a tangible
part. The presence (and absence) of the filmmaker in the image, in
off-screen space, in the acoustic folds of voice-on and voice-off, in titles and
graphics constitutes an ethics, and a politics, of considerable importance
to the viewer. Axiographics extends those classic topics of ethical debate—
the nature of consent; proprietary rights to recorded images; the right to
know versus the right to privacy; the responsibilities of the filmmaker to his
or her subject as well as audience, or employer; codes of conduct and the
complexities of legal recourse—to include the ethical implications conveyed by the representation of time and space itself.

The documentary viewer's subjectivity shifts according to whether a
politics of sexual or of spatial representation is predominant. The indul-
gence of fantasy is blocked to some degree not simply by the invocation of
a desire to know, but by an awareness that the views given originate from
the encounter between social actors on either side of the lens. The viewer's
relation to the image, then, is charged with an awareness of the politics and
ethics of the gaze. An indexical bond exists between the image and the
ethics that produced it. The image provides evidence not only on behalf of
an argument but also gives evidence of the politics and ethics of its maker.

The stamp of one person's vision across the face of the world calls for a hermeneutics of ethical interpretation as much or more than a hermeneutics of erotic interpretation.

Axiographics, then, is an attempt to explore the implantation of values in the configuration of space, in the constitution of a gaze, and in the relation of observer to observed. It parallels, something like a resistance movement, the more pragmatic, institutional discourse centered on the camera and the act of filming as the crucial moment in the overall practice of documentary filmmaking (arguments about lack of control over what occurs in front of the camera notwithstanding). Axiographics asks us to examine how the documentary camera gaze takes on distinctive qualities and poses concrete issues of politics, ethics, and ideology in terms of space.

Since documentary does not address the fictive space of classic narrative but historiographic space, the premise and assumption prevails that what occurred in front of the camera was not entirely enacted with the camera in mind. It would have existed, the events would have unfolded, the social actors would have lived and made a presentation of themselves in everyday life irrespective of the camera's presence.

Though subject to extensive qualification and subversion, this serves as a founding premise, a starting point which the documentary film viewer will accept as given until proven wrong. For scientists, what is called "mere film" or raw footage can be of great value. Unedited, not organized into any more elaborate form of textual system, it still bears significant information about the world such as the proxemic interactions that are the focus of *Microcultural Incidents in Ten Zoos.* In fiction, though, rushes (the unassembled shots and repeats of shots) have little comparable value. The unused takes commonly wind up on the cutting room floor. Only if there is a significant error (a blooper) or revealing process at work do rushes take on intrinsic importance. In this case, the piece of film shifts from being a signifier floating in discursive limbo to a historical document of what occurred in front of the camera without being necessarily for the sake of the camera. Examples would include the TV blooper-style footage that has become a commodity staple; outtakes that provide another, sometimes ironic view of the aura of Hollywood stars; and those sequences of takes through which we can see the construction of a fiction elaborate itself with more and more complexity. This last example is particularly vivid in the documentary *The Unknown Chaplin,* built around outtakes from several of his films that served as virtual sketchpads; with each take we can see his development of a gag grow increasingly sophisticated.

This difference in the documentary dimension of the shot introduces an immediate distinction with regard to the physical presence of the filmmaker. Since fictive space is imaginary, we expect the filmmaker to approach it from the outside. Camera angle, musical accompaniment, intertitles and so on—the full repertoire of stylistic devices that can signal authorial presence or narrational overtness—impinge on a fictive world that appears to retain its own coherence and consistency despite them. (When these marks of author or narration are absent we seem to enjoy transparent access to the fiction, often by means of views that seem to be those of an ideal observer, someone not responsible for the scene but available to view it and relay it to us.)

Since documentary space is historical, we expect the filmmaker to operate from the inside, as part of the historical world rather than the creator or author of an imaginary one. Documentary directors do not create an imaginary realm so much as a representation of the very same historical world as the one they themselves occupy. Their presence in or absence from the frame serves as an index to their own relationship (their respect or contempt, their humility or arrogance, their disinterestedness or tendentiousness, their pride or prejudice) to the people and problems, situations and events they film.

No stylistic devices are necessary to remind us that if what occurred in front of the camera was not entirely enacted for the camera, then this historiographic space in front and behind are of exactly the same woof and warp; they are continuous and coextensive. There is no ontological divide marked by the fabrication of an imaginary world. (The historical world may still be made over into the form of a narrative but the indexical link between image and historical referent remains in place. It locates the filmmaker as much as his or her subject.) Issues that would have been a matter of style may now become questions of skill—of how the filmmaker manages to secure the representations subsequently relayed to us.

The question posed to the spectator, then, is not what kind of imaginary world the filmmaker has created but how the filmmaker acquitted him- or herself in relation to those segments of the historical world that have become the scene of the film. Where does the filmmaker stand? What space does he or she occupy and what politics or ethics attach themselves to it?

The Gaze in Documentary

The primary markers of stance, or space occupied, are the sound and image relayed to the viewer. To speak of the camera's gaze is, in that one phrase, to mingle two distinct operations: the literal, mechanical operation of a device to reproduce images and the metaphorical, human process of gazing upon the world. As a machine the camera produces an indexical record of what falls within its visual field. As an anthropomorphic extension of the human sensorium the camera reveals not only the world but its operator's preoccupations, subjectivity, and values. The photographic (and aural) record provides an imprint of its user's ethical, political, and ideological stance as well as an imprint of the visible surface of things.

This notion is usually subsumed under the discussion of style. Of primary significance is the idea that style is not simply a systematic utilization of techniques devoid of meaning but itself the bearer of meaning. Point-of-view shots in Hitchcock may open onto a plane of voyeuristic fascination (of male characters with female ones, mostly); close-ups in Wiseman may implicate us in a dark, absurdist vision of bureaucracy and institutional power. Style, in this sense, is intimately attached to the idea of a moral point of view. Just as various prefigurative choices in the use of language signal the moral point of view of a historian, "the camera's gaze" may signal the ethical, political, and ideological perspective of the filmmaker.[4]

Style implicates the documentarist as a human subject directly; what we see, unlike what we see in a fiction, does not offer the conjectural space of a metaphor. We need not speculate whether someone who constructs a fiction like this, say the fictions of Hitchcock with their voyeuristic gazes aimed at women, regards his fellow humans in precisely the same way. In documentary we see how filmmakers regard, or look at, their fellow humans directly. The documentary is a record of that regard. The implication is direct. Style attests not only to "vision" or to a perspective on the world but also to the ethical quality of that perspective and the argument behind it.

One vivid illustration of the linkage between style as technique and moral outlook (or political point of view) arises in the relationship between the camera and its subject in documentary. Because the subjects of documentary—social actors and historical events—have a life that persists beyond the frame of the text, the camera and its gaze invoke a set of moral/political issues distinct from those associated with fiction. Some of these differences have been extremely well described by Vivian Sobchack in her essay, "Inscribing Ethical Space."[5]

Of particular interest is her discussion of documentary ethics pertaining to the representation of death, especially the moment when the passage from life to death itself occurs. Here we have documentary evidence of a most powerful kind. The difference between a fictional representation of death and a record of the historical occurrence of death itself is profound. We are made witness to something that cannot be seen literally (the exact moment of life's cessation) or metaphorically (for the most part, taboo disguises it). As Sobchack argues,

> Fictive death primarily represented by iconic and symbolic signs does not move us to inspect it, to seek out a visibility we feel—in seeing it—it lacks. Even without the slow motion ballet of death made paradigmatic by Sam Peckinpah in *The Wild Bunch*, fictive death is experienced as visible. Referring significantly only to themselves, representations of death in fiction film tend to satisfy us—indeed, in some films, to sate us, or to overwhelm us so that we *cover* our eyes rather than *strain* to see. Thus, while death is generally experienced in fiction films as representable and often excessively visible, in documentary films it is experienced as confounding representation, as exceeding visibility.[6]

We witness what exceeds our sight and grasp. The camera gazes. It presents evidence destined to disturb. This evidence cries out for argument, some interpretive frame within which to comprehend it. Nowhere is this need more acutely felt than in a film that refuses to provide any explanatory commentary whatsoever (though it does have a perspective and style): Stan Brakhage's *The Act of Seeing with one's own eyes*. Brakhage's work is traditionally assigned to the camp of experimental film where the work of the artist on the image and the heightened sense of form achieve a high degree of remove from the historical world and any claims of referentiality that the photographic image may present. Though experimental, *The Act of Seeing with one's own eyes* anchors itself to the historical world relentlessly. It presents, with almost classic ethnographic dutifulness, images of autopsies in the Pittsburgh morgue. Distortions we might expect to form the structural basis for the film—zoom shots, extreme close ups, camera movements, rapid cutting, optical printing—are quite minimal. More often than not we are asked to gaze at the slow, deliberate process of corporeal dissection, nowhere so disquieting as when this act centers on the head. More than once, the camera sits in medium shot, watching as the coroner cuts the skin loose around the back of the skull and then peels it forward and down, rolling the scalp with its attachment of hair into a semblance of a rug and then pulling this roll further down over the face until it rests, like a half-removed stocking, across the bridge of the nose. —All this to gain access to the brain, the organ, we are now graphically reminded, that this canopy of flesh and hair and skull protects.

More can be said about this extraordinary film and the effect it provokes, especially regarding its indexical bond with the objects it represents, but for now attention must go to the ethical dimension of this act of seeing, or gazing. The question is clearly of a different order of magnitude from what we would encounter in a fiction. In George Romero's *Day of the Dead,* for example, one of the surviving humans trapped within an underground shelter that is under siege by ghouls, is a scientist conducting experiments on the brains of these creatures in the hopes of learning how to control them. Some scenes present images of these fully exposed, pulsating brains, attached like some kind of glutinous red flower to the stalk of a still intact body, in a manner strongly reminiscent of *The Act of Seeing*. But the effect is radically different. In the one case we know we confront a mimetic facsimile of a dissected human brain (no human was actually sacrificed to achieve the effect); in the other we confront an indexical representation of the thing itself (human loss stands behind every frame). *Day of the Dead* may present ethical questions of its own, but they differ considerably from those of *The Act of Seeing with one's own eyes*.

As one simple example, consider the effect seeing Brakhage's film might have on a relative of one of the deceased. This issue does not arise in the Romero film. Death is imitated; it is presented as fact but not in fact.

(Relatives of the actors have the assurance that their kin lived to perform in other roles.) With the Brakhage film the degree of disturbance could be catastrophic for a relative or loved one. Here is but one issue that arises with an urgency absent from most fiction.

The link between style and ethics may be sharpened by considering how the impression of a particular form of subjectivity attaching to the camera or filmmaker carries an implicit ethical code along with it. On the one hand the viewer registers an emotional tonality, an authorial subjectivity, from specific aspects of the selection and arrangement of sound and image. This tonality and subjectivity approximate a "structure of feeling." They are manifestations of a certain orientation toward the world and they prompt emotional response. In addition, this tonality and subjectivity convey an implied ideology. They represent a specific set of propositional relationships between an object and its beholder. From this perspective, they testify to the operation of an ethical code governing the conduct of the camera/ filmmaker. This code is what legitimizes or licenses the continuing process of cinematography as a response to specific occurrences in the world.

An occurrence that gives this process particular pointedness is the moment of death. Witnessing the act of dying, which in the fiction film can only be mimicked, places an acute emotional and ethical strain on the documentary filmmaker. Different subjectivities emerge, different circumstances arise, different relations pertain between camera and subject and between camera and viewer. These differences can be illustrated by considering the camera's gaze in the following anthropomorphic categories. Each tonality or impression of subjective engagement between camera and world implies a different ethical code, and these in turn legitimize the continuing process of filming in the face of death.

—The accidental gaze: the camera happens upon the moment of death unexpectedly. The Zapruder footage of John F. Kennedy's assassination is one example, along with the television record of Lee Harvey Oswald's arraignment, which became coverage of his assassination by Jack Ruby; the "mere" or raw footage of the Hindenberg dirigible disaster is another. As Sobchack notes, such footage often incites a desire for slow motion examination, as if the moment of death can be fixed and with it some sense of explanation assigned. Such a desire cannot be satisfied, and some films emphasize this point by showing the same slow motion footage repeatedly. (This trope of slow motion as the potential source of an explanation that is not forthcoming pushes our attention elsewhere in *Roses in December* and Bruce Conner's *A Movie*, among other films.) The signs of "accidentalness" are the same signs that signify contingency and vulnerability for the documentary generally: chaotic framing, blurred focus, poor sound quality—if there is any synchronous sound at all—the sudden use of a zoom lens, jerky camera movements, the inability to foreshadow or pursue the most pivotal events, and a subject-camera distance that may seem too distant or too close on either aesthetic or informational grounds.

The accidental gaze depends on an ethic of curiosity for its duration. This is a low-order ethic to be sure, but one intimately tied to more culturally specific conceptions of knowledge and wisdom. Curiosity legitimates continuing the process of recording what has come into the camera's visual field accidentally. The reworking of the footage obtained (as we have in *A Movie* or *Report*) suggests the inadequacy of curiosity as an ethic: like a riddle or puzzle that has not yet yielded its secret, the images prompt rearrangement and modification in the hopes that we may infer the explanatory secrets they contain and thereby convert curiosity to knowledge.

As with the other ethical codes suggested here, an ethic of curiosity may also entail a pathology. A thin line separates the accidental gaze from morbid curiosity. More accurately, no clear line divides the two. Psychopathologies of desire may infiltrate any ethic, coloring the gaze with undertones of voyeurism, sadism, masochism, or fetishism. These subjectivities thwart or obstruct the implantation of an idealized ethical standard, but they need not dominate the affective tonalities of the gaze. Brakhage's *The Act of Seeing* clearly risks the charge of morbid fascination with a cultural taboo, but the film's power to disturb revolves around its avoidance of a morbidity that would allow viewers to explain away what they see as symptoms of the filmmaker's pathology.

The camera's gaze always requires distance between camera and subject. The question is how that distance is made to function, over time, as a signifier of subjectivity, ethical stance, political perspective, psychic "perversion," and ideological affiliation.

—The helpless gaze: the footage demonstrates an inability to affect a set of events it may have set out to record but with which it is not complicitous. Filmed records of public executions would be one example. Such a situation is mimicked in Peter Watkins's *The War Game* when the cameraman/reporter witnesses the unceremonious burning of dead bodies in the city streets in order to prevent contagion. Helplessness not only testifies to the filmmaker's lack of affiliation with the agency of death (this is characteristic of the professional gaze, too; see below), but also to an impulse to appeal to, dissuade, or otherwise challenge that agency, together with an inability to do so. Signs of "helplessness" might include emphasis on the spatial context and the camera's restricted location within it, particularly if there are physical barriers between camera and event. (In Watkins's case, a constable restrains the cameraman from moving closer or interceding.) Repeated zoom shots that seem to penetrate these barriers (of walls, windows, police cordons, and the like) only to withdraw behind them fix the filmmaker in a passive/active position of being able to see and record but not act or intervene.

Helplessness is a strong stylistic mark of an observer or authoring agent who feels bound to continue observing while also signaling a blocked ability to intervene. The result is often the registration of involuntary passivity, an inability to traverse the distance between camera and subject

physically. The registration and continuation of such a gaze draws legitimation from an ethic of sympathy. This code operates to allow the continuation of filming along with a heightened sense of the impasse that keeps
filmmaker and subject at a distance.

—The endangered gaze: the footage shows the filmmaker or cameraperson at personal risk. Such risk is particularly common to documentary
war footage. The most vivid example in the early days of the attack on Iraq
that began on January 16, 1991 was the reporting from Baghdad, particularly by the CNN (Cable News Network) team. Their courage and determination in the face of great danger became a key part of how their reports
were described and contextualized by CNN's own anchor people.
Sobchack argues that this form of gaze functions to absolve the filmmaker
"from seeking out and gazing at the death of others" (p. 296) by dint of
evident personal peril. (The disavowal of pathology by a demonstration of
personal risk could be, itself, analyzed, but in most cases I suspect Sobchack
is correct.)

Danger, in documentary, is real. Contingency abounds. There is, therefore, the possibility that risk will have real consequences: the endangered
camera may even record the final moments of a fatally jeopardized cameraperson. One of the most compelling examples of this gaze, if we can still
call it a gaze rather than a look or line of sight, occurs in *The Battle of Chile*
when the cameraman steps into a street only to be cut down by rifle fire.
We see the killer and witness the moment at which the bullets are fired,
their impact inscribed in every jolt and jostle of the falling man and camera
before the machine stops running and the image turns to black.

Endangerment reveals itself in the signifiers of perilous security that may
enter the frame: branches, holes and ditches, walls, the sides of cars,
doorways or window sills that provide inadequate protection; and in the
indexical bond that exists between the evidence of fatal risks we see and the
camera itself: vibrations that synchronize with explosions, shakiness that
corresponds with a dash for shelter, sudden movements that match up with
the sound of incoming artillery fire. Survival is at stake and the camera's
record testifies to the delicate balance struck between preserving the life of
the cameraperson and recording the risks undertaken by others whose fate
resides beyond the scope of filmic intervention.

What legitimates continued filming despite endangerment is an ethic of
courage. A higher priority than personal safety authorizes risk-taking. Risk
serves a greater good. This greater good can range from testing one's
individual mettle in the face of death to the selfless recording of information considered vital, including the courage and heroism of others. Adven-
turism, professionalism, and commitment to a given cause can all motivate
an ethic of courage. Like curiosity and sympathy, courage functions as an
ethic that stresses our relation to the camera and filmmaker. These ethical
codes heighten our awareness of the camera's gaze arising from a location
that carries its own emotional burden.

—The interventional gaze: the camera abandons the precondition of distance, transforming the detachment of a gaze into the involvement of a look. Intervention is usually on behalf of someone else more immediately endangered than the cameraperson him- or herself. This, Sobchack argues, is a confrontational look that chooses to place the living body of the filmmaker on the same plane of historical contingency as its subjects rather than to preserve the distance, and relative safety, afforded by the gaze. The camera becomes more than an anthropomorphic symbol and locus. It becomes the physical embodiment of the human being behind it. When it moves into a potential line of fire, it is the body of the filmmaker that has done so and a sense of acute physical risk is conveyed to the viewer. Examples occur in *Love, Women, and Flowers, Harlan County, U.S.A.*, and in the fiction film, *Medium Cool*, when the filmmakers accept endangerment in order to take their place alongside those with whom there is affiliation. In *Harlan County* and *Medium Cool*, the moment is marked on the sound track as well by off-screen voices proclaiming the danger. In *Medium Cool*, for example, one of the crew members warns the director/cinematographer, "Watch out, Haskell [Wexler]; those bullets are real." In *Love, Women and Flowers* the hazard comes from the enormous quantities of pesticide and herbicide used to grow flowers for export.

The interventional gaze is also aligned—in its creation of an axiographic space shared by historical actors who conduct a dialogue across the axis of the camera's line of sight—with the interactive mode of documentary filmmaking. The threat of death places interaction or affinity, commitment, and solidarity with those filmed on emotionally charged ground. Such moments are rare, but they indicate what stakes exist when the filmmaker chooses to act in history alongside those filmed rather than operate from the paradoxically "safe place" of authoring agent, a place that can never be made fully secure in documentary.

An ethic of responsibility legitimates continued filming while in the process of intervention. The emphasis shifts away from the filmmaker at a position of distance from others more directly endangered to a relationship between filmmaker, subject, and threat. The passage across this space is at the center of an ethic that stresses a responsibility that finds no higher goal than a direct, personal response to the threat to human life itself. Though intervention may well require courage it is a subordinated courage, a necessary support for actions required to confront the agency of death. No longer helpless and not content to register endangerment, the interventionist gaze is willing to nullify itself, to abandon filming in the course of intervening. This reverses the priority that governs the professional gaze discussed below.

An ethic of irresponsibility is also conceivable in which the intervention is participatory rather than oppositional. The camera gaze that actively sides with the agency of death legitimates itself through the same code that legitimates the taking of life in the first place. Those who filmed the results of lethal medical experiments in Nazi concentration camps functioned as an extension of the experiment itself and signaled none of the detachment that the other positions discussed here involve. Those who filmed the hanged body of the American hostage William Higgins in Lebanon as proof of his execution also displayed adherence to an ethic of irresponsibility. Rather than witnessing against the taking of life this ethic conveys a complicity with murder and with the rationale supporting it. Within the framework that legitimates killing, the gaze will appear as responsible as the murder itself, but from outside that frame a sharp reversal occurs.

—The humane gaze: the film registers an extended subjective response to the moment or process of death that it depicts. Intervention may be considered one form of humane gaze that pertains to situations where intercession may have some effect. Both the interventional and humane gazes disrupt the fixed, mechanical recording process to emphasize the human agency behind the camera, but the humane gaze occurs in cases where death cannot be prevented by intervention. Terminal illnesses provide a prime example. Like endangerment, the display of a humane gaze may absolve the filmmaker of fault for seeking out and gazing at the death of others. The display mitigates any appearance of morbidity. Like the endangered gaze the humane gaze also draws motivation from a greater good; often the goal is to help others understand and anticipate what a process like terminal illness entails. (Examples include *Dying, Erika: Not in Vain,* and *One Man's Fight for Life.*)

If it is to be separated from an interventional gaze and not limited to still images, the humane gaze requires the same barrier of distance or obstacle that describes the helpless gaze. (Since the very thing to which all these gazes give eternal life is the moment of death itself, an element of helplessness is inevitable, but for the humane gaze, it does not dominate.) Instead of an emphasis on the inability of the camera or filmmaker to intervene physically or directly, this gaze stresses a form of empathetic bond across the barrier between the living and the dead (or those whose death is imminent and those whose death is, as yet, unforeseen). Subjectivity streams outward, toward the dead or dying, rather than inward, toward the cameraperson's helplessness. The link between camera and subject takes priority over the subjectivity of the camera gaze alone.

Signs of the humane gaze include the absence of the signifiers of helplessness or active intervention together with the presence of signifiers of empathetic response, such as emphasis on the continuing proximity of camera and subject despite the encroachment of death and the direct acknowledgment of a human relationship between filmmaker and subject through dialogue or commentary. In films like *Roses in December,* where the subject has already died prior to filming, the humane gaze attempts to recover from the traces of a life departed (belongings left behind, letters, reminiscences, and photographs) those affective bonds that would have joined the one departed to his or her community. In films like *One Man's*

Fight for Life, where death is protracted, the humane gaze signifies the establishment of a rapport between camera and subject that exceeds the terms of professional responsibility to obtain a record of value to others. This film, for example, includes several exchanges between filmmaker and subject in which the dying cancer patient, Saif Ullah, confesses his normally well-disguised despair. The confessions demonstrate a humaneness to the encounter that places camera and subject on the same experiential plane of lived reality.

An ethic of responsibility, channeled primarily through empathy rather than intervention, legitimates the process of continued filming. Like the interventional gaze, the humane one gives the definite impression that continued filming is not as important as personal response. That both occur at once is what gives the text a strong emotional charge.

—The clinical or professional gaze: the film situates itself within the ambivalent space between detached recording and humane response. A. J. Liebling's remark that reporters don't always remember that what's a fabulous story for them is simultaneously someone else's disaster identifies the source of ambivalence. If the helpless gaze inverts an empathetic response to death or dying into an inability to intercede, the clinical gaze, too, steps away from empathy but from powerlessness as well. Accidental and helpless gazes are as foreign to the clinical gaze as interventional or humane ones. The clinical gaze operates in compliance with a professional code of ethics that trains its adherents in the art of personal detachment from those with whom they work. The professional seeks out what others stumble upon but chooses to signal neither helplessness nor empathy. The intent is neither intervention nor a humane response but a disciplined one inoculated against displays of personal involvement.[7]

The clinical gaze testifies to a special form of empowerment whose fairly elaborate, professional codes of conduct are symptomatic of its location at the boundaries of the ethical. It is presumably in the service of a greater good—the viewer's "right to know"—and is sanctioned by a constitutional guarantee of freedom of the press. (This is true for journalism, at least. For documentaries concerned with more extended issues than news, the guarantee may have different limits in the face of a competing right to privacy.)

This inoculation against the display of personal involvement goes by the name of objectivity. The tension within objectivity arises from the "responsibility" of the journalist to forego emotional, biased, or subjective response to events in order to safeguard his or her professional standing as detached, impartial observer. Fulfilling such a responsibility completely is seldom possible and hardly defensible if intervention might have saved a life. This is a particularly strong rebuke in cases where the event has been staged for the sake of news coverage in the first place such as the antinuclear protest in Oakland, California in 1987 that resulted in amputation of the legs of protester Brian Wilson by a munitions train or, in even more complex, cross-culturally mediated events such as the self-immolation of Vietnamese

Buddhist priests in Saigon. In these cases events may well have taken a different course were it not for the prospect of news coverage: does the journalist then have a "responsibility" to report what his presence prompts or to intercede when human lives are at stake?

Sobchack describes the sign of this gaze as "technical and machine-like competence in the face of an event which seems to call for further and human response" (p. 298), a description that places the professional on the side of the automaton. The countervailing perspective stresses the ethic of the "greatest good" and the professional's need to exempt him- or herself from intervention in order to serve that good. The right to know is a right belonging to the plurality, to all citizens, and that right is best served by allowing events to take their own course, even events planned specifically as media events from the start. Those who participate in an event must be assumed to be aware of the potential consequences, those who watch them of the potential fabrication; it would not be the place of the reporter to assume the role of parent or guardian. (Several films by Peter Watkins such as *Culloden, The War Game,* and *Punishment Park* underscore the moral ambiguity of the professional reporter and his gaze when Watkins's fictitious reporters articulate a humane response to what they see. They report what they find but also attempt to give voice to the empathetic response to violence or atrocity that a viewer might have. Without moving toward emphatic intervention or toward lending aid to those who suffer, their response serves to underscore the helplessness of the reporter, the moral intensity of the situation, the anomaly of the professional stance, and the need for human intervention even if it comes to nought.)

The ethical code of the professional subdivides into different institutional practices. Doctors, social science researchers, police, soldiers, and journalists each inflect the code of the professional and the clinical use of the gaze in distinct ways. The filmmaker or documentarian also subscribes to a professional code that may demand detachment from the antecedent reality from which he or she constructs a text. This broader sense of detachment carries us into the realm of textual representation generally and goes beyond those situations where lives are imperiled at the moment of filming. This latter (more specific and acute) case sharpens the tension between objectivity and self-effacement on the one hand, and subjectivity and protest on the other. The clinical gaze may well be an abject response, the symptom of a social pathology that carries detachment beyond a justifiable limit.[8]

This array of gazes and the ethical codes that support them bring the ethical, political, and ideological into suggestive alignment. They draw our attention to an ethics of responsibility, as each gaze signals an alternative response in the face of death; to a politics of representation and authority, as each gaze stands for what the filmmaker sees, how he or she responds, and the relay of these responses to the viewer; and to the ideology of objectivity and epistemology, as each gaze reinforces the value of the visual as evidence and source of knowledge. (Each gaze depends on detachment and the physics of camera optics to convey subjective tonalities. In this sense each gaze supports an epistemology based on scientific principles of mechanical reproduction even if they may also support other, more intuitive, empathetic, or gnostic forms of knowledge.)

Documentary Modes and Ethical Accounting

These axiographic questions regarding the stance of the filmmaker, the way in which he or she occupies space and negotiates the distance of the camera's gaze, have not been questions of primary importance in the criticism or practice of documentary film. This silence may be symptomatic of filmmakers' conventional strategy for the representation of their own presence, a strategy that has constructed a disguise for the person behind the camera's gaze. Filmmakers exonerate themselves from accountability for their bodily presence in the name of a greater good. Only the interactive and reflexive modes routinely acknowledge the presence of the filmmaker, and of these only the reflexive calls this presence into question. In the other modes, specific conventions have developed which, in a manner akin to that of classic narrative fiction, render the presence of the filmmaker as absence. These are true conventions; they could be otherwise. The movement of interactive filmmaking toward greater acknowledgment of the filmmaker's corporeal presence illustrates the force of convention. Many films built around interviews or other forms of observed engagement between filmmaker and social actors rendered the filmmaker as an off-screen presence, as a disembodied intelligence. Jean Rouch, however, marked out an alternative direction from the start in which the personal interventions of the filmmaker—the active, explicit process of shaping lived experience into mise-en-scène, the contingency of events on the dynamics of filmmaker/subject relationship—pointed to the physical presence of the filmmaker on the scene.

The distinctive formulation of the camera's (and filmmaker's) presence as absence, so common to classic narrative, poses problems of a peculiar nature in documentary. In expository documentary, for example, the presence of the filmmaker is shifted to the sound track and eliminated from the image track. The film's argument is usually carried by the sound track and despite the claim that documentary represents a fetishization of the visible per se, the fetish, if any, would here be of the Word, commensurate with a Platonic logocentrism and the denotative emphasis of the discourses of sobriety.[9] Direct address, either through an off-screen commentator or on-screen voice of authority, endorses the tradition of disembodied, universalized knowledge. Such speech, like the clinical gaze, requires the acceptance of a discipline that detaches knowledge from the body that produces it. The claims of the word exceed their bodily origin.

They are best delocalized, to be applied like a glaze to the visible scene. The disembodied quality of speech becomes a rhetorical virtue. Individuation becomes a matter of inflecting institutional discourse with the "grain" or texture of the distinctive, recurring voice. These voices—such as those of television anchorpeople and reporters—are attached to bodies that represent not personal witness, but institutional authority in anthropomorphic form.

This privileging of the word faces a crisis with every edit. With each cut the opportunity exists to reinscribe the filmmaker's presence rather than excise it. Each cut opens the gap between human agency and cinematic evidence only to anneal it again through continued exclusion. Documentary convention upholds the expectation of presence, of an ethic of witnessing, of a situated view, and yet excises the bodily evidence of presence. (Works like Ophuls's *Hotel Terminus*, Claude Lanzman's *Shoah*, Jon Alpert's *Hard Metal's Disease*, and Octavio Cortázar's *For the First Time* prove the exception.)

The ethics attached to "being there" on the scene become replaced by the ethics of objectivity and good journalism or displaced into the ethics of rhetoric and argumentation, of what can be said at a distance, from somewhere else. The edit squeezes out that "other scene" from which what the camera represents is seen. A lacuna opens, at the very moment that the edit sutures it back up, in historiographic space. We are left with a window onto the world where once there was a presence. The window stands in for that presence, representing it as a presence *in absentia*.

Axiographic questions of ethical space recall that absent but structuring presence to the scene in order to inquire into its ideology, politics, or ethics. Consider the representation of disaster. A tension between the professional code of conduct that places the filmmaker at the service of an institutional discourse and an ethical code of human responsibility to, or for, what immediately surrounds us is frequently apparent. This situated responsibility becomes displaced into disembodied, detached professional responsibility. The presence of the reporter (the effect is most acute in news reportage) attests to the authenticity of the representation but it is an authentication built on the inauthenticity of the reporter's own presence. That is, the reporter as historical social actor on the scene of human disaster must suppress any sustained and totally absorbing response to the disaster in order to preserve the distance necessary for the relay of disaster to those not bodily present. This allows the viewer apparently unmediated emotional response to the images of disaster and yet it is a response dependent upon the social act of detachment.

The news coverage of the famine in Ethiopia offers an example. Subsequent interviews with reporters who first "covered" the event (the use of the word "coverage" perfectly feeds into the consideration of space presented here) disclosed how difficult it had been to persuade the first major network (the BBC) to break the story. The interviews do not disclose how difficult it had been for the reporters to live in the face of death and respond by taking pictures of it. Such a question would be "unprofessional" for one reporter to pose to another in public discourse, since it calls into question the very foundation of the reportorial ethic. Human response may well have occurred; it may even have predominated, but, in terms of the news, it has, literally, no place. As professionals, the reporters' presence only gains credibility to the extent that it marks the place of ethical absence, of distance and nonintervention on behalf of an institutional discourse. The editorial exclusion of the filmmaker or reporter from the scene and the visual anchorage of the reporter at the scene achieve the same end: in either case the reporter's bodily presence serves the needs of an institutional discourse above all. When bodily present, it is to certify the omnipresence of the authoring agency, the news apparatus, rather than to offer witness to the response of one human to the plight of another.

The politics of space, the policing of boundaries, and maintenance of distancing devices lie behind Brian Winston's critique of the expository tradition in documentary as one that constitutes its subjects as victims. (The position of victim recalls the documentary's preoccupation with death: victimization is a maiming or murdering of the individual to produce a typification or stereotype.) When both filmmaker and social actor coexist within the historical world but only one has the authority to represent it, the other, who serves as subject of the film, experiences a displacement. Though bodily and ethically absented, the filmmaker retains the controlling voice, and the subject of the film becomes displaced into a mythic realm of reductive, essentialized stereotype, most commonly romantic hero or powerless victim. After the attempt to assist the working class to find their own voice in Elton and Anstey's *Housing Problems*, the convention of speaking for others regained primacy: "The victim would stand revealed as the central subject of the documentary, anonymous and pathetic, and the director of victim documentaries would be as much of an 'artist' as any other filmmaker."[10]

The presentation of subjects who "stand revealed" but who cannot reveal the detachment of the human subject who represents them itself constitutes a victim position. The axiographic result of this move is to place them within a mise-en-scène they do not control, not unlike the "cattle" (the trained actors) of whom Alfred Hitchcock speaks when he stresses the ultimate control of the director over audience response. Victims of famine are nameless examples; their representation provides the evidence of disaster, their anonymity licenses empathy and charity, if we see past the absent presence of the expository filmmaker or news reporter whose lack of response provides the occasion for our own.[11]

A different form of witnessing occurs in observational documentaries like the work of Fred Wiseman or Martin Bell's *Streetwise*. Unlike the interactional mode where the interaction between filmmaker and subject figures heavily, observational documentary excludes the filmmaker from the frame but not the scene. An entire ethical problematic has grown up around this "fly-on-the-wall" aesthetic of cinematography that closely replicates classic narrative style but at the same time gives evidence, through the camera eye, of the filmmaker's presence-as-absence. What effect did this unacknowledged presence have? (Pat Loud felt that her family had been turned into stereotypes in *An American Family*, a twelve-part observational record of their lives over a year.) What authority legitimates the appropriation of the images of others in the absence of an *acknowledged* human relation? (What mandate licenses observing the quarrels and fights between the husband and wife featured in *A Married Couple*; what greater good justifies exposing the survival strategies of an impoverished family in *The Things I Cannot Change*; in what context can the Yanomamö people be said to grant "informed consent" to the ethnographic films that constitute the Yanomamö series? What forms of tacit human interaction or acknowledgment can be incorporated into an observational style without the filmmaker consistently implanting him- or herself as one more social actor within the same historical space? (Gestures of acknowledgment enter into *Soldier Girls*, *Seventeen*, and *Kenya Boran* without transforming an observational style into an interactive one.)

A small but intriguing group of these questions can be pursued by asking how *changes* in a film's conventions governing the spatial positioning of the camera implicate us within the politics and ethics of the documentary gaze. Every film establishes normative patterns of its own, conventions that are part of the style and rhetoric of that one work but that draw on a repertoire of techniques and styles available to films of a similar type or to the cinema generally. When we examine observational films where direct address to the viewer does not occur, the question arises of what inflections can be given to the ethical space of the present, but absent, filmmaker. Is it possible for changes in a previously established convention or for shifts in the mode of spatial representation to signify a retroactive perspective on or a recontextualization of the implied ethics of the observation mode employed? Is it also possible for the spectator to share the geographic perspective of a camera position but not necessarily share the moral perspective of that position?

In an essay on the rhetoric of John Ford's *Stagecoach*, Nick Browne examines questions like these in relation to Ford's camera position and the viewer's moral sympathies for and against specific characters. Browne argues that although we share the physical viewpoint of Lucy, a somewhat prim, married Easterner, at the dinner table during the coach's stopover, we do not share her moral point of view. Our moral alliance is with Dallas, the outsider and prostitute, whom the Ringo Kid (John Wayne) also happens to defend.[12] After taking us through a shot-by-shot analysis of the scene at the dinner table, Browne writes, "Though I share Lucy's literal geographical position of viewing at this moment in the film, I am not committed to her figurative point of view. I can in other words repudiate Lucy's view of or judgement of Dallas without negating it as a view, in a way that Dallas herself, captive of the other's image, cannot."[13]

Observational documentary is often described as vulnerable to the predisposition of its audience. Since there is no guiding commentary and since the filmmaker is nowhere to be seen (or heard), the audience will assess what it sees according to social assumptions and habitual ways of seeing, including biases, that it brings to the film. Though not without merit, this description also neglects the degree to which strategies of textual organization themselves can inform and shape the readings we make.[14] The carefully controlled rhetorical operations of a fiction film like *Stagecoach* may also make their appearance in those observational documentaries that most closely resemble it.

Consider the predominantly observational documentary, *Streetwise*. Shot on the streets of Seattle over an extended period, the film depends on the confidence that arose between filmmaker and subject, especially the children who became the central characters, Tiny, Rat, and Duwayne. The repeated use of wide-angle close-ups and the presence of the camera during moments of intimate conversation between characters provide axiographic evidence of a rapport between filmmaker and subject (unlike telephoto close-ups, wide-angle shots indicate the physical proximity of filmmaker/cameraperson and subject). Voice-over commentary in the form of diaristic or confessional remarks by the main characters (we do not hear the voice of the filmmaker) add to the sense of intimacy. Tacit, mutual acceptance is at work. Other issues linger—whether, for example, informed consent could be explained to the subjects or given by them, the possible charge that the subject remains represented as victim, and that although the filmmaker's moral presence and accountability is figured in the specific nature of the image, it is an incomplete presence and at best a partial accountability—but the immediate question of how a change in spatial conventions affects the viewer's response calls for further discussion.

A year after the film was shot, Duwayne hanged himself in a detention cell. The filmmakers decided to return to Seattle to film the funeral and plan additional sequences dealing with this dramatic turn of events. Throughout the film up to this point the taped interviews with the street kids have amplified the tonalities of the scenes we see, something like the "masked interview" technique that sets up a situation, requests discussion of a certain topic, and then records the conversation that results observationally.[15] The voice-over monologues provide an additional point of entry and emotional orientation for the viewer without resorting to mise-en-scène or explicit interaction between filmmaker and subject. Voice-over does not do in this film what it often does in others: provide contextualizing information from experts, witnesses, or the filmmaker directly. Given the film's convention of only using conversations recorded with the street kids for voice-over, it upsets our expectations when we hear Duwayne's parole

officer say in voice-over that Duwayne wanted his ashes scattered in Puget
Sound as we see the body of Duwayne lying in a casket. At this point, we
gain "inside information" from someone outside the circle of street kids
themselves, undercutting the intimacy built up by the previous voice-over
commentary. The filmmaker has resorted to an interview with the parole
officer for information of the sort that the kids have volunteered up until
this point. We enter a different, more detached form of auditory space.

   This is paralleled by a different order of visual space. Whereas wide-angle
close shots have characterized the shooting style up until this point, the
camera assumes a position at the back of the funeral parlor while Duwayne's father and his police escort mourn in the deep background of the
shot. (The boy's father is serving a prison sentence.) The camera does not
seem to belong. It is as if the usual implication that what we see is what there
was has been inverted into a negative assertion: what we see is what we
should not see.

   This discomfort, though, runs against a common convention regarding
spatial positioning. A long shot of an event such as a funeral can suggest
restraint or respect (it is very common in fiction films) whereas close shots
might seem intrusive or distracting, perhaps morally suspect for the way
they test the ability of social actors to continue to ignore the presence of a
camera that records them in moments of heightened intimacy and vulnerability. (Close shots of a funeral in *Joe Leahy's Neighbors* have this effect: as
the grieving continues we wonder more and more about the dynamics
between the invisible filmmaker and the closely observed subjects.) But the
long shot of the funeral in *Streetwise* has the opposite effect. Axiographic
conventions are reversed. Distance suggests a self-conscious or queasy
intrusiveness, an attempt to get close enough to a private moment to be
able to photograph it when the spatial rapport evident elsewhere in the
film is lacking. Distance, instead of conveying respect, suggests an awareness of the moral dubiousness of returning not to resume Duwayne's
acquaintance but to make dramatic use of his dead body.

   The reversal of audience expectations associated with the axiographics
of funeral scenes reinforces a point made by Nick Browne: "the spectator's
figurative [moral] position is not stated by a description of where the
camera is in the geography of the scene. . . . Evidently, a spectator is several
places at once—with the fictional viewer [or the camera position and
filmmaker], with the viewed, and at the same time in a position to evaluate
and respond to the claims of each."[16] Most importantly, the shot goes
against the grain of the film's previous conventions. We are not free to
interpret it solely according to expectations and norms we bring to the film.
Instead, the altered treatment of space registers as an ethical/political/
ideological difference:

   —Ethical in raising the question of the filmmaker's responsibility in
representing the funeral. The death clearly fills a narrative function—the
authority of the gaze stems from the structural use of this death to provide

dramatic climax, closing off a portrait of street life with a powerful caution-ary moment. Dramatic form, however, comes at the expense of an embod-ied and situated gaze. It is as though the filmmaker has reasserted a hierarchical relation between camera and subject by recourse to the pro-fessional gaze, now that dramatic form requires it.

—Political in raising the question of representation as a social issue: what use may a filmmaker make of the images of others; what form of consent may fathers and (deceased) sons grant that will shield them from taking the place of victims in someone else's argument? How can the professional filmmaker work nonhierarchically with those who are not empowered?

—Ideological in pointing out how our own subjectivity is constituted, in part, by our engagement with the text and how shifts in the terms of that engagement bear consequences for us that are far more nuanced than certain "ideological effect" arguments about the cinematographic appara-tus would have us believe.[17] A significant difference in ethical space opens up between two distinct shooting styles; the cinema does far more than achieve the singular ideological effect of calling forth a transcendental subject. (If there is an overriding and overdetermining effect to the expe-rience of cinema at all, it is still subject to considerable variation at the much more concrete level of the space within and between shots.)

A similar distinction between types of ethical space takes vivid form in Fred Wiseman's film, *Model*. The segment that is particularly instructive involves observation of the production of a television commercial for Evan Picone pantyhose which is, at the conclusion of the segment, contrasted with the finished ad itself. Wiseman provides no commentary on the process of making the ad. It is not until we see the finished ad that it is completely clear that two long sequences—one observing the filming of a scene on location in New York and one observing the filming of another scene on a sound stage by a different director—are two parts of the same ad. Space in Wiseman's observation of this process is sharply segmented to produce what I have elsewhere called a mosaic effect.[18] By not guiding us through the unfolding sequence of images and events, and by only provid-ing synchronous location sound (without music or commentary), Wiseman already achieves a significant difference from the ad: his style requires a retrospective reading if it is to be fully comprehended. But the contrast between Wiseman's observational style and the rhetorically expository style of the ad is much more extensive than that:

—Wiseman stresses duration, process, labor, production, and, implicitly, the extraction of surplus value. His long takes, the inclusion of "empty" moments and repetitive actions (multiple takes of the same shot by the camera crew he observes, extended shots of onlookers who simply look on, for example) generate a sense of exhaustive observation (we must have seen everything that could be pertinent since we have seen so much that isn't). The recurrence of individuals such as the director begins to suggest some sense of psychological depth and distinctiveness (he is not simply "the director" whose generic role will even be erased in the final ad but a particular manifestation of one with his own idiosyncratic mannerisms and phrases and attitudes).

—The pantyhose ad constructs a clear, linear unification of space and action. Interestingly, Wiseman renders space in the normal realist conventions of a boundless, three-dimensional volume where social actors are readily located in relation to one another whereas, in the ad, the linear drive of the narrative takes precedence. The "real" space Wiseman observes contrasts with the constructed space of the ad. We can detect a mismatch. The ad's linearity gives rise to an Escher-like impossible space: the principal figure's movement from shot to shot turns her around so that she ends up walking back toward where she began even though she is meant to convey the impression of an alert, self-possessed businesswoman leaving home for a day at the office.

A similar irrealism occurs on the soundtrack. Whereas Wiseman gives us nothing but location sounds, the ad gives us no location sounds whatsoever (and no hints, of course, of the presence of any onlookers or a camera crew). The aural space is entirely taken up by a jingle and voice-over commentary. Meaning in the ad is obvious on the first viewing. Characters are read as types, representative of a social class rather than individualized (the principal figure who is jostled on the street by a handsome but absent-minded man has no individuated psychology: she can only be identified as "successful and attractive career woman," or some other such category). Instead of exhaustiveness, the ad stresses rapidity, immediacy, and an almost surreal collapsing of realms. We move from an on-the-street encounter between the career woman and a distracted businessman who is captivated by her appearance (especially, of course, by her legs) to a peacock-like effect (the result of the studio filming) in which another woman's leg rises to a fixed but increasingly higher position in the frame, each time displaying a different style of pantyhose, and conclude with a two-dimensional billboard-like image of the Evan Picone pantyhose package, with the name clearly displayed. The ad collapses three-dimensional social space into the two-dimensional iconic space of commodity packaging.

—Wiseman's camera gaze has a voyeuristic quality (his is an unacknowledged presence or a presence-as-absence in relation to the social actors) and yet it does not elaborate this scopophilic tendency into the more gender-specific form of voyeurism found in many fiction films. (The camera does not align itself with male characters nor does it isolate women as spectacles-to-be-looked-at.) The filming that Wiseman observes does this, but his own camera surveys the scene to include casual passers-by, housewives looking out their windows, a gay couple pausing to look on, a policeman, a street cleaner, and several others. Wiseman allows us to observe the gender hierarchy of space as organized by the film crew without duplicating it himself.

—By contrast, the advertisement's blatant voyeurism becomes clearly aligned with a hierarchical sex-gender system. Women make themselves "presentable" and men enjoy their self-presentation (is this our heroine's principal career?). When the woman is jostled by the male businessman, the camera tilts from her face and a brief exchange of looks between the characters, as the man turns her around by the waist in a well-choreographed effort to maintain their balance, to her legs. (Wiseman's own camera did not offer such a "bodypart" view nor document the advertising camera doing so; as a result of this lack of forewarning, the displacement of the gaze to her legs comes as a greater surprise than it otherwise might; Wiseman helps draw our attention to it through an axiographic difference in shooting style.) In the ad itself, desire is "naturally" displaced from the woman's face to her legs/pantyhose through the camera movement and a jingle that refers to her pantyhose ("exciting new look . . . right down to her hose") so that it does not seem lewd and objectifying so much as an informative revelation of the secret of her desirability. (The tilt downward complies with an evidentiary editing style in which what we see illustrates what we hear: "right down to her hose.") The ad, after all, is directed toward other women, not the male spectator/voyeur. The male gaze must be presented as something desirable and the fetishizing attention to the character's legs as a confidence shared between women (or between the rhetorical narrative and the female viewer): these pantyhose are the true source of desirability.

—Wiseman's representation of social space does not center around sexual attraction so much as work. What hints of sexual orientation exist are not part of a single "compulsory heterosexuality." We see individuals in sloppy dress, housewives who appear indifferent to matters of visual desirability, a gay couple looking on with apparent indifference to the glamourous appeal of the models. The body as represented by Wiseman is de-eroticized into a tool or instrument. Though exceedingly difficult to photograph according to plan, the body is relentlessly disciplined to produce the impression of the natural and spontaneous. The principal actress/model is repeatedly referred to by the director as "doll" and "sweetheart," usually in a tone of determined tolerance for her miscues and gestural errors. The repeated takes compel the actors to expunge any sense of autonomy: their motions must be fully synchronized to the will of the director who, in turn, must satisfy the Evan Picone representative observing the activity. In the historical world observed by Wiseman neither men nor women are in control of events and the orchestration of their own movements and gazes; corporate representatives of either sex assert that power.

—In contrast to Wiseman's suggestion of systemic constraint, instrumental psychology, and overdetermination, the advertisement conveys a linear, character-centered causality, but its temporality is reversed. The ad first displays a certain quality of life (female desirability) which is then posited as the effect of the subsequently revealed cause (pantyhose). Here is what

you will be like, if you buy this. A conditional tense might be applied to the
ad as it can be to films like Peter Watkins's *The War Game.* The effect,
although it comes first and is presented in the manner of a readily available,
contemporary life-style, is retroactively placed in the future. It is an effect-
in-waiting. It can belong to your future if you trigger it now by buying the
specified commodity. Space and time ultimately implode back to their
moment of genesis: the final image of the two-dimensional, iconic depiction of the Evan Picone pantyhose packaging. It has the ontological status
of a first thing even though it comes last: nothing produced it; it is not a
commodity but a primordial talisman. You, too, can play God to your own
creation. Buy this and the axiographic space of male desire and a personal
future of success and glamor will be yours. A teleology that seems so
tenuous or indeterminate in Wiseman's representation of the historical
world becomes absolutely clear: the future you want (the future we want
you to want) is yours and here is exactly how to obtain it.

The difference in the organization of space between Wiseman's observations and the advertisement's claims proposes different axiographic systems. Different values obtain. The juxtaposition of one form of ethical
space with another not only highlights some of the operations that might
otherwise be less obvious in the ad (if we did not have access to the "other
scene" of the ad's production), it also provides justification for Wiseman's
absent presence as surrogate "ideal observer." That is, some of the disquiet
that unacknowledged observation might otherwise provoke becomes displaced by the revelation of the difference between Wiseman's visual system
and that of the ad. A generalized epistophilic voyeurism (watching in the
service of knowledge) seems less problematic when what we watch seems
all the more so, where the terms and conditions of knowledge reduce to
"smart" commodity consumption, and voyeurism becomes a fetishizing
male gaze at women who take pleasure from serving as spectacle. The
axiographic issues raised by the observational mode of documentary representation are themselves displaced (or disguised) by the more acute issues
raised by the ad. Our desire to know legitimates the set of observations that
provide the evidence that the finished ad omits.

Other modes of representation raise other axiographic issues. Interactive documentaries call attention to the physical and historical presence of
the filmmaker by means of the interaction between social actors and the
camera, normally through interviews. This, in turn, raises questions of the
filmmaker's accountability to these people or social actors. Is their spatial
proximity evaded by techniques that mask the presence of the filmmaker
(presenting the comments of the characters but not the questions of the
filmmaker, for example), that recruit witnesses and experts to serve an
argument not of their own making (as we have in numerous films from
Housing Problems to the evening network news), or by subordinating the
film's argument to the point of view of its witnesses (as we find in *With Babies*

and Banners, If You Love This Planet and *Through the Wire*)? Does the film-maker appear in the frame and demonstrate his or her own style of interaction, and, even more, the lengths to which he or she will go to obtain information (as we find in *Hotel Terminus* and *Shoah*)? Is the presence of the filmmaker as someone who may well shape or determine events acknowl-edged (as it is in Jon Alpert's *Hard Metal's Disease*, Jean Rouch's *Jaguar*, and Rouch and Edgar Morin's *Chronicle of a Summer*)? Even if present mainly as an absence, is the filmmaker's ethical/political presence nonetheless reg-istered in the space between shots, in the juxtapositions that stitch together an argument and that, while recruiting social actors to an argument not of their own making, convey less a sense of misuse than of quotation? Provid-ing sufficient context for quotations (such as we find in Emile de Antonio's *In the Year of the Pig* or Loni Ding's *The Color of Honor*) allows witnesses to be judged for what they say rather than simply for how what they say is used.

Finally, reflexive documentaries that call into question norms and con-ventions of documentary practice may very well call the present but absent filmmaker into question as readily as anything else. Raul Ruiz's *Of Great Events and Ordinary People* represents the filmmaker as a social actor in the process of making a documentary about the impressions people in his arrondissement have about a national election. Ruiz appears on screen attempting to arrange an interview with the mayor (who is never seen) and his voice-over comments reflect on the very nature of the documentary and his own, situated status as a Chilean exile living in Paris, forbidden by law from becoming involved in French political affairs, including elections. His metacommentary on documentary plays off against his own dislocation as a presence-in-exile who cannot participate in what he comments on. Ruiz raises, obliquely, but as a direct result of his own acknowledged presence, the question of documentary authority: who is empowered to represent whom and with the authority of what specific discursive regime (what set of documentary conventions) shall he or she do so?

Without appearing on screen or signaling the moral uncertainties he may have, Errol Morris also establishes a reflexive position vis-à-vis the filmmaker's presence in *The Thin Blue Line*. The film examines the conflict-ing stories of two men who were present when a Dallas policeman was shot and killed. One of the men, Randall Adams, was found guilty, partly as a result of the testimony of the other man, David Harris, but Adams main-tains his innocence. Morris, however, emerges less as stalwart defender of the innocent than as ironic observer of how facts become woven into disparate and conflicting narratives (of Adams and Harris, the police, the prosecution and defense, witnesses and friends). He does not amass evi-dence with a conviction that it leads directly to the truth. In fact, he leaves us, at film's end, with the discomforting sense that although Randall Adams was almost certainly innocent, justice depends upon ascertaining truths that evade determination and cannot be guaranteed.

In most documentaries that include reconstructions, the reconstruction derives from historical, factual evidence, as in *Night Mail* and *The War Game*. The premise that historical evidence backs them up also lends plausibility to the subjective reenactments in films like *Roses in December, Las Madres de la Plaza de Mayo*, and *The Color of Honor*. Morris, however, ignores the conceit that allows the documentarist to reconstruct the mise-en-scène of presumed truth. The "truth" in this case is far more elusive, shrouded by time but even more by memory, desire, and the logical paradox that it is impossible for any statement to vouchsafe its own truth status. Morris concludes with a well-lit close-up of a pocket tape recorder presumably playing back the interview that we hear. It is described as David Harris's final interview, in which he makes it clear that Randall Adams was not guilty. But this assertion emerges from the following exchange.

Errol Morris asks, "Was he innocent?"

"Did you ask him?" Harris responds.

Morris: "He said he was innocent."

"There you go," Harris remarks, "Didn't believe him, huh? Criminals always lie."

Like the Cretans paradox, Harris's reference to criminals lying threatens to nullify Adams's claims of innocence—if he is in fact a criminal—or Harris's corroboration of Adams's innocence—if Harris is a criminal, as the film demonstrates him to be, without question.

Like the paradigmatic problem/solution structure of *Downwind, Downstream, The Thin Blue Line* ends with a solution, but this one tends to undercut itself reflexively even as it clinches the case for Adams's innocence. The power of the sequence, in large part, follows more from its narrative placement at the end of the film than from its irrefutable "proof" of guilt and innocence. Roland Barthes's claim that, in fiction, truth is a function of what comes last was never more true than here.[19]

The process of establishing distance from authorial omniscience and political authority so central to the discourses of sobriety, and to socially conscious documentary in particular, occurs through Morris's detaching his images from the indexical realm of historical reference. Instead of presenting objects such as the murder weapon in a factual manner, Morris provides a realistic but iconic drawing of a "handgun" against a white background. The image is more closely akin to the discourse of the pictorial illustration than photographic documentation. Similarly, instead of presenting the reenactment of the murder in the most plausible manner (given the apparent innocence of the condemned man), Morris reconstructs the event in several highly stylized variations. In some a Harvey's vanilla malted sails through the night sky in slow motion before splattering on the asphalt pavement, in others the camera dwells on the officer's feet rather than his face. In none of them do we receive a clear indication that David Harris, and Harris alone, committed the crime. Rather than offer visual evidence to support the most likely explanation, the reenactments illustrate the less likely, and conflicting, accounts offered by attorneys, police officers, and purported witnesses.

Though the film has a conclusion, the tape-recorded "confession" is not exactly conclusive. We are back where we began, with the word of one person against that of another, the situation in which all exposition and narrative finds itself, in fact. Morris's reluctance to rely on the indexical quality of the image to imply a truthfulness that no image can guarantee opens up an ambivalent ethical space for the filmmaker: on the one hand, by disregarding the norms by which truth is conventionally conveyed, he may be playing with or mocking the claims of a man whose life is at stake; on the other hand, by "baring the device" and making the process by which truth is constructed more evident, by showing how multiple truths based on different assumptions and motivations contend with one another, he may be inviting us to draw our own conclusions on the basis of facts and stories that do not readily admit of unequivocable resolution into a single truth. Randall Adams may indeed be innocent, but the film invites us to experience the uncertainty that licenses divergent narratives of explanation for anyone without firsthand knowledge of the original event. Morris refrains from using the power of the photographic image to appear to certify (through "authentic" reenactments) a degree of certainty that remains unavailable outside the cinema.

Given the conventions of documentary advocacy in which the socially responsible filmmaker seeks to demonstrate the validity of one interpretation over others, it remains ambiguous whether Morris's refusal to do so follows from a desire to use this actual event to shape a more complex and narrative-like film or from a desire to challenge our assumptions and expectations regarding documentary convention. In the first case, the film would come into being at the expense of "what really happened" and the power of documentary to convince us of its nature. In the second, the film operates to strengthen our subjective experience of the ambiguity of factual knowledge based on individual representations while still indicating that some representations are much more plausible than others. My own sense is that the latter is the prevailing tendency, but that this is overlaid by a competing tendency to display an ironic wit that is less an essential element in this deconstruction of expectations than of Morris's own bemused detachment and stylistic preference. Like the irony of David Lynch's *Blue Velvet*, it is a style that encourages controversy through the deliberate promotion of ambivalence.

Ethics, Politics, Ideology

As a final move in this discussion of axiographic space, it is important to place the ethical more squarely in relation to the political and ideological. I hold ethics in alignment with politics (and ideology) since the terms signify the same problematic within different conceptual frames. Ethical conduct can, on another level, be considered politically motivated, and vice versa; both ethics and politics can be seen as instances of ideological discourse aimed at the constitution of the appropriate forms of subjectivity for a given mode of social organization. There is clearly a politics to ethics as there is an ethics to politics: both are ideological discourses not simply in the sense that they seek to affect individual conduct by means of rhetoric, but in the more basic sense that they establish and maintain a specific "ensemble of social relations" that form the tissue and texture of a given cultural economy.

What we consider ethics in one system may be politics in another. The usefulness of identifying the implications of spatial representation as a matter of ethics, initially, is that this helps stress the experiential confrontation with issues and values that occur for the viewer, as they did for the filmmaker. The danger is to fail to recognize that ethical values imply an ontology, a self-contained worldview or value system, which deflects efforts at historical placement. Ethical actions then appear to be driven by timeless values rather than deriving from the code by which those with power police themselves and others as they opt for regulations of conscience and social responsibility as an alternative to coercion.[20] A system like Christianity or journalism, for example, becomes the boundary or frame that supplies the repertoire of values and the means to apply them to a given situation. We believe we need look no further since the ethical frame can be applied by its adherents to all possible situations. I introduce politics to suggest that while values may circulate within self-contained systems, they also infiltrate and sustain the modes of power and hierarchy, hegemony and control that structure such systems. A true ethics of spatial representation is also and simultaneously a politics of spatial representation. The former gives greater emphasis to the immediate, phenomenological encounter of viewer with filmmaker, the latter to the ideological patterns and relations that tend to underpin or produce this encounter.

Ethical debate can become a final resting place when it occurs within a frame that presents itself as universal. (No other possibility for correct conduct could exist.) Good is differentiated from evil; harmony prevails. And yet this sense of assurance, once we have got our ethics right, is fundamentally misleading. More often than not, ethical debate is an occasion for a great deal of posturing and self-righteousness. Valuable to a degree—it helps break the hermetic seal that poststructuralism placed around text and discourse as operations that produce effects and constitute subjectivities with minimal regard for the moral and ethical experience of subjectivity itself—ethics is, finally, an arrested form of logic. It succumbs to a position wholly within an ideology of binary oppositions justified by the moral superiority of one term over another (good over evil, truth over falsehood, men over women, property rights over civil rights).

Ethical debate is often debate of the most fervent and emotionally charged sort. Its finality depends, ultimately, on consensus that there is one natural order to things. Ethics can be said to be an ideological mechanism by which those with power propose to regulate their own conduct. This can be a means of avoiding external regulation (one function, it might be argued, of medical, legal, and journalistic ethics); of providing practical guidance for the resolution of concrete issues (a function clearly performed by the ethical codes of ancient Greece for male sexual conduct examined by Michel Foucault in his *The Use of Pleasure*); and of offering a mechanism for investigations of self-discovery. An ethical system, however, depends on unanimity regarding its appropriateness for all (or at least the suppression of alternative systems and the relegation of individual resistances to *ressentiment*, "deviance," or other categories that lack the legitimacy to challenge what prevails). As soon as two ethical systems contend for legitimacy, or as soon as ethics itself is placed within brackets, certitude dissolves. We are compelled to find some other ground for our beliefs and actions.

Rather than relying on ethics as the means whereby we can evaluate and rank documentary film practices, an alternative tack would be to defamiliarize this very practice and implant it within another one: the attempt to challenge and subvert the dominant ideology of oppositions and hierarchy and the ethics that underwrite it. Beyond good and evil lie the dialectics of a social practice grounded in differences that do not coalesce into Them and Us, Self and Other. The point is not, for example, that Wiseman's gaze is ethically more sound than an advertisement's, but that each gaze operates within a different ideological frame that still requires praxis on the part of the viewer, not self-congratulation, if static, imaginary categories of either/or are to be avoided. (Similarly, *Consuming Hunger*, falls into the same ethical trap it criticizes if its analysis of contemporary, media-orchestrated charity allows the viewer to feel smugly superior to those who donate their money for famine relief, rather than forcing the viewer to acknowledge the need for a more adequate, transformative response beyond the polarities of a Them and Us that simply shifts from victim/benefactor to dupe/critic.) Insofar as individuals are the makers of documentary texts, the ethical space they occupy with their bodies and their gazes may properly occupy us, but if we are to see documentary representation as a social discourse and institutional practice, we will also have to engage these bodies and gazes in political and ideological terms as well as in the ethical terms of good and evil that are used to hold individuals accountable.

Part II

Documentary: A Fiction (Un)Like Any Other

IV

TELLING STORIES WITH
EVIDENCE AND ARGUMENTS

Challenging the Status of Documentary

A tendency in recent writing on documentary is to stress its link to narrative. Documentaries are fictions with plots, characters, situations, and events like any other. They offer introductory lacks, challenges, or dilemmas; they build heightened tensions and dramatically rising conflicts, and they terminate with resolution and closure. They do all this with reference to a "reality" that is a construct, the product of signifying systems, like the documentary film itself. Like the constructed realities of fiction, this reality, too, must be scrutinized and debated as part of the domain of signification and ideology. The notion of any privileged access to a reality that exists "out there," beyond us, is an ideological effect. The sooner we realize all this, the better.

Some documentary filmmakers have also stressed this view. In *Far from Poland* the central question of the film is what is really happening, over there, in Poland, in a realm of which we have fragmentary and highly mediated knowledge, a realm we creatively reconstruct for our own diverse purposes. Jill Godmilow introduces herself as the filmmaker who meditates on and debates this question, inconclusively. She inverts the expository mode of documentary that relies on interviews with witnesses and archival footage by doubting the truth value of this form of evidence about the historically real. She fabricates her own version of what historical figures, social actors, might say and do. She has a companion, Mark Magill, who challenges her own reflexive inclinations: is she indulging in word and image play? Is Poland not a reality, where people live and die; can we reduce it to textual figures without reducing our sense of history itself? Godmilow withholds a concluding answer. Perhaps we have lost the possibility of such engagement. Perhaps speaking directly about the reality of speech, and its limitations, is the strongest way in which the assumptions we hold about our access to a reality that comes to us largely through media representations can be challenged. And to challenge these representations

107

to challenge historical representation and its ally, documentary film itself.

This insistence on a narrative, constructed basis to documentary under-cuts claims for the moral superiority of documentary to fiction. Dziga Vertov, John Grierson, Paul Rotha, Pare Lorentz all extolled the documen-tary as a morally superior form of filmmaking, as a responsible contributor to the discourses of sobriety. This perspective certainly facilitated the creation of national film producing agencies like the GPO and Empire Marketing Board in Great Britain, the United States Film Service, or, later, the U.S. Information Service, and The National Film Board of Canada. Documentary has set itself apart, historically, from the fiction film. Fiction was what deceived and distracted. Fiction ignored the world as it was in favor of fantasy and illusion. It was of little consequence, especially if it came from Hollywood.

Dziga Vertov took this view: "A psychological, detective, satirical, or any other picture [*sic*]. Cut out all scenes and just leave titles. We will get a literary skeleton of the picture. To this literary skeleton we can add new footage—realistic, symbolic, expressionist—any kind. Things are not changed. Neither is the interrelationship: literary skeleton plus cinematic illustration. Such are all our and foreign pictures, without exception."[1] Paul Rotha in his *The Film Till Now* had a similar opinion: "Hollywood did little to further the humanitarian uses of the cinema. . . . No, Hollywood must face the accusation of having deliberately kept people from thinking, from asking questions, from knowing how and what other people in other places were doing."[2] Documentary, even if it still relied upon images, stood apart from the illusory realm of fiction by addressing itself to the historical world and the real issues that confronted it. But this belief in redemption through an avowed social purpose has come under siege. To call the work of a documentarist a fiction like any other shocks and paralyzes the liberal mind. It places documentary's liberalism under attack and leaves precious little by way of an alternative for the socially conscious filmmaker, critic, or viewer.

This critique of documentary as a fiction like any other needs to be questioned without resorting to the assumed superiority of an analytical, essayist, and fact-based discourse. The rationalism and logocentrism that characterize the documentary tradition and its nonfiction kin in the realm of journalism, television news reporting, editorializing, and the yet broader web of legal-rational discourse that supports our political-economic system can be understood as a distinctive mode of social inquiry and conduct without any ontologically superior basis, Plato notwithstanding. It can even be argued that this is a masculinist tradition, reinforcing those values and skills of abstract analysis and symbolic manipulation that men claim as their special province. But the opposite assumption, that documentary is as much a fiction as any other, that the world we inhabit is a social construct as much as any fiction is an imaginative one, that what we find "out there" is nothing more than what our codes and systems of signs posit, this, too, needs to be questioned.

Documentary shares many characteristics with fiction film but it is still unlike fiction in important ways. The issues of the filmmaker's control over what she or he films and of the ethics of filming social actors whose lives, though represented in the film, extend well beyond it; the issues of the text's structure, and the question of the viewer's activity and expectations— these three angles from which definitions of documentary begin (filmmaker, text, viewer) also suggest important ways in which documentary is a fiction unlike any other.

The World in Documentary

Consider how we enter into a fictional world, based on the spatio-temporal dimensions of the characters' environment. This world is a unique, imaginary domain. It bears resemblance to fictional worlds in other texts, often aligning itself in groupings such as genre or movement. It also bears resemblance to our own world, especially if it is made in a realist style. It will be populated with recognizable people, objects, and places and with recognizable feeling states or emotional tonalities, but the resemblance is fundamentally metaphorical. We may comprehend this world through cognitive procedures that are distinct to fiction,[3] but we interpret this world through evaluative procedures that also depend on assumptions and values applicable to the world in which we live. To it we address questions of ideology and social value, gender and sexual representation, history and political affiliation, national and cultural identity, and so on, as well as more formal matters, and we do so metaphorically. It is a likeness rather than a replica to which we attend.

Documentary is somewhat different. Documentary offers access to a shared, historical construct. Instead of *a* world, we are offered access to *the* world. The world is where, at the extreme, issues of life and death are always at hand. History kills. Though our entry to the world is through webs of signification like language, cultural practices, social rituals, political and economic systems, our relation to this world can also be direct and immediate. Here, "strychnine poisoning" is not just a signifier lying inertly on a page in all its polysyllabic density, but a life-threatening experience. Here, "Fire," "Shoot to kill," "Jump," or "Scalpel" are not simply linguistic imperatives but preludes to action that carry life and death consequences for our physical selves. *Material practices occur that are not entirely or totally discursive, even if their meanings and social value are.*

Like people themselves, representations and texts have the potential to kill, but they lack the physical capacity to do the job directly. The Bible, Koran, and *Communist Manifesto* are three works that have left a trail of blood, among other things. But to have this effect, they must enter into the world by means of form, rhetoric, and ideology. As sources of ideas, images, values, and concepts, of systems of belief and categories of perception texts may, like past experience, shape or inflect behavior, often through a cumulative process. But matter and energy are not at their immediate disposal. The text itself cannot act upon us. It can give no orders nor take any measures. The words "Workers of the world, unite!" remain inert, mere words on a page, unless they enter into the mental disposition of a reader in such a way as to provoke or contribute to subsequent action. Texts are a realm of information, where differences circulate and signifiers slide. And as fictions or narrative, texts direct us toward worlds, inviting us to inhabit imaginatively realms often uncannily similar to our own, sometimes radically distinct, but always other than the one world we physically inhabit.

The world is where not only information circulates but also matter and energy. These physical forces can be unleashed for or against us by discourse, linguistics, or even more directly, by nature. Whatever else we may say about the constructed, mediated, semiotic nature of the world in which we live, we must also say that it exceeds all representations. This is a brute reality; objects collide, actions occur, forces take their toll. The world, as the domain of the historically real, is neither text nor narrative. But it is to systems of signs, to language and discourse, that we must turn in order to assign meaning and value to these objects, actions, and events. Occur they will; their interpretation, though, invokes the full power of our cultural system. Documentary directs us toward the world of brute reality even as it also seeks to interpret it, and the expectation that it will do so is one powerful difference from fiction.

Documentaries direct us toward *the* world but they also remain texts. Hence they share all of the attendant implications of fiction's constructed, formal, ideologically inflected status. Documentary differs, though, in asking us to consider it as a representation of the historical world rather than a likeness or imitation of it. The image of the death of an individual purports to record the actual, physical death of that person rather than a mimetic representation of death. This experiential difference is itself the subject of a videotape, *Eternal Frame*, by the Ant Farm Collective, which reconstructs historical reality by simulating the Zapruder footage of the John F. Kennedy assassination and yet achieving a decidedly different effect. (The status of the footage itself as artifact and our tendency to engage with it as a talisman come to the fore, displacing the apparent transparency of the recording with the event it records. This is comparable to the effect of the reworked historical footage in *A Movie* and *Report*.) Although we must often take the text at its word ("What you are about to see really happened . . . "), the effect of doing so produces a sharp difference which is dramatically demonstrated by the question of death.

Death may, in fact, be the underlying theme of the great majority of documentaries, as Andre Bazin hinted about the cinema generally in his essay, "The Ontology of the Photographic Image."[4] Documentaries often confront the experience of death itself directly. Even if they do not, the fragile mortality of its social actors remains always in evidence. The institutions, practices, apparatuses, beliefs and values, situations and events that impinge on this mortality provide the recurring focus for the great majority of documentaries whether they adopt a fatalistic, amelioristic, or revolutionary argument about the ways in which our bodies and mortality are placed at risk. This lends urgency to a category of filmmaking that lacks the appeal to fantasy and imagination possessed by fiction.

Documentary Representation

Documentaries, then, do not differ from fictions in their constructedness as texts, but in the representations they make. At the heart of documentary is less a *story* and its imaginary world than an *argument* about the historical world. (In *Ideology and the Image* I used "diegesis" and "rhetorical fiction" to make this distinction between the imaginary world of a fiction and the propositional world of a documentary. I prefer "argument" as a more familiar word, but I do not mean to suggest that all documentaries are argumentative, only that their representations or propositions, tacit or explicit, aim at the historical world directly.) Documentary represents the world, and it may be useful to recall some of the multiple meanings of the word "represent" since they are all simultaneously applicable here. The most prevalent usage in film criticism has been that of likeness, model, or depiction. (The idea of a model that was, simultaneously, its object, that shared in its ontological being by dint of the photographic process, was the form of representation that so fascinated Andre Bazin.)

Representation also means, according to the OED, politically representing a group or class by standing for or in place of them with the right or authority to act on their account. The House of Representatives of the United States Congress bears its name due to its responsibility to represent the population in fair and equal proportion among the states. An entire discourse surrounds the representative function of elected politicians generally, including an ethics, but other, more informal forms of political representation also occur.

In addition, representation means "The action of placing a fact, etc., before another or others by means of discourse; a statement or account, esp. one intended to convey a particular view or impression of a matter in order to influence opinion or action" (OED). Here representation is made or presented; representation amounts to making a case in a convincing fashion. Representation is allied with rhetoric, persuasion, and argument rather than with likeness or reproduction.

In sum, documentary gives us photographic and aural representations or likenesses of the world. Documentary stands for or represents the views of individuals, groups, or agencies from a solitary filmmaker like Flaherty to

CBS News or a state government. Documentary also makes a representation, or a case, an argument, about the world explicitly or implicitly. In offering our own representation of documentary here, in giving an adequate account of its properties and traditions, forms and effects, we will need to attend to all three of these meanings.

The Documentary Window

Documentary shares the properties of a text with other fictions—matter and energy are not at its immediate disposal—but it addresses the world in which we live rather than worlds in which we may imagine living. This may be partly a matter of conventions and expectations, but it makes a fundamental difference. Conditional tense documentaries such as Peter Watkins's *Culloden* or *The War Game* and historically discrepant reenactments such as the staged accounts of a policeman's murder in *The Thin Blue Line* test one boundary of documentary and narrative by directing us toward an imaginary extrapolation from the present world, based on factual evidence, but necessarily presenting *a* world rather than *the* world to us; they therefore share a fundamental trait of fiction but employ many of the conventions of documentary.

The difference between direction toward *the* world and *a* world can be illustrated by imagining ourselves in relation to a room. In fiction, we look in upon a well-lit room, overhearing and overseeing what occurs inside, apparently unbeknownst to the occupants. The opening of *Psycho*, with its slow panning shot of the Phoenix skyline that gradually zooms toward and then through a single window into the hotel room where Marion Crane and Sam Loomis discuss their lives, crystallizes this impression of looking in.

In documentary, we look out from a dimly lit room, hearing and seeing what occurs in the world around us. The opening of *The Battle of China* in the Why We Fight series evokes the war in China through edited wartime footage of Japanese bomber planes dropping their explosives on the city of Shanghai. Walter Huston's first words, coming to us in a motion picture theater or at home before a television monitor, are, "This is the battle of China." Representations are being made: cinematic likenesses arrive before us; a political argument unfolds; the concerns of citizens across the land are spoken for. Our attention is immediately directed outward toward the historical world, past or through the text, and into the realm where action and response are always possible.

We enter a fictional world through the agency of narration, that process whereby a narrative unfolds in time, allowing us to construct the story it proposes. We enter the world in documentary through the agency of representation or exposition, that process whereby a documentary addresses some aspect of the world, allowing us to reconstruct the argument it proposes. In fiction, the sense of an authoring activity or of an overt narrational process that draws our attention away from the imaginary world we have entered is normally slight and intermittent, only rarely forceful. In documentary, the sense of the filmmaker's argumentative activity or of an overt expository process that directs our attention toward the historical world is often continual and highly noticeable. Without it, we would have the impression of gazing onto the world itself rather than seeing the world by means of a text, a window, and an argument. This is indeed the case with some modes of documentary, most notably observational documentary or American cinema verité. (This is another mode that skirts up against fiction, as it stresses the sensation of overhearing and overlooking a world that happens to be drawn from some portion of the historical world, without making an overt argument about it. The argument is tacit, oblique, or indirect; it arises by implication.)

In most documentaries, we are asked to realize that the world we see is one conjured for a purpose and that this purpose is made manifest to us through the agency of an external authority, our representative, the expository agent. (It is important that we grasp the argument although not necessarily the conjuring.) The world as we see it through a documentary window is heightened, telescoped, dramatized, reconstructed, fetishized, miniaturized, or otherwise modified. Like realist fiction, documentary presents us with an image of the world as if for the first time; we see things anew, in a fresh light, with associations we had not consciously realized or attended to. An observational documentary can hide behind this effect, giving us the impression that this modified world was there all along, waiting for us to discover it. An expository documentary may also try to mask or diminish its own shaping and modifying activity so that it seems self-evident that the world is indeed cast in the image that the film proposes. This apparent naturalness of a given image of the world may be a rhetorical ploy, but it is also a vital aspect of how we come to hold views of the world that may guide subsequent action.

Their respective orientations, toward *a* world and toward *the* world, sharply distinguish fiction and documentary, but the effect of providing, as if for the first time, a memorable form for experiences and concepts that the text purports only to reveal or reflect is a common bond between them.[5] That bond frequently goes by the name of realism, one of the issues immediately raised by this conception of the documentary as a fiction (un)like any other. We are offered a world but a world different from any other by dint of its basis in history itself. We can construct a world of our own design or represent the one whose design surrounds us. In representing it we introduce the subjectivities and vicissitudes, the issues of style and form that govern discussion of any text. It is, mysteriously or magically perhaps, the world out there that we represent in documentary, and shape so as to be seen as if for the first time from a particular angle, in the grip of a particular way of seeing and a distinctive argument about its workings.

The mystery or magic stems from the re-presentation, the documentary's apparent ability to mechanically reproduce the world as it is, in all its historical uniqueness, again and again in the service of representations or arguments, often recycling images of never-to-be-repeated events in the service of sharply divergent points of view.[6]

The world, in documentary, is destined to bear propositions. "This is so, isn't it?" is the gist of the most common and fundamental proposition we find. It is the basic proposition made by realism. This question, as much or more than Louis Althusser's "Hey, you there!" is the basis for the social construction of reality and for the work of ideology.[7] In documentary what "is so" is a representation of the world, and the question, "isn't it?" has to do with the credibility of the representation. This representation can be either a re-presentation of overt propositions made *in* the historical world—the record of public speeches such as we find in *Triumph of the Will*; the representation of a case or argument *about* the world such as the claim that "This is the battle of China," mentioned above; or of perspectival propositions about the world made obliquely or indirectly by the way in which actions and events are represented. (Examples of a tacit perspective include the films of Fred Wiseman, the impressionistic memory of the Vietnam War given by *Dear America*, and the ironic tonalities of Buñuel's *Land without Bread*. Although there is a referentiality about these representations that anchors them to the historical world, they are by no means free of constructedness. They are, however, propositions somewhat distinct from those introduced by the text itself where the representation of the world serves as evidence for an argument that did not entirely predate the text.)

Consider, for example, two airplane disasters: the destruction of Korean Airline flight 007 on September 1, 1983 by the Soviet Union and of Iranian Airline flight 655 on July 3, 1988 by the United States. Although the incidents bore many similarities in how they came about, the American press represented the Soviet attack as a crime against humanity, as a blatant example of a "real" Soviet mentality of territorial obsession and wanton disregard for life. The American attack, however, was represented as an unfortunate mistake, an error or miscalculation that would never have been allowed to occur by design. And although spy theories involving American reconnaissance flights, decoy missions, and tests of Soviet radar defenses were largely dismissed as possible justifications for the Soviet attack, there were repeated hints that the Iranians had brought the American attack upon themselves by government policy that allowed civilian flights in an area the United States had chosen to defend. In both cases the evidence available was quite similar, but the uses made of the evidence were sharply different. News accounts included representations made in the world by figures like President Reagan, arguments made by the text such as accounts of the "most plausible explanation" offered by reporters and news anchorpeople, and tacit perspectives arising from such cues as tone of voice, choices of symbolic or iconic representation, and reference to stereotypic notions of national character. Each account claimed "This is so, isn't it?" and yet the accounts used similar facts in radically different ways.

The world as we encounter it in most documentary is both familiar and distinctive. Although twentieth-century culture has given us a world rich in ambiguity, indeterminacy, subjectivity, and doubt, a post-Freudian, post-Einsteinian world radically different from the Cartesian, Newtonian world that prevailed from the Renaissance to World War I or so, this is not the world that documentary usually represents. We find a more traditional vista before us, akin to the nineteenth-century fictional conventions that govern most popular cinema. Documentary represents the world of individual responsibility and social action, common sense and everyday reason; it confronts the historically momentous and the patently quotidian—all couched in the style and rhetoric of classical realism. (Realism, as we shall see, has certain distinctive attributes in documentary but shares profound kinship with narrative realism in its effect.) This is indeed *the* world we see but it is also *a* world, or more exactly, *a* view of *the* world. It is not just any world but neither is it the only view possible of this one historical world. There is an obviousness and naturalness about the world as represented that we are frequently invited to take for granted. Documentary remains distinct in its representation of the historical world, the world of power, dominance, and control, the arena of struggle, resistance, and contestation. Documentary asks us to agree that the world itself fits within the frame of its representations, and asks us to plan our agenda for action accordingly.

Khrushchev's Shoe

Unlike fiction, documentary evidence refers us constantly to the world around us. Fiction films, too, may anchor their stories in a historical reality, whether past or contemporary, and many of their elements may be authentic. (In Hollywood cinema, great care is traditionally given to the authenticity of supporting elements like clothing, furniture, weapons, locale, architecture, and so on, while great liberties may be taken with (1) dialogue and language—historical figures of any nationality speak English; (2) motivation—the need of narrative for unity and closure governs motivation; (3) character—established stars always play the central ones, and (4) sequence—the events are rearranged into linear narrative form.) Although fiction films employ elements of realism in the service of their story, the overall relation of film to the world is metaphorical. Fiction presents the likeness of actual events, motives, appearances, causality, and meaning. Fiction may well constitute an explanation or interpretation of great power, but the avenue back to the world is always by means of this detour through narrative form. There is a centrifugal pull on elements of authenticity away from their historical referent and toward their relevance to plot and story.

Documentary, on the other hand, takes up and uses an *indexical* relation to the historical world. It grounds itself in evidence that cannot be witnessed as it happens, on a first-hand basis, more than once. I am thinking here of those evidentiary claims that depend upon the photographic or aural authenticity of film as document. To see not what Hitler, Kennedy, Holocaust survivors, or Vietnam War victims looked *like* but how they themselves actually looked, we turn to documentary. As Jerry Kuehl points out, "at the heart of documentaries lie truth claims, and these claims are based on arguments and evidence. Did Khrushchev ever lose his temper in public? Film of him banging his shoe on the desk at the U.N. may not convince everyone; film of Telly Savalas wearing the Order of Lenin and banging a desk on the set at Universal City will convince no one."[8]

Documentary evidence in this sense is distinct, less because it is of an entirely different order from similar historical evidence in the fiction film (the authentic firearms, waistcoats, and wall hangings in a period film, for example), but because the evidence no longer serves the needs of narrative as such. (This is a matter of degree, but a degree that is very often registered.) Documentary evidence is not a touch of the historically real used to embellish *a* world. It is not an element deployed and motivated according to the requirements of narrative coherence. Instead, documentary evidence refers us to the world and supports arguments made about that world directly. (It is still a representation but not a fictional one.)

In sum, evidence of and from the historical world may appear in either fiction or documentary film and may have the same existential bond to the world in both. In one it supports a narrative; in the other it supports an argument. The effect of a heightened realism may be very similar in the two instances—to gain our assent that "This is so"—but the process for making this case differs in fiction and documentary, in degree if not kind. Even though the evidence has a historical basis, the argument or representation made with it does not. Representations are what the text constructs: "truth claims" not simply of what exists in the world but, in a strong sense, of what meaning, explanation, or interpretation should be assigned to what exists in the world. It is here that elements of narrative, rhetoric, style, and representation commingle.

The conventions and constraints, codes and expectations may function somewhat differently, but both fiction and documentary set out to make something from the historical evidence they incorporate. Matters of institutional discourse, textual structure, and viewer expectation constitute the heart of the difference. At issue is not only whether we see Telly Savalas playing Nikita Khrushchev banging a shoe or Khrushchev himself (though this is hardly insignificant) but also what kind of argument or story this action supports. Even if thoroughly authentic, so that the "truth claim,"

"This happened, in history" is fully validated, the action only becomes meaningful as more than an isolated incident when it is placed within a narrative or expository frame. (The shoe banging might be "noise," an incidental detail bolstering a sense of verisimilitude or realism but bearing no further significance of its own. Attaching any greater meaning to it requires a conceptual frame or explanatory scheme. This moves us away from factual accuracy to an entirely different level of engagement.)

Factual documentation serves as evidence, but evidence *of what* becomes a fundamental question. Documentary answers this question with conventions that call for evidence drawn from the historical world indexically, as it was seen and heard to occur rather than with metaphorical likenesses. (If we do not recognize the authenticity of the evidence, we may misinterpret the film as fiction. Khrushchev banging his own shoe may seem like a bad TV movie to someone who does not know what Khrushchev looked like.) For the most part, though, the preoccupation of documentary is to answer the question, "Evidence of what?"

Once we embark upon the presentation of an argument, we step beyond evidence and the factual to the construction of meaning. This is where footage such as the historical evidence contained in shots of Khrushchev banging his shoe or in the amateur Zapruder footage of Kennedy's assassination become more than isolated facts. They become pieces of evidence demonstrating the physical look of a historical event in a way no fictional likeness can ever duplicate however close its approximation. Once an argument begins to take shape, that fact begins to fit into a system of signification, a web of meanings—in the case of Kennedy's assassination, of conspiracy, of grievous national loss, of the tragic consequences of demented, individual acts; in the case of Khrushchev's shoe, of volatile and untrustworthy character, crude, bullying ways, of America's need for diplomatic wariness and military preparedness. There is never a pure one-to-one correspondence between fact and argument. For every fact, for every piece of incontrovertible evidence, more than one argument can be fashioned. In this, documentary is like fiction, but it relies on different forms, procedures, conventions, and strategies to achieve its end.[9]

Kuehl stacks the deck somewhat by choosing an example of evidence that cannot be represented authentically in a fiction because there can only be one Khrushchev and no actor can authenticate something that he himself is imitating, whereas a fictional representation of a 1955 Chevrolet can be just as authentic as a documentary representation of one. The difference lies in the uses made of the evidence: the subordination of the car to a narrative story in one case and to an argument in the other. Similarly, the function of the Bushman in *The Gods Must Be Crazy* is the classic one for the racially or culturally Other: as donor to the protagonist, assisting in the white hero's efforts to rescue the white woman abducted by a gang of marauding looters, a function whose construction is clearly documented in *N!ai: Story of a !Kung Woman*, which observes the multiple takes required to film the Bushman's triumphal return to his own family in a "natural" tone. Narrative maintains a metaphorical relation to the real whereas arguments represent truth claims about it. This may give the evidence an added force in documentary (as we shall see in discussing the film *Roses in December* later), but it does nothing to give its truth claims status as anything other than claims. Documentaries do not present *the* truth but *a* truth (or, better, a view or way of seeing), even if the evidence they recruit bears the authenticating trace of the historical world itself.

Documentary Logic: Perspective, Commentary, Argument

To speak of *a view* of the world is to return to the notion of argument generally. If narrative invites our engagement with the construction of a story, set in an imaginary world, documentary invites our engagement with the construction of an argument, directed toward the historical world. The authenticity of sounds and images recorded in the historical world (or reconstructed according to specific criteria) constitutes evidence about the world. The evidence is the material basis for the argument and has a similar relation to it as the plot (or *syuzhet*) does to the story (or *fabula*) that we construct in fiction. The evidence and commentary on it is what we physically see and hear in a documentary.

We will consider argument to be the general category for the representation of a case about the world and subdivide this category into two major parts. Perspective is the way in which a documentary text offers a particular point of view through its depiction of the world. It leads us to infer a tacit argument. Perspective in documentary would be akin to style in fiction; the argument is implied, sustained by rhetorical strategies of organization. Commentary is how a documentary offers a particular statement about the world or about the perspective it has tacitly presented. Commentary is always at a more "meta" level than perspective. It is a more overt and direct form of argumentation.

Commentary can include not only direct address (voice-over narrators or on-screen authorities, for example) but also other tactics or devices (elements of style, and rhetoric) that draw attention away from a perspective on the world and toward a more distanced, conceptual accounting of it. (This might include the particular way interviews and commentary are contextualized in the film.) These tactics or devices are not specific figures but rather any figure that departs from the stylistic expectations previously established by the text. In Frederick Wiseman's *Titicut Follies*, for example, the usual pattern of cutting from one fragmentary scene of hospital life to another, not directly related one is disrupted by a sequence of a patient being force-fed through a tube cross-cut with later shots of his preparation for burial. In the context of the established expectations, the cross-cutting becomes a commentary on the institution rather than a perspective on it.

The cross-cutting operates outside the normal editing pattern already established by the text and becomes thereby a commentary signaled not by voice-over narration but by this deviation itself.

All documentaries, not only reflexive ones, take up a specific relationship to their own commentary or perspective. Some of these possible relationships can be summarized in terms of formal properties such as the degree of knowledge possessed by the text, subjectivity, self-consciousness, and communicativeness.[10]

Degree of knowledge: What we learn may be restricted to what a single character or commentator knows or it may exceed any one source. In classic voice-over, expository documentaries like *Housing Problems* or *The Plow That Broke the Plains*, our knowledge is directly correlated to what the anonymous but all-knowing narrator tells us. In more recent variations like Emile de Antonio's *In the Year of the Pig*, Connie Field's *Rosie the Riveter*, the Black Audio Film Collective's *Handsworth Songs* or Trinh Minh-ha's *Naked Spaces*, what we learn exceeds the knowledge of any one source. These works lack a single, controlling voice; we deduce the argument from the weave of many voices. Other films align knowledge with a single character or agent. What we learn in the films of Michael Rubbo, for example *Sad Song of Yellow Skin* or *Waiting for Fidel*, is restricted to what Rubbo himself knows or learns since he places himself in the foreground as an inquiring presence. His questions, puzzlements, observations, and reflections provide the informative tissue of the film. Bonnie Klein's *Not a Love Story*, which also presents the filmmaker as an inquiring presence (this time about the nature and effects of pornography), includes a number of substantive interviews with various individuals either in the pornography industry or critical of it. Although Bonnie Klein conducts the interviews, our knowledge is not filtered through the filmmaker's sensibility as thoroughly. The interviewees provide independent evidence that contributes to an argument that seems to derive from the expository agency of the text itself rather than from the persona of the filmmaker. In both cases, though, the filmmakers assume a role akin to that of the fiction film detective or the real life investigative reporter and restrict our knowledge, in varying degrees, to their own.

A character can also provide the basic restriction on what we learn and when we learn it, but this is a fairly unusual format. It requires the filmmaker to subordinate his or her knowledge or investigative skills to those of a single character or social actor. One example of this possibility is *The Emperor's Naked Army Marches On* by Juki Jukite Shingun. The film follows Kenzo Okuzaki as he investigates the fate of several Japanese soldiers executed by their own army in the days after the end of World War II. Our degree of knowledge is virtually identical to Okuzaki's, with the result that we experience both suspense and alarm as we learn what Okuzaki learns in concert with him and also witness the confrontational tactics he employs to gain this knowledge. (The key revelation is that the officers, with their rations gone and starvation setting in, shot army privates in order to cannibalize their remains.)

Degree of subjectivity: The extent to which we experience the inner thoughts and feelings of characters or share their perspective. The prevalence of a criterion of objectivity in documentary has left the exploration of subjectivity underdeveloped. Although there are several recent counterexamples of note, most documentaries neglect the traditional forms of fictive subjectivity (flashbacks, visualized memories, slow motion, anticipations, fantasy, visual representations of altered states of mind such as drunkenness or reverie, dreams, and so forth). The primary exception is when these forms of subjectivity are adopted by the expository agency itself as a form of anonymous or omniscient but personalized, collective consciousness. Vivid examples include Alain Resnais's *Night and Fog* and Bill Couturié's *Dear America*, in which the film's own voice-over adopts the attributes of human memory and reminiscence, speaking, in the first case, as a generalized voice of conscience, and, in the second, as a recounting of individual experience. The recounting of individual experience takes even more elaborate form in *The Civil War*, where over a dozen voices speak for participants, quoting from letters, diaries, and memoirs. A similar, less intense form of collective memory governs the voice-over commentary of *Victory at Sea* as well. The commentary is less a didactic statement of how World War II was fought than a poetic evocation of what that fighting felt like: when and where it occurred, what anxieties and heroism it induced, what sounds and furies accompanied it.

Subjectivity also enters into the documentary mainstream via the preference for people, or social actors, who can present themselves before a camera with minimal self-consciousness and, more importantly, who can inflect actions or recountings with a subjective depth of feeling. Like trained actors, social actors who convey a sense of psychological depth by means of their looks, gestures, tone, inflection, pacing, movement, and so on become favored subjects. The impulse is toward social actors who can "be themselves" before a camera in an emotionally revealing manner. This is not quite as neutral and objective a preference as it might at first appear since not everyone who acts before a camera in a manner very similar to how he or she acts without it presents an appealing figure for documentary films. Priority goes to those individuals who can convey a strong sense of personal expressivity that does not seem to be produced by or conjured for the camera—even if, in fact, it is. Television personalities are a prime example, from talk show hosts, advertising announcers, and quiz masters to news reporters and anchorpeople. But so are the guests on talk shows, the "men-and-women-in-the-street" found in TV commercials, and the contestants on quiz shows.

In documentary films, the central characters are frequently individuals who convey some sense of an interior dimensionality, of a complex persona, without suggesting that the persona is a role wholly distinct from the persona they would normally present. Nanook, the central character in Flaherty's classic documentary, supplies a prime example. *Frank: A Vietnam Veteran* depends entirely on the confessional storytelling power of its only subject, Frank, a vet whose muted normalcy belies the extreme behavior he describes, just as *Portrait of Jason* relies entirely on the dramatic self-revelations of Jason, a black male prostitute with various improbable aspirations. (It need not be their "true" or "private" persona that social actors display; normal may mean the presentation of self in public space such as we find in *Primary*, for example, on the 1960 Wisconsin primary race between John F. Kennedy and Hubert Humphrey. Both men perform continuously, but the persona represented in the film seems very much the same as the persona they presented in public appearances generally.)

This tendency to seek out social actors with expressive capacity becomes one of the main avenues by which subjectivity enters documentaries. Even though the film may adopt an objective shooting style and abstain from cinematic attempts at interiority like point-of-view shots or flashbacks, expressive individuals heighten the possibility for empathetic identification and involvement on the part of the viewer. Social actors who lack this kind of expressive capacity seldom become the focus of the documentary film no matter how similar their performance is during shooting to what it is before and after. David MacDougall has spoken and written quite insightfully on his tendency to gravitate toward individuals who suggest complexity and density to their character through their everyday behavior. Lorang, the central character of the Turkana Conversations trilogy (*Lorang's Way, A Wife among Wives, Wedding Camels*), certainly exhibits this capacity with his urban experience but preference for traditional tribal ways, his skills at bargaining, and a predilection for philosophical musing that brings these films closer to Eric Rohmer's early work (*Claire's Knee, My Night at Maude's*, etc.) than to other ethnographic films. By contrast, MacDougall's later experience among Aboriginal people who were extremely reticent and disinclined to discuss their culture led him to experiment with strategies of "interior commentary" that might compensate for the absence of expressive performance.[11]

The paradoxical nature of this tendency is the desire for performance that is not performance, for a form of self-presentation that approximates a person's normal self-presentation. One of the conventional hallmarks of great acting is the ability to represent a wide range of characters; one of the conventional expectations about social actors is that their character remains stable, with continuity and coherence. In documentary we have the desire for performance stripped of the training, rehearsing, and directing that normally accompany it. This desire spans almost the entire gamut of documentary forms and modes. (The exceptions are mostly films that focus on process, objects, or concepts rather than people, films like *The Bridge, Rain, Drifters, Industrial Britain, Song of Ceylon, Naked Spaces, Kudzu, Consuming Hunger, Time Is*, or *Powers of Ten*, and even here "performance" may return as prototypical faces and body types, icons that evoke preexisting assumptions and attributions present in the audience. The long rhapsodic passages of the German people in Leni Riefenstahl's *Triumph of the Will* provide a pantheon of *volk* images even though none is given any dimensionality.)

The paradoxical sense of a performance, an expressive capacity, where the concepts of acting and performance are simultaneously disclaimed and desired, can be captured by the term "virtual performance." *Virtual*: "That is so in essence, or effect, although not formally or actually; admitting of being called by the name so far as the effect or result is concerned" (OED). Virtual performance has the power and effect of actual performance without being one. It has this characteristic by dint of its representation of the logic, or deep structure, of performance without its historical, institutional, or professional manifestations, all of which can be considered surface structure. (Computer science defines "virtual" in a similar way: unlike a library or archive, a computer's virtual memory stores bits of information without regard to their physical location. Each item is tracked by means of an algorithm that correlates physical space with logical relationships, allowing information to be readily retrieved regardless of spatial placement.)

Virtual performance presents the logic of actual performance without signs of conscious awareness that this presentation is an act. (Such awareness is what the terms "self-conscious" and "camera conscious" refer to.) Virtual performance, or the everyday presentation of self, derives from a culturally specific system of meanings surrounding facial expressions, changes of vocal tone or pitch, shifts in body posture, gestures, and so on—those very elements that actors train themselves to control at will. When Sergeant Abding in *Soldier Girls*, the tough drill instructor who puts the female recruits through grueling paces, breaks down and confesses that his Vietnam experience has left him shattered inside, we witness a virtual performance of considerable power. It has all the effects on a viewer that an actual performance would also have (as well as another: the sense of historical authenticity and privileged access). It is also typical of virtual performance in documentary in that the camera is not used to enter into an interior state of mind (via point-of-view shots, memory images, or expressive montage). The camera continues to observe; the sense of subjectivity arises from the expressive dimension of what it observes.

Degree of self-consciousness: The extent to which an expository agency acknowledges itself such that the viewer senses, "An argument is being presented to me." Self-consciousness is quite variable in fiction film—ranging from the relatively un-self-conscious style of much Hollywood film (most frequently broken by beginnings, summary montages, some comedy, and many endings) to the highly self-conscious style of early Soviet cinema, many experimental narratives, and contemporary advertising. Self-consciousness is least common in observational films, the documentary mode most akin to fiction. There is an inevitable perspective on the events and this can be taken as an implicit argument, but self-conscious, overt argument or commentary remain minimal. Expository, interactive, and reflexive films, however, depend for their effect upon our recognition that an argument is being made. The viewer's awareness of an argument, case, or representation defines these modes and establishes audience expectations in terms of demonstration or exemplification.

Degree of communicativeness: The extent to which the exposition reveals what it knows. Delays and retardations, enigmas and suspense are intrinsic aspects of both fiction and exposition. They serve to attract ("Guess what happened today?") or retain attention ("This could be the way the last two minutes of peace in Britain would look" [*The War Game*]). Enigmas arise at a local level, when we watch Nanook set about the business of seal fishing for several minutes before the purpose of his labors becomes clear, or when an elaborate sequence of cross-cutting suspends the moment of confrontation between the sons who have stayed out too long and the father who awaits their help back at the family pizza parlor in the Middletown series film, *Family Business*. They also contribute to the overall structure of documentary. Exposition generally invokes a desire to know and the promise to fulfill that desire, in time: the time it takes the argument to unfold. *The Day after Trinity* promises to provide an understanding of Oppenheimer's role in the development of the atomic bomb as *Harlan County, U.S.A.* promises to explore the heated conflicts between workers and owners in the coal mines of Kentucky.

Texts know more than they tell at any one moment. They can be straightforward or elusive in relaying that information. The desire to know addressed by many documentaries is not a timeless, ahistorical one, however. The degree of communicativeness may fluctuate as the argument unfolds, but the promise remains that all will be told and the sum total of what is reported shall be the truth. (TV news shows frequently lead into commercial breaks with a teasing reference to the dramatic quality of a news item yet to come, but when the newscast concludes, effort is made to assure us that we have received all the news there is, for now, with no emotional loose ends yet to be resolved.)

Unlike the detective film, with its paradigmatic structure of false starts and misleading clues, where the "truth" has a structural definition, namely, it is what comes last (as it is in "*Sarrasine*," the novella analyzed by Roland Barthes in *S/Z*), the documentary breaks out of a structurally determined truth to claim a correspondence between its representation of events and the truth of an external reality. Structural determination remains, however, in the assumption that the satisfaction of the desire to know calls for a linear coherence, a documentary logic that invokes a teleological world of "meaning and truth, appeal and fulfillment."[12] Delays and retardations offer hesitations, feints, suspense, and uncertainty along the long and relentless march of exposition toward the full disclosure of a knowledge it had held and possessed from the beginning. Permanent uncertainty and unresolved suspense, on the other hand, seem anathema to a tradition devoted to telling what it knows. Texts that follow this route (films of a reflexive bent like *Of Great Events and Ordinary People, Unfinished Diary,* or *Reassemblage,* for example) call this entire tradition of certain knowledge and full disclosure into question.

Another important difference between fiction and documentary stems from the specific degree of control that the documentary filmmaker may have over the events filmed. A lack of communicativeness that we would attribute, in fiction, to an intent to delay or retard the transfer of information may not, in documentary, be an attempt to withhold information at all. The information may simply be unavailable. Conversely, there may be information available that the filmmaker chooses to suppress or ignore, and it may be suppressed in ways designed to distract us from the omission. *First Contact* does not tell us that the white gold-mining brothers who made first contact with the New Guinea Highland natives some fifty years ago have been and still are married to native women; *Nanook of the North* does not disclose the differences between its depiction of Eskimo life and the much more modern patterns of existence that Flaherty found but did not film; *With Babies and Banners* does not reveal the Communist Party affiliations of some of its witnesses to the conditions of women workers in the 1930s.

Alternatively, a tangible trace of unavailable information may remain in the film as evidence of the limitations confronted by the filmmaker. The sense of an uncontrolled historical process may not only authenticate "reality," but also authenticate the documentary *representation* of that reality. It may authenticate the documentary process itself. In Sturla Gunnarson's *Final Offer,* about negotiations between the Canadian branch of the United Auto Workers and Canadian car manufacturers, his crew gains access to several of the negotiating sessions but at one crucial session, the crew, and Gunnarson, are barred, unexpectedly, at the hotel room door. This scene is left in the finished film. It contributes both surprise and suspense and can be read as an editing choice that is fully communicative in the face of a situation where important information was withheld *from* the filmmaker rather than *by* the filmmaker. Although this is an expository strategy, it is less an unalloyed testimony to rhetorical mastery than the narrational strategies of a Hitchcock are to story-telling mastery. The scene presents evidence of vulnerability as well as mastery, or, mastery in this context means displaying the way in which the filmmaker remains vulnerable to the vicissitudes of the historical world.

These categories of degrees of knowledge, subjectivity, self-consciousness, and communicativeness suggest some of the important stances a documentary can take in relation to its own argument, to the process by which it lets its knowledge be known. The distinctive ways in which these categories operate in fiction and in documentary films suggest how documentary is a fiction (un)like any other. Knowledge more often derives from an omniscient narrator than from a single character; subjectivity is more limited than in fiction and performance has a distinctive, "virtual" quality; self-consciousness is a more common component of exposition than of narrative; and restricted communicativeness may be a stratagem for suspense and viewer engagement but it may also be testimony to the filmmaker's limited control over a world not entirely of his or her own construction. At the core of these differences remains the concept of expository argument. Its characteristics need further examination.

Argument in Documentary

Argument about the world, or representation in the sense of placing evidence before others in order to convey a particular viewpoint, forms the organizational backbone of documentary. This backbone constitutes a "logic" or "economy" of the text. This, in turn, guarantees coherence. Both narrative and documentary are organized in relation to the coherence of a chain of events, which depends on the motivated relationship between occurrences (taking "motivation" in the formal sense of justification or causality). The term "narrative logic" frequently invokes this organizational principle in contemporary criticism, but since narrative is less concerned with traditional principles of logic, analysis, rhetoric, and argument than with motivation, plausibility, function, and consistency, it may be more appropriate to speak of "narrative coherence" and "documentary logic." In documentary as in fiction, we use material evidence to form a conceptual coherence, an argument or story, according to a logic or economy proposed by the text.

The argument is what we make of the documentary's representations of the evidence it presents. These representations can take a great variety of forms. Many of these provide the chapter headings for Erik Barnouw's *Documentary: A History of the Non-Fiction Film* ("Explorer," "Reporter," "Painter," "Prosecutor," "Catalyst," and "Guerilla," for example). Typical forms of nonfiction argument that we readily recognize would include the essay, diary, notebook, editorial, report, evocation, eulogy, exhortation, and description. These forms are not specific to a given medium any more than are the forms of fiction (romance, comedy, epic, and so on). Medium-specific argumentative strategies form another, complementary categorical level. These are the modes of documentary representation previously discussed (expository, observational, interactive, and reflexive). Such modes have a history and paradigmatic logic. They confer a patina of authority on the individual text by dint of its membership within a larger category of representational strategies. Various combinations of forms and modes are possible (expository reports or evocations, observational diaries or descriptions, reflexive eulogies or essays, and so on) with some combinations being more favored at given times and places than others.

Argument treats the historical world as the ground for the figure of its documentary representation. Argument gives us a sense of an authorial or expository presence. This creates the context for a particular view of the world and a particular array of evidence about it. As we have seen, argument takes two forms: it comes both in the form of a perspective on the world and commentary about the world. The distinction is between a continuous, implicit form of argumentation such as we find in observational films like those of Frederick Wiseman or the Middletown series and an intermittent, explicit form of argumentation that we customarily associate with voice-over commentary or the direct testimony of social actors. Perspective is the view of the world implied by the selection and arrangement of evidence. Films built heavily around interviews, such as *In the Year of the Pig*, *The Sorrow and the Pity*, and *Shoah*, also may present their argument primarily as a perspective, although both filmmaker and interviewees may interject commentary into their descriptions and accounts. (In all three examples above, it is very clear from his argumentative perspective where the filmmaker stands on the central issues, even without further commentary.) Commentary is the view of the world stated by the filmmaker or social actors recruited to the film. (Such "statements" need not be verbal; they can also be visual or more generally aural as we shall see when we discuss intellectual montage in documentary.)

Commentary serves to provoke a sense of distance for the purposes of orientation, evaluation, judgment, reflection, reconsideration, persuasion, or qualification between the text as a whole and the evidence it presents. Commentary allows for a recognizable moral/political overlay to be applied to the world, often using the same techniques or stylistic devices that contribute to establishing the text's representation of the world in the first place (editing, speech, camera angle, composition, and so on). This doubling is what gives the text its voice or social point of view.

The distinction between commentary and perspective can also be made by the contrast between a viewer position that is relatively active in terms of determining the moral or political theme of the text and one in which the viewer is placed in a more passive position. The first, most pronounced in observational films, could be described as "see-for-yourself" in its effect, the second as "see-it-my-way." A "see-for-yourself" perspective is closer to the experience of most fiction. In relation to viewer expectations for documentary it may seem manipulative because it is oblique. Wiseman's *High School* is sometimes regarded this way, while a highly pointed, satirical text such as *Sixteen in Webster Groves* appears more frank. Emile de Antonio's films (*In the Year of the Pig, Point of Order, Millhouse, Underground* and others) are particularly successful examples of argument by perspective (see-for-yourself) in contrast with many other interview-based films that leave us with little choice but to accept the perspective, and commentary, of their interviewees (see-it-this-way). Still other films remind us that the alternatives are not quite so stark: multiple commentaries may conflict with one another without resolution; different voices may compete for attention; a heteroglossia may prevail that says, in effect, "there's-always-more-than-one-way-to-see-it" and may also say that each "way" carries ideological/ moral/aesthetic implications with it. (*Naked Spaces*, with its three non-hierarchized commentaries representing indigenous African sayings, the thought of African intellectuals, and Western commentary about Africa conveys this possibility effectively.)

One immediate consequence of this way of representing documentary logic is that a perspective, and therefore a representation or argument, differentiates a text from "mere film" or raw footage. Once the viewer can infer a perspective, then even observations, descriptions, and "objective" reports or records can no longer be considered mechanical replicas or value-free reproductions of the historical world. Such representations do not offer a neutral fingerprint or decal of the world although they may aspire to a certain culturally determined standard for objective reportage. Put differently, objectivity is itself a perspective. Nonjudgmental, impartial, disinterested, and factually correct, objectivity nonetheless offers an argument about the world; its strategy of apparent self-effacement testifies to the significance of the world and the solemn responsibility of those who report on it to do so impartially and accurately, with a detachment legitimized as institutional discourse.

Objectivity also emphasizes the denotative dimension to situations or events in preference to subjective and connotative elements (these often figure in as "color commentary," introductory "hooks," or accentuations of particularly dramatic occurrences). But the emphasis on denotation remains a perspective. As Roland Barthes effectively argues at the beginning of *S/Z*, denotation works to legitimate scientific, critical, and philosophic discourse. And although this can be seen as a linguistic effect, it is a felt effect, one that registers as "true." (In a similar fashion apparent motion in film registers as felt or perceived motion; "to reproduce its appearance is to duplicate its reality."[13]) Denotation, then, bolsters the persuasive power of an argument. Barthes, though, dissects this support into a form of complicity: connotation and denotation refer to each other in the manner of a game:

> Ideologically, finally, this game has the advantage of affording the classic text a certain *innocence*: of the two systems, denotative and connotative, one turns back on itself and indicates its own existence: the system of denotation; denotation is not the first meaning, but pretends to be so; under this illusion, it is ultimately no more than the *last* of the connotations (the one which seems both to establish and to close the reading), the superior myth by which the text pretends to return to the nature of language, to language as nature.[14]

Though illusions, denotation and objectivity have considerable power. They cannot be disregarded, but their status as distinct perspectives, implicit arguments about the world, remains of fundamental concern.

Objectivity, in accord with realism, represents the world the way the world, in the guise of "common sense," chooses to present itself. Barthes calls this natural and commonsensical (that is, ideological and institutionally enforced) form of representation "zero-degree style." It adopts a posture of innocent neutrality in the face of the wiles of individuals, institutions, and social systems while also providing one of the foundation stones for professions like journalism and certain forms of ethnography, anthropology, sociology, and documentary filmmaking. And in each case, objectivity is not only a perspective, it also allows for more specific individual or institutional perspectives to represent themselves. (We may, for instance, feel we have an impartial view of both of the presidential candidates, John F. Kennedy and Hubert Humphrey, in the Drew Associates' *Primary*.)

Frederick Wiseman's documentaries are never quite as neutral as they seem, for example. They embody a distinctive view of institutions like hospitals, schools, and the military that sides with strategies of resistance over instrumental, bureaucratic logic.[15] But they do so through a particular selection and arrangement of sound and image, without benefit of overt commentary. In other words, rhetoric is operative, but less blatantly. It is embedded in a style that, like fiction, appears to address us only indirectly.

Likewise, television news represents the world in accordance with the criteria of objectivity, but from a perspective—at least in United States network broadcasting—that empowers the institutional apparatus for the production of news more than the viewer, and often more than those who, in fact, make the news.[16] The reality of the news takes precedence over the news of reality. And the objectivity offered clearly is constrained by decisions of what is and is not news, what should and should not be reported, what may and may not be commented upon. Like soap operas, television news presents an ongoing saga of complication, reversal, and suspense composed, in this case, of events drawn from a national political and socioeconomic drama as represented in the commonsensical terms of the dominant institutions that define this drama. Like a secondary plot, more cursory attention goes to the world of sports, culture, weather, and curious, offbeat, or exceptional occurrences in everyday life. (The offbeat or unusual highlights the difference between normalcy and deviance for a society whose collective agenda is set by, as much as reported in, the news.)

The primary point is to identify a level of authorial presence, or voice,[17] that is felt and experienced by the viewer as different from the mere replication or reproduction of the world. What we experience is less the world reproduced than represented. Perspective can embody both objective and subjective moments; it can defer to those individuals recruited from the world to speak in the film but not for the film; it can be a voice wholly embedded within stylistic choices of selection and arrangement. By contrast, commentary is a form of argument in which the voice of the film is seen or heard directly. Elsewhere I have referred to this form as "direct address." Direct address, though, tends to be most closely associated with exposition, whereas commentary in the sense meant here can occur in expository, interactive, and reflexive documentaries. (It is rare in the observational mode, although individual observational films may well contain examples, as we saw with *Titicut Follies*.)

Commentary gives didactic orientation toward the argument. Commentary guides our grasp of the moral, political view of the world offered by the documentary text. Unlike perspective, it diverts our attention from the world represented to the discourse of the text, to the representations of a documentary logic. In *The Battle of San Pietro*, for example, the commentary, in the form of John Huston's voice-over, provides an argument about the cost of battle that is at odds with the opening statement by General Mark Clark praising the fruits of victory. Huston's ironic remarks ("Last year was a bad year for grapes and olives") form the scaffolding for our construction of the argument so that we regard the images as supporting material, illustrative of an argument carried by tone more than assertions (shell-pocked fields accompany his remark about crops, for example). (*The Battle of San Pietro* also has a perspective embedded in the editing and music that places a much higher premium on the loss of Allied lives than Axis ones: we see living GIs in facial close-up, but we see their dead bodies from angles that hide or obscure their faces; with German and Italian soldiers we do not see their faces while they are alive, but we do see close-ups of them when they are dead.) [18]

Similarly, the commentary by anchorpeople and reporters in television news guides our comprehension of the events that may also be visually illustrated. The argument will usually identify the important characters or forces involved and briefly indicate what kind of narrative-like event they contribute to. Famine in Ethiopia, for example, is represented as the result of natural drought and inept organizations that create starvation and death of grand proportions. Longer-term factors such as the transformation of agricultural practices by external economic pressures and imported technologies will be ignored or downplayed in favor of a more dramatic tale of sudden and catastrophic disaster. The images, vivid and dramatic in their own right, support this argument.

This steering or agenda-setting process by those who provide commentary is even more evident in television talk shows. In both late-night talk shows, where the emphasis is on inconsequential, entertaining conversation, and in daytime talk shows, where the emphasis is often on timely, volatile issues like wife battering or drug abuse, the host guides us along an argument that, at the level of content and commentary, often appears minimal, made up on the spot, and seldom more than platitudinous but, at the level of form and perspective, is highly preconceived (i.e., this show and this host will give you a lively, informative, entertaining, but also sensitive and socially responsible window onto the world; trust us). These shows rely upon the interview for their basic structure but seldom marshal their guests into an arrangement that builds to support a particular point of view (unlike, say, Emile de Antonio's classic expository documentary, *In the Year of the Pig*). The underlying argument, the formal perspective, is more attitudinal: this host (and the ongoing show, its sponsors, and the network that carries it) cares about important issues; he or she will explore them conscientiously; he or she will ferret out evasions and show tact in the face of emotional distress; he or she will allow your own surrogate representatives—members of a studio audience—to participate in the dialogue; and we will leave you yet more aware of the full extent and possible consequences of the issues even if we offer no clear solutions. You may congratulate yourself for watching us; we will make you a more informed and empathetic person.

Commentary appears directed toward us. On-screen narrators and hosts look into the camera lens, at us. Interviewers and interviewees present three-quarter poses, carefully aligned so as not to look directly into the lens. They look at each other, lest the process of interviewing seem irrelevant. This orchestration of the gaze also subordinates those interviewed to those who speak on behalf of the program or network—the host—by restricting access to the camera lens. Guests and hosts have different rights of access to the camera. Guests normally look about fifteen to thirty degrees to the side of the camera, presumably at the host. Frontality of face, eyes, and trunk is the favored bodily position for commentators. (Hosts invariably look directly at the camera when they announce a station break; the control of time and space is delegated to them, not guests or audience.) This commonly lends a heightened awareness not of the constructedness of an imaginary world or even the constructedness of a particular representation of the historical world, but of the authoring, expository agency itself: this is the world according to Barbara Walters, Robin Leach, Oprah Winfrey, Arsenio Hall, or Ted Koppel, and the institutions for which they stand.

This emphasis on the agent of expository argumentation itself is vividly demonstrated in television advertising. If awareness can be said to be heightened by these texts, it is primarily in terms of the sense of being addressed. The world represented in the commercial, whether anchored to the historically real or fully fabricated, takes on an aura of plausibility by providing a suitable milieu for its own denotative ground: the product. But its stability and extension as a world is precarious. "Documentary logic," in this case rhetorical claims about the product, supports a believable world— but only to the extent that this world substantiates claims made on the behalf of a commodity, claims that often stretch our definition of common sense. We feel ourselves less in the presence of *a* world or *the* world than of an argument, frequently one based on wish-fulfillment or hyperbole. (In lifestyle ads that make few if any overt claims, the argument may be carried by a perspective that associates a particular form of sensibility and experience with the use of a product.) What David Bordwell has claimed for the innovative Soviet cinema of the 1920s can also be said of television advertising (even though the political intent makes an abrupt about-face): "This cinema goes beyond those narrational asides which we found in the art cinema; these films do not offer a reality [a mix of objective and subjective representations] inflected by occasional interpolated 'commentary'; these films are signed and addressed through and through, the diegetic world built from the ground up according to rhetorical demands."[19]

The construction of a world to the measure of rhetoric in early Soviet cinema was nowhere more true than in the use of intellectual montage, the combination of images, or sound and images, explicitly in order to comment on some aspect of the story. Sometimes the image chosen to make a comment would have no basis in the world of the fiction (a peacock would be imported to comment on the character of Kerensky in *October*, for example). Sometimes the image would be drawn from the world of the story itself, constituting a refrain of sorts (repeated expressions of shock on the faces of citizens as the troops attack them on the Odessa steps in *Potemkin*, or the cross-cutting between the abattoir and the slaughter of the workers in *Strike*). These alternatives are sometimes called extradiegetic and diegetic inserts or juxtapositions. In documentary, the intrusion of an image that does not belong to the world represented is a near impossibility to the extent that documentary images claim a bond to the historical world. Archival footage might be said to intrude on the present with the evidence of history, although this is less an intrusion than an amplification. The most intrusive images would be fictional ones, not even reconstructions so much as scenes from preexisting fictional films, but even here the join can be made reasonably seamless and the effect of contrasting planes of representation minimized. The documentary *The Making of a Legend*, about the making of *Gone with the Wind*, uses fiction films rather than newsreel footage to authenticate, quite effortlessly, the historical period it describes. More likely, images that support the "logic of implication" associated with commentary arrive from disparate parts of the same world in accord with principles of evidentiary editing. Smoke stacks from different factories or towns may be inserted to evoke "industry" or, today, "pollution."

Even more to the point, intellectual montage may actually *constitute* the visual representation of the world. Elements of the world required as evidence for the text's argument can be herded together from separate points of origin; their combination may not prompt the sense of a diegetic and extradiegetic distinction since they are all of the world and all in support or constitutive of the argument. In other words, since there is no fictional world to be intruded upon, intellectual montage in documentary emphasizes the overt or constructed quality of an argument, based on representations from the historical world, rather than the constructed quality of an imaginary world. It is less reflexive or deconstructive in its

potential than pointedly argumentative. It urges us to follow the logic of
the text, perhaps casting aside or questioning previous assumptions and
knowledge about the world.

Intellectual montage is more than the combination of disparate snatches
of the world according to the rules of evidence. Intellectual montage
achieves an unbalancing or disequilibrium in relation to norms, assumptions, or expectations that prevail for the viewer. It is a form of formal and,
often, political reflexivity. Insight replaces recognition, new possibilities
suggest themselves, alternatives come to light. In this sense intellectual
montage achieves its effect by means of strange juxtapositions. This was the
quality of mechanically reproduced art that excited Walter Benjamin who
saw this as a way of empowering workers. Strange juxtapositions, reassembl-
ies of the world as it is, suggest how the principle of the assembly line can
be revolutionized to subvert a logic of order and control into one of
transgression and change:

> If close-ups of the things around us, by focusing on hidden details of
> familiar objects, by exploring commonplace milieus under the ingenious
> guidance of the camera, the film, on the one hand, extends our compre-
> hension of the necessities which rule our lives; on the other hand, it
> manages to assure us of an immense and unexpected field of action. Our
> taverns and our metropolitan streets, our offices and furnished rooms, our
> railroad stations and our factories appeared to have us locked up hope-
> lessly. Then came the film and burst this prison-world asunder by the
> dynamite of the tenth of a second, so that now, in the midst of its far-flung
> ruins and debris, we calmly and adventurously go travelling.[20]

The history of intellectual montage—and the larger goal of political
reflexivity to which it contributes—is a story of suppression, distortion,
dilution, and repression. In Hollywood, Slavko Vorkapich perfected the
montage summary that became the standard means by which transformation or prolonged process was represented. A series of images would be
rapidly cut together (often joined by overlapping dissolves or other optical
effects) to evoke the various stages or periods of a process without analyzing
the labor that would go into the process. Things changed, seemingly
without effort or cost, until the story resumed at its more leisurely pace and
the fate of specific characters could be once again differentiated and
individualized from the general historical flow.

In United States documentary in the 1930s, where the influence of Soviet
film theory and practice was massive, intellectual montage never achieved
the status of a fundamental principle or commitment. A pragmatic insistence on reportage, on bringing back evidence of working-class solidarity
and struggle, took precedence. Leadership and change resided outside the
film process, in the political vanguard provided by the Communist Party.
Films depicted conflict (strikes, hunger marches, etc.) but were not themselves representations of conflict. The Film and Photo League, Nykino, and

the most sophisticated filmmaking group, Frontier Films (*People of the Cumberland, Heart of Spain, China Strikes Back, Native Land*), acknowledged the importance of the Soviet example without adopting its methods wholesale.[21]

Where pragmatism and deference to a political party did not prevail, humanism did. The emphasis throughout the 1930s, and in *Native Land*, the film that culminated and terminated the left cultural activism of the period, was on identification and empathy, the human cost of war and fascist inclinations, through characters shaped and crafted with an attention to psychological realism not radically different from that of Hollywood. Departure from individuated characters and their plight for conceptual juxtapositions or strange combinations of competing logics never took hold. The formalist concept of *ostranenie*, the "making strange" of things familiar through the manner of representation and juxtaposition; the Brechtian concept of *Verfremdungseffekt*, using alienation devices that break the empathetic bond to promote a broader level of insight; and surrealism, with its insistence on the forced juxtaposition of incommensurate realities, all seemed too distracting for principles that were direct, immediate, and obvious.

Instead, documentary or historical realism filled the bill. It let audiences see for themselves. It assumed an unproblematic transfer of motivation from activists to viewers, and it encouraged a strong identificatory bond between viewer and exemplary character. Strange juxtapositions such as those employed by Luis Buñuel in *Land without Bread*, by Dziga Vertov in *The Man with a Movie Camera*, by Eisenstein in *Potemkin* or *October*, by Franju in *Blood of the Beasts*, and by other surrealists and early French ethnographers hovered beyond the pale, unable to move beyond their status as "art" or "novelty" to that of model and foundation. To this day, the documentary of social change—especially in its classic, expository mode—remains character-centered to a remarkable degree in the United States, and the teachings of Eisenstein, Pudovkin, Dovzhenko, and Dziga Vertov together with the foremost exemplars of those strategies for a political cinema, Bertolt Brecht and Jean-Luc Godard, remain comparatively underutilized.[22]

V

STICKING TO REALITY

RHETORIC AND WHAT EXCEEDS IT

Rhetoric

Rhetoric moves us away from style, to the other end of the axis between author and viewer. If style conveys some sense of the author's moral outlook on and ethical position within the world, rhetoric is the means by which the author attempts to convey his or her outlook persuasively to the viewer. Pragmatics is that part of communications theory concerned with the effect of messages on their recipients and rhetoric is the means by which effects are achieved.[1] Rhetoric, too, may rely on cinematic techniques (as well as others not specific to the cinema like syllogisms or appeal to common sense), but its emphasis is less on meaning than effect. Rhetoric is therefore not independent of style but, rather, a different way of regarding it. Style as personal vision concerns us with the author; style as rhetoric concerns us with the audience.

Aristotelian rhetoric takes up the ways in which any argument can gain persuasive support. One avenue is through evidence: factual material recruited to the argument (witnesses, confessions, documents, objects: those material representations brought from the world for us to see and hear). Another is "artistic proof," those persuasive strategies deployed by the speaker or author on his or her own behalf. Evidence in documentary often depends on the indexical bond of the film image with what it represents. Artistic proofs, though, depend on the quality of the text's construction, the persuasiveness of its representations or truth claims. These proofs Aristotle divided into three categories:

—Ethical: Proofs based on the projection of the morally or ethically unassailable character of the speaker. This proof is often assigned to on-screen commentators and television anchorpeople as well as to the journalistic principle of "balanced reporting" and the general sense of unbiased or "fair" treatment of a subject. (Ethical integrity may be assessed in relation to the text as a whole and its expository agency even if there is no identifiable speaker, narrator, filmmaker, or other human representative for the film's commentary or perspective.) The speaker, if there is one, embodies the voice of calm reason, offering us the benefit of dispassionate analysis, or, if emotion is called for, as it is in the Why We Fight series, *Roses in December*, and *Shoah*, the commentary will appeal to a common sense of injustice, inhumanity, barbarism, or madness.

To the extent that the speaker becomes known by name, the value of a "good name" is paramount. Television newscasters must appear to live exemplary lives. Were they to conduct themselves in a questionable manner that becomes the subject of public scrutiny, their ethical credibility would be placed at risk regardless of the merit of the suspicions. Gary Hart's demise as a viable presidential candidate in 1988 centered precisely on this point. For several years, Hart's ethical proof of his suitability for the office revolved around his principled demeanor and the quality of his ideas. His personal conduct had remained strictly compartmentalized outside public view until he challenged the press to scrutinize his private life, virtually defying them to prove that his ethical stature could be undermined. When they did so and found his conduct at odds with his public presentation of himself as a man of principle and close family allegiances, his ethical credibility crumbled. Hart's insistence that he be judged "on the issues" now rang hollow since he himself had introduced the issue on which he was found inadequate.

—Emotional: Proofs based on appeals to an audience's emotional disposition. This proof is often assigned to compelling images in television news, to music in some documentaries, and to juxtapositions that attach feelings of empathy or repulsion to subjects in a novel way. An example of a juxtaposition of this kind would be Tony Schwartz's classic anti-Barry Goldwater political campaign message, produced for Lyndon Johnson's 1964 presidential campaign, in which a cute little girl picks petals from a daisy accompanied by a countdown that concludes with the roar and mushrooming cloud of a nuclear explosion; at the end, we hear Johnson speak on behalf of peace. The campaign message depends on prior knowledge of Goldwater's pronuclear position to associate him with reckless annihilation. (Emotional proofs in general depend on our preexisting emotional attachments to representations.) Lifestyle ads offer similar proofs: various "The night belongs to Michelob" ads associate this particular beverage with romantic adventure between handsome men and seductive women in a sultry, erotic world of alleyways, barrooms, and the studied fashionability of urban consumer culture.

Sometimes an emotional appeal will be made by an ethically credible commentator. In this case, it will be important to demonstrate that the emotional response of the commentator does not stem from personal vindictiveness or intolerance but articulates the shared response of decent people everywhere. "Decent people everywhere," of course, refers to the speaker's intended audience; it may not be quite so all-encompassing as its rhetorical underpinning would have us believe. The emotional appeals in the National Film Board of Canada's record of an antinuclear speech by

Helen Caldicott, *If You Love This Planet*, and the pro-war film by the U.S. Department of Defense *Why Vietnam*, build on the common moral ground assumed to exist between speaker and viewer. Those who oppose the antinuclear or pro-Vietnam War movements will feel excluded from an appeal whose emotional basis assumes that its opponents are morally culpable.

—Demonstrative: Proofs based on demonstration or example, where convincing the audience takes priority over the demonstration's factual merits. The demonstration may be real or apparent without rhetorical consequences so long as it is persuasive. Evidence has a role to play here, but a demonstrative proof concentrates on making evidence persuasive, not on ensuring that it is fair, accurate, or even authentic. Since falsehoods damage an argument if they are discovered, demonstrative proofs often rely less upon false claims than on half-truths. To take a hypothetical example, an ad for a paper towel product might claim simply that it is more absorbent than other brands, leaving unsaid that it does so only marginally, costs twice as much, may stain some surfaces, and leaves smudge marks on windows.

Rhetoric involves making a persuasive case, not describing and assessing damaging or less appealing facts, though their disclosure would be necessary to a well-informed judgment. The Why We Fight series, for example, celebrates the United States as the land of freedom and democracy in sharp contrast to the demagogic, dictatorial regimes in Nazi Germany, fascist Italy, and totalitarian Japan. The proof's ability to convince resides in its evocation of a conventional image of America, one that has a historical, factual basis but which also glosses over such severe problems as racial discrimination, inequality between rich and poor, and intolerance for opinions and practices outside an established normalcy (such as homosexuality, atheism, and communism—a triad, in fact, often linked together in many right-wing demonstrative proofs of American weakness). How America can be a cherished, free democracy in the face of these problems would require a far more elaborate argument, one that would detract from the primary goal of painting a clear-cut picture of good and evil.

Rhetoric courts the viewer as style reveals the author. But rhetoric is not synonymous with overt commentary; it includes the argumentative aspects of any text. A text can be persuasive without being overtly so by speaking from a tacit or implied perspective. The filmmaker can decline to address the viewer directly without rejecting rhetoric as such. To argue otherwise would be to assign rhetoric to cases of open appeal such as we find in advertising, propaganda, and the early Soviet cinema, clearing the ground for a neutral, nonrhetorical domain of aesthetic remove.

Although this classification is not uncommon and seems to undergird some of the representations of objectivity in journalism and the social sciences, its assumption that persuasion and ideology are localized phenomena that can be activated in or eliminated from any given text, is not really tenable. The scientist, like the journalist, must still convince, especially if what is reported is unexpected or unusual. Rhetoric comes into play even if it is more constrained in its tactics by rules governing scientific or journalistic reporting. To those within the discursive community, accepted rhetorical ploys may seem both normal and neutral (such as claims of disinterestedness on the part of the reporter even if funding grants, status, and careers are at stake). Rather than demonstrating the absence of rhetoric, this demonstrates its effectiveness: a message gains in its persuasiveness by appearing independent of the personal presuppositions, biases, or vested interests of its speaker. Whether persuasion operates overtly or tacitly becomes a question of means rather than of fundamentally different modes of discourse.

Rhetoric may also be at odds with style, not in terms of "propaganda" versus "pure art" but in terms of mixed messages. The definition of ideology applied here—as the way by which subjectivity becomes aligned with commonsense notions of reality and elaborated doctrines regarding the real—means that some ideological systems may be overt, well-demarcated, and consciously attended to, such as organized religions or beliefs about what is manly, feminine, or parentally wise, whereas other ideological systems may be tacit, poorly demarcated, and unconsciously acted upon, such as homophobia, male chauvinism, Oedipal rivalry, or even an unquestioned certainty of the individual's free subjectivity, subject to no one. We arrive at the first set of ideologies as concepts through "commentary," or explicit arguments we adopt as our own. We arrive at the second set of ideologies as orientations or subjectivities through "perspective," or tacit arguments we make our own through routine, repetition, and habit. As historical beings we inevitably exhibit a mix of these two forms of subjectivity, and there will be cases where conscious beliefs are at odds with unconscious behavior.

This, in turn, means that a documentary may address us on more than one level and with more than one argument. Like narrative fiction, documentary may convey mixed, ambivalent, or paradoxical messages. Its authors may hold mixed, ambivalent, or paradoxical views of their subjects and of their own presence in relation to others; their subjectivity may be highly alloyed rather than all of a piece.

An early formulation of this notion by Jean-Louis Comolli and Jean Narboni remains a fertile one. They discuss the relation of fiction films to ideology and identify as one of their categories:

> films which seem at first sight to belong firmly within the ideology and to be completely under its sway, but which turn out to be so only in an ambiguous manner. . . . The films we are talking about throw up obstacles in the way of ideology, causing it to swerve and get off course. . . . Looking at the framework one can see two moments in it: one holding it back within certain limits, one transgressing them, An internal criticism is taking place which cracks the film apart at the seams.[2]

The concept of ideology applied by Comolli and Narboni associates dominant ideology with capitalism and the cracks and fissures of the double-edged films with resistance or refusal that stands outside ideology, putting it on display. This part of their position seems more time-bound than their idea of a double system at work that requires attention to how levels—of style and rhetoric, say—may interact conflictually. (The allegiance to an Althusserian belief in scientific, Marxian knowledge that exists outside ideology and to an identification of ideology with *an* ideology— that of capitalism—are the portions of their argument that seem bound up in late '60s formulations of ideology.) A double system requires a double hermeneutic: attentiveness to both the ideological and the utopian elements of a text, its relation to what is and its proposals of what might be. This potential of a text for ambivalence, paradox, parody, or deception (and self-deception) invites both suspicion—is the text saying something more or other than what it seems to be saying?—and revelation—what is the text manifestly saying?[3]

One recurring example of this double system involves the professional stance we have already touched on. This stance often seems to bear the sign of a lack, a lack of *human* response to the events that unfold so that others, the viewers, may see, witness, and experience what someone else reports dispassionately. The reporter remains "free" to move on, to take up other stories and events, rather than become engaged in the forms of human response that he or she may very well report on (relief to victims of disaster, for example). But the text may show signs of the strain between the professional and the humane. Tone and intonation may shift, the gaze may linger, formality may crack. This was once far more common in journalistic reporting than it is now. We need only think of some of Edward R. Murrow's wartime radio reports to gain a sense of how the human may couple with the professional,[4] but the increased institutionalization of the news media has marginalized personal response to specific formats ("Geraldo," and other, similar TV talk shows, "color" commentators, and cultural reviewers, especially film reviewers, for example). These marginalia, unfortunately, present the personal as an unalloyed show of emotion rather than an ambivalent tug between professional ethics and personal response. In some documentaries this tension between the human and the professional surfaces as a conflict between establishing rapport with subjects and reporting about these same subjects. The role of the reporter, filmmaker, or commentator as a professional in the midst of what will be one of many reports over a lifetime comes into tension with his or her immediate presence as friend and confidant to those encountered.

In *Thy Kingdom Come*, for example, our on-camera commentator and interviewer, Anthony Thomas, visits Jim and Tammy Bakker's Heritage USA. We meet Kevin, a handicapped young man of seventeen who lives, alone, in a large house the Bakkers built for the handicapped children of America. (When others will join him is left undetermined.) Early in our encounter, the camera follows Kevin down one corridor, along another, and into a bedroom. The camera tracks left and slows down while Kevin continues in his wheelchair to the left, then slows, turns, and moves to face the camera. This uninterrupted take, which lasts noticeably longer than any of the shots before or after it, is not only a *tour de force* in its own right—with strong echoes of the memorable tracking shot in *Primary* that follows John F. Kennedy into a building, through hallways, backstage and then out onto the stage where he delivers his campaign speech—it also works to heighten the viewer's feelings of suspense and identification with Kevin, whose ability to navigate through this large and lonely structure receives tangible demonstration. But the discussion that ensues makes it clear that Kevin is here to serve as evidence in someone else's argument: he explains how he is expected to act as an advocate and promoter—or tout—for Heritage USA in exchange for his room and board.

Thomas's thinly veiled indignation at Kevin's treatment quickly bypasses Kevin's own situation as Thomas returns to the main subject of moral concern: the self-serving, insensitive quality to the Bakkers' opportunistic charity, and the materialistic preoccupations of the religious right generally. In doing so, the text articulates at the level of rhetoric (in the address it makes to the viewer) a compassionate and socially concerned morality but at the level of style (in its relationship to its own sources of evidence) it sacrifices personal response for general denunciation. The tension spawns a morality of self-serving, insensitive opportunism.[5]

Thy Kingdom Come does not crack open the dominant ideology from an unintentionally or unwittingly progressive/Marxist viewpoint as Comolli and Narboni suggest a text with its own "fifth column" subtext might. The documentary never steps beyond the morality it condemns, but by making an overt argument against self-serving morality and then adopting the very quality it has just condemned, the documentary eviscerates itself. It serves as a vivid demonstration of how difficult it can be to escape at an unconscious level of subjectivity and ideology what may be condemned at a conscious level as immoral or unethical. And it suggests how this tension may be felt all the more powerfully when it is oblique or implicit rather than an overt theme (where it would be subject to further subversion).

A similar reflection of values criticized on one level and repeated on another occurs in Fred Wiseman's documentaries. Here, in films like *Titicut Follies, Hospital, Welfare,* and *High School,* Wiseman presents evidence of how public service institutions structure demeaning exchanges between public servants and their clientele. In numerous instances this process yields an objectification of the client that Wiseman's unblinking gaze makes apparent. The individual becomes classified as a type for whom procedures or formulaic routines are prescribed. Those dimensions of self that exceed the prescriptions remain as a form of excess, testimony to a dehumanizing process that Wiseman documents with unflinching persistence. Or is it "tactless" persistence?[6] Wiseman objectifies his clientele, the people he films, especially those who staff these institutions. Eileen McGarry has shown how Wiseman favors institutional users over their keepers by means of unflattering extreme close-ups, the inclusion of scenes that involve protest or pleas for help on the part of the clientele coupled with repression or routinization on the part of functionaries, and a sense of black humor that might also be considered part of an absurdist view of institutional life.[7]

Wiseman seems to treat these functionaries with the same cold, objectifying scrutiny that they accord their clients (students, patients, cases), but we might also argue that Wiseman, unlike Thomas, aligns himself with the powerless in hierarchical relations of surveillance, dominance, and control. Wiseman's repetition in his own perspective of the values he simultaneously criticizes in others does not betray the self-serving and opportunistic ends of the professional reporter, crusader, or documentarian as much as it signals affiliation and commitment to one side of a hierarchy over another. It can be more closely compared to an affinity for Kevin over and against the Bakkers and their Heritage USA complex rather than the instrumental use of witnesses to serve potentially selfish ends. This is a distinction worth making since it separates Wiseman from the debatable ethics of objectivity and the professional gaze and places him in the arena of another ethics and debate: that of commitment, advocacy, and critique. The comparison and contrast between Wiseman and Thomas, though, serve to indicate some of the questions that are at issue when we begin to consider style, rhetoric, and ethics as multileveled and potentially contradictory dimensions of documentary representation.

Technique, style, and rhetoric go to compose the voice of documentary: they are the means by which an argument represents itself to us (in contrast to the means by which a story does in fiction). The voice of a documentary gives expression to a representation of the world, to perspective and commentary on the world. The argument expressed through style and rhetoric, perspective and commentary, in turn, occupies a position within the arena of ideology. It is a proposition about how the world is—what exists within it, what our relations to these things are, what alternatives there might be—that invites consent. "This is so, isn't it?" The work of rhetoric is to move us to answer, "Yes, it's so," tacitly—whereby a set of assumptions and an image of the world implant themselves, available for use as orientation and guide in the future—or overtly—whereby our own conscious beliefs and purposes align themselves with those proposed for us. We become better qualified through the knowledge provided us by the text's argument and through the subjectivity conveyed by its rhetoric to take a specific position within the arena of ideology. Documentary reference to the world around us is not innocent. Like pleasure, knowledge is not innocent. What it includes and excludes, what it proposes and suppresses remain issues of significance. Gaps and fissures suggest that something exceeds the grasp of the text and its ability to secure agreement. It is to questions of such excess that we need now turn.

Excess

Fiction films are burdened by excess. Some things exceed the centripetal force of narrative. In David Bordwell's *Narration in the Fiction Film*, this excess is everything that cannot be absorbed within a theory of narrative comprehension: "causal lines, colors, expressions, and textures become 'fellow travelers' of the story."[8] These formal qualities fail to add up; excess is the random and inexplicable, that which remains ungovernable within a textual regime presided over by narrative. The qualities listed above could be extended to include acting or performance (a glaring "excess" almost entirely ignored in all of modern theory); spectacle; identification not with characters or situations but with the moving image as such (what Christian Metz has argued forms our primary identification with cinema); "triggered" emotions that are carried outside the fiction or perhaps the movie theater and that cathartic theories do not accommodate like fright from horror films, aggression from action films, or sexual activity from pornography; and the stylistic excesses that accompany melodrama, musicals, and much animation.

The notion that what is excess lacks organization or pattern is disputable. It may be better to say that in narrative films excess is what does not fit into a given analytic scheme; it is the noise that remains when we agree upon limits for what will pass as information. As Charles Altman argues, "the more a static notion of dominance leads us to concentrate on a specific definition of textual unity, the more elements there are that fall outside the bounds of that unity," and thus the more we need a concept like that of excess: "Unless we recognize the possibility that excess—defined as such because of its refusal to adhere to a system—may itself be organized as a system, then we will hear only the official language and forever miss the text's dialect, and dialectic."[9]

And as Dana Polan chronicles in a recent article, considerable attention has gone to examining "non-narrativized affect" in film, contesting the notion of an always dominant narrative principle in favor of a more fluid and pluralistic conception of the text.[10] An instructive example of this kind of approach is Richard Dyer's essay, "Entertainment and Utopia," where he explores the musical film genre in terms of sensibility rather than logic. He refers to qualities of "color, texture, movement, rhythm, melody, camerawork" in order to show how they help establish what a utopian world of energy, abundance, intensity, sincerity, and community would feel like in the classic Hollywood musical.[11] Such considerations move us away from referentiality in its most immediate form to matters of style—especially realism—but they also illustrate how excess in one system can quickly become meaning in another.

Excess can exude a romantic appeal. It can be conceived as that which exists outside the law (the law of narrative, or of Oedipal desire insofar as narratives are tales of male desire and its quest for a suitable object). In this way, excess becomes less a countervailing system of organization, less a challenge to the dominance of the law that asserts its pride of place, than testimony to the centrality of that law. To term something "excess" is to concede its subordination to something else. Like the concept of marginalization, excess forfeits any claim to autonomy. Without a dominant system, excess would not exist. In this regard, excess and marginalization are both akin to the Marxist theory of class whereby the working class exists as a class only because of and in relation to the dominance of a ruling class. Without the one there would not be the other. And although the working class can be taken as an object of romanticization, it might be better seen as the site of resistance, qualification, contestation, and revolt against the dominant system from which it gains identity. Excess, too, can be regarded not only as things the theorist chooses not to examine, as inchoate outlaw forces, as a romantic emblem of elusiveness or difference, but also as the oppositional principle within a dialectical system. (In Richard Dyer's essay, this notion is worked out in great detail through the oppositional qualities of the mundane everyday world and the exuberant world conjured by song and dance. In documentary, this notion of a dialectic may apply to the contingency, indeterminacy, and vicissitudes of life that evidence pattern but only after the fact.)

If excess tends to be that which is beyond narrative in fiction films, excess in documentary is that which stands beyond the reach of both narrative and exposition. Narrative is like a black hole, drawing everything that comes within its ambit inward, organizing everything from decor and clothing to dialogue and action to serve a story. Narrative has a place in documentary, but a less dominant one generally. If there is a comparable black hole, something that attempts to provide an organizing dominant, it would be the combined principles of narrative and expository argument. (Not all documentaries are expository, and some eschew the narrative shape of most observational documentary. These alternative modes of documentary raise somewhat different questions about excess.) Excess is that which escapes the grasp of narrative and exposition. It stands outside the web of significance spun to capture it.

Does this excess have a name? I would argue that it has a simple and familiar one: history. As the referent of documentary, history is what always stands outside the text. (Other qualities may stand outside a given analysis, such as color, texture, or performance. They are excesses of a different order.) Excess is an outlaw against the dominance of the text's own system. Always referred to but never captured, history, as excess, rebukes those laws set to contain it; it contests, qualifies, resists, and refuses them. And like the concept of excess advocated by Charles Altman, history as excess is a system of its own. It is more than a simple matter of exclusions or incommensurates, more than the lawless confronting the lawful. As Altman puts it, "Far more penetrating are those instances when the dominant legal system confronts laws of another order. The case has followed its course through the legal system, but the killer still has not been executed. They all know the law, but they refuse to leave the Greensboro lunchroom. The law prescribes a course of action, a well-motivated narrative, but other laws break away from the prescribed pattern."[12]

Fredric Jameson puts it this way when he tries to differentiate Louis Althusser's concept of history from most other, poststructural concepts that reject the existence of any referentiality outside of language and discourse: "We would therefore propose the following revised formulation: that history is *not* a text, not a narrative, master or otherwise, but that, as an absent cause, it is inaccessible to us except in textual form, and that our approach to it and to the Real itself necessarily passes through its prior textualization, its narrativization in the political unconscious."[13] And Hayden White, from a formalist point of view, also drives a sharp wedge between the written history (with which the documentary shares a common referential bond) and historical existence as such: "I will consider the historical work as what it most manifestly is—that is to say, a verbal structure in the form of a narrative prose discourse that purports to be a model, or icon, of past structures and processes in the interest of *explaining what they were by representing* them."[14]

The impossibility of perfect congruence between text and history stems from the impasse between discourse and referent, between the signification of things and things signified. Representation serves to bridge that divide, however imperfectly, self-consciously, or illusionistically. Explanation, like ideology, provides strategies of containment designed to account for historical reality by, in White's analysis of historical writing, giving reality the shape of a narrative, or, more generally, by proposing a dominant concept, be it narrative closure, teleological destiny, structuring cause, or grand theory around which the historical realm can be made known. In every case, excess remains.

Bertolt Brecht pointed to one kind of excess particularly pertinent to the documentary text when he argued that a photograph of the Krupp munition works does nothing to explain the reality of that enterprise: its forced labor practices, its margin of profit, its ties to the Nazi regime, and so on. Explanation, like narrative, takes time. Every photograph bears witness to an excess that eludes it: that of time itself as the necessary precondition for history and historical understanding. A series of images might begin to provide an argument about the munitions industry or Krupp in particular. With time and movement (or with captions that amount to a written version of the same thing), we enter the realm of explanation, but excess still remains.

What forms does excess take? What resists containment most forcibly? Death, as already noted, is one form of monumental excess. *The Act of Seeing with one's own eyes* ranks as one of the most unwatchable films ever made not because, like *Night and Fog, Memorandum,* or *The Museum and the Fury,* it deals with atrocity beyond the reaches of the human imagination, but because it represents death as the mundane, ubiquitous thing it is, or shall be, for all of us, without any attempt to account for it. The film is all evidence, almost entirely bereft of exposition or narrative. The excessiveness of that evidence—its ability to exceed any explanatory frame—permeates every shot. The lack of any sound whatsoever, even of scalpels and water hoses, further deprives us of any dominant within which the fact of death might take its place as one datum among many. Unlike Robert Gardner's *Forest of Bliss,* which details many of the funeral rituals practiced in Benares, India but also organizes them into a poetic pattern of negotiations and dialogue, commotion and purpose, music, prayer, and ritual, *Act of Seeing* stands as a relentless gaze at a historical reality no structure, no code or system, no-thing, can contain.

Excess in documentary takes the forms it does in fiction (acting or performance, spectacle, primary identification with the image as such, triggered emotions, and stylistic excess) as well as ones that hinge more directly on documentary's historical referent. Among these, the exotic, local, sacramental, and complex are frequent sources of excess. The exotic resists all attempts to naturalize it with words attending to appearance, function, value, or meaning. The words are familiar and the explanation reasonable but an excess remains. The exotic remains different, beyond familiarity. And if there are no words of commentary, as in the Turkana Conversations Trilogy, narrative and argumentative structures invariably encourage us to attend to matters other than the exotic such as the wedding negotiations in *Wedding Camels,* Lorang's character and place within Turkana society in *Lorang's Way,* or the position of his first wife, Arwoto, in *A Wife among Wives.* Part of the fascination of all ethnographic films, in fact, is their ability to both represent the exotic—difference, otherness—and contain or naturalize it, to make it familiar. The difference remains; however familiar it might be made, it continues to stand outside the law of our society and our representations of what it might be.

The local provokes a sense of excess in its very ability to elude more global or contextualizing description. Individuals may be selected for central roles in documentary because of their ability to perform engagingly before the camera or for their representativeness. (Nanook defined this practice; Paul, the unsuccessful but fascinating Bible salesman in *Salesman,* Joe Levine in *Showman,* Kennedy in *Primary,* Dedeheiwä in *Magical Death,* N!ai in *N!ai: Story of a !Kung Woman,* Bob White, leader of the Canadian auto workers union in *Final Offer,* the Loud family in *An American Family* are some of those who occupy the pantheon of documentary performances.) The attempt to probe an individual both to understand that person and to use that person to reveal larger patterns or socially representative practices always produces excess. Aspects of the person elude the frame within which he or she is placed. Dimensions of their behavior reveal a resistance to or subversion of patterns that could be seen as typical. As with every close-up that assumes the face is a window to the soul, an excess remains.

Other documentaries seek to offer a portrait of an individual, sometimes against the backdrop of a social issue, but here, too, excess persists. Mick Jagger in *Gimme Shelter*, Bob Dylan in *Don't Look Back*, Marjoe Gortner, the child evangelist, in *Marjoe*, Hugh Hefner in *The Most*, Eldridge Cleaver in *Off the Pig* (a.k.a. *Black Panther*) , and both Koumiko in Chris Marker's *The Koumiko Mystery* and Fidel Castro in Michael Rubbo's *Waiting for Fidel*—two films that in many ways explode the enigmas this genre usually prefers to mask—all these characters escape the framework designed to capture them. The excess that surrounds them attests to what is treated as little more than a cliché in *Citizen Kane*, "I don't think any word can explain a man's life."

The local can also mean the culturally, geographically, institutionally, linguistically, or economically specific. These material dimensions to lived lives form a reticulated web of complex interrelationships which, even if they can be represented by visible evidence, are seldom exhausted by it. The persistent, wave-like dance rhythms in *Bitter Melons*, the rugged, barren geography of *The Battle of San Pietro*, the density of family relations in *Family Business* or of bureaucratic ones in *Welfare*, the vivid vocal inflections of migrant workers in *The Back-Breaking Leaf* or of working women in *Rosie the Riveter*, and the economics of daily subsistence in The Netsilik Eskimo series or in *Cree Hunters of the Mistassini*—these fragments of a historical existence fascinate and inform, but the information never vanquishes the fascination. Concepts, categories, and generalizations may place or contain these practices and qualities but the sheer otherness, the persistent fact of excess, remains. Documentary evidence, the ability of photographic images and recorded sounds to re-present the compelling likenesses of things, operates in tension with the documentarist's urge to move away from the concrete and local in order to provide perspective, if not knowledge, of what we see.

Clifford Geertz conveys the complexity of this dilemma in his account of Gilbert Ryle's concept of "thick description," the attempt to render the motivational and interpretive complexity of everyday exchange such as the occurrence of an eyelid movement that may be an involuntary bit of physiology (a blink) or a highly charged piece of social encounter (a wink). "Thinly" described an encounter might be rendered as an eyelid contraction. More "thickly" put, a specific instance might be interpreted as "'practicing a burlesque of a friend faking a wink to deceive an innocent into thinking a conspiracy is in motion.'"[15] The task Geertz sets for anthropology lends itself quite handily to the goal apparent in many documentaries where evidence and argument take the place of what he calls inscription and specification:

the distinction, relative in any case, that appears in the experimental or observational sciences between "description" and "explanation" appears here as one, even more relative, between "inscription" ("thick description") and "specification" ("diagnosis")—between setting down the meaning particular social actions have for the actors whose actions they are, and stating, as explicitly as we can manage, what the knowledge thus attained demonstrates about the society in which it is found, and, beyond that, about social life as such.[16]

And in a remark that seems to hint at an acknowledgment of the excess that still remains, Geertz comments, "Anthropology, or at least interpretative anthropology, is a science whose progress is marked less by a perfection of consensus than by a refinement of debate. What gets better is the precision with which we vex each other" (and ourselves, it might be added).[17]

The sacramental is a term used here to describe those practices or events that are not what they seem. They operate on the level that Roland Barthes considered the level of connotation and myth: they are a second-order system that takes a sign whose meaning is already established in a given social context and uses that sign as the signifier for a new, more heavily connotative meaning. A vehicle, especially one for passengers, carrying its own power-generating and propelling mechanisms for travel on ordinary roads denotes a car. But this sign can now become a signifier for another, supplemental meaning: power, freedom, and adventure, say, or safety, economy, and serviceability. The supplemental meaning attaches to the primary or denotative meaning but is less self-evident; membership within a society or at least a subculture or "interpretive community" that shares common understandings about the nature of things at a connotative level becomes a prerequisite to comprehension. In some circles of American culture, for example, to be offered a drink connotes liquor or a cocktail and not water, soda, milk, or any of the other beverages a person might understand to qualify as "a drink."

Another example would be the Christian sacrament of Communion or the Eucharist. To someone not familiar with this practice, the consumption of foodstuffs might seem of primary concern while the ritualistic elements of the event might appear extraneous, oddly excessive compared to other food-taking practices or, simply, as noise. The token amounts of nutrient consumed are an important clue that the event is not devoted to allaying hunger or satisfying dietary requirements, but it is a considerable leap from the visible evidence to a full understanding of the sacrament itself.

Events of this sort are not uncommon in documentary. One major example is the subgenre of ethnographic films concerned with trance, an activity where what we see is never exactly what it appears to be since a nonvisible, altered state of consciousness informs the event. Films like *Dance and Trance in Bali*, *N/um Tchai*, *Les maîtres fous*, *Torou et Bitti*, *The Divine Horsemen*, and *Magical Death* find themselves obliged to provide commentary to explicate the events we see as an alternative system of meaning. At other times the films lapse into silence, leaving us to experience what they cannot explain. Since it is precisely the combination of these two perspectives that constitute shared understanding within the community where the sacrament occurs, these films, as well as other more sporadic representations of the sacramental, invariably testify to an excess they cannot contain.

Finally, complexity can also be regarded as a source of excess. Documentarists who set out to explain something or argue a case in the manner of a historian or sociologist encounter the vexing limitations of film and video as media of analysis. Unlike reading, viewing does not normally occur at the viewer's own pace but at a fixed rate determined by the need to create apparent motion. What might be read in an hour could only be spoken in several hours, requiring that commentary be pared down considerably. Written titles or intertitles can be presented, but only at a rate comfortable for slow as well as fast readers, and when spoken in a film or video text, words compete for our attention with other sounds and a stream of images. On a page these words can receive our undivided attention.

If the historian, sociologist, social critic, or activist who resorts to print feels that the medium requires severe restrictions on how much can be said and accounted for, this is all the more true for documentary texts. An excess remains, and within that excess we can often discover some of the complexity a longer, more leisurely examination of the same issue, from the same perspective, might have addressed. (Complexity is not the same as exhaustiveness or total explanation; the slippages, sleights-of-hand, feints, deceptions, and distractions that figure into the rhetoric of artistic proofs, though, loom larger, are more readily felt or registered for what they are in texts that have less time and more restricted analytic tools at their disposal.)

This loss of complexity, the hemorrhaging of excess, is a standard complaint about television news and, sometimes, journalism generally. What might take up several columns of print in a newspaper and may lead to article-length consideration in magazines or journals gets reduced to ninety seconds of air time. Formulaic explanatory devices replace the search for specificity and context (the element of the local): Soviet-American relations revolve around confrontation, backstage maneuvering and suspicion—even if the topic is detente or arms reduction; political activity centers on the federal government and reports of what political figures represent the case to be, with an undertone of ironic self-awareness that these are representations, not independently determined facts, but without concerted effort to obtain such facts; urban riots ignite from a single match—a shooting, confrontation, or indignity—and the simmering factors of economic deprivation, problematic community leadership, ethnic and racial interrelationships, and political histories of responsiveness or indifference become demoted as too complex to examine or even denied importance as "not news," not far enough outside the pattern of the normal and everyday to warrant attention.

These forms of leakage occur in the more extended analysis afforded by documentaries as well. Despite its eleven-hour length, Ken Burns's *The Civil War* clearly does not settle the more than a century-long debate about the war and its significance. In fact, the *Newsweek* issue of October 8, 1990 devoted its lead story to the series and highlighted many of the "partisan passions" and continuing debates raised but not resolved by the series. Particularly interesting are the claims of radically different readings in the North and South. *Newsweek* reports that some Northerners regarded the series as "essentially neutral and objective," some Southerners took it as an "outrageous slander and insult" to their ancestors, while other Northern scholars, "especially blacks, regard *The Civil War* as accurate on the major historical points but subtly undermined by sympathy for the colorful rascals and noble, long-suffering patricians of the Confederacy." The film carefully avoids giving a definitive interpretation; viewers appear to interpret it in relation to different existential contexts.

Other films generate an excess through the specific focus they choose. *The Day After Trinity*, for example, concentrates so closely on Oppenheimer's own life and his own perceptions that major decisions on the use of atomic weapons, such as the decision to drop the first two bombs on civilian populations in Japan, are glossed over. *Ethnic Notions* details the kinds of stereotypes of American blacks that appeared in film and television for decades but presents little consideration of how these stereotypes were received by either white or black Americans: the film assumes that if they were shown they were believed. Although the film demonstrates how the stereotypes derived from white fears and projections, it doesn't question whether at least some viewers might have also noticed this or contested it. *Rosie the Riveter*, *With Babies and Banners*, and *Union Maids* all represent some of the complex issues revolving around women in the workplace in the 1930s and '40s without also acknowledging the large, contentious role played by the CPUSA (Communist Party, U.S.A.). *Dear America* takes a tack that seems to sidestep the problem of complexity altogether: it eschews comment or explanation entirely in favor of a cinematically sophisticated attempt to recreate aspects of the physical and subjective experience of the average American soldier fighting in Vietnam. (It shares in this ambition with *Platoon* which also strives to recreate the experience of Vietnam without passing judgment on the legitimacy of American involvement.) The excess that leaks out, in this case, has the potential to join up with the various assumptions and perspectives of viewers to provide evidence for a wide variety of attitudes toward the war. (This phenomenon occurs in a great deal of observational documentary as well.) What remains as yet another level of excess still beyond the reach of every account of this war is acknowledgment of that other experience that would relativize the American soldier's: the experience of the Vietnamese whose civil war it was.

Material, historical evidence exceeds all strategies of containment. Even more than fiction, where the text may motivate virtually everything that we see and hear (motivate in the sense of provide justification for its presence), documentary must constantly bear the burden of historical excess itself. It must also bear the burden, and glory, of the compelling quality of this historical evidence. Those signs or representations we see and hear of the historical world bear an indexical relation to their referent. Sound and image appear to reproduce the uniqueness of historical situations and events, engendering a perpetual oxymoron or paradox. What is unique cannot be reproduced; what is reproducible cannot be unique. But there are the photographic likenesses of Hitler, Mussolini, and Hirohito, reappearing on screen every time Walter Huston says, "If you see these men, don't hesitate." There are the churning, tumbling bodies of concentration camp victims sliding into their mass grave every time *Night and Fog* is shown, and there are both the performers and the utterly unique potpourri of audience members in *Monterey Pop*, luminous likenesses of what is over and done with recycled onto a motion picture screen.

The Indexical Bind

Representation preserves uniqueness, although it does not dispel the sense of paradox. Representation involves one thing standing for another, an image or recorded sound standing for that from which it was "taken." "Taken" is in quotation marks because this taking is nonsubtractive: the thing remains, imparting information to the representation but not at the expense of any of its own matter or energy. It is, however, a potential theft at a more metaphorical level: information about a thing can be implanted into a text as one sign among many in new and unexpected ways; its connotative dimension can be altered, its meanings multiplied, strange juxtapositions can be made. The claims that photographs are both windows onto and thefts of the soul are not without legitimacy. "Taking" suggests what is peculiar to the indexical sign: a close physical or existential bond seems to exist between referent and representation.

Charles Peirce was perhaps the first to describe this relationship in detail:

> Photographs, especially instantaneous photographs, are very instructive, because we know that in certain respects they are exactly like the objects they represent. But this resemblance is due to the photographs having been produced under such circumstances that they were physically forced to correspond point by point to nature. In that respect then, they belong to the second class of signs, those by physical connection [i.e., the indexical].[18]

The indexical bond of photochemical and electronic images to that which they represent, when formed by optical lenses that approximate the properties of the human eye, provides endless fascination and a seemingly irrefutable guarantee of authenticity. Authenticity stems from the image-forming process itself; it is not determined by verifying of the style of a brush stroke or a signature, an authenticity that guarantees "de Kooning-ness" or "Renoiricity" rather than a bond between image and referent. But the primary importance of this indexical quality to the photographic image (and magnetic sound recording) is less in the unassailable authenticity of the bond between image and referent than in the *impression of authenticity* it conveys to a viewer. Even if the indexicality is fabricated—as certain trompe l'oeil techniques of set design, lighting, and perspective or the computer-based technique of digital sampling can do—the effect or impression of authenticity can remain just as powerful. What Christian Metz said about the effect of apparent motion in cinema also applies to indexicality: "to reproduce its appearance is to duplicate its reality."[19]

The indexical bond, however, is not enough to produce the impression of a unique historical referent reproduced as image. Photographic images ("photographic" will stand for all those photochemical and electronic image-making techniques that establish an indexical bond) re-present the visual field before a lens but they have no ability whatsoever to distinguish, or to allow us to distinguish, the historical status of that field. A photographic image of Lauren Bacall, Mary Tyler Moore, Madonna, or Ronald Reagan will enjoy an indexical bond with its subject regardless of whether it is a candid shot of the subject in his or her own backyard or a highly crafted depiction of the subject in the thick of a performance.

Fiction generally and the star system specifically depend on this effect. But the movement remains centripetal. When we recognize a star appearing in a new role, we take it less as documentary evidence of how he or she occupies a historical space and more as an anchor and reference point from which we depart, moving into the specificities of this narrative and its imaginary world. The indexical bond remains, but its evidentiary value is sharply discounted: make-up and costume disguise the person's normal physiognomy; gesture and action become attributes of a character; accent, tone, and inflection depart from the evidence we have of the star outside his or her roles. How will Meryl Streep acquit herself in this role, within this world, with these tendencies and traits? The indexical bond to what was filmed before a camera (and recorded by a microphone) remains, but what appeared before the camera was itself shaped and altered to fit within a fiction. Our attention flows inward, to comprehend and interpret a story set in *a* world rather than outward, to understand and assess an argument about *the* world.

At one level then, filmed fictions take advantage of the same indexical bond as do documentaries. (The establishing shots of Mount Rushmore in *North by Northwest* are every bit as indexically bound to their referent as are similar shots in any travelogue.) In what way, then, does the indexical image provide evidence of the historical world or within what limits does that evidence exist?

> Only a photographic lens can give us the kind of image of the object that is capable of satisfying the deep need man has to substitute for it something more than a mere approximation, a kind of decal or transfer. The photographic image is the object itself, the object freed from the conditions of time and space that govern it. No matter how fuzzy, distorted, or discolored, no matter how lacking in documentary value the image may be, it shares, by virtue of the very process of its becoming, the being of the model of which it is the reproduction; it *is* the model.[20]

André Bazin made his point clearly enough: the "sticky stuff" that he also likened to an amber that preserves what it entraps perfectly, makes no discriminations about the ontological or historical status of its subject: it is the photographic *image* that shares in the being of the model. The image gains a historical authenticity regardless of the historical status of what it represents. "*Voilà,* this is how it was," or, with a succession of images and apparent motion, "This is how it is, this is duration itself and the object caught within it." The image stands as evidence, it reproduces what could only occur once, and yet it is *not* the model, not the thing itself, and not evidence whose ontological status is unassailable.

"Is it the real Ella Fitzgerald or is it Memorex?"—a question asked of viewers/auditors who of necessity must answer based on an indexical representation (the TV commercial's recorded sound track) of Fitzgerald's voice in any case. This quandary, or existential paradox, where we are expected to make a distinction that entails its own logical impossibility, is not unlike the paradox of the indexical image.[21] It is evidence, but not irrefutable evidence. It is the model but it is not the model. The indexical quality of the image proclaims its authenticity but this is also a self-substantiating claim akin to the remonstration by the Cretan that he is telling the truth as he tells us that Cretans always lie. The "Ella Fitzgerald" paradox is also analogous to the Shroud of Turin paradox. The shroud tells us that it is the death mask of a human being, but is it the death mask of the historical Jesus? Are we to see in this quintessence of indexicality the likeness of Jesus Himself or just that of a human figure? The *likeness* is authentic, but the *historical* authenticity remains in doubt.

What this points to is that the guarantee of authenticity we may feel in the presence of the documentary image is a guarantee born of our own complicity with the claims of a text. The image and the text—its conventions and techniques—combine to provide the basis for our inference or assumption that the photographic image's stickiness has within it the stuff of history. There is no other guarantee than the inference we ourselves make, based, often, on very good evidence such as the similarity between the photographic image we see and others of the same subject (for public figures and well-known places and events), on explicit assurances of authenticity by the film itself, and on our familiarity with everyday conduct and how it differs from fictional representations. Films that deliberately falsify their assurances, however, such as *No Lies, David Holzman's Diary,* or

Daughter Rite, remind us of how readily the historical and the indexical bonds can be brought in or out of alignment and take sharply to task our own willingness to lend credence to an image's status as evidence.

André Bazin himself acknowledges that the image is not its own guarantee and our trust in it can be a blind one when he mounts an extended criticism of Charles Frend's *Scott of the Antarctic.* The film is obviously a reconstruction and a narrative. Much of the delicacy of determining the evidentiary status of the images is lost, but Bazin catches the crux of the matter when he refers to the location shooting: "The extent to which his [Frend's] film is a pointless undertaking is even more evident *when one discovers* that it was made among the glaciers of Norway and Switzerland. The realization that these settings, although they may bear some resemblance to the Antarctic, are nevertheless not the Antarctic, is enough of itself to destroy any sense of drama with which the subject would otherwise be charged"[22] [italics mine].

When does one discover such a fact? Is it, for the average viewer, in noticing the color, density, sheen or texture of the ice? Is it, in fact, from anything within the frame itself? In a great many instances, including this one, I suspect the answer is no; admissions or clarifications that arrive from outside the film reveal that the indexical bond between image and referent, which remains as vivid and compelling as ever, is between the image and a referent other than one inferred or assumed. Such external information is sometimes necessary and sufficient to radically realign our perception of a film.

This alone is enough to undercut the claims to a privileged ontological status sometimes made on behalf of documentary, but there is more. Not only is the historical authenticity of the image subject to uncertainty; the meaning it bears as evidence, even if it is authentic, is subject to interpretation. Facts make sense only within systems of meaning. Such systems are multiple and sometimes conflict with one another. The link between evidence and system is tenuous. Facts and the concepts we employ to grasp them can be described as "labels for points of view voluntarily adopted by the investigator."[23] The same evidence, or facts, can often be placed quite convincingly within more than one system of meaning, or given more than one interpretation. Court trials often hinge upon precisely this fact and involve not only matters of circumstantial evidence but the meaning of documentary evidence itself. For this reason, the status of the photographic image in legal proceedings is far from cut and dried and it may serve us well to recall the caution exercised there.

Two recent examples may suffice to make the point. At the trial of Symbionese Liberation Army captive Patty Hearst, surveillance camera videotape recordings were introduced as evidence. These recordings showed Ms. Hearst as a participant in a bank robbery. She was armed and she pointed the gun in the direction of some of the people held within the bank. (There was no sound track to determine what was said.) The prosecution argued that the tape demonstrated that Ms. Hearst was clearly an active, willing member of the Army and deserved the same treatment as they did. The defense admitted that the images were authentic, that she had been in the bank during the robbery and had held the gun, but that the images did not reveal her state of mind or motivation. The defense argued that she was an unwilling participant and acted only as a result of threat, coercion, and brainwashing that gave her no viable alternative. The second example was the trial of John DeLorean for conspiring to traffic in drugs. Mr. DeLorean was entrapped by federal agents who recorded on videotape the transactions that prompted his arrest. What was said was also recorded. The prosecution claimed that Mr. DeLorean's comments and actions presented an open and shut case. The defense argued, again, that the tape was not what it seemed, that it bordered on a recording of the sacramental in the sense described here. Mr. DeLorean was only *appearing* to go along to see how far these men would push the matter, and even if he did conclude the transaction he had intended all along to report the matter and use the deal to provide the police with the proof they would need to distinguish his report from hearsay or idle speculation about someone's motives. (A comparable defense emerged in Washington D.C. mayor Marion Barry's trial for drug use: he did what the images show but his motivation was not what the prosecution claimed it to be.)

By changing the motivation underlying an action the meaning of the action is radically changed. But a photographic image represents the visible event, not the motivation. Subjectivity eludes its grasp. The very indexicality that makes the image or film so convincing can serve to mislead the viewer all the more powerfully when inferences are drawn based on assumptions, conventions, suggestions, or attributions that the image invokes or prompts but cannot substantiate.

Documentary, then, shares with fiction the advantages and liabilities of the photographic image's "sticky stuff." Indexicality plays a key role in authenticating the documentary image's claims to the historically real, but the authentication itself must come from elsewhere and it is often subject to doubt. Our willingness to suspend disbelief in the face of the "living likeness" such images convey supports the fascination, pleasure, and power to persuade that documentary affords; it is also a willingness we tender more often on faith than reason.

Referentiality depends not only on the image and its properties, but also on larger textual effects. Documentaries like *Dead Birds, Microcultural Incidents in Ten Zoos, Why Vietnam,* or television news employ a continual process of labeling, for example. A commentator identifies the historical dimension to images we see: the voice places the image in time and space, it provides background information, it names individuals we may not otherwise know, it supplies a historical context, and suggests an interpretation. A young Dani boy becomes "Pua," an older man "Weyak," and their actions representative ones for the culture they belong to. In *Microcultural*

Incidents, as in *Nanook of the North,* the commentary directs us to those aspects of the image that are deemed most revealing or indicative: cultural differences in the interaction among family members at a zoo become focused on specific body movements, fluctuations in spatial relationships, tendencies for initiatory or prompting actions to attach to one family role more than another, and so on.

Here the image's stickiness, its indexicality, provides the evidence, but the commentary guides us toward those aspects of the image that are most important to the argument. At the most general level, this process identifies the documentary text as such: we believe the authenticity of what we see and hear because we are told that what we see is evidence of historical occurrences, not fictional simulations of them. At a more local level, commentary provides a selective anchoring of the image. It selects out some detail and places it within a conceptual frame or explanatory grid. It encourages us to move past questions of construction or fabrication to the brute facticity of the image as historical decal or imprint.

Labeling also proposes attributes. As Sol Worth has observed, young children attribute qualities to an image mainly on the basis of prior knowledge. A photograph of a doctor leaving the scene of an accident without stopping may still elicit the attribution of "good doctor" despite this evidence to the contrary, whereas older children, and adults, more commonly infer meanings from the specific structure and context of the image. Labeling techniques in documentary propose attributes that may well skew our own inference-forming process toward those meanings favored by the text. Some texts may well be haunted by an excess of possible or even self-evident meanings or implications that labeling has overlooked or suppressed.

The commentary in *Obedience,* for example, describes how the test subjects are led to believe that they are inflicting electrical shocks on "learners" whenever the learner makes a mistake. Since the degree of shock admissible moves across a scale that ends in "Danger" and since the "learner" is an accomplice of the experimenter, coached to emit screams and then lapse into silence at the highest voltages, the test subject faces a profound crisis: administering shocks elicits signs of acute distress but the impulse to stop flies in the face of emphatic requests from a scientist to continue. The experiments are a matter of historical record, but this documentary representation of them could be fabricated as easily as not. The only individual not performing in the usual sense of the word is the test subject; these individuals could be easily replaced by performers who would act out the part of the conscience-stricken subjects.

But the commentary assures us that this is a record of actual experiments, that the test subjects do *not* know that the shocks they apply never reach the learner, that the results we see are the results that actually happened. This assurance that what occurred was an event within the historical world itself and not a simulation of it transports the viewer into a highly distinct moral position. We witness other humans wrestling with the possibility that they have done physical injury to fellow human beings, possibly even killing them. The hesitations, the protests of concern, the desire to be relieved of responsibility, the gestures of fear and anxiety (hand to brow, the sudden, jerky motion used to send an electrical charge rather than a firm flip of a switch, the both nervous and guilty glances toward the scientist)—all these bear an awesome, distressing authenticity that can discomfort the viewer immensely.

Subjectivity and Identification

The commentary in *Obedience* compounds its effect by guaranteeing the very objectivity of the camera's gaze: the camera was hidden behind a one-way mirror so that its presence could not affect the subject in any way. This guarantee, of course, also effects a disquieting shift to the axiographic space of the clinical or professional gaze. The very objectivity of the gaze seems to cry out for some further and human response. A camera looks in, recording what it sees, the fact of acute emotional distress making no impression upon it. Neither helplessness nor intervention, neither endangerment nor human empathy attach to it. The very relentlessness of the gaze, in light of evidence that it was present during an event of severe trauma, gives professionalism, or objectivity, a disturbing undertone. This effect, though, derives not simply from the indexical quality of the image but from the direct address guarantees made to us that the events are unstaged and the evidence completely authentic. (These classic experiments by Stanley Milgram could not pass the requirement of "informed consent" that prevails today, but to Milgram's credit, the test subjects were debriefed after the trial and suffered no lingering after-effects, or at least none were reported.)

A fictional rendering of this same experiment would probably rely on building an identificatory relationship between viewer and test subject. Continuity editing and a psychological realism would replace the unblinking long takes and medium shots of the hidden camera. Psychological or emotional realism selects aspects of a scene in accordance with their emotional importance to characters. In this situation, such a realism might rely on a series of shots such as (1) medium shot of the subject at his or her test console, (2) close-up of subject testing the learner, (3) medium shot of learner giving an incorrect answer, (4) close-up of subject hesitant to deliver the shock, (5) close-up of subject's hand near the electrical switch, (6) close-up of subject's imploring look at the scientist, (7) medium shot of the scientist from the subject's point of view, refusing to excuse the subject from his or her task, (8) close-up of subject grimacing as he or she decides how to extricate him- or herself from the horns of the dilemma, (9) close-up of his or her hand as he or she raises it and throws the switch, (10) medium shot of learner issuing a well-timed howl, (11) close-up of the subject's distressed response.

This type of decoupage with its carefully constructed space presupposes the stopping and starting of the action to facilitate the best camera positions. Its use would destroy the reality effect achieved by the professional gaze of a hidden camera as it records an uninterrupted series of events. And yet the larger goal of psychological realism is not beyond the reach of documentary. Forms of identification and subjective engagement are entirely possible. They can add yet another dimension of affect to the indexical quality of the image.

Identification is used here as a particular type of emotional proof. Our previous discussion of emotional proofs described them as a rhetorical strategy designed to elicit preexisting feelings and attach them to a given argument. Evidence of atrocities, for example, is a standard emotional proof for documentaries concerned with violence or war. Little in the way of identification with the specific historical victims is required; the effect derives from the photographic, or aural, evidence of the atrocity itself.

Identification, by contrast, is a form of emotional proof tied to the particulars of situation and character. It involves a tie between the viewer and the intersubjective domain of the character. Rather than being presented from the exterior only, identification requires that characters be presented from the interior as well. Identification comes from being drawn into an empathetic attachment to a particular character's situation, even if this character represents a type, rather than from tapping a preexisting disposition. (Hitchcock illustrates this point vividly when he draws us into identificatory relationships with psychopaths and murderers by means of subjective point of view shots in *Psycho, Strangers on a Train,* and *Shadow of a Doubt.*)

Subjectivity and identification are far less frequently explored in documentary than in fiction. Issues of objectivity, ethics, and ideology have become the hallmark of documentary debate as issues of subjectivity, identification, and gender have of narrative fiction. But this divide is a matter of aesthetic convention and historical circumstance. Nothing precludes the documentary from incorporating moments of identification nor from pegging them to the indexical linkages it has to the world.

Subjectivity has particular importance in a great many national cinemas outside of Hollywood, especially in European and Latin American work from the 1960s and beyond. (In Hollywood it serves to tie us more closely to central characters and their fates in ways that seldom make access to interior states of mind or their mutual correspondence a fundamental issue or source of formal crisis.) Generally associated with a modernist viewpoint that stresses a nonlinear, ramifying world of uncertainty, anxiety, and political ambivalences, subjectivity serves to emphasize the relativity and even incompatibility of points of view and the ambiguity of experience. Documentary, on the whole, has not endorsed a modernist perspective.

Subjectivity has not been joined to indeterminacy, ambiguity, and relativity but rather to a rational, commonsensical view of the world. We observe in documentary the everyday world of social action and photographic realism. This is clearly *a* view of the world, not the world as such, but it is not just *any* view of the world, as a fiction might be. It is the obvious and natural world of everyday life; it is a world represented with the indexical "wham" that photographic images can provide; it is an argument set amidst those contending discourses of power, dominance, control, and the strategies of resistance, qualification, debate, contestation, and refusal that accompany them. Subjectivity functions differently in such a realm.

A comment made about the work of Jean-Luc Godard, who has frequently skirted the boundaries between documentary and fiction with his pronounced emphasis on an expository voice, an argumentative rhetoric, and a collage style, suggests how subjectivity might function in many documentaries as well: "Instead of claiming the ability to plunge into the mental life of the character, the narrator creates those portions of that mental life which can play a part in the tissue of self-conscious address to the viewer."[24] The force is centrifugal, away from the story and toward the mode of address or to the historical world, rather than inward toward a more richly, densely realized imaginary world.

Documentary subjectivity functions in a similar way. Rather than draw us into a vortex of personal psychology through sustained and systematic use of point-of-view editing, subjective images of memory and anticipation, or subjective interpretations of altered states of mind (such as drunkenness or euphoria), documentary subjectivity strengthens the sense of human engagement within the historical world. Subjectivity lends a greater sense of aura to the world around us. (I use "aura" in the sense proposed by Walter Benjamin: "The authenticity of a thing is the essence of all that is transmissible from its beginning, ranging from its substantive duration to its testimony to the history which it has experienced."[25] Although photography stripped things of their aura, for Benjamin, my argument is that subjectivity heightens the *impression* of aura in documentary film.)

Subjectivity in this sense may be used in a manner similar to visual evidence in documentary. Such evidence need not be organized into the tightly knit forms of continuity that prevail in classic narrative film. Great disjunctures of time and space can occur without prompting any sense of disorientation or of strange juxtapositions. These leaps, for example, from farmers hoeing a field, to soldiers marching, to fighter planes, to rubble— all shot in different times and places—can fit together quite neatly in support of commentary (as they do in *Why Vietnam,* for example). Similarly, subjectivity may be intermittent and less than full-blown. It may not attach to a specific character, but attempt instead to convey the feel or texture of an event or experience as does the cross-cutting between close-ups of swooning faces and medium shots of the young Paul Anka performing on stage in *Lonely Boy.* These shots, which adhere to the norm for point-of-view editing in other ways, fail to provide a particular character for us to identify with. Instead they both allow us to observe the *folie à deux* between singer and followers, and to share the subjective space of the fan empathetically. Fragments of the world and moments of subjectivity play a part in the tissue of the argument, in the provision of a voice for the film; as in Godard, elements of narrative become subsumed by something else—self-conscious address itself or perspective and commentary on the world around us.

Consider *Las Madres de la Plaza de Mayo*, a film that examines the prolonged struggle of a group of mothers to determine the fate of their "disappeared" children in Argentina. The film's structure centers on images of the mothers marching in front of La Casa Rosada in Buenos Aires combined with testimony by individual mothers about their particular experience. During the interview with one mother the film cuts away to a scene presented in an entirely different register. Instead of seeing the mother in a traditional medium shot, in color, the film shifts to a black-and-white, slow-motion scene depicting the abduction of her son by a group of unidentified men. The scene is highly subjective, representing what she might have seen had she been there (she tells us that she was not home when the disappearance took place). It is similar to a flashback but it is a conditional flashback, of what might have been, rather than a memory of an event witnessed directly.

This scene, placed in the context of a documentary interview, strengthens the indexical bond already established between the image of the mother and the historical events she describes. These subjective images serve to anchor her testimony to lived experience that we are asked to witness with her, imaginatively, empathetically. Unlike traditional illustrative images such as those in the Why We Fight series that represent, say, industrial productivity in the United States to support the commentator's statements about American power, these images do not derive from the historical world directly. Like fiction generally, they are a simulation or facsimile of the world, not decals or imprints of it. And they are a subjective simulation, representing the shape the mother's imagination may give to an event that haunts her and motivates her protest. This is evidence of a different order. It heightens our emotional relationship with the character, the mother, and it does so by means of narrative, fictional techniques employed for documentary, rhetorical ends. The effect is less to draw us toward a story than toward the affective, experiential dimension of lived reality.

Similar moments occur in *Roses in December* (when the film recreates the abduction and murder of four nuns), *The Thin Blue Line* (when the film repeatedly represents the murder of a police officer, varying each representation in accordance with different versions of the event), *The Color of Honor* (which opens with a highly nostalgic, softly lit, rose-colored impression of a Japanese American home in the days before World War II, before examining the detention camps and telling the story of those Japanese men who served in the United States military), *First Contact* (which subjectifies its black-and-white archival footage taken by the first white men to live among a particular group of Highland New Guineans into a haunting, impressionistic series of shots rendered in slow motion, with musical accompaniment, as though it came from a tribal collective memory, and further amplifies it with testimony given in the present with conventional interview footage), *Dear America* (which relies on visually stunning battle footage and rock and roll songs to recreate the subjective experience of the combat soldier as the sound track carries the spoken words of the letters such soldiers sent home), *The Atomic Cafe* (during its culminating rendition of nuclear holocaust drawn from archival source material—pronuclear propaganda films—whose very claim to the factual status of evidence the film has already undercut), *Fire from the Mountain* (as it renders the archaic, mysterious power of the mountain to both shelter and inspire Omar Cabezas and the other pioneer Sandinistas), and in *Cane Toads* (where we have shots taken from the point of view of the toads, most notably from inside a packing crate as a toad travels across the Australian landscape in a box car).

In many cases the subjective sequences are unclaimed by any one character. They serve as a subjective voice, offering a perspective not commonly found in documentary, loosely but clearly attached to the experience of its subjects and with which we are invited to identify. In the context of an argument about the world, rather than a story about a world, these moments reclaim a dimension of human experience that had been lost in the movement toward an observational stance and scrupulous nonintervention. They rejoin subjectivity to the objective: they add a perspective that runs the risk of being dismissed as fiction but that also offers the benefit of rounding out our sense of the human within the arena of history. Narrative technique enters here as well as in the tendency toward a focus on character, crisis situations, suspense, and closure or in the affiliation between expository discourse and the reliance on narrative structure to offer a moral perspective or political judgment (as discussed by Hayden White).

The tendency is not new. We see traces of it in passages from *Victory at Sea* (especially the landing at Guadalcanal), *The Battle of San Pietro* (when a man and a dead woman are joined, by the editing techniques of psychological realism, into a figure of grief) and in *Rouli-roulant* (an NFB film from 1966 that treats the skateboard as *Fire from the Mountain* treats its mountain, as full of an enhancing, mysterious power that flows, here, from board to adventurous youth), among others. What is new, perhaps, is the degree to which such elements of subjectivity have become an accepted part of documentary representation. Historically, the risk of subjectivity has lain in its potential to color or subvert objectivity, the prized goal for many. The new journalism, the intellectual critiques of objectivity and even of participant-observation, the increased prevalence of "soft" news and subjective reporting styles in local television news, along with the *auteur*-like status of

the reporter as personal witness and, sometimes, trusted friend (epitomized by news anchorman Walter Cronkite in the United States but also
represented by talk show hosts like Phil Donahue and Oprah Winfrey, by
documentary filmmakers like Michael Rubbo and Jon Alpert, and by film
essayists like Godard and Raul Ruiz) have all contributed to this limited but
increased acceptance. All demonstrate how subjectivity can be brought to
bear upon discourse about the world. Well removed from the essentially
fictional domain of docudrama (stories based on fact but performed by
actors and scripted from both documents and conjecture), these subjective
moments remain anchored in the lived reality of the historical person.
They offer a distinct and revitalizing form of referentiality to today's
documentary.

Historical Recognition and Authenticity

One final aspect of referentiality requires examination. The "sticky stuff"
that attaches image to referent not only attaches indiscriminately to what
occurs before the camera, without regard to its status as historical evidence,
and not only has the ability to invite identification with subjective images
as well as objective ones; this stickiness also requires recognition by the
viewer before it can come into play. If we lack familiarity with the historical
events whose semblance attaches to the sounds and images we view, then
these images may lack the referential power documentary requires of them.
And with this lack comes the loss of one of the pleasures distinct to
documentary. The point may be obvious when we think about it, but it has
several repercussions for how we engage with a text and what we take from
it as an argument or story. Documentary is a fiction unlike any other
precisely because the images direct us toward the historical world, but if
that world is unfamiliar to us, our direction will just as likely be toward a
fiction like any other.

Home movies are an extreme example. Such material, often close to raw
footage in its lack of expository or narrative structure, has clear documentary value for those of whom it offers evidence. Usually this is a family or
small circle of friends. More broadly, it can be viewed as ethnographic
evidence of the kind of events deemed filmworthy and the modes of
self-presentation regarded as normal (for commemoration before a camera) within a given culture. But in order to take on evidentiary value, the
footage must be recognized for its historical specificity. The viewer who
says, "Ah, that's me eight years ago!" has a radically different rapport with
the footage than the viewer who has no inkling of who this figure in the
image is. (But were the viewer who only recognizes a human figure to
recognize, subsequently, that this is a friend, to see not only general
resemblance but an indexical bond stretching across eight years of time,
the effect of discovery would be equivalent.)

Recognition involves a sudden click or shift of levels as information, sensory impressions, arrange themselves into a larger gestalt. In this case, the shift is from the recognition of a human figure to its placement as a particular, historical figure. A face in a crowd becomes the visage of a friend. The man stricken by an assassin's bullet in the Zapruder footage becomes John F. Kennedy, President. The central character in *Don't Look Back* is not just a young performer but the elusive, mischievous figure of Bob Dylan. The animated figure giving a speech to a crowd of thousands in *Triumph of the Will* suddenly becomes not just another political orator but Adolf Hitler. The characters of Colonel Mandrake, President Muffley, and Dr. Strangelove suddenly become variations of a single person, Peter Sellers. The character of Howard Hughes in Francis Coppola's *Tucker* becomes the well-masked person of Dean Stockwell and the young hot-rodder and farm boy, Falfa, in *American Graffiti*, becomes an indexical record of a young Harrison Ford.

This recognition of a historical specificity anchors the image in its full indexicality. It cannot float freely as an exact but unspecified likeness, set free from historical contingency amidst the ethers of general resemblance. This congealing of historical density occurs in three stages: (1) the recognition of the body as such (an important element in *Roses in December* and in *The Act of Seeing with one's own eyes*); (2) the recognition of a typicality that places the body and person within a time and place (the soldier of World War II, Vietnam, or Mexico in 1920; the "man on the street" of 1929 or 1988; the crinoline dress that identifies the postwar period or the mini-skirt of the sixties and the punk costumes of the early eighties); and (3) the recognition of a specific person, unique to all of history, however typical or indicative they may also be. (This anchoring can, of course, be mimicked so that we lend credence to the historical authenticity of people and images when we ought not: fictions disguised as documentaries such as *Culloden*, *The War Game*, *No Lies*, *David Holzman's Diary*, and *Daughter Rite* may deceive, and anger, us for the deceptiveness with which they represent the historical world. Films like *Spartacus*, *Burn*, *Heaven's Gate*, *Ashes and Diamonds*, or *Lucia* may fascinate partly for the array of historical details they provide alongside their fictional stories.)

Though our own assumptions about the solidity and reality of the historical world may lead us to think otherwise, these forms of indexical anchorage are highly variable. What is one person's historical evidence is another person's fiction. The first two levels of referential anchorage are shared by fiction and documentary and hence provide no guarantees. The last level, where we recognize a figure as that of a specific historical personage, not only leaves open questions of how they have been recruited to a text and subjected to representations peculiar to it, it also lacks universality. Figures clearly identifiable as well-known historical personages in one viewing context may be no more than actors like any others in a different context.

A typical American audience watching Robin Spry's *Action*, about the

1970 October Crisis in Quebec when the federal government declared martial law, may feel no particular click of recognition when presented with authentic images of historical figures like Pierre Trudeau, René Levesque, Rupert Cook, or Robert Bourassa. The same audience may take Tisuka Tamasaki's *Patriamada* as a pure fiction, even though it places its fictitious trio of central characters in the thick of historical figures and events such as the demonstration of a million Brazilians in Candelaria Square on April 10, 1984, the presence of Sonia Braga in an unrehearsed interview at the Square, and the documentary footage of Governor Brizola and military President Joao Figueiredo, and even though, in a move reminiscent of Godard, the adaptation of many of the speeches by progressive Brazilian industrialist Antonio Ermirio de Morais for the fictitious character of Rocha Queiroz (who represents the progressive, prodemocratic wing of industrial capitalism within the story).[26] Similarly, a non-U.S. audience may not identify all of the historically authentic elements that occur in *Medium Cool* such as the police's use of tear gas and bullets to disperse protesters or the speeches by Hubert Humphrey and other Democrats that appear on TV screens within the film, likening them to other narrative representations of history rather than to the comparable moments of threat and danger in a film like *Harlan County, U.S.A.*

The compact we strike with the text we see has a determining effect on the historical status we lend to its images. Tied indexically to what appeared before the camera, we are left to determine if the sounds and images we attend to also occurred in or outside of social history, within the web of fabrications needed to construct the time and space of a story or within the folds of a larger history. No guarantees exist. Cues, conventions, prior knowledge, and previous experience all contribute to the compact made, but it also remains subject to change and inflection. The centripetal force of a narrative may sweep up sporadic historical referents into its imaginary realm, as it does with the historical details fondly supporting most Hollywood fictions; a more uneasy balance may exist, such as we find imaginatively proposed in Woody Allen's *Zelig* or his *The Purple Rose of Cairo*; the balance may rest on the side of the historical documentation as it does in *The War Game* or *No Lies*, at least until we comprehend the fabrication; or our compact may be entirely on the side of the historical evidence as it most commonly is in documentary. Even here, the matter cannot be put to rest since there are still those strategies of style and rhetoric that will make of evidence what they will. Our compact extends to the perspective and commentary attached to evidence and moves well beyond the subject of our immediate concern which is, simply, the nature and status of the image's indexical bond to its referent in fiction and in documentary.

We can summarize the ways in which various forms of indexicality function in relation to representations of the real by considering three quite different types of representation: television news, commercial advertisements, and pornography. Although ads and pornography may seem to be at the margins of documentary, all three rely upon establishing and guaranteeing an indexical bond between what they represent and the historical authenticity of that representation. They help us see how the three options of the indexical "sticky stuff" of the photographic emulsion and magnetic sound recording, the direct address labeling of things, and subjectivity, which can all occur in any one text, also tend to appear more often in some types of work than in others. The variables can be tabulated as follows:

Creating an Impression of Authenticity

	NEWS	PORNOGRAPHY	ADVERTISING
Indexical Bond to Historical World	*STRONG* (real events)	*STRONG* ("real" sex)	*WEAK* (putative claims)
Direct Address Labeling	*STRONG* (reporters)	*WEAK* (observation)	*STRONG* (direct address)
Subjectivity	*WEAK* (objective ethic)	*STRONG* (fantasy)	*STRONG* (utopian)
Recognition of Specific Social Actors	*STRONG* (historical figures)	*WEAK* (actors, body parts)	*VARIES* (celebrities, stereotypes, actors)

News relies on the guarantee of authentic images and the labeling of appropriate elements of what we see and hear. Pornography depends on the authenticity of its sexual representations (unsimulated and physically—if not emotionally—real, unlike the love, or sex, of most narrative films) and the subjective rendering of experience, often in the less fully character-centered manner of much documentary, stressing feeling or tone more than interior states of mind. Advertising employs indexicality at times to authenticate the testimony of witnesses as unrehearsed (even if, in fact, it is rehearsed), to persuade by means of the ethical proof or role model offered by well-known spokespeople, and to guarantee the existence of its product or service in the historical world no matter how far-fetched the world with which it is associated in the commercial. Advertising also relies on subjectivity to render the tone, rhythm, and texture of experience even if this is not intimately tied to an individual character's perspective. (A vivid comparison of the uses of subjectivity would be the astonishingly vivid and poetic treatments of liquids, ice, and citrus fruit in Slice commercials, or of the strong but soothing iconography of milk in generic dairy industry commercials in contrast to the treatment of the potentially poisonous glass of milk that Cary Grant brings to Joan Fontaine in Hitchcock's *Suspicion*.)

These general patterns in the use of the indexical bond to draw the text and the historical world into distinctive alignment also raise the question of general styles of representation and the overriding importance of realism as a documentary style akin to, but once again, different from the realism of narrative film.

VI

THE FACT OF REALISM AND THE FICTION OF OBJECTIVITY

Realism in Documentary Film

As a general style, documentary realism negotiates the compact we strike between text and historical referent, minimizing resistance or hesitation to the claims of transparency and authenticity. Along with the more specific matters of perspective and commentary, personal style and rhetoric, realism is the set of conventions and norms for visual representation which virtually every documentary text addresses, be it through adoption, modification, or contestation.

Yet, documentary realism is not the realism of fiction. It possesses antecedents and characteristics of its own; it answers to needs and suggests tensions that differ from those of narrative fiction. In fiction, realism serves to make a plausible world seem real; in documentary, realism serves to make an argument about the historical world persuasive. Realism in fiction is a self-effacing style, one that deemphasizes the process of its construction. The vision or style of a realist filmmaker emerges from the rhythms and textures of an imaginary world, from aspects of mise-en-scène, camera movement, sound, editing, and so on that seem at first natural, inevitable, or simply at the service of the story. The "vision" of the documentarist is more likely a question of voice: how a personal point of view about the historical world manifests itself. Leni Riefenstahl's paean to fascism, *Triumph of the Will,* or Grierson's tribute to fishermen, *Drifters,* voice similar but contrasting points of view: the celebration of men in action, an enchantment with ritual, and for Riefenstahl, fascination with ceremony and its power to define a common cause; for Grierson, respect for the ordinary working man and willingness to contribute to the common good. Similar stylistic techniques come into play but the end result is a distinct mix of style and rhetoric, authorial personality and textual persuasion, that differs from that of fiction.

Realism builds upon a presentation of things as they appear to the eye and the ear in everyday life. The camera and sound recorder are well suited to such a task since—with proper lighting, distance, angle, lens, and placement—an image (or recorded sound) can be made to appear highly similar to the way in which a typical observer might have noted the same occurrence. Realism presents life, life as lived and observed. Realism is also a vantage point from which to view and engage with life. In classic Hollywood narrative, realism combines a view of an imaginary world with moments of authorial overtness (commonly at the beginning and end of tales, for example) to reinforce the sense of a moral and the singularity of its import. In modernist narrative (most European art cinema, for example), realism combines an imaginary world rendered through a blend of objective and subjective voices with patterns of authorial overtness (usually through a strong and distinctive personal style) to convey a sense of extensive moral ambiguity.[1] In documentary, realism joins together objective representations of the historical world and rhetorical overtness to convey an argument about the world. Schematically, the differences look something like this:

TYPE OF CINEMA	TYPE OF WORLD	AUTHORIAL ADDRESS VIA	VIEWER WORKS TO INTERPRET
Classic Hollywood	Imaginary, Unitary	Style and Plot, Realism	A Singular Moral
European Art Cinema	Imaginary, Fragmentary	Style and Plot, Modernism	Pervasive Ambiguity
Documentary	Historical	Commentary and Perspective, Rhetoric	An Argument*

In each case a claim is made that "This is so, isn't it?" Such claims build on the indexical quality of the image and a realist style of representation. But realism in fiction relates primarily to sensibility and tone: it is a matter of an aesthetic. Realism in documentary, marshaled in support of an argument, relates primarily to an economy of logic. Realism underpins rationalism more than an aesthetic. It supports a commonsensical view of the world, one where a reasoned perspective appears to subordinate and mobilize passion for its own purposes rather than orchestrate feelings to address or resolve contradictions that remain intractable to reason or that

---

* As discussed in chapter 4, "argument" may be too emphatic and too closely aligned with rationalist discourses of sobriety. In some documentaries, rhetoric yields to poetic or evocative exposition, stressing the formal organization of the message rather than its persuasive effects; in other films representational strategies may give way to more reflexive ones, also calling greater attention to the message and the nature of argumentation than to a specific argument. This table is a general overview of documentary; it breaks down somewhat when we examine each of the four modes of documentary representation in detail.

follow from patterns of social organization (hierarchy, dominance, control, repression, rebellion, and so on). Ideological entailments follow in either case, but the starting point and emphasis differ. Documentary realism is not only a style but also a professional code, an ethic, and a ritual.

Neorealism and Documentary

Documentary realism as buttress for rationalism begins with the beginnings of cinema in the travelogues and news reports of the Lumière cameramen and others and becomes elaborated into something of an aesthetic and political agenda with Dziga Vertov, Flaherty, and the British school of documentary under John Grierson. The aesthetic dimension remained underdeveloped and even less openly discussed than in Hollywood. Documentary had a social mission to perform. It set itself apart from the spectacle and clamor of fiction, as we have already seen. But with the neorealist movement in postwar Italy, documentary realism gained a fictional ally in relation to its ethical calling as a responsible, if not committed, form of historical representation. Neorealism, too, placed its faith in reality, but sought an aesthetic more than a logic that could serve that faith. Neorealism, as a fiction film movement, accepted the documentary challenge to organize its aesthetic around the representation of everyday life not simply in terms of topics and character types but in the very organization of the image, scene, and story. Its success and limitations help sharpen the difference between fiction and documentary.

The strong causal connections of the well-made Hollywood film that motivated every line of dialogue, every off-screen glance, every camera movement and cut fell away, leaving serendipity, contingency, and chance. The time and space of lived experience gained an imaginative representation in films like *Paisa, La Terra Trema, Shoeshine, Bicycle Thief,* and *Umberto D.* Such films melded the observational eye of documentary with the intersubjective, identificatory strategies of fiction.

These films worked less to subordinate characters to the great narrative machinery of dramatic rise, climax, and resolution than to suggest an autonomy to individual lives that happened to contain small dramas of their own. Conversations faltered; actors conveyed the awkwardness of first encounters and the clumsiness of actions not rehearsed to a smooth grace. Events occurred on location, outside the conjurings of a studio set; the harsh, high contrast lighting came from whatever was available at the scene, replacing the sculpted shades of key, fill, rim, and backlights all carefully balanced, positioned, and softened; the plots left many things unexplained or unstated; events took on a laconic quality.

André Bazin captured the feel of such a realism when he wrote of the last episode in *Paisa*: "This fragment of the story reveals enormous ellipses—or rather, great holes. A complex train of action is reduced to three or four brief fragments, in themselves already elliptical enough in comparison with the reality they are unfolding."[2] The sense of a vaster, untold, and untellable realm of experience and insight, which resulted from a rhetorical ploy in classic fiction, results, here, from the narrative structure itself. In classic fiction, the sense of a greater plenitude within the bounds of the story, but beyond the reach of the narration, is what Roland Barthes dissected as a rhetorical ploy in *Sarrasine*: "And the Marquise remained pensive," uses pensiveness to signify the inexpressive, "as though, having filled the text but obsessively fearing that it is not *incontestably* filled, the discourse insisted on supplementing it with an *et cetera* of plenitudes."[3] Neorealism reconstitutes the form of subjective experience and our own halting attempts to lend narrative shape to our lives.

Robert Kolker, in his excellent study of an international, modernist cinema, takes up the attack on Hollywood that we have already heard from Dziga Vertov and Paul Rotha, but now on behalf of a new alternative: Italian neorealism.

> They did battle against what they saw as a cinema of escape and evasion, uncommitted to exploring the world, and seeking instead to palliate its audience, asking them to assent to comedic and melodramatic structures of love and innocence, of unhappy rich people and the joyful poor, of crime and revenge, the failure of the arrogant and success of the meek, played by stars of status and familiarity in roles of even greater familiarity. It was a tradition of cinema that asked little of the spectator besides assent and a willingness to be engaged by simple repetitions of basic themes, a tradition that located the spectator in fantasies that had the reality of convention.[4]

Neorealism, like documentary, but in the tradition of a socially conscious *trompe l'oeil* aesthetic, set out to establish as complete a congruence as possible between its representation of reality and the lived experience of postwar Italian reality. Within it, individual characters elude reification into objects or symbols controlled by the powers of narrative. We cannot love or hate them without first having to face the hurdle of their humanity.[5] The image and, through temporal extension, the shot, puts its quality of being "sticky stuff" at the service of historical representation. Strange juxtapositions, expressionistic techniques, the smooth continuities of classic narrative and psychological realism drop away to leave unadorned moments, strung together with something of the catch-as-catch-can, see-for-yourself quality of documentaries at the mercy of events beyond direct control. There is in this the art of artlessness, of "the refusal to make more of the image than is there, and an attempt to allow the fewest and simplest faces, gestures, and surroundings to speak what they have to say and then to move on."[6]

And yet, this refusal to make more of the image never forbade narrative structure itself and the fabrication of a fictional world. As Luigi Chiarini wrote, "Facts speak through the suggestive force of neo-realism; not as brutal documentary, because absolute objectivity is impossible and is never 'purified' out from the subjective element represented by the director."[7] At the level of the individual scene, the subjectivity might be highly muted. As Bazin notes regarding the Florence episode of *Paisa*, in which a young Italian searches the city for her fiancé only to learn of his death, this discovery strikes her like a stray bullet, as a ricochet from the news of a wounded partisan: "The impeccable line followed by this recital owes nothing to the classical forms that are standard for a story of this kind. Attention is never artificially focused on the heroine. The camera makes no pretense at being psychologically subjective."[8] But this oblique quality is precisely the aesthetic technique needed to convey the force of the accidental and tragic as they converge in this one incident. It serves to heighten a subjective, empathetic bond between viewer and character without resorting to the centripetal pull of continuity editing, subjective point-of-view shots, and a musical crescendo.

The contingent, coincidental tone of the plot replaces these centripetal alternatives for building empathy between audience and character. Fresh, raw, compellingly "real," the "ricochet" plot remains a technique aimed at audience engagement on an intersubjective plane. Such a structure, though aesthetically powerful, does not provide the "logic" documentary requires. In fact, it moves in the opposite direction, toward that asymptotic congruence with the real that documentary must avoid, ultimately, if it is to constitute a representation or argument about the real.

The controlling presence of narrative form is more directly felt in the overall structure of neorealist films. Neorealism not only provides a repertoire of techniques for giving the formal effect of representing a reality that evades the control of the filmmaker—a repertoire put to imaginative use in documentary by observational filmmakers where the argument is tacit or implied by the perspective—it also lapses back toward the very conventions at an overall level that it avoids at a local one. The documentary tradition of the victim described by Brian Winston gains powerful support from neorealism: "Flaherty's contribution to the notion of the documentary (the individual as subject, and the romantic style) when mixed with Grierson's (social concern and propaganda) leads directly to privileging 'victims' as subject matter."[9] The very objectivity of the style, its tendency to catch at a glance the drama-laden moments of ordinary lives, simultaneously stresses the passivity and endurance of the poor and working class. Fate—and, for Bazin or Flaherty, faith—loom large. Wonder, and a child-like state of reverence, lead, when things go wrong, to disappointment and resignation, or vague intuitions of conspiracy. Emotional tugs of sympathy occur at the edges of almost every scene and add up to a pathos that is close to melodrama in its intensity.[10]

The emphasis in neorealism remains with story more than argument, with a fictional representation more than a historical one, with imaginary characters more than social actors. It breaks with some of the conventions that seem to separate fiction from documentary most sharply: the compositional quality of the image; the remove of the world of the image from the domain of history; the reliance on continuity editing; the tendency to motivate, in the formal sense of providing a plausible justification for the presence of objects, characters, actions, and setting as much as possible.

Like the observational documentary, neorealism eschews overt commentary for perspective or vision but it also avoids many of the ethical issues that the taking of a perspective entails for the documentarist. Although the impression may be otherwise, the lives of the characters we follow, whether played by nonprofessionals or not, terminate at the borders of the frame and at the conclusion of the film. The filmmaker need not be accountable for what happens next to them, in history, even if the aesthetic force of the film is to suggest that we, the viewers, ought. Neorealism retains the fictional quality of metaphor: it presents a world *like* the historical world and asks that we view it, and experience the viewing of it, *like* the viewing, and experience, of history itself. Neorealism demonstrates the ways in which narrative can be placed at the service of a documentary impulse by imparting a sense of autonomy to the image and shot, by developing an elliptical style of editing, by constructing a weakly motivated, coincidental form of plot, and by placing all these devices at the service of a world rendered with objective accuracy and subjective intensity. Although qualities such as these have been taken up by documentary, neorealism remains just the other side of the boundary between fiction and fact, narrative and exposition, story and argument.

Types of Realism

Neorealism is one particular form of realism situated in history and identifiable as a movement. Realism can also be considered from a less historical perspective in terms of at least three levels or types of mimetic verisimilitude: empirical, psychological, and historical realism.

Empirical realism can be considered the underpinning for naturalism, but its potential uses extend beyond a style devoted to the accumulation of factual detail and the accurate placement of characters and objects within specific milieus. It also provides the foundation to what Michael Schudson, in his *Discovering the News*, refers to as the "naive empiricism" of journalists up until, roughly, the Treaty of Versailles and the acceptance of propaganda (or rhetorical suasion) as a convenient tool for governing. The naive empiricists did not segregate fact from value, objective from subjective; "they believed that facts are not human statements about the world but aspects of the world itself, given in the nature of things rather than a product of social construction."[11]

Ien Ang uses empirical realism in her *Watching Dallas* to describe the factual, socially recognizable aspects of the Ewing family world that exhibit its distinctive place within 1980s America: particular styles of clothing and cars, the architecture and furnishings of the Ewing mansion, even certain colloquialisms and references to topical events.[12] "Dallas" is not a show that could be considered naturalist by any stretch of the imagination, but this level of realism is clearly at work, placing melodramatic issues within a world built up from pieces of a recognizable social environment. Those historically accurate replicas and facsimiles of costumes and weapons, times and places that figure in historical narratives like *Ben-Hur*, *Spartacus*, *Revolution*, *Heaven's Gate*, and *American Graffiti* perform a similar function, anchoring the story to a ground of empirical realism at the level of fact and detail.

More generally, we might consider empirical realism to be the domain of the indexical quality of the photographic image and recorded sound. "Mere film"—isolated long takes, amateur footage, scientific recordings—these types of cinematographic record depend for their value on their indexical relationship to what occurred in front of the camera. Empirical verisimilitude provides no guarantee of historical accuracy at the higher level of significance or interpretation, as we have already noted, but it does secure an existential bond between image and referent whether it is a particular evening gown worn by Sue Ellen in "Dallas," the grimaces and hesitations of subjects in Stanley Milgram's experiments seen in *Obedience*, the 1960s cars driven by Terry the Toad, John, and Curt in *American Graffiti*, or a distinct set of gestures and spacings peculiar to the greeting rituals of Turkana women in *A Wife among Wives*. This quality of empirically accurate observation stands behind all forms of camera surveillance as well, although here, too, ambiguities immediately arise when it comes to interpretation, as the trials of Patty Hearst and John DeLorean and such fiction films as *Blow Up*, *Blow Out*, and *The Conversation* demonstrate.[13]

Empirical realism, the indexical bond of image and referent, stylistic naturalism—this family of patterns of verisimilitude does not exhaust the most common understandings of realism. A broader sense that "life's like that" arises most profoundly at a psychological rather than empirical level. Psychological realism conveys the sense of a plausible, believable, and accurate representation of human perception and emotion. In stylistic terms, it may depart sharply from the empirical underpinning it relies on for part of its "reality effect." Extreme states may be realistically represented by extreme styles—as expressionism, which attempts to convey mood and tone accurately by means of form, demonstrates. It is also at this level that a Stan Brakhage or a Picasso can claim a realist motivation to their formal innovations as ways of addressing accurately how we might perceive the world outside the constraints of social convention and routinizing experience.

Most commonly, though, psychological realism involves a recognition that characters and situations are lifelike in a universalizing way. Both "Dallas" and *An American Family*, both *Platoon* and *Dear America*, both *No Lies* and *Not a Love Story* locate themselves within concrete situations set in a specific time and place, but they also invite their audiences to acknowledge the emotional chords struck as common ones, as the ties that bind us one to another, wherever we might be. Jealousy and love, trust and fear, humiliation and anger—these emotions take off from the plane of the concrete and move toward a more universal realm of shared experience. Fictional style and documentary rhetoric strive to emphasize that commonality, to draw us in, to make the experience of characters and social actors stand for the experience we (despite myriad distinctions among this "we") might also have and that we, the audience, can have empathetically.

A prime example of a psychological realism that departed radically from any literal empiricism of time and place was the Live-Aid concert of July 13, 1985. Broadcast to as many as two billion people across the world via thirteen satellites, Live-Aid had twin, empirical roots in the actual concert by famous performers and in the empirical fact of starvation in parts of Africa. What resulted, though, was a universalization of subjectivities that allowed concern to manifest itself in an AT&T advertising jingle done for the program as a rearrangement of the previous "Reach out and touch someone" campaign. This epitomized an ethic of good intentions that reduced the starving to the abstract, nameless category of victim. Commentary or perspective on the human, political, or economic reasons for hunger fell by the wayside. Instead, someone else's misery became an occasion to celebrate our own (white, Western) compassion, a compassion conveniently in harmony with musical pleasure, television entertainment, and effortless identification by means of familiar icons. The empirical fact of hunger and the empirically authentic images of the starving were subsumed into a narrative accounting that, as African critics of the event pointed out, denied individual dignity and overlooked African forms of aid to the stricken regions, in order to reinterpret events in a universalizing, psychologically realist, and therefore highly loaded manner.[14]

Realism aids and abets empathy. The constructedness of the story or argument itself may be readily admitted. as it is in almost all musicals, cartoons, pornography, ethnography, and expository documentary, but the empathetic or identificatory bonds are very rarely treated as constructs: they transcend the fabrication, they triumph in spite of it, they rely on the complex dynamic of suspended disbelief or an acceptance of things we know to be other than what they seem. In *Singin' in the Rain*, Gene Kelly consciously arranges a sound stage to evoke a romantic setting in which to serenade Debbie Reynolds: his actions blatantly disclose what illusionism normally hides—the fabrication of scene and mood; his feelings for Cathy Seldon (Reynolds), though, are still meant to be understood as genuine. We are meant to identify with a feeling of romance, not its fabrication.

Fans of "Dallas" may say things like, "Do you know why I like watching it? I think it's because those problems and intrigues, the big and little pleasures and troubles, occur in our own lives too. You just don't recognize it and we are not so wealthy as they are."[15] The exaggeration is noted but, rather than serving to expose the fabrications of the narrative, it only stresses a *fact* of social difference across which common problems readily travel. Similarly, an appreciative viewer of *Lonely Boy* may say that the documentary lets him or her feel what it is like to be a young man who makes a Mephistophelian pact to transform himself willingly into the image of a young, "lonely boy" that will make him a star even as we see and hear how this image is carefully constructed. The image may be contrived and the text may display its own contrivances as well as those of its subjects, but the sense of realism remains: it really is like this; this is Paul Anka, as he is; he is human, like me, even if he is only what he chooses to appear to be.

A similar, enigmatic realism pervades *Don't Look Back* where the "real" Bob Dylan remains an elusive figure. We emerge with the sense of a psychologically realistic portrait of elusiveness and of the ability of performers to confuse us about their level of performance both on and off stage. An identificatory bond takes shape in relation to this complex game of self-presentation. But a complex game of levels of knowingness and quests for a "real" self are not a necessary part of documentary realism. Documentaries like the Middletown series, Fred Wiseman's studies of institutions, the majority of film biographies like *Antonia, The King of Colma, The Most, The Day after Trinity*, and social biographies like *Reds, Rosie the Riveter, With Babies and Banners* evince a more straightforward realism that promises fairly direct access to the emotional states and psychological make-up of specific individuals. Whether enigmatic and self-conscious or clear and direct, psychological realism poses as a transparency between representation and emotional engagement, between what we see and what there is.

Although psychological realism may depart from the mimicry of normal perception to convey unusual states or feelings, it is most often associated with a "zero-degree" style that minimizes its own status as part of a socially constructed reality in order to maximize the impression of direct, immediate access to the emotional reality it represents (in documentary) or fabricates (in fiction). This style derives most forcefully from the classic Hollywood film and the principles of continuity editing. Such editing relies heavily on the formal principle of motivation: each cut is justified not for its own sake but for how it serves to efface itself in order to maximize our identification with character, scene, action, and story. Maintaining consistent screen direction and eye-line matches across cuts; editing in relation to movements that draw attention away from the cut; building, in general, a sense of coherent physical orientation and spatial volume that centers on the intersubjective realm of character relations leads to the achievement of a realism that directs all of our curiosity, anticipation, empathy, and suspicion to the realm of the story itself.

A similar style prevails in many documentaries where the measure of success might be that the film draws attention to the issue it addresses and not to itself. (A documentary filmmaker once remarked to me that she considered a film successful if the audience discussed the issue and not the film.) A documentary "zero-degree" style effaces itself sometimes in favor of the domain of individuated characters (as in many observational films), generally in favor of the historical world and the representations made about it (as in many expository films where evidentiary editing illustrates the point in ways harmonious with these patterns of psychological realism). Documentary editing, evidentiary or otherwise, tends to conform to guidelines similar to those for Hollywood continuity editing, but screen direction, eye-line matches, and cuts on movement may be less strongly linked to specific characters. A great deal of the editing in the Why We Fight series and in *Triumph of the Will* (the two works share some of the same footage) achieves continuity not in relation to any one character we come to know but through cuts on movement that retain screen direction, line, volume, or eye-line match with social actors who come and go. They function, at a formal level, primarily as a pivot or relay for the flow of images (crowd scenes where people look off-screen right or left followed by cuts to what they presumably see are a prime example). These scenes also exemplify the concept of a social subjectivity where our own identification is brought into play but less with any one individual than with the sense of collective participation itself.

In fiction the sound track often assists in the creation of continuity. Lines of dialogue, music, and sound effects can all carry across a cut, helping to minimize any jarring effect since our attention is given over, in part, to the continuing sound. Documentary relies on similar sound bridges with great frequency. The most significant contrast lies in the difference between dialogue, which is normally attached to specific characters and their spatial surround, and commentary, which has the license to roam disembodied, calling on images from diverse times and places to support its points. Because of this license, documentary continuity may be less coherent in terms of geographic consistency, spatial contiguity, or orientation from the standpoint of an individuated character. The continuity instead derives from the logic of the commentary which the images illustrate, counterpoint, or metaphorically extend.[16] Jumps in time and space that would be disruptive in the fiction film unless motivated through a character (through memories, fantasy, anticipation), can, in documentaries that rely on evidentiary editing, be easily and smoothly assimilated.

Raul Ruiz, in fact, addresses part of his self-reflexive *Of Great Events and Ordinary People* to this very property of "logical discontinuity" when we hear a voice-over commentary describe how the film will construct space with shot/reverse shots of two people in the street. We see two intercut series of images of a Parisian street with an unindividuated social actor in the foreground, the series performing no other function than to construct a spatial relationship. In another instance, Ruiz, speaking in voice-over, announces, "One of the film's themes is the peculiar dispersal of documentary across a series of heterogeneous objects," after he has presented a series of still-life images whose only continuity, in this case, is their evocation of the classic oil painting genre.

The commentary in Ruiz's film reflexively demonstrates the achievement of continuity at the same time it puts the construction of such continuity on display. Unlike the forms of self-confessed constructedness found in *Singin' in the Rain* or *Lonely Boy* that still allow for subjective engagement with an imaginary or historical world, this construction arrests attention. The "heterogeneous objects" illustrate no representation of the world as much as their own representationalism. No argument is made apart from the one directed at the strategies of documentary itself. They do not allow a process of identification to continue; blockage occurs. The logic of discontinuity, the logic of evidentiary editing, and the construction of a representation are put on display such that we must attend to the display rather than the referent.

Realism in Poststructural Perspective

Through most of the seventies and the beginning of the 1980s, poststructural criticism had realism under siege. The attempt to represent a world illusionistically had the quality of deceit about it. The critique of illusionism argued that not only were we encouraged to overlook the fabrication involved but also the apparatus that supported the fabrication: the cinema as institution and industry. "The cinematic apparatus," to use a phrase of some popularity, schooled viewers to occupy passive, masculinist positions in relation to stories involving active males and desirable females. Narrative policed the flow of sounds and images, holding them "on track," insuring that their temporal succession remained motivated by the requirements of the story. Realism contributed the lynchpin to this operation, drawing our attention past the apparatus and machination, past the enunciation and its ideology of containment, past the seeing to the scene and its imaginary, lifelike autonomy. Documentary, which often seemed to endorse realism and its effects uncritically, merited little discussion since, no matter what issue it addressed, it remained a prisoner to the ideology of the style and system it used to address that issue.[17]

Other writers have contested this view, and, even more importantly, have begun to suggest viable alternatives that question whether entire aesthetic systems or specific "apparatuses" achieve this sort of unitary effect. The best poststructural critiques of realism never claimed it was monolithic in any simple way, but they also drew attention away from the specific text as a source of unique interpretive problems in order to stress its value as example or symptom of a larger mechanism. Countercritiques to this poststructural tendency have offered a better sense of what diversity in structure, strategy, and response might mean. This has come about through the introduction of different methodologies such as phenomenology and neoformalism, and through attention to previously neglected or too readily generalized aspects of realism such as the social dynamics of viewer-response, the cognitive process required to comprehend fiction films, and concepts like excess and masquerade.

A provisional and contingent, situated appraisal of realism can serve us well. The poststructural critiques of realism never offered a very satisfactory perch for the criticism of specific works: since the effects were generalizable, the individual work became a demonstration of how specific tactics achieved the same general results time after time. The possibility that specific tactics might yield significantly different results even though they continued to rely on realism for their effect did not receive systematic consideration, nor did the possibility that different viewers might have very different readings in ways that did more than demonstrate idiosyncrasy among viewers. Tania Modleski's *Loving with a Vengeance,* Ien Ang's *Watching Dallas,* and David Morley's *The "Nationwide" Audience* suggest how class, gender, nationality, and history all contribute to significant differences in how texts are understood even when the texts are fundamentally realist in their style.

The poststructuralist critique of realism may be best seen, and used, as a misplaced manifesto for the avant-garde. This critique almost always implicitly calls for what Laura Mulvey makes explicit: "The first blow against the monolithic accumulation of traditional film conventions (already undertaken by radical film-makers) is to free the look of the camera into its materiality in time and space and the look of the audience into dialectics, passionate detachment."[18] Drawing most frequently on the theories of Bertolt Brecht but giving them a strongly formalist orientation by valuing the disruption of the classic form of illusionism and psychological identification with characters, such calls tend to write off mainstream cinema and realism as retrograde. In doing so, they move outside the arena of popular culture and its debate and enter the realm of experimental art and avant-garde politics. These critiques are richly suggestive in their denunciations and proposals, in their ability to locate ideologies of sexism, racism, and class at the levels of form and apparatus even more than content, and to provoke thought about alternative systems and forms. But if we wish to apply our theory and criticism to works that remain within the popular mainstream, as most documentaries do, without driving them all into the same ideological corner, a more open-ended conception of realism and its possible effects will have to be entertained.

The most compelling critique of realism involves the subordinated position of women, not simply in terms of roles but also in terms of narrative structure. Although they may be contested and qualified, arguments for the pervasiveness of fetishistic and voyeuristic relations between a masculine viewer and a female image as object of visual pleasure have great persuasive power.[19] Such a dynamic exists in documentary as well, although since we encounter individuated characters less consistently and find both space and time less tightly organized around them, it is not so common for entire texts to be organized around such a dynamic (the films of von Sternberg and Hitchcock provide two immediate examples of fictional work that is).

In keeping with the tendency of documentary to bridge evidence and argument, the concretely historical and the conceptual generalization, the issue of gender may revolve more abstractly around the body. How shall it be represented? What subjectivity can be attached to it when it is not an imaginary construct to begin with (a fictitious character) but a participant in the historical world (a social actor)? What elements of sexism pervade not only the roles and subjectivities made available to women in the world but the representations of the body as image and Other (male or female)? And what responsibilities accrue to the filmmaker when people, made more widely known by their exposure on film, resume their lives after the film, possibly subject to insult or injury as a result of the film?

Such questions are the exception in fiction. Risk or injury to the actor, rather than the character, is required before they are posed. They arise in the aftermath of tragic incidents like the crash of the helicopter that took three lives during the filming of John Landis's portion of *The Twilight Zone*. They arose in the wake of *9 1/2 Weeks* when reports surfaced that playing her (masochistic) role had affected Kim Basinger personally. Such questions are central to documentary representations of the human body, however. In fact, the presence of such issues in pornography vividly demonstrates its status as documentary when it comes to matters of the body: what subjectivity operates in performers who engage in sexual encounters designed primarily to be documented; what self-image arises for performers whose bodies are rendered as appendages to sex organs, and what responsibilities arise when, as in most contemporary pornography, the act of intercourse takes place in defiance of almost every known precaution against the risk of AIDS? Some of these questions are taken up again in chapter 7, where we will try to show how sexism in documentary may revolve more around issues of power than pleasure, control than fascination, distance than identification.

Realism, then, has both empirical and psychological dimensions that repeat some of the objective, subjective polarities of our culture. Documentary realism also presents a pointedly historical dimension. It is a form of visual historiography. Its combination of representations *of* the world and representations *about* the world, of evidence and argument, give it the ambivalent status that the word "history" also enjoys: history is at once the living trajectory of social events as they occur and the written discourse that speaks about these events. We live in history but we also read histories. We see documentaries but we also see past them. We engage with their structures but we also recognize a realist representation of the world as it is.

Historical or documentary realism refers to those aspects of realism that are distinctive to documentary. Not only is there the empirical element of an indexical link between image and referent (usually presumed to be a historical referent), not only is there the psychological realism of subjectivity and empathetic engagement, there is also a historical realism that gives questions of style a distinctive ring in documentary.

Epistephilia

A realist style supports an illusionistic mode of reception. Even if the style of the text is blatant, the blatancy is motivated by the pathetic fallacy: stylistic vividness evokes or mimics qualities of the world represented. In fiction film, realism aligns itself with a scopophilia, a pleasure in looking, that often establishes a masculine position for the viewer where the pleasure of seeing male characters comes from recognizing and identifying with a potential ego-ideal and the pleasure of seeing female characters comes from activating sexual, voyeuristic, or fetishistic desire. Historical or documentary realism may well retain some of these characteristics but they are seldom quite so dominant as they are in fiction, where heightened attention to subjectivity brings ego-centered and libidinous relations to the fore. More likely, documentary realism supports—in addition to identification, voyeurism, and fetishism—an illusionistic mode of reception where style vivifies the physical texture and social complexity of the historical world itself.

Documentary realism aligns itself with an epistephilia, so to speak, a pleasure in knowing, that marks out a distinctive form of social engagement. The engagement stems from the rhetorical force of an argument about the very world we inhabit. We are moved to confront a topic, issue, situation, or event that bears the mark of the historically real. In igniting our interest, a documentary has a less incendiary effect on our erotic fantasies and sense of sexual identity but a stronger effect on our social imagination and sense of cultural identity. Documentary calls for the elaboration of an epistemology and axiology more than of an erotics.

The subjective dynamics of social engagement in documentary revolve around our confrontation with a representation of the historical world. What we see and hear ostensibly reaches beyond the frame into the world we, too, occupy. The subjectivity John Grierson exhorted the documentarist to support was one of informed citizenship—an active, well-informed engagement with pressing issues such that progressive, responsible change could be accomplished by governments. Other subjectivities are also possible—from curiosity and fascination to pity and charity, from poetic appreciation to anger or rage, from scientific scrutiny to inflamed hysteria—but all function as modes of engagement with representations of the historical world that can be readily extended beyond the moment of viewing into social praxis itself.

The credo that a good documentary is one that draws attention to an issue and not itself follows from the documentary's epistephilic foundations. Engagement is the aim more than pleasure. But both engagement and pleasure presuppose an exterior object, a target for cathexis or concern. And both stop short of erasing the gap between subject and object, viewer and representation, self and Other. Both, in fact, depend upon an aesthetics predicated on the preservation of distance (if not distanciation). (Were there no distance, the text itself would dissolve back into the world it represents and our engagement would be with this world directly.) The realist illusion of transparency complicates this aesthetic of distance by denying its omnipresent activity, but realism *is* a style, a form of textual construction, and a means of achieving specific effects one of which is the appearance of a nonproblematic relationship to representation itself. We seem to enter into a subjective relationship to the represented world aided, rather than impeded, by the work of rhetoric and style.

Humphrey Jennings's classic documentary, *Listen to Britain*, exemplifies the fusion of subjective and objective representation with an overall style that may seem surprisingly modern in its absence of voice-over commentary. Though apparently observational in this regard, it fractures the time and space of its scenes from the visible world of wartime Britain into a large number of dissociated impressions. The result is a poetic form of exposition rather than the observation of life unfolding before a subordinated camera. *Listen to Britain* presents situations and events in the spirit of evocation and remembrance: recognize this, remember that. In many instances the evocation is objective in the sense that the camera's gaze attaches to no specific human agency. We are not prompted to ask, "Whose gaze is this?" when we see shots of industrial Britain, of women at work bobbing and nodding in time to music coming from the factory loudspeakers, of men stoking the furnaces of a steel mill. But at other moments, we are invited to adopt the subjective perspective of specific social actors. This is most often true in the concert scenes when singers, pianists, and orchestras perform for representatives of a hard-working, culturally appreciative nation. Repeatedly the camera singles out members of the audience and then, using eye-line match editing, constructs a reverse-angle, point-of-view shot of the performance. Sometimes the pattern is the classic A/B/A where we return to the audience member to note his or her facial response to the music.

These classic forms of subjective editing depart from the unstated convention of fiction films that point-of-view shots develop around characters with whom we come to identify (by following their initiation of and response to a series of actions and events). Although point-of-view reaction shots tied to an undifferentiated audience are quite acceptable in fiction, they are not the lifeblood of narrative subjectivity, only a secondary variation. In documentary, though, such shots can become the foundation for a *social* subjectivity. This is subjectivity dissociated from any single individuated character. Our identification is with the audience as a collectivity, anchored by subjective shots that align us with specific audience members but without any prelude or follow-up that gives these particular members meaning or significance beyond their representative quality and position as emotional relays within the film.

By this means Jennings evokes the social subjectivity of viewing, or listening, itself. We share the spatial position of audience members at the wartime concerts. They become a mirror for our own act of viewing and listening to Britain. They represent pleasure that derives from shared, subjective experience. Jennings creates a form of affiliation through point-of-view editing while also emphasizing the social dimension to this affiliation rather than a strictly personal one.[20] We engage with a historical realism that represents collective experience subjectively.[21]

This relationship of subjective engagement retains, as a basic prerequisite, distance. The irony of this distance is that it supports the impression that we have achieved a direct form of engagement that has bypassed and even replaced the need for any other, more direct engagement with the world. What documentary may produce (like fiction) is less a disposition to engage directly with the world than to engage with more documentary (or fiction). The aesthetic of epistephilia, like that of scopophilia, nourishes itself, not its own alternative or replacement. We come to value and look forward to the pleasure of engaging the world at a distance, looking out through the windows of our theaters and living rooms onto a world that truly remains "out there," with all the assurance this provides about the importance of our engagement with a historical world that we have simultaneously postponed in order to attend to a representation of it. This paradoxical aesthetic will come under further scrutiny in chapter 7, where the question of distance will be pursued in relation to issues of power and control.

Authenticity and Documentary Realism

As we have seen, historical realism does not support the same aesthetic as fictional realism even though it uses many of the same techniques, nor does it necessarily support the same forms of subjectivity. By the same token, realist style in documentary plays a somewhat different function from the one it has in fiction. Fictional realism has most often been celebrated for its self-effacing quality. It allows unimpeded access to the world of the representation. And yet different directors have different styles that are noticeably distinct. These distinctions contribute to the sense of a personal vision, individual perspective, or unique point-of-view on an imaginary world. When we encounter a predominance of point-of-view shots within a fictional world heavily centered around the fascination and danger of heterosexual relationships, we enter the world of Alfred Hitchcock. When we encounter a tightly organized series of modulations in camera placement, movement, and character action along with a highly attenuated sense of emotional expressivity, we enter the world of Robert Bresson.

In documentary, style plays a somewhat different role. Individual film-makers do display different styles in a manner similar to fiction film directors and these differences define different perspectives on the world, but realist style in documentary also grounds the text in the historical world. It is a mark of authenticity, testifying to the camera, and hence the filmmaker, having "been there" and thus providing the warrant for our own "being there," viewing the historical world through the transparent amber of indexical images and realist style.

Even if a fiction film is shot on location, as neorealist and many Holly-wood films of the postwar period were, the centripetal force of the narrative draws such signs of authenticity into the woof and warp of the story; the location becomes one more signifying element, more or less well motivated in relation to the plot. In *Call Northside 777*, for example, the authentic urban locations enhance the indexical or empirical realism of the reporter/detective story while in *Niagara*, the location shots of a thunderous Niagara Falls serve to underscore the psychological realism of a story of infidelity and murder. In either case, the gravity of an imaginary world draws the location photography into its force field, holding it in place as one more element of plot and story.

In a documentary, location shooting is a virtual sine qua non. (Staged re-creations fail this basic requirement but usually adhere to strict claims of fidelity to actual events. This may also cause them to forfeit the peculiar fascination of engaging the historical world itself as Bazin noted in his comments on *Scott of the Antarctic*.) Location shots do not require motivation in relation to a plot line; instead their motivation lies in the documentary impulse itself: to represent the world in which we live. Compare, for example, two highly similar opening sequences, those of *Louisiana Story* and *Touch of Evil*.

Touch of Evil begins with a tour de force. The first shot is a long take that sets the entire film in motion. The camera travels near and across the Mexican-American border, picking up the crucial bits of evidence that will sustain the story. A man plants a bomb in a car; newlyweds Mike and Susan Vargas stroll from Mexico to the United States; Mike has broken up part of the Grandi gang; the car with the bomb contains another man and a woman, Linnekar and Zita; the two pairs of characters cross paths at the border but no one takes Zita seriously when she complains of a ticking noise in her head; a moment later the car explodes, disrupting Mike and Susan's kiss. They won't get another one until an hour and a half later, at the end of the film.

The opening draws us into an imaginary world with enormous rapidity. A highly unstable equilibrium prevails, full of darkness, uncertain borders, ambiguous and missed communications. A bomb explodes, precipitating yet further confusion and creating the experience of loss or lack that drives the remainder of the narrative forward (the loss of life and the lack of romantic solitude). The location has the air of authenticity of the sort we expect in fiction. Border towns are *like* this: danger and intrigue surround us at every step, the night is full of mystery, people live in jeopardy of wandering across lines they ought not cross, one's identity and self are put at risk. The metaphorical power of fiction operates at full force. Even though the scene was shot in Venice, California—hundreds of miles from the Mexican border—Welles has caught the likeness of a border town that we recognize as real (probably more on the basis of how such places figure in other fictions than of our own experience).

Flaherty, on the other hand, catches the thing itself: Petit Anse Bayou in Southern Louisiana (or at least a vividly indexical representation of it). Like Welles's *Touch of Evil*, Flaherty's film also features a fluid, poetic camera and a strong sense of rhythmic movement as we enter into the world of the bayou, first noting small, distinctive features such as lotus leaves and exotic birds before picking up the trail of the young boy, Alexander Napoleon Ulysses Latour (played by a nonprofessional actor from the bayou). Unlike the omniscient camera movements of *Touch of Evil* that choreograph the cold destiny of numerous characters, *Louisiana Story* brings us into alignment with the point of view of the boy. We see the bayou as he sees it and share his pleasure in the discovery of a young raccoon and his sense of excitement in a subsequent hunt.

There is more enchantment and mystery here than threat and danger. A long, graceful tracking shot passes through the swamp with its clusters of silvery Spanish moss, picking up the boy in the far background as he steers between the trees. The brightness of the grays (more silver than drab gray) contrasts with the deep black of Welles's night-for-night photography. The water may be everywhere and dark but it supports a world of brightness and wonder. Shots of an alligator prompt Virgil Thompson's score to sound deeper, more ominous notes, but when Napoleon beams an enormous broad smile at the young raccoon, the music shifts to a lighter, cheerful key: generic convention assures us this will be a happy story.

"Story" is, indeed, an apt word since Flaherty's film is barely distinguishable, structurally, from Welles's baroque fiction. Flaherty, too, relies on actors; he, too, constructs his opening to present the basic tonal values he wants to establish and to introduce a disruption, lack, threat, or disequilibrium. The explosion of the car in *Touch of Evil* is matched by the explosion of the bayou itself. The bursts of soil and vegetation abruptly interrupt Napoleon's hunt and dwarf the power of his little rifle. Just as the romantic interlude sought by Mike and Susan is massively disrupted, so too is Napoleon's relation to his beloved bayou, in this case by an oil derrick.

The largest difference is not in the fabrication of a fiction versus the found quality of Flaherty's world but in the method by which construction proceeds. Welles worked from a script, the equivalent of a composition or orchestral score; Flaherty worked without one, composing his scenes ex post facto in the editing process.

His editor, Helen van Dongen, describes the nature of this process well. She writes, "The choice of these scenes [for the opening] and their continuity was not decided upon *a priori*."[22] The selection and arrangement depended on content, spatial movement, tonal value (the shades of black and white), and emotional content, a somewhat ill-defined quality analogous to what we have identified as the goal of psychological realism. This realism grows more powerful, for van Dongen, as shots are brought into association with one another. After describing in some detail how her criteria led to the juxtaposition of the first two shots of the film, van Dongen concludes,

> The final continuity is the result of a long period of shifting scenes [camera shots], now in one combination, then in another, until first some, then more, impose their own combination upon you. When in their right combination the scenes start speaking. . . . Once the final continuity is reached one can read or analyse step by step all the factors which caused two or more images to demand to be in a certain continuity. The other way around seems to me to be impossible—unless everything, from the very first conception of the idea, is calculated beforehand.[23]

Her final sentence might be read as a tribute to documentarists like Flaherty (or, even more, their editors) who can achieve as powerful an effect as a Welles with their hands tied behind their back. Instead of planning everything in advance, a Flaherty will photograph whatever his spirit moves him to record and only later discover the rhythms, tones, values, and meanings that are at least partially embedded in the screenplay with which Welles begins. The end result is no less constructed, no less a creature of Soviet montage theory in this case than *Touch of Evil* is of a long-take style. In fact, *Louisiana Story* is in most ways far more a companion piece to *Touch of Evil* than its opposite even though it presents itself as documentary. We may affiliate Flaherty with poetic realism rather than film noir, but the fictional elements of the film are never far from sight.

What restores the documentary balance—apart from the film's own claim to historical specificity as "an account of certain adventures of a Cajun boy who lives in the marshlands of Petit Anse Bayou in Louisiana"— is the representation of indexical fidelity. The images (much more than the sound with its musical score and lack of synchronous location recording) attest to the historical facticity of the bayou. The swamp has not been fabricated or recreated. Flaherty was there. He has brought back images— poetic, wonderful images—that celebrate that land and affirm the harmony people can enjoy with it even in the midst of technological change and commercial exploitation. The location photography escapes from the relatively weak force field of a "slight narrative"[24] to achieve relative autonomy. We are invited to observe what we see not simply as an imaginary world of mystery and enchantment but as an argument about how enchantment and mystery can be discovered in the historical world itself.

As indexically forged evidence, the location photography testifies to the nature of *the* world and to the active presence of Robert Flaherty within it. He was there, in the realm of alligators and moss, pirogues and raccoons, and he now presents these images as testimony not only to a personal vision, not even simply to a perspective on the historical world, but as testimony to the very existence of such a world. What the Hollywood musical always insisted was a question of will—put on a happy face, smile and the world smiles with you—Flaherty argues is an aspect of reality itself: the world *is* a place of hope and optimism, of boyish wonder and childlike playfulness. We do not need will power so much as an ability to see. Documentary realism will help us see what we may not yet have seen, but which is there, in the world, awaiting our discovery.

Documentary realism, then, testifies to presence. The filmmaker was there, the evidence proves it. Rather than moving us into an unproblematic relationship to an imaginary world, it provides a foothold on the historical world itself. To see what we would have seen had we been there, to see what would have happened even if the camera had not recorded it—these impressions of reality anchor us to the world as it is. Rather than effortless transport into the nether regions of fantasy, documentary realism transports us into the historical world of today through the agency of the filmmaker's presence. (In television news, reporters serve as agents of presence who dutifully stand before capitols, angry crowds, blazing fires, battlefields, stock exchanges or fields of wheat; they serve as the sensory receptors of a larger news gathering organism whose head and heart remain at a remove.)

Realist style undergoes an inversion in documentary. Rather than bringing the sensibilities and vision of the filmmaker to the fore, it situates the filmmaker in the historical world. The helpless, accidental, humane, interventionist, and professional gazes testify less to a metaphorical vision of the world than to the real presence of the filmmaker in the face of historical events beyond his or her control. The shaky camera shots of *The Battle of San Pietro* seem less the artistic embellishment of a creative vision than evidence of risk and danger that required no invention. Those occasional moments in an observational film like *Soldier Girls* or the much more frequent moments in an interview-rich film like *In the Year of the Pig* when an individual looks directly into the camera and acknowledges its presence are not entirely or, often, even partially disruptive. Rather than shattering the realist illusion of an autonomous, imaginary world such moments authenticate the presence of characters (or social actors) and filmmakers on the same plane of historical coexistence.

But just as the indexical quality of the image is no guarantee of its historical authenticity (only of the bond between image and what was present before the camera), so realist style may be less a guarantee of historical reality—that which always exists *elsewhere*—than of the historically real recording of a situation or event, whatever its status. Signs of presence—of recognizable people, places, and things, of familiar sounds and images; signs of incomplete control over what occurs or how it unfolds—imperfect framing, missing elements of action, loud background noises—such signs may be less evidence of the historical world than of the real recording of a world whose status as representation remains open to question and debate. These signs testify to presence, but not necessarily to the presence of historical reality. They more properly testify to the presence of the recording apparatus and the reality of the recording process, which we, often on faith, assume to have occurred in the face of pell-mell contingency.

Thus visible, audible clapper boards and the rough beginnings or ends of takes authenticate the act of recording itself—here we are, they announce; this is what was said or done—rather than the historical authenticity of what gets recorded. The empirical fact of such recording, represented as taking place in the historical world, underpins objectivity. Whatever challenge might be put to the veracity of what is said, the reality of the recording itself, the authenticity of the representation escapes debate. The filmmaker was really there. We have a heightened sense of the actual process of recording what was said and done. This sense may be imaginatively constructed—as it is in the hand-held combat camera style of the attack on Burpelson Air Force Base in *Dr. Strangelove* or the impromptu, morally loaded exchanges between filmmaker and civil defense personnel in Peter Watkins's *The War Game*—or it may be more securely rooted historically—as it is in *Harlan County, U.S.A.* or *The Sorrow and the Pity*. It is an *impression* of authenticity based on the reality of representation more than the representation of reality.

Realist style offers indexes of a filmmaker's presence on the scene through the metaphoric nature of the camera gaze, his or her direct acknowledgment by filmed subjects (most frequently masked in observational films and emphasized in interactive ones), the use of voice-over commentary, location sound, and dialogue. As much as it presents a personally inflected world, style demonstrates how the historical world inflects the person. Realist style acts as evidence of physical presence in the world, of the authenticity of sound and image, and of the filmmaker's limited power over the world with which he or she engages.[25]

Realism, Distance, and the Professionalization of Objectivity

Realism requires distance. As we have already seen, realism supports an epistephilia that arouses curiosity about objects whose knowability is limited only by the physical capacities of camera and filmmaker. The enforcement of distance may therefore seem quite weak. But the documentary apparatus—if we might apply that word, somewhat tentatively—persists by never collapsing the distance between itself and the world reported. Television news is a prime example, and closer to being an "apparatus" than the work of an individual like Flaherty. Reporters bring back news of the world, but neither they nor we, the viewers, are encouraged to tarry. Our engagement is meant to be with the news *show*, with the flow of events chronicled or dramatized. To linger, to experience the full flowering of empathy and identification, to make an issue one's own threatens not only to transform news into propaganda (or civic mobilization), but also to eradicate the precondition and *raison d'être* for its existence. Without distance, epistephilia yields to praxis: to the pleasure of active, participatory engagement, practical rather than practicable involvement.

To erase epistephilic distance and engage the world directly, as a participant, is not the same as erasing questions of representation. People represent themselves, and others, just as texts and social actors do. What happens when we engage in praxis may still occur within an institutional discourse or signifying practice, a regulatory set of codes or conventions. Praxis, though, eliminates the distinctive bounds of textual representation. But texts often guard against their own elimination by encouraging a continuous, self-contained cycle of production and consumption that postpones any more direct form of praxis. Desire and need become deeply invested in textual representation. A compulsion to repeat draws us to another text rather than to the historical world to which such texts may refer. This is true not only for us, the viewers, who come to documentary with our own expectations and a desire to fulfill those expectations in terms of a representation and argument, but also for the filmmaker whose professional presence in the world requires the perpetuation of distance.

Unlike activists, who make a cause their own, filmmakers, like anthropologists, must retain a measure of remove, no matter how compassionate or dedicated they may be. Their loyalty remains divided: between making representations and taking on the issues represented. Their ritual compulsion is to repeat the act of representation and forge it into a profession and career. Though their presence is required by the historical world, their allegiance to it is equivocal: part belonging to the codes and conventions of documentary and the institutional bonds these engender, part to the struggles and dilemmas, prospects and qualities of the world they address.

Objectivity, for example, requires an interpretive community, a cohort of like-minded individuals who will have some agreement about the terms and conditions that guarantee this form of distanced presence in the world. No one individual could institute a regime of objectivity, nor adumbrate the conventions governing a common form of subjectivity such as expressionism. All texts are overdetermined and historically situated, including this one. Accountability is also splayed: between those with whom one shares a professional ethic and a practitioner's craft and those about whom one shapes a film or text. These divisions accompany the act of representation. They take on particular pointedness for the documentarist who addresses aspects of the historical world and, in doing so, forgoes other forms of more direct engagement.[26]

Those who do otherwise tend to be exceptions, by definition. These are individuals who resort to film or video to convey to others what matters deeply to themselves. The issue takes precedence. Film is but a tool. A recent example is the production of *Sadobabies*, a film about runaway teenagers in San Francisco who, having escaped from parental abuse, form an extended family of their own in an abandoned high school. May Petersen, the filmmaker, has used the film to lobby city officials. Her goal: to establish a no-questions-asked shelter for runaways in San Francisco.[27]

Such cases are rare since those who are committed to a particular issue are more likely to enlist the help of professional filmmakers than to take up that task themselves. Perhaps the most notable example of such a combination of commitments in the last few decades was Newsreel in its early years. For most participants in the filmmaking collective, the primary commitment was to the political issues and leftist movement of the sixties. Over time, as the need for refined filmmaking skills became more evident and the dilemmas of divided loyalty more pointed, Newsreel experienced the same kind of division that had occurred with the New York Film and Photo League in the 1930s: those with the strongest commitment to film remained, hoping to make more ambitious films, and others, with primary commitments to the issues of the day, aligned themselves with specific political groups or parties.

Objectivity and Documentary Discourse

Many documentary filmmakers regard themselves as a polity of one. They do not belong to a news gathering apparatus such as the ones operated by the major television networks, wire services, or government sponsored agencies like BBC, CBC, RAI, or ORTF. They are not compelled to adhere to the policies and guidelines that such organizations may codify. They do, however, belong to a looser fraternity of the like-minded. Lacking institutional authority, this like-mindedness can be other than homogeneous. Sharp differences can arise, vivid debates may ensue. Advocates of an observational style may find the tactics of an interactive filmmaker exceedingly noisome and those who feel the documentarist's first principle is to direct attention to an issue, not the film, may express great exasperation at the seemingly irreverent, formal self-consciousness of the reflexive filmmaker. If a community, documentary filmmaking is not a coherent one. Within distinct subcategories, however, the sense of shared purpose and common principle can be quite strong.

To a considerable extent these communities of practitioners have shared a belief in the importance of objectivity. The word, though, may have different shades of meaning as we move from one community to another, being most vividly and rigorously defined by the codes and constraints of the institutional agencies and most sharply challenged by reflexive practices. For a news gathering and disseminating apparatus like a television network, objectivity provides a legal safeguard against libel. It helps differentiate documentary from fiction (particularly that small slice of documentary known as news but also investigative or background reports). Objectivity means reporting what was said and done in the historical world, and if it was said by or done by other major institutional apparatuses, most notably, the state, objectivity means passing on official accounts with a minimum of skepticism or doubt. (Should doubt later be substantiated, as it was with Watergate, the My Lai massacre, the Iran-Contra affair, or the cases of the "disappeared" in Argentina, this basic posture allows such events to be described as anomalies and exceptions attributable to the corrupt few rather than to political institutions in their totality.)

Although a "naive empiricism" once seemed adequate—when things were what they seemed and people said what they meant—it was no longer so in the period following World War I. The barrage of propaganda unleashed during the war by the Committee on Public Information in the United States under George Creel, beginning in 1917, culminated in the Treaty of Versailles, which more than one commentator has chosen as the symbol of a new age of social relations based not on the "iron cage" of totalitarian controls but on a "soft machine" of dissimulation, manipulation, and disinformation.

Objectivity has its virtues for the individual reporter as well. In a world of half-truths and staged events, it can offer self-defense. The reporter who passes on the official remarks of a public figure, when he may also know, but be unable to prove, that the remarks are not altogether accurate, has done his job all the same. (This adherence to the denotative and literal is also a prime defense of schizophrenics in the face of mixed messages and double-binds.) Objectivity requires accuracy of description, not interpretive acumen. The reporter who reports the facts, and nothing but the facts, cannot be held accountable if those facts later prove to be manufactured. Like the indexical image that preserves what occurred before the camera with fidelity—be it fictive or historical—the reporter's prose captures the facts as received—be they designed to dissimulate or the raw stuff of spontaneity. The reporter is a conduit, shielded from criticism by a professional gaze and an ethic of objectivity.

As a member of a professional community, good standing among one's peers depends more heavily on accuracy than explanation, on adherence to an internal code of objectivity than on offering correct interpretations that may contradict the ones given by historical figures. If Senator Joseph McCarthy asserts that the State Department housed 159 communists and their sympathizers, or 92 or 51, then this is what an objective reporter is obliged to pass along, personal doubts notwithstanding. (To write, "Senator McCarthy made the ridiculous and totally unsubstantiated claim today that . . ." or "No independent evidence can be found to substantiate Senator McCarthy's inflammatory claim today that . . . " would put the author in the position of determining what is and is not fact. In a world where such determinations have become exceedingly difficult, better to present the facts, not challenge the legitimate institutions of the culture, and let others with less to lose provide the divergent interpretations or countervailing details.)

In such a situation documentary realism vouches for the reporter's presence. Gestures, pauses, atmosphere, tone—the glistening surface of appearances is rendered only as one who was present could. Because the reporting agent effaces itself and thereby gives the impression of expunging bias, documentary realism validates the historical authenticity of what was said and witnessed, even if it does not assess it. Realism not only supplies evidence about the world, it also gives evidence of the filmmaker's loyalty to a community of cultural representatives: documentarists, journalists, reporters. Documentary realism testifies to the institutionalization of observers observing. What might have seemed an odd form of detachment becomes a professional mode of social engagement. The realist code of location photography and sound, of physical presence "on the scene" and the various forms of documentary gaze that follow from it, of style and rhetoric that constitute an argument about the historical world within the bounds of permissible conventions—these all supply evidence that works to authenticate the subject matter, legitimate the filmmaker or reporter, and validate the canon of objectivity. That this validation is self-confirming need not destroy its effect: the repetition of a ritual or approach can become its own justification, generating a sense of trust based on the naturalness with which what could be questioned is instead taken for granted. This is often precisely what we mean by common sense.

If the meaning of objectivity extends beyond impartiality to an emphasis on the isolated fact, the recounting of discrete events, a commonsensical mode of explanation, and the avoidance of any totalizing social theory (be it theological or secular, reactionary or radical), then considerable room for alternatives remains. Walter Lippmann and John Grierson were among those whose position was not very different in principle from George Creel's fervor for wartime propaganda: facts are little more than bare bones; the modern world has a plethora of them. What the average citizen needs is not a steady stream of facts, passed on by organizations fearful of going out on a limb, but interpretation, which might in other arguments be called editorializing, persuasion, orientation, ideology, propaganda, or, as here, representation.

It is into this interpretive arena that most independent documentarists have stepped. Objectivity moves into an easier balance with at least some elements of subjectivity. Personal expression is possible along with testimony to one's presence in the world. The subjective engagement of the viewer becomes a matter of rhetorical concern to the filmmaker (as Helen van Dongen's commentary on the opening scene of *Louisiana Story* indicates), and the elaboration of an argument becomes overriding.

Interpretation builds on facts, however. Its forms and its canons of validation depend upon referentiality, an evidentiary base, and documentary logic. Argumentative rhetoric must adhere to at least some strictures regarding an objective stance even if subjective, interpretive, or emotional elements enter the picture. Like Walter Lippmann, Curtis MacDougall, author of the widely used textbook, *Reporting for Beginners* (later retitled *Interpretative Reporting*), wanted reporters to orient their readers to the meaning of events by interpreting them: "the most successful newspaper men and women of the future will be those with . . . the ability to avoid emotionalism and to remain objective, descriptive styles, the power of observation, and, above all, the ability to comprehend the meaning of immediate news events in relation to broader social, economic, and political trends."[28]

Ethical proofs have consistently relied upon the avoidance of emotionalism as evidence of fair-mindedness, coupled with spontaneous amazement, disbelief, fear, horror, amusement, and so on as evidence of a "natural" or commonsensical human response to events that call for such display. (This emotionalism, of course, was precisely, what was absent in the initial description of the explosion of the space shuttle Challenger and so abundant in the eyewitness radio account of the Hindenberg disaster). Stars and celebrities like Sally Field, Mary Ann Hartley, Lily Tomlin, and Kenny Rogers, who spoke on behalf of the victims of Ethiopian famine, did so with clear compassion. Their already established status together with their heartfelt response lent ethical proof and legitimacy to a specific type of charity: the avoidance of political rhetoric or action; indifference to causal factors in favor of the dramatic effects of famine; stress on urgency and immediate aid (albeit short-lived); appeal for individual witness of a symbolic form (giving money for redistribution as food but leaving institutions and power untouched); and emphasis on unity, common cause, and collective well-being that provides a social reward for personal altruism.

Other constraints on documentary logic include a presumption in favor of verifiable facts; the accurate documentation of claims or interpretations; the selection of institutionally accredited experts and the identification of any vested interest that may pertain; the balanced presentation of opposing views (usually restricted to those views held by representatives of dominant or legitimated institutions); the reliance on historically bona fide social actors, places, situations, and events rather than fictional composites or reconstructions (unless the fictions are identified and restricted to what can be shown to have a historical basis); the avoidance of the direct advocacy of specific measures if it might seem to subordinate a report to a totalizing theory; and a respect for those other codes and rituals (like the constraints of realism in the representation of expressive states and subjective experiences) deemed appropriate by the interpretive community of like-minded documentarians.

These constraints operate in Marlon Riggs's documentary about racial stereotyping, *Ethnic Notions*, for example. The restrained, dignified voice-over commentary conveys distress at the continuation of stereotypes and revulsion at their virulence. The evidence of stereotypes derives from authentic artifacts such as ashtrays shaped like Negroid lips and clips from popular films that illustrate the Sambo, Mammy, or Coon caricatures. Experts are identified by institutional affiliation and convey their personal opposition to the practice of stereotyping even as they provide social and historical explanations for its occurrence. No one speaks in defense of black stereotypes but the experts' explanations offer a form of balance. They shift the level of the problem from personal sickness, or recrimination, to a question of broader social understanding. And, like many other historical documentaries made primarily for public television, *Ethnic Notions* adheres to the basic tenets of the expository mode of documentary representation, especially with respect to the unfolding of a documentary logic by means of evidentiary editing. (By contrast, Riggs's *Tongues Untied*—on black gay experience—shatters conventions in complex and unexpected ways.)

Observing Observers

These representational constraints, which impinge upon and shape documentary realism into something distinct from fictional realism, also affect the documentarians themselves in important ways. Like narrative convention, these constraints provide a centripetal force field that draws practitioners in and keeps them in place. It is clearly a place apart, separated off by loyalty to a code, ethic, and ritual that revolve around the social practice of representing the historical world.

If all social activity involves processes of communication and exchange that occur within culturally determined or inflected codes, frames, or contexts, then the idea of standing apart in order to represent and interpret what occurs elsewhere is not a radically distinct or peculiar activity. The assignment of this task of standing apart to experts of various kinds— historians, critics, sociologists, journalists, documentarians, and so on— with attendant questions of hierarchy, authority, power, and legitimacy is much more prominent in oligarchic societies that are also democratic, where institutions or discursive formations arise that have responsibility, and power, for communication, social representation, and interpretation. (Institutions like the press and the communities of historians or documentarians have something like "observer status" but they also acquire a power of their own.) The social and historical conditions that spawn a set of potentially competing interpretive elites require a study of their own. It is far from natural and obvious to have organized groups of observers and interpreters, although it may often seem to be precisely that. Questions of interpretation therefore bring us face to face with the politics of representation.

Representation that involves arguments (or interpretations) of the historical world necessarily draws us into the realm of law: into those patterns of regulation and control that give a social system coherence. Representations moralize about this law: for or against, conservative or liberal, reactionary or radical. What Hayden White says of the historian applies quite well to the documentarian as well: "The more historically self-conscious the writer of any form of historiography, the more the question of the social system and the law which sustains it, the authority of this law and its justification, and threats to the law occupy his [sic] attention."[29] Without issues of law, legitimacy, and authority, the self-consciousness or sense of detachment that seeks to represent the historical world as rhetorical argument or interpretation would not exist. White's assessment of Richerus of Reims applies, interestingly enough, to documentarists as well: "We can legitimately suppose that his impulse to write a narrative of this conflict [one which involved him directly] was in some way connected with a desire on his part to represent (both in the sense of writing about and in the sense of acting as an agent of) an authority whose legitimacy hinged upon the establishment of 'facts' that were of a specifically historical order."[30] The rights to representation and authority become central issues in this "place apart" from which the documentary tradition stems. These issues also confront the critic or theorist. I, too, argue for and against. I, too, have a social purpose, a desire to address issues and concepts in documentary as a historical participant in a process of change. If reflexivity identifies the place apart from which scholarship originates, it is not to close the circle of formal reflexivity, but to open the process of political reflexivity by locating this place apart within the compass of history itself.

John Grierson first put the issue in civic terms. The filmmaker demonstrated his own civic responsibility by helping others orient themselves to the issues of the day. It might happen, as it did in *Smoke Menace*, that the argument presented coincided with the interests of a sponsoring agency (in this case the British gas industry, which wanted to convert coal-burning furnaces and fireplaces to gas ones). Grierson saw this as a harmonious marriage of public interest and self-interest. In his terms the objective of films like *Smoke Menace*, *Housing Problems*, and *Industrial Britain* was to demonstrate the beneficence of government and industry "so that people would accept their industrial selves, so that they would not revolt against their industrial selves"[31] or, regarding the task of the film unit at the Empire Marketing Board, "Its [E.M.B. publicity, education, and propaganda] effect in six years (1928–33) was to change the connotation of the word 'Empire.' Our original command of peoples was becoming slowly a cooperative effort in the tilling of soil, the reaping of harvests, and the organization of a world economy."[32] Like Richerus of Reims, Grierson seeks to establish "facts" of a specifically historical order, ones that further the aims of industry and government.

The politics of representation are clearly joined here. Recent critics of Grierson's political agenda have even disputed the ennobling, civic-minded sense of mission in which he attempted to cloak the British documentary. Peter Morris, in his thoroughly researched essay, "Re-Thinking Grierson: The Ideology of John Grierson," locates Grierson's thought squarely within turn-of-the-century neoconservatism that deemphasized romantic individualism and international capitalism (in deference to the nation-state), stressed the need for central coordination and control through a technocratic and managerial elite (organized by the state), and distrusted reasoning with the masses, who lack the capacity to act in their own best interest.[33] Grierson's vision of a documentary film movement would be one such managerial elite, designed to provide the guidance the masses could not provide for themselves. Rather than the progressive, socially conscientious movement he styled himself as representing, Grierson's Hegelian devotion to a state that guaranteed an order the average man could not sustain let alone create actually underpinned a documentary film movement that might be better understood as "authoritarian with totalitarian tendencies." In either case, interpretation simultaneously introduces questions of power and authority.

This represents a different perspective from one that regards the canons of objectivity and the reportorial as an odd form of alienation, disenfranchisement, or social paralysis. Georg Lukacs once wrote, "The journalist's 'lack of convictions,' the prostitution of his experiences and beliefs is comprehensible only as the apogee of capitalist reification."[34] Lukacs also argued that a preference for description over narration occurs when the felt possibility for action diminishes. Zola only describes the horse race in *Nana* as a piece of verisimilitude, whereas Tolstoy narrates the horse race in *Anna Karenina* as an integral part of his characters' lives.[35]

Engagement at these subjective, identificatory levels has always been the goal of classic realist fiction, and what Georg Lukacs says about the difference between Zola and Tolstoy has bearing for the difference between a news report and a documentary:

> In Scott, Balzac or Tolstoy we experience events which are inherently significant because of the direct involvement of the characters in the unfolding of the characters' lives. We are the audience to events in which the characters take active part. We ourselves experience these events.
>
> In Flaubert and Zola the characters are merely spectators, more or less interested in the events. As a result, the events themselves become only a tableau for the reader, or, at best, a series of tableaux. We are merely observers.[36]

Lukacs's distinction, though, misunderstands the ways in which historical representation always operates within a political frame where power
and knowledge are inextricable one from the other. Descriptions, empirical recountings, observational modes are not partial or inadequate versions
of more totalizing practices, not failed Marxisms, but alternative political
perspectives, presenting arguments and offering interpretations even if
they appear to lack conviction or to anaesthetize engagement.

News reportage urges us to look but not care, see but not act, know but
not change. The news exists less to orient us toward action than to perpetuate itself as commodity, something to be fetishized and consumed.
Even though news has never shunned the dramatic or ignored narrative
and myth, it employs them in a context where the process of framing,
setting an agenda, and promoting certain assumptions over others foster
the position of viewer-observer.[37] The enormous emphasis on electoral
politics in the news, for example, only underlines the point: candidates
and races are objects of spectacle and dramatic structure more than the
focal point for participatory engagement. In fact, only half the eligible
voters in the United States vote in presidential elections. Everyone, however, is represented as an active participant in such elections, a subject
position adequately served, apparently, by attending to the news rather
than voting.

Lukacs's description of Scott, Balzac, and Tolstoy proposes another form
of engagement that is more participatory. We move from observation as a
form of alienation and commodity reification to a form of empathetic
involvement. To experience is to become involved. Experience provides
the ground for knowledge and ideology. Epistephilia shades toward gnosti-
philia, a term we might use for knowledge not dependent on distance,
objectivity, and reasoned analysis alone but also on empathy, identification,
feeling, tone, and sensibility.[38] Typicality (the congruent resonance between the local and the global, the specific and the general in terms of
historical process and social subjectivity), the affective engagement of the
viewer with social tensions and pleasures, conflicts and values—move the
viewer away from the status of observer toward that of participant. Something is at stake. Namely, our very subjectivity within the social arena. The
move beyond observation to experience (coupled with understanding and
interpretation, discovery and insight), opens up a space for contestation.
Lukacs located the beginning of this process in experiential qualities of
narration, which offer both pleasure and recognition, involvement and
awareness simultaneously. Brecht held out for reason joined to passion,
Lukacs for insight embedded in classic narrative structure. In either case,
ideological struggle and political change follow from changes of habit that
art, and the art of documentary, can provoke.

Always a representation and an argument in the sense meant here,
objectivity as code, ethic, and ritual stands at some remove from "the truth."

Its limitations may be well known to its critics, and even to its adherents. Rituals do not have to be believed to be practiced. They may have values other than the guarantees they promise rhetorically or by implication. Clearly, in observational documentaries, for example, objectivity as a non-intrusive, nondidactic mode of representation does not guarantee any sort of value-free or unambiguous access to situations and events. Such an objective approach eschews commentary but remains fully laden with perspective, allowing films by Leacock, Pennebaker, Wiseman, Churchill and Broomfield, MacDougall, and others to establish moral positions, incorporate subjective strategies, deploy rhetorical devices, and convey a personal style or voice. They may do so in ways that continue to make them unlike fictions, but they also share with fiction those very qualities that thoroughly compromise any rigorous objectivity, if they don't make it impossible. This impossibility is also evident in the more standardized and enforced objectivity of journalism.

Objectivity has been under no less siege than realism and for many of the same reasons. It, too, is a way of representing the world that denies its own processes of construction and their formative effect. Any given standard for objectivity will have embedded political assumptions. In broadcast journalism, these might include belief in the legitimacy of capitalism, the state, the nuclear family, and the expert; in the distrust of dissenters and protesters, and certainly of the use of violence unless authorized by the state. (In this case even terrorism can then become legitimate: witness reportage of the policies of the PLO, Iran, and Libya versus coverage of the United States military's air raid on Khaddafy's home in Tripoli.) In documentary, these assumptions might also include belief in the self-evident nature of facts, in rhetorical persuasion as a necessary and appropriate part of representation, and in the capacity of the documentary text to affect its audience through its implicit or explicit claim of "This is so, isn't it?"

Finally, objectivity may operate, particularly for those who work within the institutional apparatuses that enforce its practice (like television networks or major newspapers) as a "strategic ritual." Rather than a sign of alienation or an anomic social order per se, objectivity has a functional value for the individual: it helps defend him or her against mistakes and criticism. As Schudson notes, "In this view, objectivity is a set of concrete conventions which persist because they reduce the extent to which reporters themselves can be held responsible for the words they write."[39] For the individual documentary filmmaker, though, it is precisely the opportunity to be responsible, to respond to the world through argumentative representation, that motivates and sustains a position requiring, simultaneously, engagement and distance. Objectivity functions more as rhetoric than ritual although here, too, it may also help forge a collective identity among those with a shared sense of how objectivity should inform a text (such as observational filmmakers).

The Elusiveness of Objectivity

Objectivity has at least three meanings that bear on the discussion of documentary representation: (1) An objective view of the world is distinct from the perception and sensibility of characters or social actors. The objective view is a third-person view rather than a first-person one. It corresponds to something like a normal or commonsensical but also omniscient perspective. (2) An objective view is free of personal bias, self-interest, or self-seeking representations. Whether first or third person, it conveys disinterestedness. (3) An objective view leaves audience members free to make their own determination about the validity of an argument and to take up their own position in regard to it. Objectivity means letting the viewer decide on the basis of a fair presentation of facts.

The first, formalist definition is useful for differentiating whose view a camera represents. The camera can represent itself as a technology, a photomechanical, scientific recording of what occurred before it, but it can also represent, more anthropomorphically, the view of a character (through point-of-view shots, for example), or of the viewer (when we share the point of view of characters), or the authoring agent (when it demonstrates traits of omniscience or foreshadowing, for example, through selection of detail or high-angle views). This definition, however, leaves a considerable amount of murky ground precisely where we might think the term objectivity would offer clarity: a great many expressive, and subjective, effects can be achieved without attaching them to characters, viewers, or the authoring agent as such. The systematic difference between an "objective" shot that shows a character in the frame and an objective shot that shows the same thing, not from the point of view of the character, but in the mood or style that corresponds to that character's sensibility is also vague. This definition also fails to differentiate sharply between the point of view of the filmmaker or the narrating/expository agent (the enunciating mechanism itself) and non-character-based views generally. We may say the view does not "belong" to a character and does not convey his or her particular sensibility, but the view may be more or less indicative of the authoring agent's perspective. It may range from the highly matter-of-fact to the highly expressive. Our ability to assign a camera view to a character to determine whether it is subjective or objective proves singularly unhelpful in relation to less formal, more socially pertinent questions of objectivity.

The second definition—the absence of perceived bias—presupposes some englobing framework that can subsume personal bias and self-interest. This framework is, for individual filmmakers, the interpretive community of filmmakers that share a style, conventions, and a perspective, and—for journalists and reporters, along with anthropologists, sociologists, ethnographers, and other members of the scientific community—it is those institutional structures that regulate and control the shape of news and interpretation (networks, publishers, universities, and professional societies).

What objectivity masks in this case is the specific point of view of institutional authority itself. Not only is there an inevitable concern with legitimation and self-perpetuation, other, more historic and issue-specific forms of self-interest and partiality may also prevail, often in the all-the-more-powerful form of unacknowledged predispositions and assumptions rather than stated interests. The disposition toward invasive surgery and strong regimens of drug therapy in American medicine compared to a British and European preference to let the body heal itself would be one example; the abhorrence of terrorism in American journalism as an irrational, hateful practice with no justifiable origins compared to the disposition toward representing it as the last resort of the dispossessed and disenfranchised, in Middle-Eastern reporting, would be another.

The third meaning—of a non-propagandistic openness allowing the viewer to decide for him- or herself—may still acknowledge that discourse, even if objective, seeks to persuade and convince. It does so, though, without recourse to patently biased arguments and without attempting to maneuver the viewer into a singular position of support for one of many alternative positions. Objectivity stands at a remove, above the fray. The point of view or argument advanced may clearly favor one position over others, but the choice of concurrence is not foreclosed. At the far extreme from the objective text, then, stands that form of exhortation known as propaganda.

This conception, too, is flawed. The free choice allowed the viewer is only partly that. Rhetoric remains at work, even in the domain of the most intensely scientific discourse. Propaganda is not as far away as one might think; ideology is always in the air, and the "free subject" is itself a concept of debatable soundness. As Paul Feyerabend notes in his discussion of Galileo's defense of a Copernican universe, the task was not to effect a move from myth to science, or from the fantastical and misguided to the rational and true. If anything, it seemed the other way around: a tried and trusted, scientific system had to be overthrown in favor of one with coherence, simplicity, elegance, and explanatory power but also with untested implications and a strong hint of the absurd. Any conversion would have to be brought about "*by irrational means* such as propaganda, emotion, *ad hoc* hypotheses, and appeals to prejudices of all kinds" (italics Feyerabend's).[40] And Thomas Kuhn adds, in his own study of science as a self-perpetuating community like any other, "We shall not, I suggest, understand the success of science without understanding the full force of rhetorically induced and professionally shared imperatives like these. Institutionalized and articulated further . . . such maxims and values may explain the outcome of choices that could not have been dictated by logic and experiment alone."[41]

We are reminded finally of Roland Barthes's persuasive description of denotation, and the realm of objectivity which it supports, as "the last of the connotations."[42] It has a power and an effect that is real even if its claims for privileged status are not. Objectivity—like the documentary that fails to locate itself in relation to the historical world and presents an argument that appears to fall from the sky, from some place apart from the historical process of social construction and communication of which it is an inevitable part—has the appearance of an existential paradox. It appears to certify that descriptions, interpretations, explanations, and arguments remain above the fray. Objectivity distinguishes itself from the system of communication and exchange of which it is a part. It does not take on the subjective, expressive, ideological colorations present in the discursive web of social relations of which it is a part.

The impression of disinterestedness is a powerful reassurance and a seductive ploy. What objectivity itself cannot tell us is the purpose it is meant to serve since this would undercut its own effectiveness (lest that purpose be one that adopts the shroud of objectivity itself as a final purpose: the pursuit of truth, the quest for knowledge, the performance of service for the common good). And yet what we need to know above all else about this complex and highly persuasive form of discourse is the purpose to which it is put. When the solid ground that appears to form its base is shorn away, when the empirically verifiable fails to answer more fundamental questions of assumptions and goals, we return once again to the shakier, less comforting ground where human subjectivities prevail and purpose is all.

Part III

Documentary Representation
and the
Historical World

VII

PORNOGRAPHY, ETHNOGRAPHY, AND THE DISCOURSES OF POWER

Christian Hansen, Catherine Needham, Bill Nichols

When a Difference Becomes Otherness *

The preceding chapters have attempted to draw out the similarities and differences between documentary and fiction. They have stressed the ways in which documentary stands for a distinctive relation to the historical world. They have tried to avoid ontological claims that would privilege this relation in terms of its truth value. Yet documentary trades heavily on its own evidentiary status, representative abilities, and argumentative strategies. If truth stands as a cultural ideal or myth within a larger ideological system that attaches it to matters of power and control, it also stands in close proximity to documentary. The scientific use of film brings this relation to the fore and perhaps nowhere more than in ethnographic film where the criteria of scientific investigation butt up against the narrative, poetic, expressive, and subjective dimensions of documentary.[1] In essence, this alliance of science and documentary, especially ethnographic film, within the discourses of sobriety suggests that the highly problematic representations of the Other in fiction will be overcome. The parallels between ethnography and pornography described here suggest otherwise.

Issues of truth and science may seem far removed from the nether world of pornography, but such films depend heavily on their claims to give us "truthful" representations of sexual performance. What is more remarkable is the extensive parallelism between ethnography, which we may initially assume has better represented other peoples and their cultures than narrative fiction films have, and pornography, which has seldom done anything but represent women as the objects of male desire. One avenue by which we may begin to assess the proximities and parallels between

---

* Please see the Acknowledgments for a description of the evolution of this chapter.

pornography and ethnography in terms of documentary representation is to examine the figure of the Other.

Patterns of hierarchy engender the figure of the Other. An economy that manages the circulation of this figure of Otherness comes into play. It involves distance as control and difference as hierarchy (*economy*: from the Greek *oikonomos*, household manager).[2] This particular "home economics" guarantees superiority and autonomy but does so, paradoxically, in relation to a fundamental dependency (on the Other) from which there is no escape. The Other becomes the precondition for the imaginary assurances of sublime independence. Those on each side of the divide must enjoy or endure a unity that erases a multitude of differences in the name of eternal constancy. As Sartre observed in his seminal *Anti-Semite and Jew*, the construction of the Other serves to support a sense of solidity and impenetrability in place of the contingencies of indefinite approximations and difference:

> We have demonstrated that anti-Semitism is a passionate effort to realize a national union *against* the division of society into classes. It is an attempt to suppress the fragmentation of the community into groups hostile to one another by carrying common passions to such a temperature that they cause barriers to dissolve. Yet divisions continue to exist, since their economic and social causes have not been touched; an attempt is made to lump them all together into a single one—distinctions between rich and poor, between laboring and owning classes, between legal powers and occult powers, between city-dwellers and country-dwellers, etc., etc.—they are all summed in the distinction between Jew and non-Jew [or Self/Other—BN]. This means that anti-Semitism is a mythical, bourgeois representation of the class struggle, and that it could not exist in a classless society.[3]

Both ethnography and pornography benefited from the turn against a Victorian insularity and public prudery that had emphasized the disciplinary requirements of good breeding (in both senses): to be one of Us required demonstrable separation from Them. Etiquette, dress, and demeanor joined with specific forms of social knowledge and cultural ideal to distinguish Otherness on an everyday and persistent level. But Victorian distinctions began to crumble at the turn of the century. High modernism and its *épater la bourgeoisie* current (as manifested in surrealism, dadaism, and even in the Soviet constructivist eroticization of industry and machine); the suffragette movement; changes in fashion, music, and public conviviality throughout the twenties; anthropology with the ascent of participant observation in the field in the early 1920s and the great African expeditions beginning with the Dakar-Djibouti mission of 1931-32; the growth of urban centers with their cosmopolitanism and anonymity; and the increasing importance of that great socioeconomic "in between" known as the middle class with its disregard for tradition and its openness to transformation—these and other factors promoted a redrawing of fault lines and alliances within the social imaginary. Native people were not only obstacles and threats to be tamed or eliminated but also societies to be understood. Sexual expressivity was not only a secret of the boudoir and potential taint on one's character but a route to self discovery. Both the assured tone of anthropology texts, which assumed other cultures deserved serious study as much or more than military domination, and the popularization of half a century of an increasingly open recognition of sexuality, ranging from Freud to Hugh Hefner's "*Playboy* Philosophy," attested to the remarkable assimilation of the Other (other cultures, women, and sexuality) to institutional discussion.

And yet this is but half the story. The fact that there was once an undercurrent of dissent regarding this assimilation and liberalization suggests that the practices of cultural relativism and sexual experimentation retain the economy of Otherness (and of repressive desublimation, in Marcuse's terms) that they at first seem to destroy. Michel Foucault's *History of Sexuality* reverses commonsense parlance to argue that we have witnessed the emergence of a discursive economy designed to regulate sexuality. Instead of liberation from patriarchal interdictions we have the subjugation of sexuality to therapeutic discourses. The advantage of this "open" discussion lies in the complexly intertwined relation between pleasure and power that follows. As Foucault describes the languages of sexuality—from the medical examination to parental rules of behavior—they all circle around pleasure and power:

> The pleasure that comes of exercising a power that questions, monitors, watches, spies, searches out, palpates, brings to light; and on the other hand, the pleasure that kindles at having to evade this power, flee from it, fool it, or travesty it. The power that lets itself be invaded by the pleasure it is pursuing; and opposite it, power asserting itself in the pleasure of showing off, scandalizing or resisting. . . . These attractions, these evasions, these circular incitements have traced around bodies and sexes, not boundaries not to be crossed, but *perpetual spirals of power and pleasure* [italics his].[4]

Although more radical ethnographies and pornographies may propose alternative economies to the regulation of Otherness, the assumption of this chapter is that classical ones do not. (These alternatives are discussed further below.) Pleasure and power entwine themselves around fulfillment and knowledge. Technologies of knowledge set to work, producing carnal knowledge on the one hand, cultural knowledge on the other. These technologies—discourses, disciplines, institutions, social practices—define, regulate, and distribute bodies of knowledge; they are the material base where epistemology and ideology meet. (The value of words like "technology" is that they propose a physical *vehicle* or *motor* for ideology, a material mechanism or process by means of which ideology takes shape.) And like other forms of ideology, these technologies usually present themselves as authoritative and obvious, as "mere" tools for the production of a knowledge that transcends them. Carnal knowledge, the stuff of desire, often seems on first impression as free from ideological constraint as the objectivity of science. Pure passion and subjectivity, pure truth and objectivity—these modes of being-in-relation-to-the-world appear to escape the bonds of mere civility or convention. They transport us to another realm, turn us toward the light, free us from our tired assumptions and comfortable habits. And yet, despite this transport and liberation, the Other remains.

These economies of Otherness do not overcome the very dynamic of Otherness they need and preserve, often in the form of paradox and ambivalence. Ethnography and pornography rely heavily on those qualities of fiction (un)like any other that documentary provides: in ethnography, this involves the indexical representation of patterns of culture; in pornography, the indexical proof of sexual engagement. (Though embellished by a story, the actors' sexual performances have a basis in fact; the forms of *trucage* used to simulate physical peril or hazardous action in most fictions are disdained, as is prophylaxis that would safeguard the "star's" physical well-being.)

Both ethnography and pornography make use of narrative but also threaten to arrest or displace it. The referential window onto the historical world of cultural practices and physical bodies, the clinical focus of the evidential gaze, the tendency to linger on moments of descriptive elaboration that hold the temporal rhythm of suspense and resolution at bay— these elements underscore differences from classical narrative fiction. Rather than meaning that these discourses of the carnal and cultural transcend the dynamics of self and other at work in narrative, the differences set the terms and conditions for variation on a theme, not its abolition.

The Story of Otherness

Four different perspectives on the representation of the Other in fiction begin with the truism that fiction is a fabrication. With that premise we enter a realm in which the Other, like fictional narrative itself, stands in a metaphorical relation to the culture from which it arises. (Like everything else, Otherness, too, is fabricated.)

One metaphorical relation involves the cultural stereotype. The figure of the Other represents that which cannot be acknowledged or admitted within the culture that engenders it (in precisely the manner described by Sartre). The Other embodies evil or chaos, excess greed or indolence, horror or monstrosity, the nefarious and the destructive. The inscrutable and scheming Oriental, the hypersexual and athletic black, the arrogant but lifeless white, the treacherous and deceitful Latino, the savage and barbaric Indian—these stereotypes of the Other propose a rogues gallery of the forbidden: knowledge in ruthless pursuit of self-interest, sexuality without bounds, power-hunger without compassion, dependencies without loyalty, calculation or forethought without morality. One might surmise, as Sartre did, that such dreaded forms of conduct, like those ascribed to the Jew by the anti-Semite, are displacements of class conflict and projections of anxiety stemming from a culture of commodity relations. These and other stereotypes (such as *femme fatale*, virgin, madonna, wife) are not unique to fiction, but they receive full-blown embodiment in many stories, occupying the same order of fictive reality as other characters, and figuring into complex forms of emotional engagement for the viewer.

Second, the cultural Other can be understood in relation to the mechanisms of narrative per se. The Other, as a projection and construct, functions as a threat or obstacle to the hero in pursuit of a goal. In this regard, classic Hollywood cinema offers a revealing catalogue of the ways, in which Otherness can be understood as symptoms of our own dis-ease, denial, and anxiety. The status of the Other as a projection or fabrication, however, means that classic fiction has enormous difficulty representing other cultures outside of their function within a system of opposition and identity. And when the Other becomes protagonist, more than Otherness is sacrificed. What remains unrepresentable is the Other's difference. The Other (woman, native, minority) rarely functions as participant in and creator of a system of meanings, including a narrative structure of their own devising. Hierarchy and control still fall on the side of the dominant culture that has fabricated the image of the Other in the first place. Monsters, aliens, Indians, and killers—the vast array of Others, at best, compel some acknowledgment of a common bond between protagonist and themselves but almost never carry this process through to the point where it becomes altogether clear that the monster is fully and entirely a creature of the system that represents it. (This monster-of-our-own-creation theme may be the point of films like *Psycho, Taxi Driver, The Godfather,* or *Good Fellas,* and this may help expose how the economy of Otherness operates, but it does very little to clear a space in which Others might represent themselves.)

This means that popular fiction films can support readings that make it more evident how the Other is a projection and a fabrication. Such readings, however, do not reward our desire to know others in their complexity and difference. Even when the Other serves less as villain than as donor—as an auxiliary or helper to the hero, a function that allows for a more nuanced rendering of difference—the need for narrative closure precludes any sustained adoption of the place of the Other. The Other still stands as threat or guide, assistant or informer, exotic temptation or mysterious host, humorous foil or technical expert, as object of or obstacle to the hero's quest, and not as an autonomous focal point of identificatory investment. From *Little Big Man* to *The Mission* and from *Birth of a Nation* to *The Three Amigos* or *The Golden Child,* the Other as villain or donor becomes one more figure revolving around the central position of the hero. (Even though *The Golden Child* features a black actor, Eddie Murphy, as hero, the film fails to move him into symbolic or cultural alliance with that Other culture in which he locates the prized child; he remains an embodiment of the classic (white) hero of western narrative. *Dances with Wolves* fares much better; Kevin Costner's alliance with the Sioux is so extensive that he ends up more Sioux than white.)

Moving inside the experiential realm of the cultural Other requires moving outside the experiential realm of the white, male, Western hero. More commonly, though, the motives and actions, traits and impulses of the Other become drawn into the centripetal field of the hero as organizing principle. Narrative momentum builds around the protagonist, spiraling back to where it began (restoring equilibrium, eliminating deficiency). Everything that happens along the way requires a functional motivation to help the narrative achieve this act of conservation. The presence of donors and villains must be "motivated" in relation to the protagonist's dilemma or quest. And if the protagonist is "one of us" (white, Western, male, middle or upper class, and so on), the place of the Other will always be in a relation of difference to the hero rather than in relation to the terms and conditions of his or her own cultural context. Even films sympathetic to the Other's point of view such as *Guess Who's Coming to Dinner, The White Dawn, Tell Them Willie Boy Is Here, Little Big Man, Broken Arrow, Dances with Wolves, Cry Freedom, A Dry White Season,* or *A World Apart* have their dramatic center at the point where an alien culture and alternative values effect transformations in "one of us" rather than in "one of them."

Occasionally Hollywood filmmakers try to do it the other way around and move "inside" the rhythms and values of another culture in a more holistic way than simply as "local color" or descriptive passage. The result is seldom satisfactory. In describing his "problem" in making a film about the Pharaohs of ancient Egypt (*Land of the Pharaohs*), Howard Hawks confided, "I don't know how a Pharaoh talks. And Faulkner didn't know. None of us knew. . . . It was awfully hard to deepen [the scenes] because we didn't know how these Egyptians thought or what they said. . . . You kind of lose all sense of values. You don't know who somebody is for and if you don't have a rooting interest, and you're not for somebody, then you haven't got a picture."[5] The exceptions to the dilemma posed so tellingly by Hawks are as rare as the exceptions to the treatment of the nude in Western oil painting as described by John Berger in his *Ways of Seeing.*[6] Seldom is the Other represented so that something of its singularity and distinction appears instead of the stereotypical or projected. (Some exceptions might include *Brother from Another Planet, Born in Flames, Chan Is Missing, The Kitchen Toto, Stand and Deliver, My Beautiful Laundrette, Killer of Sheep,* and *To Sleep with Anger,* but most of these are films on the margins of mainstream, commercial cinema, even when their narrative construction is fairly conventional.)

Once we begin with a protagonist who represents "us" to a large extent, the place of the Other will be subordinated to this figure. The actions and qualities of the Other as villain or donor will serve to elaborate on the character of the hero. The death of anyone represented as Other is never of inherent significance, for example. Its importance comes from what it allows the narrative to reveal of the protagonist. The Other's life, and death, no longer belong to the historical world of its own culture; they become recruited to the imaginary world of the fiction. In *The Great Santini*, for example, the murder of Santini's son's black friend, Tooma, is crucial to the son's own maturation but its impact on Tooma's wholly dependent mother is left unexamined and scarcely suggested.

Third, the very concept of narrative calls for interrogation. Perhaps it is not just a problem of a donor or villain subordinated to the protagonist's destination and the narrative's goal, but that this trajectory is itself a manifestation of a teleology all our own. The poststructural critique of Western humanist thought—including its traditional antitheses of Marx, Freud, Nietzsche—relegates all such discourses to the category of master narrative: accounts that subsume all that they survey to one controlling story line, leaving little if any room for anomaly, difference, or Otherness. Although his account smacks of the same overgeneralization and disregard of particular differences found in 1970s theories of ideology and critiques of the "cinematic apparatus," Craig Owens puts the case against the narrative project of global explanation, teleological projection, and narrative closure cogently:

> For what made the *grand recits* of modernity master narratives if not the fact that they were all narratives of mastery, of man seeking his telos in the conquest of nature? What function did these narratives play other than to legitimize Western man's self-appointed mission of transforming the entire planet in his own image? And what form did this mission take if not that of man's placing his stamp on everything that exists—that is, the transformation of the world into a representation, with man as its subject? In this respect, however, the phrase *master narrative* seems tautologous, since all narrative . . . may be narratives of mastery.[7]

Fourth, and finally, at a more strictly cinematic level, the (mis)representation of the Other can be said to take place in relation to the gaze of the camera.[8] Not only are women presented within stereotypical roles that deny difference and complexity, that stand as projections of masculine anxiety more than as embodiments of feminine experience, they occupy a distinct position within the dynamics of the camera gaze. Women, as Laura Mulvey put it, are to-be-looked-at; they are objects of desire and spectacle.[9] Male characters are to be followed, as active agents of narrative development; they are objects of identification. What is more, the different views of male and female figures gets transferred to the fiction: the camera represents male characters looking at female ones while female characters are the objects of such views rather than their instigators. Mulvey goes on to argue that male viewers identify with male characters and experience sexual desire for female characters. (Mulvey assumes that male viewers will share the subjectivity of male characters and women viewers that of female characters.) She also notes how classic narrative cinema denies women viewers the pleasure of either identification (to identify with male characters is inappropriate and with female ones masochistic) or desire (male heroes are more the subjects of desire than objects; and desire for female heroines is simply not considered).

Although her assignments of identification and desire for the viewer need not be so fully determined by anatomy, the main point that there is a sexual politics (as well as a racial and class politics) to the gaze of the camera remains compelling.[10] (In this revised reading, there is fundamental agreement that an alliance prevails between camera, sound, and white, dominant, masculine subjectivity that relegates other subjectivities to a subordinate Otherness rather than perceiving them in terms of a relativist difference.) The degree of complicity Mulvey finds between formal structure in classic narrative and the representation of women as the principal Other of male desire is made apparent by her final call to destroy the "satisfaction, pleasure, and privilege" of this cinema in order to prepare for another, feminist one.

Different Forms, Similar Problems

If narrative film has a problematic track record in its representation of the Other it has also helped fabricate, we might think documentary film would fare better. The realm of the Other as constituted in the social imaginary can become the subject of a documentary, displacing the protagonist who is "one of us," and instead offering a representation of the historical world that centers on terms and conditions that prevail elsewhere. Ethnographic film clearly belongs within this category. It has extended our sense of what another culture might look and sound like: what qualities reside in space and movement, dress and demeanor, speech and expression, ritual and social practices.

The idea of potentially enlightening news from afar seems quite remote from the realm of pornographic representation. But it too centers around a portion of our historical world where the terms and conditions of engagement depart from those that prevail in everyday life. Pornographic film extends our sense of what an unbridled sexuality might look and sound like in a manner quite similar to ethnography's rendering of other cultures. In relation to heterosexual pornography, the liberated Other clearly does not represent women, who remain as much Other as one could imagine, but sexuality itself. (In this sense, there is an ironic parallelism between pornography and Foucault's concept of sexuality in *The History of*

Sexuality. Both present "technologies" of sexuality with minimal regard for the sensibilities and subjectivities of women.)

Ethnography and pornography correspond to discourses, technologies, and ideology surrounding mind and body, respectively. How do the dominant discourses of masculinism and late capitalism establish a context or system of constraints that help structure these two domains? And, more precisely, how is it that the pornographic imagination and ethnographic imperative share a series of close structural parallels? In what ways does the liberal imagination address the Other? What are the terms of address? What distinctions and boundaries are upheld between the body of Western patriarchy and the physical presence of the Other, between the mind of Western patriarchy and the cultural practices of the Other?

The films under consideration here belong to the mainstream tradition in each case. More exploratory or experimental work and alternative practices (such as the exchange network for pornographic home video-tapes, gay and lesbian pornography, reflexive and interactive ethnography) require additional discussion. Typical pornographic films include *Deep Throat, Behind the Green Door, I* and *II, Talk Dirty to Me, I* and *II, Romancing the Bone, Debbie Does Dallas, I* and *II, The Private Afternoons of Pamela Mann, Taboo I-IV,* and *The Devil in Miss Jones.* Typical ethnographic films include *Dead Birds, The Hunters, The Lion Hunters, Microcultural Incidents in Ten Zoos, The Nuer,* the Character Formation in Different Cultures series, *Four Families, Les maîtres fous,* The Netsilik Eskimo series, the Yanomamö series, and *Margaret Mead's New Guinea Journal.* The individual differences among the ethnographic works are considerable. This account dwells on underlying similarities to question the mechanisms involved in the production of Otherness itself.

Strange Bedfellows

What does it mean to say pornography and ethnography share a discourse of domination? For one thing, they represent impulses born of desire: the desire to know and possess, to "know" by possessing and possess by knowing. Each is structured hierarchically. In pornography, male subjectivity assumes the task of representing female subjectivity; in ethnography, "our" culture assumes the task of representing theirs. The appropriateness of these tasks, though sometimes given a historical context, remains, for the most part, an assumption, responsibility, or power, conferred by dint of membership in the interpreting community rather than through negotiation with the interpreted community. The cultural and historical facts of colonization, patriarchy, and masculinism are treated as a context—of which these two discourses remain aware: the burdensome practices of dominance and repression no longer suffice. Ethnographic

filmmakers express a will to understand rather than dominate, a development with antecedents as far back as Sahagun's remarkably sophisticated
and disinterested representation of Aztec culture.[11] Pornographic filmmakers express a will to sexual liberation rather than repression, an
attitude that overturns two millennia devoted largely to subordinating
sexuality to reproduction and suppressing the physical evidence of sexuality itself.

Each discourse, then, constantly produces and reproduces a "reality" (a
manifestation of power and a system of constraints) while at the same time
disavowing its own complicity with a tradition it appears to contest. Neither
succeeds. Distance as control and difference as hierarchy infiltrate where a
rhetoric of detachment or liberation holds sway. An economy of control
and hierarchy persists despite the promise of escape.

Pornography is part of a larger discourse of sexuality and the organization of pleasure, and ethnography is part of a larger discourse of science
and the organization of knowledge. But our culture makes ethnography
(science) licit knowledge and pornography (sexuality) illicit, carnal knowledge. Ethnography is a kind of legitimated pornography, a pornography of
knowledge, giving us the pleasure of knowing what had seemed incomprehensible. Pornography is a strange, "unnatural" form of ethnography,
salvaging orgasmic bliss from the seclusion of the bedroom.

For centuries the discourses of sexuality and knowledge have been held
apart. Beginning at least as early as Plato with his vision of an education that
banishes frenzy, passion, and "improper" identificatory models, and culminating with Descartes's mind/body split, knowledge becomes master of
pleasure, and science becomes the tool whereby one discovers, learns
about, and disciplines sexuality. The distinction between a Greco-Roman
"aesthetics of experience," concerned with a regimen to regulate and
control desires that were not in and of themselves categorized into the
good and the bad, the approved and censorable, and a Christian codifica-
tion and classification of specific practices as acceptable or sinful with
minimal regard to circumstance or the quality of bodily performance,
though central to Foucault's history, is something of a nicety.[12] Our study
has as its location only the latter and the "aesthetics" of pornography
belongs squarely to the modern world's preoccupation with the confession
(and interview) as a mechanism for the extraction of pleasure and knowledge. The cinematic representation of sexual activity *is* in the form of the
confessional; we watch and listen, we experience and learn from this
discursive relay rather than from the activity itself. We deploy a *scientia
sexualis* to understand, label, codify, and cure sexuality.[13] It is this yes/no,
either/or Cartesian thinking, this binary and hierarchical deployment, that
is essential to the structure of pornography and ethnography. In each, the
mind is privileged over its accompanying body and those other bodies we
know vicariously—the Nuer doing chants or Debbie doing Dallas. We

experience concepts and images of knowledge or possession instead of direct, face-to-face encounters that might place us at risk. We remain securely positioned within an imaginary opposition of Them/Us rather than immersed in a flux of difference.

While the Cartesian mind/body split may be paradigmatic of both practices, it must be emphasized that each is ostensibly about a different side of that dichotomy. Pornography is the representation of the physical manner in which we may engage with another (and the Other). It raises existential questions about bodies and their use, about good and bad sex, about desire and its bodily manifestation.

Ethnography is the representation of the conceptual manner in which we may engage with another. It raises epistemological questions about the mind and its use, about good and bad encounters, skimpy or "thick" description, desire and its sublimated manifestations.[14] Ethnography turns on how cultural activity occurs, where it happens, who it happens with, what its participants look like, how they speak, and what meanings we can make of what we see. In a similar fashion, pornography poses questions of how sex is initiated and how it ends, where sex happens, who sex happens with, what aroused sexual actors (both people and their genitalia) look like, and especially what the sex act itself looks like when staged before the camera. Both rely on a documentary impulse, a guarantee that we will behold "the thing itself," caught in the indexical grain of cinematographic sound and image. The documentary impulse answers the need for evidence, living proof of the Other's bodily manifestation and our capacity to know it.

Issues of Representation in Pornography

The story pornography has to tell centers on sexuality. Pornography dwells on the experiential tones and textures of sexual activity. The activity may involve social ritual but its representation favors viewer arousal more than understanding or analysis. Understanding is both a pretext—especially in pornography before the liberalization of censorship laws when claims of "redeeming social value" had legal significance—and a result that appends itself to the embodiment of feeling. We may understand what an orgy is like, for example, somewhat better after watching *Taboo* but our attention is drawn to its experiential and expressive dimensions rather than conceptual or functional ones.

Mainstream pornography represents a phallocentric order symbolized by male desire and a universal masculinist order, naturalized as a given. The phallus stands in for sexuality and power. All men desire the same thing as signified by the activities of their penises. These socially constructed activities raise the organ to the level of a signifier, the phallus. The phallus provides an index or standard of power and authority. The penis as phallus—symbol of sexual potency—is the "true" star, celebrated in count-less close-ups. A pornographic film is in many ways the story of a phallus. The questions are: What preoccupies or excites it? For whom does it offer fascination? What does it do when excited? What tale of encounters with the flesh can it provide? What rhythms and motions does it prefer or impose? Through what cycles and rituals does it pass?

In *The Devil in Miss Jones*, the heroine negotiates, in purgatory, for a chance to experience the sexual pleasures she had denied herself in life. The narrative then moves her through the stages of a sexual education. But, on returning to purgatory, she learns that her "time is up." She must proceed to hell. In hell, following Sartre's *No Exit*, this now sexually excited woman is consigned to a room with a sexually inert man. She is in constant proximity to his dysfunctional phallus but denied all access to it (has she forgotten what she learned about masturbation?). It is revealing that hell in this instance also signifies the film's end. Where the phallus has no tale to tell, there is no (mainstream) pornography.

In keeping with the three-part division of facts, practices, and ideals maintained by institutions or discursive formations, narrative pornography and ethnography begin with the fact of the body and its sexual/social propensities; each examines the actions, rituals, and roles pertinent to it; each also implies a utopian domain in which contradiction dissolves without dissolving the pornographic or ethnographic formation itself. We may then ask just what form of myth or cultural ideal pornography and ethnography propose.

For pornography this ideal can be termed a "pornotopia" visited by an ideal spectator. Pornography proposes an ever-renewed and continually satisfied desire; it offers the perpetuation of desire. Difference is constantly discovered and placed in the service of pleasure. The desirability of the Other is stressed; Others avail themselves for desire. It is a world in which We *have* Them, a world of lust unbound.

Sexual actors are watched, while cultural actors are watched over. The paradigmatic representation of these two states is symbolized by voyeurism in pornography and the panopticon in ethnography. Voyeurism symbolizes an economy based on seeing but not being seen. The panopticon, a design for prisons where a guard in a central watch tower could look into cylinder-like stacks of cells surrounding this tower, symbolizes an economy of knowledge predicated on distance and control centered around a single, all-seeing vantage point.

Certain genre-like features recur as pornography constantly proposes variations on the ultimate pornotopia. We find, for example: semi-individualized stars; the absence of villains (males do not compete for women but share them or find that women refuse to discriminate among eligible men); women as "experiential" donors (contributing to the progress of the protagonist's serial adventures), or, if the woman is the protagonist, men as "educational" donors (contributing to her accumulation of sexual expertise and enthusiasm); unflagging phalluses, and copious, visible ejaculations of semen as the most common resolution to narrative suspense.[15]

Pornography also presents two alternating modes of viewer engagement: narrative action and descriptive/erotic contemplation. This differentiation parallels the structure of the musical. In scenes of narrative action, enigmas arise, actions unfold, and character development occurs. In scenes of contemplation, narrative movement comes to a halt for the duration of an event (sex or song); redundancy abounds. In terms of the narrative the important point is that "sex takes place"; its duration and detail belong to another order of engagement.

Moments of erotic contemplation invite identification with the singularity of a given sexual encounter whose narrative outcome is readily known from the outset. (Contemplative moments of sexual encounter are miniature narratives in their own right, with a clearly defined beginning, middle, and end, but they are entirely self-contained: when they end they leave little that is unresolved; they remain open only to repetition.) If musical numbers idealize social relations (imbuing work and romance with a utopian aura), pornography idealizes sexual relations (imbuing sex with both a documentary realism and a mythic idealism). Each offers its idealizations as moments of contemplation that comply to their own internal norms for rhythm, pace, and duration rather than to those of the surrounding narrative.

The process of knowing by means of possessing that prevails in classic heterosexual pornography places the narrative at the service of documentation. Knowledge and objects cannot simply be acquired or taken; the act or process of knowing/possessing must itself be described and documented in far greater detail than what any plot requires. This detail is indispensable to pornographic convention. Evidence of sexual engagement overwhelms the development of a story even though it remains fully in the service of a particular subjectivity and gender-based ideology.

This departure from the needs of narrative progression into a realm of sexual demonstration resembles not only the structure of musicals, with their seemingly disruptive songs and dances, but also a tendency in early cinema that gave priority to the exhibitionistic display of remarkable sights. As Tom Gunning puts it, this "cinema of attractions"

> directly solicits spectator attention, inciting visual curiosity, and supplying pleasure through an exciting spectacle—a unique event, whether fictional or documentary, that is of interest in itself. . . . Theatrical display dominates over narrative absorption, emphasizing the direct stimulation of shock or surprise at the expense of unfolding a story or creating a diegetic [fictional] universe. The cinema of attractions expends little energy creating characters with psychological motivations or individual personality. Making use of both fictional and non-fictional attractions, its energy moves outward towards an acknowledged spectator rather than inward towards the character-based situations essential to classical narrative.[16]

Musicals and pornography seem to be subsequent manifestations of this alternative use of cinema. The sex act is an excursion toward pleasure and fascination, identification and transgression—pure subjectivity—and away from the Law. It must be treated in special ways to remain "contained" within social, textual, and fictional boundaries. This, too, leads to tension between fiction and documentation.

Documented sex seeks to reduce the narrative to a mere pretext. The narrative rationalizes or motivates the sexual encounters which then become the principle source of viewer engagement. On the other hand, narrative seeks to reduce the sex act to an internal, descriptive element, rationalized or motivated by a concern with character development and story. (The general absence of narrative from stag films and, more recently, from compilation videos that offer a series of sexual encounters without narrative linkage results in films that lack the same degree of subjectivity and identification between viewer and characters; they provide sexual stimulus without a narrative overlay of thematic meanings and goals.) Although the narrative appears to license the sexual imagination, it remains at risk. It may become simply a pretext for the material evidence of documented sex as the necessary, and sufficient, basis for the desired effect.

The ambivalence or oscillation between narrative progression and documentary evidence makes it extremely difficult, if not unhelpful, to treat pornography as a subset of fiction and narrative texts. Analogies with the musical genre are very suggestive, but even in as elaborate an analysis as Linda Williams's in her book, *Hard Core: Power, Pleasure and "The Frenzy of the Visible,"* they still tend to flatten the experiential effect of viewing into a unity that pornography constantly disrupts. In pornography, narrative is never as secure as it is in musicals. The documentary and exhibitionistic dimensions loom too large. Linear narrative and moments of stasis comingle. Neither progression nor contemplation alone encompasses the phenomenon. (This is a fundamental difference between pornography and other narrative genres such as the musical.)

Pornography imposes certain conventions on the structure of individual scenes that contribute to a narrative effect, even if it is limited or different from that of other genres. The basic unit is a situation or event exemplifying sexual engagement between actors/characters, organized and photographed from the perspective of an ideal spectator. This contrasts with ethnography where the basic unit is a situation or event offering an example of cultural specificity presented from the perspective of as ideal an observer as field conditions allow.

In both cases, camera and sound, sequence and structure anticipate the logic of what an ideal spectator would want to see of sexual or social activity. We occupy this "ideal" position, seeing what we need to see, when we need to see it. This orchestration, naturalized and invisible, serves to channel and control the investment of desire. Narrative logic prevails in that details only arrive at the moment when they have optimal explanatory power. Establishing shots lead us into scenes; close-ups increase our sense of knowledge and access; they make explicit what we might otherwise have to infer. Continuity editing directs attention to the event rather than its staging or organization in terms of shots. These patterns offer a psychological realism in which editing embraces the rhythms of a "natural" curiosity. This socially constructed, and ideological, form of curiosity supports both ethnographic and pornographic representations.

Narrative action in pornography features the desiring (male) subject and the behavioral expressivity of sexual actors. The classic parallel plot structure of commercial cinema frequently occurs: one plot involves an adventure, the other involves a romance, with the ending resolving both plots through an event common to both. (*His Girl Friday, Bonnie and Clyde,* and *Die Hard* illustrate the tendency.) In pornography, though, the adventure is sexual and the romance carnal. Pornography offers visible evidence of sexual practice more than of courtship rituals which are often conspicuously absent. Again, as Linda Williams demonstrates quite thoroughly in *Hard Core,* pornography usually adopts the plot parallelism of musical films. The story and the musical interludes (or sexual encounters) occupy distinct but compatible spaces. Frequently, what occurs in song, or sexual encounter, is a response to previous events in the story which halts the linear advance of the plot momentarily. The song or sex act, though, prepares us for yet further advances of the plot. A vivid example of this process is *Taboo,* where the central character, the mother, comes to discover through a series of generally dissatisfying sexual encounters that the best sex is also the most heavily repressed: incest with her son. (The sex acts also trivialize or derail the narrative through their preponderance, duration, and the minimal degree of character development; this leaves pornography and narrative in a precarious relationship. The "call and response" pattern is always imbalanced.)

In pornography an iconography of sexual desire abounds, giving representation to the physical manner in which we (males) engage with an Other. Pornography features icons of desirability (young, athletic bodies; casual but fashionable dress; comfortable domestic spaces; rustic nature). It features pleasure-seeking behavior by both male and female subjects. "Good" sex, measured in terms of personal gratification and the desire for more, provides a primary goal, figured by images of orgasmic bliss which are often accompanied by cries of ecstasy and musical crescendos.

Pornography and ethnography dwell on the body as a socially significant site. They extract, respectively, pleasure and knowledge from that site, while at the same time demystifying and familiarizing it. Through the body, the domestication of the Other occurs. In pornographic films, the body is an instrument of sexual performance. Thanks to their extended isolation in close-ups, sexual body parts appear to function independently from character or personality. The iconography of pornographic films includes "anatomy lessons," clinical close-ups of sexually engaged genitalia. Bodily performance features lips, breasts, legs, arms, vulvas, clitorises, and penises as instruments and targets of desire.

Though clearly part of a distinctly Western discourse on sexuality and the body, this fragmentation or anatomization does *not* share in the oil painting tradition of bodily idealization, or its cinematic celebration in the work of Kuleshov or Dziga Vertov, although it does display the same, dehumanizing result.[17] "Dürer believed that the ideal nude ought to be constructed by taking the face of one body, the breasts of another, the legs of a third, the shoulders of a fourth, the hands of a fifth—and so on," John Berger tells us. The result is dehumanizing.[18]

Pornography does not idealize in this way. Instead, it scrutinizes the individual body as something less than the sum of its parts. Pornography relies on the singular body of the individual performer for authentication. (Orgy scenes, such as the ones that conclude *Behind the Green Door, II* and the bisexual videotape, *Innocence Lost,* may sacrifice identification with specific individuals, but dependence on singular bodies for purposes of authentication remains total.) Pornography, in its fragmentary shooting style, remains subject to the critique Berger offers of the nude as an expression of Western humanism: "The result would glorify Man. But the exercise presumed a remarkable indifference to who any one person really was."[19] For all the anatomy lessons we receive, character development proves extremely hazy.

Pornography and ethnography depend on the assurance that what the spectator sees really happened. It is important that events typify the particular domain of cultural or sexual practices that they represent. At the same time these representations must be recognized or accepted as evidence of highly concrete, historically material events occurring among specific individuals. Unlike the metaphorical or allegorical typifications of a fictional universe, these typifications depend on their historical authenticity for validation. It is not reality that is at stake but the impression of reality, the impression conveyed by the conventions of historical realism.

In documentary this impression of reality extends to the actual course of events; the actions, words, and gestures; the states of mind of participants, and the outcome or resolution represented. In ethnography and pornography, concreteness centers on the evidence that the cultural or sexual practices represented occurred as depicted, in historical as well as cinematic space, without trompe l'oeil effects to create the illusion of sexual practices or cultural activity.[20] A pornographic film is considered bogus by viewers (perhaps not even pornographic at all) if the male actors simulate orgasm (if they simulate intercourse it may not even seem pornographic to censors). Likewise, it is anathema for an ethnographic filmmaker to fabricate cultural practices, or, even more, to project possible consequences from actual events. Various evidentiary strategies function to guarantee the authority of the film through the credibility of the events depicted.

In pornography this function is carried out primarily by images of penile ejaculation ("cum shots"). This is an ironic documentation that requires violation of the "real" sexuality it represents. The phallus is the central element of the mise-en-scène; after an appropriate interval devoted to its stimulation, it arrives at its moment of truth, *le petit mort*, and showers the cinematic frame with its discharge. Like proofs of witchcraft or divinity, this outward and manifest sign offers visible proof of an inward and subjective state.

The problem of an equally irrefutable and visible proof of female orgasm, at a physiological level, both leads to the convention whereby male orgasm stands in for female orgasm and to attempts to convey female orgasm by more indirect means. *Deep Throat* epitomizes the first tendency; the conclusion to *Insatiable II*, with Marilyn Chambers's whole body shuddering with pleasure while engaged with both a male and female partner, epitomizes the latter. The more typical representation of the male ejaculation engenders a remarkably paradoxical iconography. Testimony to pleasure occurs in the visible proof of ejaculation per se (and in the sounds of ecstasy) rather than in the acts of intercourse or fellatio which would render the penis invisible. We are left with a symbolic representation of what would have occurred had the needs of the observer not taken priority. Intromission becomes onanism, the pornographic "proof" of sexual activity. (This onanism differs sharply from masturbation: it is not a self-administered pleasure and is seldom acknowledged as a source of pleasure in and of itself; rather, it is treated as what it is, a convention that forbids the occurrence of orgasm in out-of-sight places.)

Issues of Representation in Ethnography

Whereas pornography addresses the domain of sexuality, ethnography addresses the domain of knowledge. Ethnography may also stress experiential forms of knowledge, but the texture and tonalities of physical actions, although they may be erotic, are represented within a frame of conceptual understanding more than arousal. Arousal, should it occur, as a certain folklore claims it does with the photographic nudes represented in *National Geographic*, would be considered inappropriate, tactless, or perverse. To respond to suggestiveness or allure when neither is intended is a misreading of the text, subject to discipline. A properly disciplined response overlooks visceral reaction to grasp the conceptual or functional place of dress, ornamentation, and bodily display in a social context. It treats sexual arousal as a lapse or sign of bad taste.

Ethnography's symbolic representation of power and authority centers on the male. The male as "man"—symbol of cultural achievement—is the star of ethnography, celebrated in close-ups as the talking informant. Ethnography represents a masculinist order—symbolic of male structures of experience and knowledge subsequently naturalized as universal. Men (ethnographers and informants) know; they guard the domain of reason, logic, conceptualization. The male stands in for culture and power.

Films like *N!ai, A Wife among Wives*, and *The Women's Olamal* offer some corrective to the male norm. Melissa Llewelyn-Davies's *The Women's Olamal*, for example, recounts the struggle of a group of Masai women to have a necessary fertility ritual performed by the men of the tribe who are intensely reluctant to do so. The film's focus lies with the travails of the women, their subjective experience, and the negotiations they conduct, but all of this is in relation to the prevailing ethnographic film aesthetic, with its presumption of a gender-blind objectivity. None of these ethnographic films initiates a feminist or postfeminist mode of representation that might compare to gay and lesbian pornography even when a woman is the filmmaker.[21]

Ethnography also proposes an ideal: an "ethnotopia" of limitless observation. Ethnography invokes an ever-renewed and never exhausted curiosity; it strives for the perpetuation of curiosity. Difference is continually discovered and placed in the service of scientific comprehension. The fascination of the Other is stressed; it avails itself for knowledge. It is a world in which We *know* Them, a world of wisdom triumphant.

Paradox governs the pornotopic and ethnotopic ideals. Paradox stems from distance, power, and the need to control, tame, or eliminate threat. In both pornography and ethnography, the images of the Other serve to propagate the notion that "they" are all alike in some special "meta" way. In pornography, for instance, women are almost always the one-dimensional locus of male desire. In *Debbie Does Dallas*, what really happens is that Dallas does Debbie. In *The Devil in Miss Jones*, the narrative revolves less around what Miss Jones does (this is the level of narrative pretext), but what is done to her (the level of erotic spectacle). In both cases, the proposed "heroine" is more object to an external point of view than subject of her own. As in traditional melodrama, women occupy the position of protagonist only to betray their inability to initiate or control a narrative.[22]

Likewise, ethnography is an essential tool for the anthropologist who hopes to tell us something about ourselves by telling us about a more *sauvage* version of ourselves. Ethnography uses the actions of the one to signify the actions of the many, the assumption being that Yanomamö and Nuer and !Kung are all of a kind albeit best represented by those who possess a peculiar mix of Lukacsian typicality and incipient "star quality"— some form of felt resonance with our own conceptions of personality and charisma as discussed earlier in terms of "virtual performance." In Robert Gardner's *Dead Birds*, we are told that the Dani, as a race, enjoy war; we are then shown the Dani in ritual warfare. Just as the actors in a pornographic film are used to put forward evidence of pleasure, the Dani are used, as objects, in someone else's argument (about man's warlike nature).

In *Magical Death*, Napoleon Chagnon describes the trance activity of

Yanomamö leader Dedeheiwä as analogous to the personal, folksy ways of a country doctor concerned with the well-being of his patients as fellow humans. The function of both great anthropological generalization and small quaint descriptions (the nature of trance, the wrestling matches with evil spirits) is similar to what Roland Barthes analyzes in "The Great Family of Man" photographic exhibit.[23] Common modalities of social function and subjectivity prevail across geographic, racial, and cultural disparities. Man (*sic*) circulates across cultures as a universal term of endeavor and value. Individual differences are circumscribed by an essentialism of gender rather than being allowed to stand as incommensurate differences.

Classic ethnographic film belongs to the humanist tradition of men celebrating the achievements of "Man." Ethnography is less narrative-centered than pornography, but often gives considerable priority to the development of (primary male) characters and the organization of a causal chain of actions. Parallelism between the advance of the story and moments "out of time" like songs or intercourse is more rare. It does occur routinely in trance films, however, such as *Trance and Dance in Bali*, *Magical Death*, and *Les maîtres fous*. Character development, viewer identification with individuated representatives of another culture, the acquisition of knowledge, and linear exposition are more central than they are to pornography.

Expository actions feature the inquiring (usually male) ethnographer and the behavioral expressivity of (predominantly male) social actors. The classic expository structure of a problem and its solution, or an event and its explanation, is common. This can be considered to parallel narrative closure based on the elimination of a disturbance to an existing state of affairs (the removal of a lack of some kind) or to qualify as a subcategory of it (where what is found lacking is most often knowledge).

Ethnography offers visible evidence of cultural practices, stressing the most cinematically accessible dimensions (public actions more than private preparations, moments ripe with spectacle or self-absorption). The "crisis structure" of observational film (a narrative concept in which ordinary people are put to a test) frequently occurs (in *Nanook*, *Dead Birds*, *The Hunters*, and *Joe Leahy's Neighbors*, for example).[24] In other cases a descriptive or more open-ended structure may prevail (as in *Dani Sweet Potatoes*, *Chronicle of a Summer*, or The Netsilik Eskimo series), but basic narrative principles continue to operate whereby the bulk of the film accounts for the changes between beginning and end (in process, perspective, situation, degree of knowledge, or type of question posed). We leave having the sense—both classic narrative and exposition take pains to provide it—that all accounts have been settled.

In ethnographic film an iconography of cultural authenticity prevails, usually indicative of an "untouched" state, sometimes of acculturation (as in Jerry Leach's *Trobiand Cricket* or Dennis O'Rourke's *Cannibal Tours*). Ethnography features icons of authenticity and specificity that give representation to the rituals, customs, speech, and everyday behavior that typifies the Other. "Good" behavior, measured by a lack of inappropriate self-consciousness and the ability to participate fully with one's social cohorts, marks the ethnographic goal, figured by images of "natural" or typical activity and their accompanying sounds.

In ethnographic practice, the body is an instrument of cultural performance. Sometimes presented holistically, sometimes fragmentarily, and often naked (or nearly so), the body is where culture comes to life. Individual physical actions give a literal embodiment to culture. Raymond Birdwhistle's *Microcultural Incidents in Ten Zoos*, Alan Lomax's choriometric studies, and much of Margaret Mead's work, such as *Trance and Dance in Bali* and *Childhood Rivalry in Bali and New Guinea* break the actions of the body down into their component parts. Such work uses close-ups and body fragmentation in much the same way as pornography but now in a scientific spirit. The idealization aspired to is that of the "typical native and his (*sic*) actions," but the concrete specificity of the individual body remains essential to authenticity.

Some advocate a "holistic" shooting style that addresses the dependence on the singular body with a dictum, "Whole Bodies and Whole People in Whole Acts: Close-up shots of faces should be used very sparingly, for entire bodies of people at work or play or rest are more revealing and interesting than body fragments."[25] Such a dictum, seldom followed with any rigor in pornography, gives rise to a tendency toward "mere footage" or cinematic data rather than text. (The distinction is one of degree more than of kind.) Long-take, wide-angle, long-shot shooting styles do offer a means to authenticate and individuate simultaneously, but an underlying tension remains: idealization lingers in the desire to transform individual practice into typical practice. Though sometimes assigned a name and even personality, the value of an individual's action lies in its generalization, its typicality within the culture in question.

The body itself looms as the "star" of pornography and ethnography. The accretion of star quality to the bodies of some (Nanook, N!ai, Marilyn Chambers, John Holmes) is the condensation of a much more general principle that makes the body, and its parts, the focal point of iconographic convention.

In ethnography we find a number of generic elements: semi-individualized stars, the absence of villains, and women in positions of subordination. (Villains would introduce a prescriptive morality, a story of good and evil, to a world that anthropologists normally constitute as a "good object" in its entirety. Evil usually enters from the outside, if at all, in the form of colonization, postcolonial interventions, and problems of acculturation.) Two modes of viewer engagement similar to those of pornography are emphasized—narrative actions and descriptive presentation—with ethnographic priority going to the latter. The description of events typifies the culture in question for an ideal observer. Principles of narrative structure string descriptive events together, often in unexamined or undertheorized ways, but narrative is at less fundamental risk than in pornography. This is largely because specific events do not invite erotic contemplation (this, recall, is bad taste) but the comprehension and placement of events in historical time, which is fully commensurate with narrative representation.

The weak narrative structure into which events fall substantiates, tauto-logically, the voice of commentary, which provides conceptual knowledge of difference and strangeness. The odyssey or quest of *The Hunters, The Lion Hunters,* or *Nanook of the North,* the symbolic, ritual actions of *Les maîtres fous* and *Magical Death*—these loose narrative frames not only offer closure; they shape events into the form of an explanation (a beginning followed by an ending where the difference between the two is accounted for by the middle) which the commentary can then certify. To become entirely caught up in the contemplation of specific events—in their rhythm and gestures, tones and textures—poses the risk of losing one's detachment.

But detachment is not only part of fictive experience (the awareness of having chosen to suspend disbelief) but a prerequisite for ethnographic knowledge. Moments of potential contemplation seldom provide the de-gree of flight from narrative that sexual acts do in pornography. They arc more heavily regulated (represented frequently as illustration or example) to comply with the requirements of a knowledge that must know/possess at a distance, across the space of descriptive accuracy and scientific objec-tivity. Moments of contemplation seldom seem beyond the Law. They remain grounded in the moral perspective afforded by a narrative (explan-atory) structure even though they may exert a fascination of considerable risk and magnitude.

Ethnographic film offers an impression of authenticity by means of the arrival scene. This represents an ironic form of coming into the presence of the Other that certifies difference (the difference between the ethno-graphic visitor and his/her subject) and makes unity impossible.[26] The ethnographer steps onto the scene, confiding to us his/her travails and hardships. The arrival scene offers an outward and manifest sign of the inner, subjective state of participatory observation. The irony is that the representation of the required subjectivity diminishes the material reality of encounter itself. Problems of interpretation, negotiations regarding space, supplies, physical assistance, the right to film or photograph, and the numerous everyday rituals of communication and exchange between human subjects slip from view. More important is the impression that the ethnographer was there and that his or her representation is, therefore, to be trusted.

The omission of problematic aspects of communication and exchange is particularly striking in *Joe Leahy's Neighbors,* a follow-up to Bob Connelly and Robin Anderson's *First Contact.* As described in chapter 2, the film is entirely about spatial negotiation—over tribal land that has been leased (or sold) to Joe and is now the target of repatriation by some while others want to strike similar deals for their own land—the filmmakers' own presence, though, is only fleetingly acknowledged, in joking asides, but is never itself the subject of serious negotiation. We are left with a symbolic displacement of the forms of engagement that would have occurred were the needs of observation not given priority. The film displaces dialogue regarding the filmmakers' space to dialogue regarding the subjects'.

Some films present a literal arrival scene. *The Ax Fight*, for example, revolves around a violent conflict that erupts just as Timothy Asch and Napoleon Chagnon start to film among the Yanomamö in the village of Mishimishimaböwei-teri; they wisely organized the film around their extended efforts to make sense of what they unexpectedly encountered upon their arrival. More often, the function of the arrival scene is achieved metaphorically, by the act of filming. The actual process of filming requires both presence and distance, the same duality that the arrival scene serves to guarantee. As long as the camera intervenes, a state of detached presence underwrites the representation. A more direct reference to the conceit of the arrival scene can involve a metaphoric, and reflexive, reversal such as the film-within-a-film sequence in *A Wife among Wives*, where encouraging the Turkana women to film the filmmakers' belongings underscores the sense of strangeness and unfamiliarity. In either case, the act of filming itself announces the distance that is both requirement for observation and guarantee of difference.[27]

Diane Kitchen's *Before We Knew Nothing* departs interestingly from this convention in that the act of filming never seems to get beyond the arrival scene and its usually suppressed complications. The film details the difficulties of establishing rapport, sharing space, and understanding protocols, rituals, and events. This process of cross-cultural negotiation, rather than an argument about the other culture, becomes the focus of the film. Our attention becomes drawn to what we normally pass over en route to more authoritative knowledge. Like *The Nuer*, *Before We Knew Nothing* renders many of the terms and conditions that underwrite ethnographic authority problematic in revealing ways.[28]

Both literal and metaphorical arrival scenes authenticate an event necessarily distorted by the process and requirements of authentication. Evidentiary demands radically alter existential experience. Heisenberg's principle holds sway: the need for evidence alters the real and places it within generic/formulaic/semiotic constraints. This is a function of imaginary relations, mainly the demand for distance so that power may have the space across which it can operate (and concomitantly display its ethics, politics, and ideology).[29]

The arrival scene is part of a larger pattern of communication and exchange across cultural boundaries. This larger pattern also takes on certain common characteristics in ethnography and pornography. In pornography, it could be termed the one-night stand. Promiscuous relations guarantee a lack of mutually binding commitment and long-term intimacy. In ethnography the comparable pattern is termed "field work." An extended but limited sojourn "in the field" as a professional *rite de passage* also guarantees a lack of mutually binding commitment and long-term intimacy. At the same time this pattern underwrites a potentially life-long series of forays and interventions.

Love and "going native" pose risks to the principles of free association and objective assessment. Each restricts the sexual or ethnographic protagonist's freedom to respond to new situations, possibilities, and challenges. Love, and a shift of cultural allegiances, create a historically conditioned sense of commitment that dissolves the detachment necessary for the extraction of pleasure and knowledge within the economies of a porno- or ethnotopia.

The Commonalities of Disparate Domains

Ethnography and pornography share at least four structural qualities that perform important functions in the maintenance of their representational authority.

Both pornography and ethnography rely on distance but seldom distanciation. Distance, a separation between subject and object, is the prerequisite for sight, realism, desire, and power. It is necessary for the imaginary relationships of identity and opposition, duality and stereotype, hierarchy and control; it is also necessary to the imaginary coherence of realism when it invites us to overhear and look in, unacknowledged.

The objects of both pornography and ethnography are constituted as if in a fishbowl; and the coherence, "naturalness," and realism of this fishbowl is guaranteed through distance. The fishbowl effect allows us to experience the thrill of strangeness and the apprehension of an Other while also providing the distance from the Other that assures safety. The effect of realism is to allow the spectator to dominate the Other vicariously without openly acknowledging complicity with the very apparatus and tactics of domination.

Second, both domains strive to contain excess. They hold pure subjectivity and total strangeness in check; they place them within a regime of the conventional and familiar. Argumentation, rhetoric, science, exposition, and narrative are the explanatory net around those strange and mysterious acts to which the image and its synchronous sound bear witness. Voice-over commentary recuperates images that defy mastery.

The need to resort to commentary is made particularly acute in trance film (*Les maîtres fous*, *Tourou et Bitti*, *Trance and Dance in Bali*, and *A Curing Ceremony*, among others). In *Magical Death*, we see the Yanomamö village leader, Dedeheiwä, take a hallucinogenic powder that sends him into a trance in which he froths at the mouth, rolls on the ground, dribbles green mucus from his nose, and makes unfamiliar gestures. The ethnographer, Napoleon Chagnon, accompanies the synchronous sound in voice-over.

He informs us that Dedeheiwä is defending his villagers from the magic of an enemy group. This authoritative voice explains each of his actions in detail and renders them, in the aggregate, comparable to the ministrations of a country doctor.

Because the actions of Dedeheiwä do not mean what they would normally (in our experience) mean (pain, illness, madness), the spectator must turn to the voice-over for clarification. But the result is that the images come to underscore and buttress the commentary; their excess is drained away. In this way, the voice-over constructs a narrative for the film. Like a narrative, this voice-over cues our expectations (he is taking the drug that will give him magical powers . . .), marks the moment of climax (he engages with dangerous spirits that may take his life . . .) and announces closure (Dedeheiwä rests, victorious). Dedeheiwä's trance becomes subsumed by allegory and analogy; the ethnographer explains the magic of *Magical Death* away.

Third, based on the indexical quality of the image, empirical realism captures details, specificities, and techniques; actions, rituals, and processes such that their representation conforms to their actual, historical occurrence. Empirical realism suggests that what we see occurred much as it would have occurred were we not there to see it.[30] Upon this empirical cornerstone each practice adds elements of psychological realism, involved with the subjectivity of characters, structures of feeling associated with the specific forms of interaction among characters, and historical realism, given over to a realist representation of lived social experience and its meanings.[31]

Both pornography and ethnography also depend, fourthly, on narrative and expository realism. Realism makes its subjects captives. As Gloria Steinem notes, pornography "begins with the root *porno*, meaning prostitution or female captives and ends with *graphus*, meaning writing about or description of."[32] To both practices realism brings with it the baggage of a Western tradition that conflates description with representation, information with knowledge, evidence with sight. The description stands in for the described, erasing any gap between form and meaning:

> The Cartesian cogito, in which self is immediately present to itself, is taken as the basic proof of existence, and things directly perceived are apodictically privileged. Notions of truth and reality are based on a longing for an unfallen world in which there would be no need for the mediating systems of language and perception, but everything would be itself with no gap between form and meaning.[33]

We achieve in our realism that "lost" state of oneness that never was by fixing it in a form that gives it an apparent reality we can never share, except at a distance—via a vanishing point that recedes from us and a vantage point that holds us in check. Like realism which presumes a continual refinement of representation until it becomes one with reality, science has been thought of as continually developing toward some knowable and obtainable truth (the apotheosis of which are the Grand Unification Theories of physics). But while narrative realism has more to do with what we would call the nonauthorized gaze, a gaze that opens onto fictions and fantasies, bearing perhaps some relation to Freud's primal scene, the expository realism of science operates as the legitimate bearer of the gaze, sanctioned under the watchful eye of the Law and opening onto truth and knowledge.

The Paradoxes of Sexual and Cultural Knowledge

Both pornography and ethnography promise something they cannot deliver: the ultimate pleasure of knowing the Other. On this promise of sexual or cultural knowledge they depend, but they are also condemned to do nothing more than make it available for representation.

In pornography the paradoxical state of the viewer revolves around pleasure:

—We are pleased and yet not pleased entirely.

—We extract pleasure but never the pleasure that is (only) represented. We defer our own pleasure, perhaps indefinitely, in favor of those who represent its fullest satisfaction (the actors). We cannot break the narrative illusions of pleasure without breaking the illusions of narrative.

—We are caught within oscillations of desire and pleasure. We acquire a desire *for* this oscillation per se. This leads to the deferment of the satisfaction of desire in favor of the perpetuation of desire itself.

In ethnography we encounter the paradoxical structure of knowledge:

—We want to know and yet not know completely. We seek to make the strange known, or, more precisely, to know strangeness. We want to *know* it but to know it *as strangeness* as such, to know that by being beheld as strange, it continues to elude full comprehension. The motivating force of curiosity persists, conserving the strangeness of what we seek to know.

—We extract knowledge and yet never the knowledge that is represented (which is *their* knowledge). We defer the full knowledge available to those who represent it, perhaps indefinitely. We cannot break the expository illusion of knowledge without breaking the illusion of exposition.

—We are caught within oscillations of the familiar and the strange. We acquire a fascination *with* this oscillation per se, which leads to a deferment of the completion of knowledge in favor of the perpetuation of the preconditions for this fascination.

These oscillations amount to an ambivalence. The ambivalence cannot be overcome within the realm of the imaginary where pornography and ethnography base themselves. Ambivalence goes back to the self/Other relation of identity and opposition in the Lacanian imaginary. (The imaginary derives from Lacan's story of the child's mirror-phase where he or she discovers that reflections of oneself, like the visual image of another, appear to exude a solidity and mastery not accessible to the self; this image then forms the basis for identity and desire prior to language and the symbolic representation of self with signifiers like "I.") We cannot help but be ambivalent about the image of an Other that is essential to our own identity but not under our corporeal or mental control. Kaja Silverman writes, "As a consequence of the irreducible distance which separates the subject from its ideal reflection, it entertains a profoundly ambivalent relationship to the reflection. It loves the coherent identity which the mirror provides. However, because the image remains external to it, it also hates that image."[34]

Ethnography and pornography operate within the inauthentic dialectic of this ambivalence as do other forms of mimetic art. They console with mastery, which has often been associated with a sadistic or fetishistic pleasure. These two discourses also offer submissive fascination devoted to prolonging moments of rapture and suspending movement toward resolution, which some have associated with masochistic pleasure. These pleasures oscillate. The oscillation allows cultural or sexual practices to become known, or controlled, while also allowing these discursive practices to remain in control. Ethnographic and pornographic discourses retain control through the fascination they exert by means of these paradoxical, ambivalent pleasures.

Ethnography and pornography are condemned never to escape an economy of domestication. We are condemned to settle for a pleasure/knowledge that, with its aftertaste of ambivalence, testifies to the struggle for power, control, and the elimination of risk. We desire to know, but not to know everything; we want to be pleased but not pleased entirely. We have the power to perpetuate this state; ambivalence is its trace.

Moments of Risk and Subversion

Troubling moments arise that can signal the limitations or assumptions within which these two forms of representation function. In pornography, two forms of potential "trouble" within the films discussed here are lesbianism, often recuperated by being structured for a male gaze, and love, often recuperated as receptive to open or swinging relationships. Another risk would be the absorption of characters in their own pleasure. This might include the absence of the cum shot (ejaculation might occur out of sight, less as a spectacle than a personal pleasure, indifferent to our gaze). Absorption might also include the loss of the performers to the ideal spectator when they no longer tacitly arrange themselves as though at the behest of an invisible, orchestrating presence. Videotapes currently circulating through informal exchange networks among participant-producers (couples who record their own sex acts in order to exchange their videotapes with others) suggest something of this possibility. They operate within a distinct, if still dystopian, economy.

In ethnography a persistent threat is that of going native. This threat is held in check by institutional discipline. In this case the "discipline" discredits the loss of objectivity or the forfeiture of appropriate methodology implicit in total absorption into another culture. Unauthorized accounts by those who lack institutional legitimacy often provoke retaliation that is symptomatic of this threat to the discipline. (The works of Carlos Castaneda, and Florinda Donner's *Shanbono: A True Adventure in the Remote and Magical Heart of the South American Jungle* provide examples.)

Altered states, often recuperated by voice-over commentary of explanation and allegory, are another potential threat similar to the threat of characters absorbed in their own pleasure. Altered states signify a "loss" of the informant or subject to the ethnographer and induces the need for recovery. The ethnographer feels compelled to help us see what is going on when it is no longer empirically self-evident. (Rouch's *Tourou et Bitti*, with Rouch's determination to provoke and record a trance that is never fully explained, is something of an exception. *Trance and Dance in Bali* and *Magical Death* are more the norm.)

Alternatives

If we are to imagine alternatives to these regimes as they have existed, more than moments of potential trouble and subversion is necessary. One alternative might be described as an erotics. This would mean more specifically the eradication of the power, hierarchy, and control produced by distance and voyeurism. In ethnography, similar alternatives might be termed dialogue, heteroglossia, political reflexivity, and the subversion of ethnocentrism. All of these alternatives would require distanciation from the ethnographic effect of hierarchy and control. They would remove the stigma of going native by removing the disciplinary will to knowledge that results in paradoxical and ambivalent experience.[35]

These alternatives call for an end to pornography and ethnography as they have existed. They dissolve the oppositions of Them/Us, Self/Other, male/female that mask hierarchy as difference. These alternatives arise as voices from "the other side" that insist on being heard. They call into question the pornographic imagination (control, dominance, objectification, voyeurism). The call for a new pornography is not a choice between eroticism and "hard core" pornography. The more radical call is for a dissolution of the mechanisms of hierarchy while retaining the possibilities of the explicit. The most crucial hierarchy is the one that treats the penis as the representative of the phallus, as the signifier of mastery and control itself. Linda Williams writes, when erection, penetration, and ejaculation are no longer the primary, self-evident measures of male pleasure, then a realm of female pornotopia may be at hand. . : . If the sexual other is ultimately unknowable, then all the more reason to desire this knowledge, especially now that what was once the "other" has begun to make the journey herself. A pornographic speculation about pleasure that begins in the "other place" of a heterosexual feminine desire and pleasure, that constructs meaning in opposition to the unknowable mystery of masculine desire and pleasure, and that journeys to the male other would now seem possible. It remains for women to decide whether to undertake this journey.[36]

Alternative forms of representation also challenge the ethnographic imagination. The classic humanist virtues of empathy for others and a yearning for the ideal; an ethic of tolerance, good will, and understanding; and a methodology of field work coupled to participant observation—these structures burden us with a prefabricated Other no matter how lovingly this Other is observed. The most vivid embodiment of a lovingly fabricated Other may still be the splendid dioramas in the Africa Hall at the Museum of Natural History in New York.[37] The embalmed animals testify to an encounter where one side always had the final word. The challenge is to listen to what uncontained, unembalmed, self-representing others have to say; to evoke the give and take of conversation that matters as crucially to the one as to the other rather than represent, explain, describe, or interpret others in ways that matter very little to anyone but ourselves. As Trinh Minh-ha says of anthropology, "A conversation of 'us' with 'us' about 'them' is a conversation in which 'them' is silenced. . . . Anthropology is finally better defined as 'gossip' (we speak together about others) than as 'conversation' (we discuss a question). . . ."[38]

The pornographic and ethnographic imaginations have had their liberating effect (pornography from a stultifying Victorian censorship, ethnography from a smug superiority to other cultures), but neither remains defensible. The hierarchical, hegemonic, institutional interests they serve are all too apparent.

VIII

REPRESENTING THE BODY

QUESTIONS OF MEANING AND MAGNITUDE

"It's starting to rain again. The rain had slacked up a little bit. They've backed the motors of the ship for just holding it, just enough to keep it from . . .

It's burst into flames! Get this, Scotty. Get this, Scotty. It's crashing, it's crashing, terrible. (In a choked-up voice throughout), Oh, my—get out of the way, please—it's burning, bursting into flames and it's falling on the mooring mast and all the folks in between. . . . This is terrible. This is one of the worst catastrophes in the world. (Sobs) . . . Four or five hundred feet into the sky. It's a terrific crash, ladies and gentlemen, the smoke and the flames now, and the plane is crashing to the ground, not quite to the mooring mast. (Sobs, chokes.) Oh, the humanity, all the passengers, teeming around here. I don't believe . . . I can't even talk to people whose friends are out there. It's a . . . (sobs), I can't talk, ladies and gentlemen, honest; it's a laid-down mass of smoking wreckage, and everybody can hardly breathe. I'm sorry; honest, I can hardly breathe. I'm going to step inside where I cannot see it. Scotty, that's terrible. (Sobs) I can't . . . Listen, folks, I'm going to have to stop for a minute because I've lost my voice. This is the worst thing I've ever witnessed."

—Live radio commentary on the crash of the Hindenburg dirigible, May 6, 1937

"There seems to be a major malfunction."

—NASA's voice-over commentator during the explosion of the Challenger space shuttle, January 28, 1986

229

A moment erased from the subsequent narrativization of the Challenger space shuttle disaster was this initial response by NASA's own voice-of-God narrator. As the enormous, brilliant burst of exploding fuel ripped the entire rocket into fiery shards, the narrator could only concede that the malfunction was major. Language as regulation and control, language as anaesthetic for the emotions: the voice of NASA speaks in a register that abolishes the feeling and pain of the individual even as tragedy strikes. Unlike the appalled but helpless commentator at the Hindenburg disaster, NASA's spokesman had acquired the ability to represent the hazards of flight, the risks of missions, and the experience of death with the detachment of empirical science and faceless bureaucracy.

These words have been lost; not a single report has referred back to them. NASA's own vision was superseded by a national dramaturgy that sought to render the perfunctory and mechanical as destiny and sacrifice. This spectacular obliteration of human lives cannot be taken quite so lightly by the body politic. These are not just any lives, but individuals made into representatives of the American ethos, the national imperative to mobility, ascendance, conquest. The "malfunction" may not have been theirs but America's national destiny lay in their hands, or so the dramaturgy that quickly enveloped the event would have us believe. Those seven individuals required recovery, not in the flesh, but in the spirit, as exemplary embodiments of cultural ideals, thereby reaffirming a shared sense of national purpose.

The grotesque juxtaposition of event and commentary, evidence and statement points toward the very disjuncture this chapter sets out to explore. The report of a "major malfunction" raises the question of how any narrative or expository frame can be of an order of magnitude commensurate with the magnitude of what it describes.[1] Narrative and exposition are alway forms of miniaturization that seek to encapsulate a "world" that bears some meaning for us. Documentary presents a world we take to be congruent and coterminous in quality and nature with the one in which we act rather than re-presenting an imaginative transposition of it. In documentary people act as agents in history, not narrative, regardless of how persistently we give meaning to history by means of narrative. What structure might documentaries have that will conjure or restore for the viewer those orders of magnitude appropriate to the full dimensionality of the world in which we live and those who inhabit it?

Mortality, Myth, and Magnitude

This question seems particularly fitting for documentary film form since this form activates conventions that prepare us to expect a privileged status for the indexical link between sign and referent. Our apprehension of this link anchors the image in the specificity of a given moment. Such moments are understood as subject, at the moment of filming, to the vicissitudes of history rather than the coherence of narrative. Some quality of the moment persists outside the grip of textual organization. The issue of magnitude goes beyond formal pattern per se and the search for structure, style, and system commensurate to that which is represented, for these are achievements whose satisfaction is fundamentally *aesthetic.* Considerations of magnitude take us further, toward an awareness of what is fundamentally incommensurate and the *praxis* required to address it. As such, issues of magnitude rejoin issues of rhetoric and political reflexivity. To add yet sharper focus, emphasis will fall to the body and the recurring question of what to do with people, of how to *represent* another person when any representation threatens diminution, fabrication, and distortion.

The quotations that launch this chapter are more exclamations than descriptions. The raw spontaneity impelling them reveals assumptions and predispositions about the relation between observer and event that more well-honed utterances might not. The sense of rhetorical "design," the effort to enlist language to fulfill specific designs on the listener, has little purchase here. The utterances do not stand removed from history through the polish of aesthetic or rhetorical form. Though spoken on behalf of others—as commentary—these voices implant themselves in history as commonsensical, spontaneous (and thereby ideological) responses to immediate experience. They acknowledge in a more direct way, therefore, the mortal threat of obliteration, the urgency of control, the will to power, and the central place of language as an arena in which system and necessity struggle to prevail despite immanent chaos. At the "zero-point" of reflexivity or rhetorical design, they nonetheless achieve the effect produced by reflexivity or rhetoric in less spontaneous, more crafted texts: the invocation of magnitudes that exceed any text. The ceaseless slide of signifiers breaks apart: we have a glimpse across the gulf between representation and experience.

Questions of magnitude are always questions that run not so much against the grain as beyond it, outside the constraints of any given system. These two quotations, though polar opposites in their tone, are attempts to stop up the leakage of meaning threatened by disaster. They signal, through hysteria on the one hand and bureaucratic numbness on the other, the radical difference between a discursive system (language) and experience, or its aggregation, history. "History is *not* a text, not a narrative, master or otherwise. . . . History is what hurts, it is what refuses desire and sets inexorable limits to individual as well as collective praxis."[2] A magnitude of excess remains. It is a specter haunting what can be said or written.

Questions of magnitude return us to the problem of the relationship between a sign and its referent, a relation largely dismissed within the semiotic and poststructural universe of the discursive "prison-house" that seldom moved beyond the strictly textual relations of signifier to signified.[3] Documentary, though, requires awareness of an antecedent reality before it can come into being as a specific form of representation. *The issue of magnitude involves a tension between the representation and the represented as experienced by the viewer.* Remove this tension, enter a realm of aesthetic engagement, and the specific qualities and questions of documentary no longer apply.[4]

At issue here is the experience of a subjective condition triangulating viewer, representation, and represented. Our concern is with the expressive modalities brought into play even by descriptive or "objective" representations that turn our attention to an antecedent, historical reality. This can be considered an aspect of ideology where ideology is at its most affective. Ideas, concepts, and values cannot be simply announced if they are also to be believed. In this, dialectical, sense, the culture provides the "base" for those activities of economic production through which things—physical objects like the human body—take on the significance of signs within human communication and exchange. Cultural production invites our consent to an assigned place within the signs and meanings of social space. It renders the flat, objective givenness of the world into a complex realm of intersubjective meaning and values.

The human subject requires introduction to this viscerally engaging realm so that attachments can be made between desire and the world disposed around us. Visceral experience must be rendered meaningful. We require an imaginative sense of what it means to belong or participate (what community is like); of what conditional states participation engenders (what it would be like if . . .); of what forms of subjectivity accompany these possibilities (how would it feel if . . .), and of the *form* within which subjectivities become incarnate (how would it look, what patterns would pertain if . . .). From such intangibles—the imaginary and symbolic realms within which rhetoric trades—come motivation and purpose, discipline and self-control, belief and advocacy, in short, all those magnitudes of subjectivity that position us in relation to what exists, what is appropriate, and what is possible.

Magnitude, then, raises questions not only of indexical correspondence between a text and the visual world but also of ideological correspondence between a text and the historical world. The magnitudes opened up by a text are not merely a matter of naming something of profound importance but, more tellingly, of situating the reader in a position where these magnitudes receive subjective intensity. Questions of magnitude pertain to our experience of a text rather that its formal structure or cognitive comprehension.[5] These questions move us toward a *politics* of phenomenology, a recognition of the priority of experience not as a structure to bracket and describe but as the social ground or foundation for actual praxis.

Central to this question is our experience of the body. Documentary film insists on the presence of the body. It exerts a relentless demand of *habeas corpus*. Like the legal system, documentary discourse insists on the principle that we must be presented with the body. Witness and testimony, deposition and refutation, accusation and denial—all depend on direct encounter and physical presence.[6] The cinema in general cannot leave the incarnation of characters or social actors to the viewer's imagination. An indexical bond prevails between the photographic image of the human body and the more abstract concept of historical or narrative agency. We may imagine Hamlet or Jesus to have whatever likeness we, and our culture, choose to assign, but the image of Martin Luther King, Jr. delivering his "I Have a Dream" speech or of the Chinese citizen who stopped an entire line of tanks with his body during the Tiananmen massacre of June 4, 1989 cannot be separated from their photographic likenesses.

Though memorable, neither Sir Lawrence Olivier's nor Sir Richard Burton's Hamlet enjoys ontological superiority to any other performer's work, but John F. Kennedy's "Kennedy" will always be of a decidedly different order from Martin Sheen's, or any other actor's "Kennedy." A photographic likeness offers evidence of a life as it was lived and experienced in the flesh, within the constraints of the historical, physical body itself. And yet that likeness in and of itself is insufficient evidence. It is but a frozen moment, an artifact, that requires the animating force of time, narrative, and history to gain experiential meaning. An *awareness* of the tension between representation and that which is represented, of magnitudes beyond representation, is the foundation for praxis informed by a text.[7] Here is where cinema, as André Bazin acknowledged in the final sentence of his famous essay, "The Ontology of the Photographic Image," "is also a language."

To Reach Out and Yet Not Touch Someone: Spectacle or Vivification

Consider the opening of *Roses in December*. The opening newsreel-like footage that begins the film reminds us of that time when the body is no longer evidence of life but death. *Roses* begins with the disinterment of four American women murdered in El Salvador, among them Jean Donovan, a lay missionary for the Catholic Church. The graphic, clinical nature of the camera's gaze, or stare, disturbs profoundly. The sight of a body pulled out of its grave by ropes only to flop inertly on the dusty ground, the physical residue of what had been a human residence, approaches the unwatchable. The tension between what we see and what it represents may exceed all bounds. Such images testify to the problematics of the professional or clinical gaze.[8] What ethical (or political) perspective authorizes such a sight? What response can we as viewers have? What effort is called for to restore the full magnitude of a life that has reached its termination? By what means and to what ends can the absent life that inhabited this inert body be given representation, however incomplete and partial?

These questions involve engagement within an ideological, value-saturated domain. The issue of magnitude, though, receives pointedly incomplete address within the terms Western culture has traditionally reserved for it. Whether speaking of an individual considered "one of us" or of the Other, neither the symbology of martyrdom nor the iconography of victim, neither the emotional state of sympathy nor the benevolence of charity provides an adequate frame of reference. These icons and feelings depend upon the maintenance of the very distance their emotional valuation is meant to overcome. They offer a subjective state of being for the one who reaches out that enforces separation just as romantic love sustains a state of being in love that, to persist, requires unrequited passion. (The AT&T jingle bidding us to "reach out and touch someone," used in special ads sponsoring the Live-Aid concert for famine in Ethiopia is apt, for a telephone company: the gesture exonerates us from physical contact which it offers to simulate.) Victims and martyrs float in the timeless realm of the ill-fated or exemplary; sympathy and charity must be bestowed, not negotiated. These terms all uphold Otherness as a precondition for their existence rather than overcome it.

The question of magnitude involves a different order of engagement. The terms remain emotional, experiential, visceral. At issue is vivification, rendering *felt* what representations only allude to. Affective ties must be forged obliquely, between viewer and representation but in relation to the historical referent. Vivification is not identical to persuasiveness, though it may be an essential part of it. (What becomes most vivid is the excess that remains after evidence and argument, rhetoric and conviction have had their say.) Vivification is not at all similar to spectacle, though it may contribute to it. Spectacle is more properly an aborted or foreclosed form of identification where emotional engagement does not even extend as far as concern but instead remains arrested at the level of sensation.

What vivification involves is more closely aligned with a felt sense of contradiction, dilemma, or existential paradox.[9] This is a specific aspect of those participatory, conditional, and subjective states of being (what it would be like if . . . and so on). They embody a sense of disparity between what is and what might be. These states of being are the means by which political reflexivity becomes more than a formal exercise as well. The magnitudes that require restoration circle around nascent structures of feeling, experiences as yet uncategorized within the economy of a logic or system, something like what Roland Barthes described as the "third" or "obtuse meaning" in certain images from Eisenstein,[10] a meaning that might serve to subvert rather than destroy narrative. Similarly, magnitude might subvert those comforts discourse provides (structure, order, distance, closure) without destroying the very condition of its own emergence (the discursive formations themselves).

How, for example, can the body be both an agent and an object? How can it be testimony to life and evidence of death? How can a person live, subject to the vicissitudes of history, and yet be remembered as somehow transcendent, available for mythic reinterpretation? How can an economic system that destroys its environment not destroy itself? How can what appears to be difference and equity on one level become hierarchy and control on another? Systems that produce subjects who are multiple, split, and layered provide a rich spawning ground for contradiction and paradox. A text may vivify these tensions and thereby heighten our own awareness and experience of contradiction or paradox as a step in the process of disentangling, recasting, or transforming them.

What calls for vivification, therefore, is not the sound and fury of spectacle, not the empirical realities of facts and forces, but the experiential awareness of difference that, in the social construction of reality, has been knotted into contradiction. Texts, precisely because they operate as miniaturized and more formally controlled domains, make this possible in specific ways. They bring to mind the difference, for example, available for remaking, between a representation and that which is represented, between text and context itself, and, with it, the difference between the physical body and the discursive representations we make of it. Reality itself is available for reconstruction; texts may give us our first glimpse of what something is "really like," offering, as if for the first time, a representation of what is posited to have always been there. As Walter Benjamin suggested, this process, perhaps intrinsic to mimetic art, accelerates greatly in the industrial (and postindustrial, postmodern world). With the loss of "aura" everything is freed from its position inside tradition. Everything is available for representation, and remaking.[11]

The historical context enters documentary in a distinctive way, as excess and as a subtext. To move, persuade, or convince; to address and at least appear to resolve contradiction, to bring home a sense of magnitude present *in absentia*, the text must acknowledge and work on history. To the extent that symbolic action is a way of making a difference in the world, the world must be brought into the domain of the symbolic rather than simply referred to or reflected as something intrinsically distinct from such action. As Jameson puts it,

> The symbolic act therefore begins by producing its own context in the same moment of emergence in which it steps back over against it, measuring it with an eye to its own active project. The whole paradox of what we are calling the subtext can be measured in this, that the literary work or cultural object itself, *as though for the first time*, brings into being that situation to which it is also at one and the same time a reaction [italics mine].[12]

The sense in which a preexisting reality receives representation as though for the first time may be particularly acute with written fiction where those indexical anchorages so crucial to the documentary are absent. *In Cold Blood* and *Ragtime* give palpable texture to what had been, though real, far more elusive prior to these textualizations. The texts enter an imaginative terrain for which few other guides are available. A documentary dealing with the Holocaust or apartheid enters a terrain where history has already been textualized over and over again, in images as well as in words. And yet, the sense that this reality now comes before us, as though for the first time, remains powerful. This is largely because reality is represented with an eye to the text's own project, its own argument. But it is also because the text locates on the person of its subjects, as it were, the tensions, conflicts, contradictions, and paradoxes of a historical moment, making them real, as though for the first time, because they are rendered with a specificity they have never had before. There is little need to fear, for documentary, the effect Jameson notices at work in much written literature, where this impression of reality becomes credited entirely to the text, where an illusion persists that "the very situation itself did not exist before [the text created it], that there is nothing but a text, that there never was any extra- or contextual reality before the text itself generated it."[13] The represented instance clearly existed before the camera. What may not have existed prior to representation is the meaning, value, and affective experience of this situation or event in the subjectivity of others. History awaits us outside the text, but aspects of its magnitude may be discovered within.

To witness, in *Shoah*, the Israeli barber who repeatedly deflects and delays the line of Claude Lanzman's questioning away from the vividly remembered reality of being a barber in a Nazi death camp, shaving the heads of those about to die, or the inability of the former diplomatic courier to sit calmly before a camera when asked to recount his experience of entering the Warsaw ghetto so that he could take a first-hand report of the conditions to the Allied leaders (he breaks down and insists the camera withdraw), places us in front of representations that attest to a historical reality that takes on orders of magnitude experienced as though for the first time, in this particular moment, in relation to these specific people and their bodily display of trauma that time cannot heal. In the PBS documentary *Arab and Jew: Wounded Spirits in a Promised Land* Palestinian workers describe how they pass border checkpoints easily in the mornings, when their arrival at Israeli factories is required on economic grounds but when arms and supplies could also be smuggled *into* Israel. In the evenings, though, they are harassed, delayed, and detained on their trip back to occupied territory. Punctuality is no longer an issue and the lesson of power can be taught at the leisure of the powerful. The representation of this pattern affords us, as though for the first time, a feeling for the magnitude of contradictions that manifest themselves in the tense, frustrated, and yet submissive bodies of those who must not resist too openly the control of speech and movement exercised upon them.

The mortality of the body presents a continual challenge to documentary. It eludes all strategies of representation. It is, in the crucial moment of its occurrence, unrepresentable. Vital *signs*, representations, provide us with a boundary across which life can pass surreptitiously, but they remain indifferent to the fate of the values we assign or the feelings we attach to it. Death is the deduction or cessation of something within, unseen.

Representation turns to those vital signs that provide an oblique index of what cannot be shown directly like the unconscious. These signs are both medical (pulse, EKG, etc.) and social (bullet holes, stab wounds, scenes of mass destruction). These latter signs are familiar ones in the age of "modern" warfare and mass death. The ethical/political/ideological issues they raise are of significant magnitude themselves. *Consuming Hunger* addresses precisely this issue with regard to the famine in Ethiopia, *Blood of the Beasts* in relation to the urban abattoir, *Night and Fog* with regard to the Holocaust. How can we vivify the contradictions of an event that is itself constructed of the unimaginable, the unwatchable, the unbearable? Fiction, with its simulation of the historical, is at its most superfluous in such cases. Films like *Sophie's Choice, The Pawnbroker, The Holocaust, Playing for Time,* and *War and Remembrance,* which represent the death camp experience of specific individuals, exert a centripetal force that obscures the relation between the representation and its historical referent. Performance, character development, and narrative structure insinuate themselves, as does the quality of "gloss"—that polished or lacquered look of reconstructions, make-up, and costume whose power to simulate is of a very different order from the power of the documentary image to authenticate. What we see is no longer the referent represented as though for the first time, but as it has been rendered many times before, long enough to constitute an iconography and structure, a sourcebook for stereotype and spectacle. Something other than fiction like any other is called for, and documentary form offers one possible avenue of approach.[14]

Bodies at Risk and the Prophylactic Measures Taken

With documentary film we tender belief that the referent has the same status as that of our own bodies. Its mortality is as much at stake as our own. Death is not a simulation but an irreversible act. At stake is representing the indignities and hazards flesh is heir to with sufficient magnitude to escape the security of comfortable responses of charity or sympathy to martyrs and victims.

The spectacle of the Hindenburg and Challenger disasters underscores a primary preoccupation in this century: risks of erasure. What the Hindenburg dirigible represented as accident, the Holocaust represented as policy. What the *Nacht und Nebel Erlaß* (Night and Fog Decree) of December 7, 1941 authorized (the secret, unexplained removal of citizens from their homes and neighborhoods by paramilitary forces) became the backbone of institutionalized terrorism throughout Latin America (the "disappearance" of dissidents and critics). Inclusion within collectivities carries risk— be it the virulence of anti-Semitism and racism, or the more temporary risk of sharing an elevator, an airplane, a hypodermic needle, or football stadium. The risks of automobile and airplane accidents make everyday life a scene of violent, sudden departure in an unexpected sense while terror-ism and sabotage place the individual life at the hands of a chilling mixture of technology and desperation. Actuarial tables attest to the heightened risks of insecticides, food additives, car emissions, and industrial pollutants. The terrifying power of cancer to turn the body against itself now combines with the capacity of AIDS to prevent the body from defending itself. The vicissitudes of modern life propose a landscape of biosocial hazard on a scale unimaginable only a decade ago. All those diminutions of self that the continuing hierarchies of race, sex, and class impose combine with these threats of erasure to place the body under siege. Visible, enduring testi-mony to the body's persistence becomes all the more important as threats of its permanent erasure become more pervasive.

Posing a threat from another direction are risks of possession. Econo-mies of colonization or, in a more tempered jargon, corporeal manage-ment, operate to take over effective control of the body, to safeguard it, to regulate its activity, to oversee its movements. "Our bodies, our selves" was once a feminist slogan but it also announces the risks of self-possession. The slogan converts the body into a commodity. Proprietary rights must be assigned to the body's rightful "owner," one's self. The self then doubles as an entity distinct from the body it seeks to control while remaining, in another sense, a wholly owned subsidiary of that very body. This produces an existential paradox: your self *owns* your body, but your body *is* your self. This knots up difference into contradiction. The paradox goes to the heart of questions of representation: how to represent taking control of some-thing as a liberating act without replicating the imaginary, hierarchical patterns of control itself?

The prevailing metaphor for the custodial, therapeutic, punitive, or emancipatory management of the body is prophylaxis. Constraints and safeguards applied to the body, adopted willingly, accepted as necessary constraints on the free flow of difference, have great currency in an age when elemental fluids of life (semen and blood) are also fluids of death, literally poisonous carriers of a lethal virus. All the way from airport security checks to Foucault's four main sites for the production of sexuality—the female body, the child as desiring subject, the procreative couple, and the "perversions" of the non-procreative—patterns of bodily discipline take hold that, by their very nature, testify not to power and security for the body, but threat, contagion, and the loss of control. Some risks of posses-sion are, if accepted, reasonable risks, for our own good, but diminutions all the same. Some enable others to do to us what their license allows, in the name of one cultural ideal or another, the realization of which may be at our own bodily expense.

The body is the battle site of contending values and their representation. Images of the stable, fixed, and secure serve as a kind of talisman, warding off the mutable, vulnerable, and malleable qualities of the body. A vast repertoire of popular myths and heroes complements the stereotypes and biases of sexism and bigotry to form a cultural diorama in the social imaginary. Popular heroes and stars, with their idealized appearances and memorable feats, offer icons of imaginary solidity or perfection. Ideologies in the narrow sense of organized belief systems flatten contradiction, ambiguity, or difference into either/or polarities of universal applicability. Voice-of-God narration and newscast anchormen, or, on occasion, anchorwomen, with their stentorian truth claims, offer a potential support system for the stabilization of these ideologies, or "commonsensical" positions. Celebrities, while they last, present another. The male hero of the Rambo series and, in a more white-collar vein, the Michael Douglas villain of *Wall Street* propose models for being in the world in which a solid coat of character armor guarantees both indestructability and impenetrability. The cyborg visions of *Robocop, The Terminator,* "Max Headroom," and *Bladerunner* carry the tendency to a logical conclusion. The cyborg simulacrum replaces the original body and many of its flaws or inefficiencies while giving humanoid representation, including desire, to a machine.

These images of the body reorganized according to a managerial paradigm attempt what Jean-Paul Sartre suggested the anti-Semite, as prototype for those whose identity depends on an Other constructed from their own imaginary projections, attempted:

> How can one choose to reason falsely? It is because of a longing for impenetrability. The rational man groans as he gropes for the truth; he knows that his reasoning is no more than tentative, that other considerations may supervene to cast doubt on it. He never sees very clearly where he is going; he is "open"; he may even appear to be hesitant. But there are people who are attracted by the durability of a stone. They wish to be massive and impenetrable; they wish not to change. Where, indeed, would change take them? We have here a basic fear of oneself and of truth. What frightens them is not the content of truth, of which they have no conception, but the form itself of truth, that thing of indefinite approximation. It is as if their own existence were in continual suspension. But they wish to exist all at once and right away. They do not want any acquired opinions; they want them to be innate. Since they are afraid of reasoning, they wish to lead the kind of life wherein reasoning and research play only a subordinate role, wherein one seeks only what he has already found, wherein one becomes only what he already was. This is nothing but passion [bound up in imaginary oppositions and identities—BN]. Only a strong emotional bias can give a lightninglike certainty; it alone can hold reason in leash; it alone can remain impervious to experience and last for a whole lifetime.[15]

Like hatred and its mythologies of the immutable, narrative and expository argument set out to arrest the uncertainties of time, to turn teleonomy (goal-seeking behavior with variable purposes and goals) into teleology (measurable movement toward a predefined and unalterable goal). The problem posed foreshadows the solution offered; the disequilibrium at the onset prefigures the restoration of balance at the conclusion; the quest of the hero determines the path of the narrative toward success or failure. Narratives impart a predetermination to the passage of time; they constrain the flow of events to those pertinent to the resolution of the dramatic conflict the narrative itself constructs.

Narrative, be it in the form of fictions or historiography, offers consolation in the face of indefinite approximations. It offers a morally textured, ideologically inflected means of accounting for temporal difference, what we commonly call change. Narratives, like mythologies, are the discursive systems into which we translate historical contingency in the hopes of arresting it, at least in our representations, so that facts, practices, and ideals can be organized into patterns of meaning available for adoption, contestation, subversion, or overthrow. We may know that narratives are socially engendered forms of prophylaxis against historical vicissitude. We may choose to believe in them all the same. Their use in documentary film, and the orders of magnitude they may obstruct or reveal, raise the question of representational form: how can situations and events, the bodies of individuals and the exchanges between them be represented in a text so as to promote an apprehension of magnitudes discovered or revealed, perhaps even as though for the first time? Even more pointedly, how can those often represented as Other reappropriate their own images, reestablish their own places, and reclaim their own bodies, especially when they have been routinely displaced from the position of author or authority? The risks of bodily erasure and of corporeal prophylaxis that pervade our cultural epoch make these questions urgent.

Reflexivity and the Purpose of Magnitude

Questions of magnitude also raise issues of purpose. To what end do we seek to confound any simple sense of truth, any reassurance that things are, indeed, just as they seem? Fundamental motives arise from aesthetic, spiritual, and political ground: to make us see our relation to the world anew through the experience of form; to bring us to an awareness of a goal-seeking pattern greater than personal or material purposes at work in the world; to join us one to another in pursuit of the common good. Most contemporary film theory stresses the confluence of the formal and the political, leaving the spiritual as a detour into idealism. This tendency may be a reaction against established, Western religions that promote a transcendental, anthropomorphic spirit rather than an immanent, ecological, or cybernetic one. The teleology of "God's will" replaces the teleonomy of goal-seeking systems.[16] Be this as it may, our primary focus here will be to try to understand how formal choices and strategies in documentary representation open up possibilities of apprehension in aesthetic, spiritual, and political terms.

What is vital is the discovery of the incommensurateness between representation and historical referent, the refusal of containment and closure, and the defiance of totalizing explanation (master narratives of every variety). The paradoxes of representation itself can come into play (the presence-in-absence of the referent, and the filmmaker; the indexical illusion of an ontological bond and the textual fact of semiotic production; the dilemma of the one who will speak for the many, saying what others might have said, yet saying it with a self-conceived rhetorical force that renders it felt and believed, not just heard; and so on). These paradoxes can be heightened and their presence acknowledged. But this may lead only to a formal rather than a political reflexivity. What is needed beyond this is a vivification of existential paradox, lived contradiction itself, those tensions and conflicts that exist between the text and its world, that give form to its context and also inform the text in ways that can be apprehended.

This latter point requires amplification, particularly for documentary, where facts and the apparently simple reflection of social practices are readily admitted but more subjective and experiential dimensions are often disallowed. (Witness the refusal of the American Academy of Motion Picture Arts and Sciences to nominate either *The Thin Blue Line* or *Roger and Me* for an Academy Award—each film was apparently "too subjective" or "too personal" to fit institutional definitions of documentary production.) The very possibility of what I am describing also rejects the notion that narrative or realism exert monolithic effects. On the contrary, although they establish priorities and constraints, they remain susceptible to global forms of transformation as well as to local fissure or contradiction. Such moments afford the opportunity to subvert the frame within which narrative and realism occur. This may be the work of troubled texts (with intermittent lapses or subversions) or troubling ones (with a systematic procedure for overturning our assumptions), the work of, say, *The Battle of San Pietro* or *Sans Soleil* respectively. Both troubled and troubling texts can call into question the "This is so, don't you agree?" invitation of ideological discourse to give assent to what others propose. The result is to open out onto that amplitude of experience beyond the ideology of unity or wholeness by intensifying the very antinomies, the logical scandals, inherent in narrative.[17]

> In the cinema we sense this break between a story and its presentation every time gaps appear in the events or reversals crop up in the standard conventions of the genre. . . . everything, in short, which calls attention to the work of style retards the unmediated flow of illusion and lifts the film experience from the obsessions of the imaginary to the realm of symbolic exchange.[18]

A less formal and more political formulation of dashing illusions occurs in Louis Althusser's essay, "The 'Piccolo Teatro': Bertolazzi and Brecht."[19] In discussing Bertolazzi's *El Nost Milan* Althusser concentrates on the gap between the melodramatic plot and interstitial moments of apparent emptiness when "the people" of Milan take to the stage less to embody the reality of historical experience than to set up a radical contextualization of the melodrama and its potentially all-absorbing dilemmas. This counterpointing exposes the artifice of the self-generated dialectic of the melodrama in contrast to the more intractable dialectic of history. The marginal context qualifies the melodramatic center of the text, rendering it strange. We see the relation of melodrama to historical struggle in a new light, as though for the first time, because this relation has been taken up into the text as the reality of a contradiction: "This silent confrontation of [the melodramatic characters'] consciousness (living its own situation in the dialectical-tragic mode and believing the whole world to be moved by its impulse) with a reality which is indifferent and strange to this so-called dialectic—an apparently undialetical reality, makes possible an immanent critique of the illusions of consciousness."[20] As in the work of Brecht, what is at stake is a renunciation of the transcendental subject and the egocentrism of individual consciousness. To promote an awareness of magnitudes in excess of the self among spectators or viewers, "Brecht's world must necessarily exclude any pretensions to exhaustive self-recovery and self-representation in the form of a consciousness of self."[21]

This exclusion of a pretense to exhaustion, or the fullness of closure and resolution, carries consequences for individual characterization. The consciousness of any one character cannot contain or realize the totality of the text's conditions, however reflexively. A radical decentering must occur that affects the spectator or viewer precisely as a result of its oblique representation in the play, a representation not relayed through identification with the consciousness of a single character. The relation between individual consciousness and the social practices of the culture that have produced it *cannot* be openly, didactically proclaimed (as I am attempting to do here) and still be grasped experientially (though it may be understood). As Althusser puts it,

> This relation ["between consciousness of self alienated in spontaneous ideology . . . and the real conditions of existence"] is necessarily latent in so far as it cannot be exhaustively thematized by any "character" [or spoken commentary—BN] without ruining the whole critical project: that is why, even if is its implied by the action as a whole, by the existence and movements of all the characters, it is their deep meaning, beyond their consciousness—and thus hidden from them; visible to the spectator in so far as it is invisible to the actors—and therefore visible to the spectator in the mode of a perception which is not given, but has to be discerned, conquered and drawn from the shadow which initially envelops it, and yet produced it. . . . In other words, if a distance can be established between the spectator and the play, it is essential that in some way this distance should be produced within the play itself.[22]

Raised political consciousness, then, addresses the contradiction between individual consciousness and a historical dialectic. It attends to those magnitudes that implant themselves in the person, the body, and its consciousness, and yet exceed it. Vivification must be a product of the text itself, an oblique or reflexive evocation of magnitudes referring us to the context, the social ground, which informs it so it may, in turn, inform us.

Conceptualizing the Body

The various forms of reflexivity discussed in Chapter 2 stand available to documentary, although some become more favored at a given moment than others. (At this point the introduction of narrative strategies, and reflexive moves based on them, seems to be at the center of attention while ironic strategies still seem largely premature for a discursive practice that has lagged behind the modernist tendencies prevalent elsewhere.) Reflexivity opens up possibilities for the representation of the body that fracture more conventional approaches. Reflexivity helps move the viewer outside those systems of sympathy, charity, martyrdom, and victimization that limit the apprehension of magnitude to a secure and unthreatening set of protocols for "reaching out." Reflexive strategies challenge the predestination of victims and disasters, and place inside the text the formal means for an experiential awareness of excess, of that which exceeds the frame, including social praxis itself. They begin to complicate the already complex but somewhat static sense of space within which documentary films position the body of social actors.

Documentary space, though literally depicted on a flat surface, can also be thought of by means of a geometric metaphor. In this more metaphoric sense, the spatial disposition of the body occurs along three axes. These axes constitute a prefiguration of bodily representation. (The axes are conceptual rather than real.) They provide the armatures for a repertoire of styles. (Stylistic choices would follow from this initial act of conceptualization.) Just as the classic tropes of metaphor, metonymy, synecdoche, and irony provide a prefigurative ground for the representation of history, so these axes offer a prefigurative framework for the representation of the human body.[23] These axes, then, would offer the armatures by which the body gains full dimensionality as a socially meaningful entity.

These axes mark out three distinct yet overlapping domains: (1) a narrative domain of motivated time and the body as causal agent, or character, (2) an indexical domain of historical time and the body as social actor, or person, and (3) a mythical domain of ahistorical timelessness and the body as cultural exemplar, icon, fetish, or type. We might also term these the "X" axis of narrative plot development, the "Y" axis of historical reference, and the "Z" axis of myth, spectacle, and captivation with the "to-be-looked-at-ness" of the image. (The fetishized object of desire and the transcendent image of the star are important nodes along this third axis.)

Narrative in Documentary

Characters are the agents whereby narrative structure gains coherence and completion, and secondary characters are a function of the strategic moves required for the central character or protagonist. Mythic identifications and historical references get attached to a moving chain of situations and events, actions and enigmas that sweep (or drift) toward a conclusion. Complex strategies of "narrative work"—of rhetorical suasion and conflict resolution (condensation, displacement, secondary revision)—propel the story toward its rendezvous with closure, that end-point dimly discernible in the lineaments of the beginning.

In *Roses in December,* for example, Jean Donovan's life receives narrative coherence from acts that are described rather than depicted since this portrait of her emerges after her murder. The narrative frame includes the imaginative reenactment of the crime itself and an investigation undertaken by the filmmakers (less in order to determine who did it than to learn about a historical situation where murder has acquired a form of [perverse] legitimacy). Elements of narrative plotting inform us that Jean Donovan grows up happily, makes friends, enjoys herself; then she changes her priorities, devotes herself to others, establishes an important love relationship, serves the poor in El Salvador and is, because of this, raped and killed by government soldiers. Home movies, snapshots, archival footage, and the testimony of others provide the retrospective narrative trajectory Donovan herself appears to have enacted. And they do so primarily for the reason suggested by Hayden White rather than any more pyschopathic one: "If every fully realized story, however we define that familiar but conceptually elusive entity, is a kind of allegory, points to a moral, or endows events, whether real or imaginary, with a significance that they do not possess as a mere sequence, then it seems possible to conclude that every historical narrative has as its latent or manifest purpose the desire to *moralize* the events of which it treats."[24]

This function of narrative receives a distinct inflection in documentary. The charged nature of space as an ethical domain, discussed in Chapter 3, comes into play quite vividly in a film like *Roses*. The newsreel footage that records the moment of disinterment allows us to contrast this professional or clinical gaze with a voyeuristic one. The professional gaze is the documentary equivalent of the voyeuristic gaze, but differs in basing itself upon an "objective" view of the scene rather than a subjective one. Both the professional and voyeuristic gazes betray the linkages between power/desire/knowledge that require distance, control, and a disciplined body, a preference for the economy of possession over that of erasure. It is these forms of discipline that *Roses in December*, and other films, attempt to exceed by using narrative devices to address interior magnitudes attributable to the historical person rather than a narrative character.

Documentary has traditionally taken an ambivalent position regarding interior states of mind—particularly in its cinema verité mode where the outer surface of the body, including utterances, takes on the charged importance of a naturalism. Description holds higher priority than narration, to use Georg Lukacs's distinction, because it allows for a greater sense of authenticity based on depicting what other observers would agree had physically occurred. Factual detail has a similar priority in expository documentary for the same reason.[25]

One of the recurring themes in recent works like *Roses in December* is their effort to represent interiority, to narrate as well as describe. Specifically, *Roses* offers an imaginative reconstruction of Jean Donovan's last hours, from her drive to the airport to pick up the other nuns through their detention at a roadblock, their abduction, sexual violation, and cold-blooded execution. It is all shot in tinted black and white and uses dramatic camera angles to convey a foreboding tension. The sequence relies more heavily on the cinematic apparatus to achieve the markings of interiority than on the performance of actors to re-present the four murdered women. Indeed, no-body can replace the bodies that have been historically extinguished. We never see any individuated characters or the faces of any actors. The only sign of human agency that we see during this entire sequence, in fact, is a single hand on the steering wheel of the women's van.

Narrative action takes place here in only minimal association with acting or performance. The one glimpse of the hand is little more than a physical marker of the place of narrative agency. The killers are not individuated. They are not visible at all: no close-ups, no dialogue, no physical movements that can be read as signs of expressivity. Their implied or off-screen presence only serves to circumvent the problematics of an event that might otherwise seem to lack human instigation altogether.

Other films take different tacks toward a representation of interiority without resorting to full fictional enactment. In *Frank: A Vietnam Veteran*, as in the much earlier *Portrait of Jason*, interiority comes from the intensely idiosyncratic and subjective nature of Frank's account of acts of atrocity he committed in Vietnam and the acts of desperation that followed him back home. The bulk of the video is a medium close-up of Frank's "talking head." The subjective element grows from our own subjective response to his style of presentation, his intonation and expression, his tone, and his attitude toward his own past. We move past a descriptive recounting into a far more subjective zone of fascination and repulsion, identification and rejection, moral evaluation and political reckoning that parallels the fictional device of a character/narrator who recounts his/her own story in the hope of gaining our understanding (as in André Gide's *The Immoralist* or Ralph Ellison's *Invisible Man*).

Nicaragua: No Pasarán concludes its portrait of the struggle to defend Nicaraguan sovereignty with an ominous, poetic sequence of American C-135s loading and taking off from a jungle airstrip. Instead of location sound, these telephoto images of lumbering leviathans accompany an eerie, rhythmic Laurie Anderson song, "Here Come the Bombs." (The effect is reminiscent of the phantasmagoric collage of found footage that concludes *The Atomic Cafe*, an ironic re-presentation of 1950s United States government documentaries proclaiming the necessity of nuclear deterrence and the virtues of nuclear energy.) In *Las Madres de la Plaza de Mayo*, as in Michel Brault's *Les Ordres* (on the detention of Quebec citizens under the Canadian War Measures Act in October 1970), the process of interiorization relies on the re-creation of dramatic moments when, in each film, police officers break into an apartment to arrest "subversives." *Las Madres* renders the event in blue-tinted, slow-motion black and white photography with the voice-over commentary of one of the mothers of the disappeared.

Except for *Les Ordres*, which is closer in structure to the docudrama tradition of fiction based on topical events, these films avoid extended performances by actors. In *Roses in December*, a performance as such would be highly troubling, presenting the dilemma of four bodies too many. Fictive performance departs from the indexical compact grounding the reception of documentary. (As something that is culturally based and historically specific rather than ontological, the indexical quality of "non-acting" is more an impression than a reality.) These almost entirely invisible actors in the reenacted rape and murder scene are little more than what Stephen Heath has called "animated entities," pointing out that a lack of physical individuation can be a legitimate feature of the narrative agent/ actor as such. This sequence offers a subjective vision of how specific, historical individuals confronted the moment of their own death as it delivers the body of Jean Donovan to that site at which the film begins and to which meaning must be assigned.

This sequence contrasts instructively with a parallel one in *Salvador*, Oliver Stone's dramatic depiction of recent Salvadoran history as witnessed by an American journalist played by James Woods. Woods's character, like Thompson in *Citizen Kane*, allows for a *You Are There*-like recreation of historical events. Archbishop Romero's assassination, for example, occurs just after Woods and his Salvadoran girlfriend take communion. He becomes an eyewitness to the mass mayhem that ensues when government troops attack the mourners at Romero's funeral service, and it is Woods who introduces us to the liberal but weak-willed American ambassador who, at the decisive moment, capitulates to his advisors and gives the Salvadoran military access to the American matériel they need to defeat the revolutionaries' major initiative.

Among Woods's acquaintances is a plucky young American woman who works with the poor and disabled. She remains rather peripheral to the film's development until, as with other characters we have met, the film shifts away from Woods to follow her momentarily. The moment chosen, of course, is a fateful one. It begins with her driving to the airport, continues as she and three nuns leave, and concludes with their brutal rape and murder by soldiers in civilian dress. In the next scene (but how much later we do not know), their grave site is discovered, the ambassador arrives, gives instructions, and expresses outrage—suspending the aid he will later restore. The bodies are pulled from their common grave with ropes, and James Woods arrives to cradle his friend's dead body and mourn her loss.

The sequence has an uncanny effect, partly because it is unanticipated (we have only minimal clues that this character represents Jean Donovan) and partly because the event, particularly the discovery and disinterment, is rendered with camera shots and dialogue strikingly similar to the archival news footage in *Roses*. Despite this similarity, though, the effect is markedly different.

In *Salvador*, the character's death works mainly to tell us something about the narrative, particularly about the character of the protagonist—his compassion and decency despite appearances and the immoral nature of those around him. "Cathy," the Jean Donovan character, functions as a donor, adding complexity to the hero's character by sharpening the moral contrast between him and the Salvadoran government. Stone underscores this latter point by depicting the rape extensively. In *Roses* it is only mentioned verbally. Stone goes so far as to show a blouse being ripped from one of the women in a conveniently placed beam of light. The sight of her exposed breast shocks and distracts. It reminds us how readily the fiction film will put scopophilic voyeurism in the place of "professional" objectivism. This specific treatment of the rape scene, and this close-up shot in particular, shifts the moral shock that we feel in *Roses in December* on seeing the four dead bodies removed from the earth to a voyeuristic and sadistic register, and earns for the film all the criticisms of the "to-be-looked-at-ness" of its female narrative characters.

This sequence in *Salvador* also "authenticates" the narrative by attaching it to (a re-creation of) an historical event. In *Roses*, Jean Donovan's death serves mainly as the stimulus for the film to tell us something about this person, particularly about the quality of her life and the reasons for her murder. The emphasis becomes what the film can tell us about a life, rather than what a life can tell us about the film. In *Salvador*, the event becomes exemplary of the fictional universe and its characters. A fictional or diegetic frame contains it. It can only exceed this frame metaphorically (the fiction may be *like* real death, *like* the real death of Jean Donovan) rather than existentially. The film moves along its narrative axis without pausing to contemplate the question to which *Roses* devotes itself. It is just another fictional death, powerful in its effect, informative in its placement, disturbing in its representation, and fundamentally removed from the historical realm to which it metaphorically alludes.[26]

Narrative fiction can answer more fully to the question of what is feels like to occupy a given body, to present a certain character, to walk the divide between that moment of spectacle which depends on the physical presence of the person and those moments of narrative that rely on the actions of a character. The incarnation of characters by people (social actors) holds us to the surface of subjectivity in as much as interior states must be displayed on the skin of the actor. But, like the novel, the cinema also has means of engendering subjective states apart from the skills of the actor. The full weight of the cinematic apparatus can be brought to bear in the constitution of an arresting subjectivity. As Barry King notes, "the projection of interiority becomes less and less the provenance of the actor and more and more a property emerging from directorial or editorial decision . . . . [W]hile film increases the centrality of the actor in the process of signification, the formative capacity of the medium can equally confine the actor more and more to being a bearer of effects that he or she does not or cannot originate."[27] These directorial and editing decisions can, of course, be taken up by documentary as well.

One formidable aspect of the generation of an imaginary interiority by the apparatus occurs in the discourse about stars that has its own institutional base outside of films proper. (It is part of the extrafilmic but cinematic institution of motion pictures as an economic industry that manifests itself in talk shows like "Entertainment Tonight," in guest appearances with Johnny Carson or Arsenio Hall, in gossip columns, in fan and lifestyle magazines like *People* and *National Enquirer*, in books and articles, and in posters, billboards, and photographs.) This discourse lends an overarching unity to the disparate roles a star may play by stressing the characterological consistency of the star him/herself. By contrast, the documentary film that mobilizes the "Z" axis of mythic or fetishistic representation cannot rely on this discourse for assistance (unless it is a documentary about a well-known cultural figure). It may draw on the extrafilmic and extracinematic discourses that surround people in the public eye, but, even more suggestively, such documentaries may generate their own discourse about individuals in order to lend greater coherence to the character they construct.

A film like *Roses*, then, incorporates two elements that are usually separated between the fiction film and its institutional context: on the one hand, it re-presents the social *performance* of people (social actors), usually in a manner closely allied to realist acting codes, and, on the other hand, the film generates *testimony* about this social performance or life. This testimonial evidence is built into the text. This contrasts to what in fiction remains a function of ancillary texts or social rituals such as the emulation of stars' fashion or gesture. (The forms of testimonial discourse that appear in *Roses* include the recruited mix of evidentiary sources described above as well as the subjectivizing strategies of reenactment that move toward an exploration of interiority.) The combination of performance by social actors and testimony about their lives serves as the two principal sources of evidence, just as perspective and commentary serve as the two principal forms of textual statement or argument.

The documentary combination of these two usually cross-referenced but differentiated strategies for the fabrication of mythic figures and narrative characters is not a stable one. The changes of register and voice (commentary and observation, interview and read letters, home movies and official press conferences, etc.) fracture "performance"; it becomes more intermittent and available to multiple interpretations. (*Daughter Rite*, for example, reconstructs a (fictive) mother through source material similar to what *Roses in December* uses, but places greater emphasis on the process of memory and family history, in part by using scripted performances by the two "daughters.") Subjective identification with character can be seen to be constructed more readily; its sources are both immediate (in the text) yet diverse (drawn from different discourses). The imaginary unity of character becomes eccentric. Its center, like that of documentary, lies outside itself, in the historical surround and the enunciative strategies used to represent it.

History in Documentary

Documentary texts recruit people but they continue to be historical figures functioning as members of a social collectivity. The historical domain, open-ended and contingent, lies at right angles to the closure of narrative. Indexicality and representations of authenticity disrupt the hermetical seal of narrative. They turn us toward highly localized situations and events. Mythic identification and narrative characterization may be attached to historical people, giving them dimensions greater or less than their "real-life" measure, and existing in tension with the unpredictability of a teleonomic system. The actions and motivations of people whose subjectivity is split, layered, and multiple can only be placed within the molds of icon or character at a price that must be reckoned case by case.

The sense of the historical person is very strong in individual scenes from observational documentary. Such filming roots itself in the present moment of filming, which immediately becomes a representation of a historical moment once this moment begins to figure into a larger text. There is a strong sense of indeterminacy, openness, specificity, and responsiveness to situations and events observed without foreknowledge of their outcome or most telling moments. A vivid sense of the historical present, shorn of narrative (re)organization or mythic elaboration takes hold in individual scenes from *Hospital, Primary, Lorang's Way, Salesman,* and television shows like "Cops." The structuring of a text from this footage, though, returns us to the domains of narrative and myth. Observational films rely upon these domains as armatures for character development as much as any other mode.

Unlike historical fiction, documentary lacks the problem of finding itself with a body too many, namely that of an actor. When an actor reincarnates a historical personage, the actor's very presence testifies to a gap between the text and the life to which it refers. It reduces representation to simulation. Documentary, by contrast, faces a scarcity of resources when it forgoes the use of actors. Its problem is to represent a historical person as such but within a narrative field as a character—an agent of narrative functions— and within a mythic or contemplative field as an icon or symbol—the recipient of psychic investments. Documentary faces the dilemma of a body too few. Actual historical being must also serve as the plastic material for the construction of the agent or character of their own narrative and the icon or persona of their own myth.

Documentaries that accept the burden of a body too many, those that adopt reenactments of historically based events, such as *Les Ordres*, *The Color of Honor*, which evokes the fate of a typical Japanese family at the time of the internment policy for Japanese-Americans during World War II, *Louisiana Story*, with its enacted story of a typical Cajun boy and his family, *Carved in Silence*, which recreates many of the everyday events in the lives of Chinese immigrants who were detained for long periods before being granted admission to the United States, or *The Thin Blue Line*, which reenacts the murder of a policeman, trade documentary authenticity for fictional identification. The "extra" body of the actor mediates our access to the historical event; techniques of lighting, composition, costume, decor, mise-en-scène, and acting style offer an alternative mode of entry and present a different, sometimes conflicting set of criteria of authenticity for the viewer.

The dilemma which André Bazin noted in discussing Stalin and the Soviet cinema also holds true for persons still living: in order to function within a narrative frame, the historical person must suspend his or her historical agency and assume the more static function of a mythic or narrative figure whose full trajectory is known.[28] This is only partially problematic for the deceased historical figure where memory, veneration, and storytelling occur in any case, but the living person is susceptible to the adoption of these very myths as aspects of his or her own self-presentation, a process Bazin found at work in the life of Stalin. (Historical figures begin to pattern themselves after or attempt to qualify the representations that have been made of them, a process Benjamin also noted, principally with the politician and star.)[29]

One refreshingly direct resolution of this conflict between mythic stasis, narrative closure, and historical contingency occurs at the end of *For Your Life*. In this film about a drug rehabilitation program for Oslo youth, one of the key characters is Lone, a young woman who continues to lapse back into drug use when she leaves the program. Rather than offer traditional narrative closure and a moralizing perspective on Lone and the problems of rehabilitation, Endreson's personal voice-over commentary simply remarks, "The film must stop here, in November, 1988." As he says this, we see Lone shake hands with the sound recordist (reminiscent of the farewell in *Soldier Girls* with Private Johnson) and then walk off down an Oslo street. The film makes no further attempt at closure than that.

Being contingent, the historical axis provides evidence more than argument. Argument derives from the narrative and mythic domains. *Roses in December*, for example, offers a wide array of historical evidence. The disinterment of the dead bodies provides the most disturbing evidence of all. Its presence as news footage intensifies the disturbance by invoking the problematic ethics of the professional gaze. *Roses in December* refuses to endorse this mode of observation, evidentiary though it may be. Instead, it offers, in the arrangement of its sequences, a supplemental, human response that joins fact and value, body and meaning, thus restoring magnitudes to self, and Other, that professionalism and voyeurism obscure. The elegiac structure of the film directs the uncontained excess of the newsreel footage—the queasy sense of flouted taboo (staring at the dead)—toward the ethically lived life of a person. Death, the zero point of meaning at the level of the individual life, is recuperated within a larger social, political, religious frame.

Roses bestows meaning without following the trajectory of the mythologizing impulse that remade the bodies of seven lost astronauts into icons of progress and pioneering spirit, into exemplary figures whose historical agency had to be arrested so that they could be fixed in the pantheon of American mythology. Instead the film situates the person as a historical agent whose actions are reconstituted and, in some measure explained, or morally accounted for, within a filmic representation made up of a complex balance of historical reference, narrative characterization, and mythic idealization.

The success of *Roses in December* hinges on its ability to sustain questions of magnitude involving subjectivity and dialectics which its biographical treatment of an individual life provokes. In dealing with a deceased individual, the film can only present its central character as a structuring absence in need of reconstitution. In this project it departs quite sharply from the historical documentary based on interviews and archival material that attempts to reconstruct a past event, rather than an individual life. *Roses* is more similar to those fiction films that set out to recover a past life, beginning at a point from which we may ask, "How did this come to pass?" In setting itself this task *Roses* bears a resemblance to *Young Mr. Lincoln*, although it avoids the suggestions of a monstrous dimension to the (patriarchal) hero and it begins with the tragic assassination, the counterpart of which still lies beyond the concluding horizon of John Ford's film. Still closer analogies are perhaps with *Citizen Kane* (particularly in the stress on the enigmatic, in the use of a largely invisible reporter who travels afar to seek out the insights of those who knew the character, in the multiplicity of voices and evidentiary sources, and in the catalytic, galvanizing force of the moment of death), but *Sunset Boulevard*, *The Power and the Glory*, and *The Barefoot Contessa* also share a similar structural strategy.

The question of balance among these three domains is a crucial one and looms as a serious problem in many documentaries about historical events.

In works such as *With Babies and Banners, Union Maids, The Day After Trinity, Seeing Red, Word Is Out, Solovki Power, Lodz Ghetto,* and *The Wobblies,* the tendency arises to forfeit an independent explanatory frame for the one provided by participant-witnesses themselves. (The current centrality of public television funding for feature-length documentaries and the application of conventional journalistic notions of balance seem to have eased the problem, unfortunately for the wrong [retrograde] reasons.) Oral histories tend to function in historical documentaries as pieces of argumentation rather than as primary source material still in need of conceptual organization. This may be in keeping with a desire to dispute conventions of authority and foster a more heteroglossic form of recounting, but most documentaries have not yet found a way to signal the reflexive turn this stance would represent, if theoretically informed. They do not distinguish between conveying the recollections of others and contesting received notions of history as the product of voices that claim the authority to represent it. Instead they appear to offer a more naive form of endorsement to views that remain partial, at times self-protective, and incomplete rather than suggest the foundation for an alternative conception of history itself.

Even within this more modest framework of witness and testimony, issues of perspective and tone arise that bear upon the question of magnitude. Foremost is the out-of-history status of the interview itself. We no longer witness social actors engaged in historical situations and events but in reflection and recall of such events. Like voice-over commentary, the voice of witnesses comes from elsewhere, from someplace on screen but outside the field of historical engagement itself, apparently. Restoring the full magnitude of complex subjectivities, multiple perspectives, and contingency to historical process is therefore a daunting prospect. Archival footage frequently offers us the sense of the body *in* history, the person as historical figure, whereas interviews offer something closer to the boundary between a disembodied recounting and an embodied enactment.

As well as the quasi-historical status of interviews and oral history themselves, there is also the question of voice or authorial tone. Whether specific individuals can be featured as witnesses central to the very structure of a film and then qualified and contested by other aspects of the film without running the risk of appearing to disbelieve, discredit, or mock them raises important questions of strategy and authorial tone. *The Thin Blue Line* gives signs of something less than full respect for several of its witnesses, especially a heavy-set, female attorney for the defense and three eyewitnesses whose testimony seems hardly credible, as a result of specific choices of framing, musical accompaniment, and cross-cutting. This element of authorial perspective generates a sense of irony that comes at the characters' expense. The difference between this tone and that of *Roger and Me* is that Morris appears to abet characters who also undercut themselves whereas Michael Moore structures encounters in order to undercut others.

A prime example is Moore's interview with Miss Michigan; she tries to show sensitivity as an individual to a poverty that her beauty queen role cannot address (as Moore knows full well), but he compels her to become a demonstration of this disjunction through his insistent questioning. Ironically, Moore shows more appreciation for Deputy Fred Ross, who evicts tenants delinquent with their rent with a simultaneous display of compassion unperturbed by consequences.

Trinh Minh-ha's *Surname Viet Given Name Nam* adopts an even more complex strategy involving staged interviews with nonprofessional actors (Vietnamese women living in the United States who represent Vietnamese women living in postwar Vietnam). These reenactments are based on the transcription of interviews done with women living in Vietnam which were published in French and then translated and rearranged by the filmmaker into a scripted English version. This reenacted testimony is then presented through a strong stylistic filter that calls for very expressionless and monotonal delivery, that sometimes provides subtitles and sometimes does not, that moves characters in and out to the center of the frame or has them turn their backs on us, and that truncates a personal story at a moment of heightened drama (when a woman is about to say whether she ever saw her husband again after they were forcibly separated by government agents).

These devices definitely achieve a reflexive effect—we realize that the factual information, however emotionally laden, is secondary to the problems posed around language and representation, especially issues of translation—but they also attenuate the nature of historical reference to the point where the witnesses seem the opposite of those in, say, *With Babies and Banners*: instead of having the final say on what happened, the women become instruments of a historical narrative, or myth,that is primarily the filmmaker's. The mythic element seems strongest in the stylistic weightings that present seemingly more liberated images of Vietnamese women living in the United States rather than under the oppressive conditions of both Communism and traditional Vietnamese patriarchy. This is offset by hearing the women themselves continue to give voice to the same oppressive ideology of subordination and hearing the filmmaker's voice-over enumeration of the four virtues and three submissions that define female subjectivity in Vietnamese culture. Placing this description over images of more "liberated" women creates an undertow of doubt about how much benefit they reap from coming to America.

Surname Viet refers to interviews as an "outmoded" documentary convention and severely stylizes their construction during the reenacted interviews with women living in Vietnam, but the film also conveys an impression that the interviews remain valuable as evidence for the film's own argument: internalized patriarchal values oppress Vietnamese women wherever they live. This theme raises unresolved issues of its own. Why, for example, give such emphasis to the failures of the Communist government when neither it nor American-style democracy provide a context in which patriarchal oppression can be overcome? Does the root of the problem lie elsewhere: in Vietnamese family structure, in gender roles and subjectivities, or in a Confucianism alluded to but only indirectly? We cannot be sure from what we see nor can we see what the filmmaker proposes as a progressive direction or appropriate target for struggle. In terms of historical representation, issues of magnitude seem flattened by the limited explanation provided for the persistence of women's oppression in Vietnamese culture by either the interviewees or the film's own commentary.

Myth in Documentary

Mythic icons or exemplary figures give concrete representation to cultural ideals and psychic desires. They are imaginary projections, or fetishes, answering to needs that arise within the body politic or the unconscious. The evasion of time and history is what the image of the star, the social stereotype, and the fetishization of the female all have in common. The mythic domain arrests a singular moment, a transfixing glimpse at an otherwise obscure object of desire, and renders it indelible. It tries to seize the moment and make it perpetual. If it is of sufficient force, mythic identification places a blockage in the way of narrative development or historical referentiality. In less arresting forms, the mythic is an integral part of how we experience both narrative and history. (A "great men" theory of history and a woman-as-spectacle mode of narrative pleasure have this element of mythic projection in common. Each must find ways to implant exemplary icons and arresting figures on historical or narrative terrain, through a narrative of personal psychology determined by and responding to its historical surround in the first case, by fictional motivation for the spectacle as in the case of the female showgirl or male voyeur in the second.)

Although the fascination of mythic icons requires concrete representations, the process may find the fragility of the human body a source of acute discomfort. Bodies age. They betray changes of temperament, acumen, and physical ability that mark them as "shadows" of their former selves, as past their prime, as people whose moment has come and gone. Death itself poses the most acute embarrassment of all. The massive acts of commemoration that surrounded the death of the seven astronauts aboard the space shuttle Challenger, the funeral ritual marshaled on the occasion of John F. Kennedy's death, the extraordinarily passionate desire of thousands to participate in the burial of the Ayatollah Khomeini, and the far more modest effort to mark the death of Jean Donovan with a film devoted to her memory all suggest something of the momentus impulse that seeks to turn fallen heroes into icons.

This very process of mythologization works in two directions, transforming the dead into the eternally remembered and taking from the living something of their historical specificity. A terrible objectification occurs that accounts for the eerie disquiet that the living embodiment of a myth (or even the presence of a star or advertising model) can evoke. The absolutely essential, physical body of such myth-bound figures has become uprooted from its historical context. It has undergone a transformation, a virtual transubstantiation. The body of the historical person is used to impersonate some more mythic (either exemplary or cautionary) possibility for self-presentation. But how can the body present itself if it is wearing a (mythic) disguise? Like the nude of classic oil painting, such bodies are condemned never to be themselves. Once made into an icon, symbol, or stereotype, the individual is erased. The challenge for films like *Roses in December, Witness to War, Who Killed Vincent Chin?*, and *The Life and Times of Rosie the Riveter* is to sustain a sense of magnitude that individuates as well as sublimates, that acknowledges the tensions among historical person, narrative agent, and mythic persona.

Sacrifice and the Body

These three conceptual domains of bodily representation take the fact of the human body and rework this physical "stuff" into a literal embodiment of social practices and cultural ideals. In each case we find the body recruited and trained for a given set of practices, and modeled after an ideal toward which it is aimed. For each domain we can assign specific practices and ideals:

(1) The domain of the mythic: the practice of social control and the ideal of transcendental sacrifice.

(2) The domain of narrative: the practice of knowledge and the ideal of wisdom.

(3) the domain of history: the practices of labor and the sex-gender system (production and reproduction) and the ideals of creativity and love.

Of particular note is the connection of myth and sacrifice. The cultural ideals associated with each of the three domains are, of course, mythic in terms of providing ahistorical goals for historical action, but the linkage of sacrifice with the mythic itself might seem paradoxical. On the one hand the mythic icon or exemplary figure has the appearance of permanence and solidity; sacrifice, though, implies forfeiture, the loss of permanence. The resolution of the paradox comes through a process in which the desire for personal immortality is exchanged for a socially defined, mythically commemorated immortality. The individual lives on in the shared memories of others, through the iconic forms in which these memories can be venerated: (soldier, missionary, teacher, revolutionary, parent, captain of industry, national hero,) and so on. Transcendental sacrifice provides a brilliant means of disposing of the body in a socially valued way. It allows for an enormous investment in the materiality of bodily presence while also compensating for the vicissitudes and vulnerabilities of the flesh. Ideally (in terms of hegemonic practices), sacrifice functions transcendentally, as an internally valued and voluntarily enacted practice. But, in terms of hierarchy and dominance, sacrifice can also be imposed on others unilaterally, both in a ritualistic and stereotypical sense. The individuality, and the lives, of others are sacrificed to the maintenance of cultural ideals by those with the power and need to do so.

Negative Space

To stretch the geometric metaphor a little further, texts may move in a negative as well as positive direction along each axis. A given text may challenge the apparent fullness and total presence associated with positive values. This is a principal function of reflexive operations generally, though they may be directed at one domain more than the others or at issues of a different order entirely. The "classic" narrative with its sense of closure and coherence; the body as icon, myth, or stereotype; historical referentiality as direct one-to-one correspondence: each of these conceptions wavers as a text moves toward the opposite end of each axis. In lieu of representations of fullness and presence we have: (1) the counternarrative of modernism; (2) antimythologization or historical situatedness, what Stephen Heath has called the "figure" of dispersal which thwarts a perfect overlay of narrative character and mythic icon on the representation of a person's contextually rooted consciousness (what Trinh Minh-ha would describe as "difference"); and (3) the self-referentiality of a discourse that uses its voice to locate its own status and authority in socially and existentially contextualized terms rather than in a preexisting authority of which it is merely the (infallible) agent.

Counternarrative

These forms of "negative space," in fact, have become a focus of increasing interest for many filmmakers with quite varied effect. Negative values along each axis do not abolish patterns of interference in favor of a deconstructive monotone; these texts, too, embody palpable contradictions that engage us diversely. They also disrupt the geometric metaphor of spatial coordinates by dislodging the notion of an origin or center, a zero-degree point that less contestational works posit through their reliance on the codes of realism.

Counternarratives, for example, often exhibit the following qualities, identified by Peter Wollen.[30]

Narrative intransitivity—episodic construction, digressions, and interruptions. Marker's *Sans Soleil,* Sankofa's *Passion of Remembrance,* and Godard's *British Sounds* share this characteristic.

Estrangement—"multiple and divided characters, commentary," breaks in identificatory mechanisms between viewer and character.[31] *Poto and*

Cabengo uses intertitles to distance us from the level of character involvement; *Far from Poland* includes scenes in which the filmmaker's motives
and strategies are challenged directly by another character.

Foregrounding—"making the mechanics of the film/text visible and
explicit."[32] This is one of the key aspects of formal reflexivity as previously
discussed.

Multiple diegesis—heterogeneous worlds, ruptures between different
codes and their normal representational value. Documentary normally
constructs a less cohesive world since it is less tightly bound to the actions
of a set of imaginary characters who require a coherent context to effect
believable acts. Gaps and fissures can be filled in with reference to and
knowledge of the historical world. Fragments of the historical world can be
torn out and represented as evidence in a particular argument. Wollen's
point, though, takes on significance when documentaries begin to challenge or refute the argumentative posture per se, as in Ruiz's *Of Great Events
and Ordinary People* when Ruiz, in voice-over, speaks of documentary's
propensity for heterogeneous objects and shows us a series of still-life
compositions that have no bearing on the social issue the film ostensibly
addresses—a French national election. Though coded as evidence, these
images are no longer evidence about the historical world but about the
proclivity of (Griersonian) documentary to assemble disparate images on
its own behalf.

Aperture—"intertextuality—allusion, quotation, and parody."[33] This is a
form of irony that challenges the originality of speech and exposes the
degree to which what we say has already been spoken elsewhere, in our
culture and its ideological propositions. This is a pronounced quality in the
work of Godard. It figures in all the films by Trinh Minh-ha where multi-
vocal commentaries draw on preexisting texts without placing them in
hierarchical relation to one another. It is a central issue in *Thriller*, where
the basic assumptions inscribed in the libretto of *La Bohème* become the
target of extended scrutiny (why does Camille die?). It is also crucial to *A
Song of Air*, which reworks the images and meanings of a father's home
movies into a metacritique of both home movies and family life. (The film
is made by the daughter whom we see in these home movies.)

Unpleasure—"provocation, aiming to dissatisfy and hence change the
spectator."[34] This may be a deliberate aim in some cases, and it may be a
specific value for some, who mistakenly associate Brecht's alienation effects
with the discourses of sobriety and the artistic equivalent of the Protestant
work ethic. In other cases, it may be a side-product of disrupting expectations and undercutting conventions that is not valued unless channeled
toward a specific mode of discovery, insight, and transformation. Unpleasure, in other words, can change the curious spectator into a bored one, or
the paying spectator into a resentful one. The narrative frustrations built
into *Surname Viet Given Name Nam*, for example, do not seek to displease for

the sake of displeasing, as those of Godard's *Vent d'est* or *Numero Deux* seem to do. Instead they guide the viewer toward another level of reading and problematic that would otherwise have been relegated to the background. The reliance on fictional strategies in Peter Watkins's *The War Game* to construct a conditional tense of what it would be like if a nuclear war occurred also does not simply produce unpleasure as a thematical goal but instead, by reliance on a conditional structure, transfers to the viewer the need to construct an alternative future through social praxis itself.

Wollen also addresses the tendency to contrast fiction with reality as a seventh characteristic of countercinema.[35] (In documentary the reverse contrast occurs: a reintroduction of subjective and narrative elements into a domain once governed by a canon of objectivity.)

Antimyth

Antimythologization requires a resolute effort not to represent social actors in a manner that essentializes or fetishizes their attributes. Showing an individual as "a product of their times" is not sufficient. (This can readily fuel a classic "great men" [*sic*] theory of history, where Lukacsian typification yields to the exemplary stereotype.) A more radically decentered notion of the individual that cannot be gathered back up into the ready-made mold of the icon or hero comes into play. The difference can be sharpened by contrasting *Abortion Stories: North and South*, which explores how women's lives are affected by their access to abortion procedures in different countries, with *Speak Body*, which conveys something of what the personal experience of abortion is like. *Abortion Stories* has considerable use-value as a documentary. Its array of witnesses identify key political issues and place them in a feminist context. No one favoring the right to abortion could complain very forcefully that the film fails to subvert or undercut the mythic dimension to bodily representation. *Abortion Stories* represents its witnesses in positive mythic terms, as models and exemplars. This is an important aspect of political struggle as presently conducted, whatever we may have to say about its problems and limitations in a larger, more theoretical frame. As in *Roses in December*, though, the tendency toward mythologization is held in check; it remains rooted in the historical context where courage and contestation manifest themselves. The women witnesses are not represented as vehicles for a timeless truth or divine injunction. This results in a judicious balancing of representational possibilities within the positive domains of history, myth, and narrative.

Speak Body takes a different tack. Kay Armatage presents women's voices off screen while we see fragments of female bodies and hear personal, diaristic commentaries about the experience of abortion. The shots fail to cohere into images of singular women but neither do they function like those fragments of lips, hands, eyes, breasts, hair, and legs that recur incessantly in advertising. Instead, the shots work as a form of counteridealization. The camera roams across swaths of skin without regard for the most aesthetically pleasing angle or the most suggestive composition. The lighting is fairly harsh, almost clinical. The emphasis is on the physicality, the imperfect reality of flesh, the body as an everyday object whose capacity to reproduce life brings urgency to its representation. The risks and fears that accompany abortion, the sense of loss, the impression of a literal tearing away of life receive acknowledgment in a context that weighs these realities against other considerations that may leave abortion as a choice that must be made. The film does not wind up in a position of advocacy, nor does it isolate exemplary figures who can give personal witness to the intensity of the dilemmas. It demythologizes the female body, avoiding the hazards of fetishization, essentialism, and the construction of heroes without stepping outside the arena of historical struggle itself.

A similar distinction can be made between *N!ai* and two other works: Diane Kitchen's *Before We Knew Nothing* and Paula Gaitan's *Sky*. John Marshall's film has many fascinating qualities to it, not least the incorporation of footage from many of his previous films made among the !Kung. The weave of old and new footage offers a longitudinal view of N!ai as girl, young woman, wife, and mother. Interviews and observational sequences describe the present condition of the !Kung, and N!ai, including their relationship to external aid from missionaries, the entreaties of South African army recruiters, and their "exotic" value to both tourists and professional film crews. (Marshall includes an extended observational sequence of another film crew rehearsing the !Kung in "natural" behavior for a fiction film (which happens to be part of the final scene in *The Gods Must Be Crazy*).

N!ai allows a vivid sense of the historical person to emerge that enjoys all the benefits of cinematic illusionism (a careful process of individuation with a full and complex personal psychology that is clearly situated in volumetric space). As in *Abortion Stories*, the mythic representation of N!ai makes her an iconic representative of the typical (not as "average" but as embodiment of fundamental tensions and contradictions within contemporary !Kung culture). *Before We Knew Nothing*, by contrast, is a more personal account of the filmmaker's stay among the Ashaninka Indians of the Amazon rain forest. It resists individuating characters and assigning a personal psychology to them. The people with whom Kitchen stays do not become reduced to natives one and all. They exhibit marks of idiosyncrasy that differentiate one person from another, but the film does not give emphasis to this form of psychological anchorage in the characters. A stronger sense emerges of the social collectivity as a palpable force, one which commands Kitchen's attention and subtly governs the nature of communication and exchange. Invisible and elusive, it nonetheless functions as the more pertinent historical referent, partly because individual social actors are not given the pride of place as icons or characters. A dialectic something like that described by Althusser in regard to *El Nost Milan* comes into play where what does not happen takes on greater importance than what does.

Similarly, *Sky* refuses to individuate people. Like *The Nuer,* it moves among individuals freely, without invoking identificatory mechanisms or providing personal information. *Sky* utilizes a more rigorous narrative structure than *The Nuer,* however, moving toward an allegorical critique of metropolitan "civilization" by means of a nonsequential representation of the Xingo acting out their creation myth. The historical placement of specific people and actions remains elusive, edging toward a poetic or openly allegorical pattern of organization, rather than an explanatory or identificatory one.

Our Marilyn takes a quite different approach to questions of the body and myth but also moves toward an antimythologizing position. Brenda Longfellow ponders the cultural, masculinist uses of the bodies of "our Marilyn," Marilyn Bell, a Canadian who was the first person to swim across Lake Ontario, and "their Marilyn," Marilyn Monroe, whose body epitomized the process of constructing oneself in the (projected) image desired by an Other. The film's female commentator speaks in a personal tone of how her own growth through adolescence took place in relation to these two incommensurate icons. The commentary moves the viewer into a position of critical assessment, looking at each Marilyn in relation to the other and to the mediating perceptions of the off-screen narrator.

The film's two Marilyns are not mythic figures for us to incorporate into our own pantheon of heroes and heroines. They are examples of the process of fetishizing the historical. They pose alternative possibilities for the female body, while the film refuses to represent either as an unproblematic icon, waiting for adoption. For example, *Our Marilyn* utilizes archival footage and reenactments to invert the normal dramatic curve of athletic achievement as springboard to the social status of hero. A great deal of the film's running time is given over to a rhythmically entrancing reprise of what would (conventionally) be the largely overlooked core of Marilyn Bell's accomplishment: the actual swim across the lake, some of which is archival footage and some of which is reenactment. This insistence on situational specificity, subjectively conveyed, works against the mythic icon of the intrepid swimmer as national hero that subsequently took shape in the Canadian media. Similarly *Our Marilyn* subverts the easy extraction of arresting, to-be-looked-at images of the other Marilyn by providing a historical context for that process and by reworking archival footage into slow-motion images that invite analysis more than identification. *Our Marilyn* and *Speak Body* both refuse the forms of narrative pleasure grounded in a masculinist scopophilia criticized by Laura Mulvey. They do so without denying alternative pleasures that stem from images of the female body as the site of experience and political struggle.

Self-Referentiality

Self-referentiality thwarts the illusionistic representation of the historical person as readily as the representation of narrative character or mythic icon. Reflexivity can operate to occlude the sense of realist access to the social actor. The operations of *discours* that call attention to the situated nature of discourse itself (that it is between "you" and "me" rather than issuing from an omniscient, disembodied entity unattached to a historical person or place) can either foreclose access to the real altogether or stress the mediated nature of its representation before us. Foreclosure is extreme and mostly occurs in experimental films like Paul Sharits's *T,O,U,C,H,I,N,G,* or George Landow's *Remedial Reading Comprehension.* The sense of strongly mediated access is more common. David Rimmer's *Cellophane Wrapper*, Al Razutis's *A Message from Our Sponsor* and Stan Brakhage's *Window Water Baby Moving*, for example, all retain a clearly identifiable historical referent (factory work, pornography in juxtaposition to television advertising, and childbirth, respectively) but block any impression of a realist representation. *Poto and Cabengo* and *Surname Viet Given Name Nam* make language itself one of their subjects, prompting the viewer to consider how thoroughly language, including documentary film language, constructs the reality—including the reality of "the person"—that appears to be beyond it, safely anchored in the realm of the historical.

The relationships among these different domains of history, myth, and narrative can be represented diagrammatically.

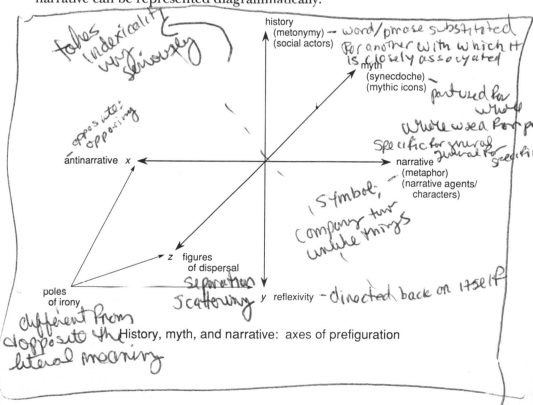

History, myth, and narrative: axes of prefiguration

Crisis and Magnitude

These questions of magnitude, representation, and the body constantly manifest tensions between representation and referent for the viewer of documentary. The documentary form poses distinct problems, such as how reflexive operations may decompose the dominant notions of subject, person, icon, and character. Questions of magnitude also provoke crisis moments in documentary when the balance of person, character, and icon is put to the test. This is the moment when ideology, as representational propositions about the world, comes into contact with the text's conceptualization of the human body along the armatures of history, myth, and narrative to determine the proportional weight of each domain and the purpose to which it shall be put.

As Frank Lentricchia has it, "In the moment of linkage [between form and ideology], form would seize and direct ideological substance, transform it into power over the subject-audience; it would turn our ideology, in both senses [as culture and as lived experience] over to a disciplinary intention. . . . The aesthetic moment of linkage, then, is the manipulative moment at which the subject-audience is submitted to the productive force of ideology."[36] In place of the "manipulative moment" we may substitute *the crisis moment*, which presents the viewer with the choice of consent or contestation. However termed, the linkage itself is indispensable.

Questions of magnitude carry us into the realm of ideology, contradiction, paradox, and excess. The utopian longing for actual community, which rhetoric frequently evokes, risks being sent on a detour to the kingdoms of narrative and myth, away from heightened awareness and a raised consciousness. The specter of a political unconscious looms. (In his book of the same name, Frederic Jameson identifies the political unconscious as the repressed site of meditation on the destiny of community, where community proposes an intersubjective realm beyond the monadic regime of desire.) The text itself becomes a site of contradiction. Narrative strategies and mythic processes seek resolution for those social contradictions they must represent if the text is to exert a hold on us but which they can only register as "logical scandal":

> [W]hat can in the former [history] be resolved only through the intervention of praxis here [in the text] comes before the purely contemplative mind as logical scandal or double bind, the unthinkable and the conceptually paradoxical, that which cannot be unknotted by the operation of pure thought, and which must therefore generate a whole more properly narrative apparatus—the text itself—to square its circles and to dispel, through narrative movement, its intolerable closure.[37]

Magnitude in this regard aligns itself with those various strategies by which a text may represent an awareness of its complicity with "logical scandal" and thereby alert us to the gap between resolution by praxis and by aesthetic form. Irony, distanciation, deconstruction, reflexivity, the formalist concept of *ostranenie*—these and other reflexive tactics operate to achieve the effect of opening out onto magnitudes not otherwise anticipated. There is not merely the flat announcement of something more that escapes the frame, but the subjective experience of excess, the discovery—usually unanticipated, sudden, or dialectical—of a magnitude of existence beyond containment. At this crisis moment, our response to the "This is so, isn't it?" of hegemonic ideology hesitates and wavers. We glimpse an alternative domain on the horizon of the existing conditions of existence and in opposition to it. Interior, subjective dimensions, given external form by cultural production, present contradiction, paradox, and dialectics with experiential force.

Documentary, with the "stickiness" of those indexical images that refer us back to the historical, makes it particularly hard to let this discovery remain within the province of a formalism, a play within codes, a deconstruction of unity into its disparate parts. "The documentary effect," as it were, turns us back toward the historical dimension and the challenge of praxis with a forcefulness born of the text's almost tangible bond to that which it also represents as though for the first time. The very process of miniaturization that narrative containment requires proves particularly susceptible to a restoration of scale when the extension of what we see appears to be the world in which we live. Realism, too, has this effect. When the conventions of documentary, realism, and reflexivity combine, they result in a crisis moment where the vivification of magnitude can take place. Form and ideology intersect; representation and referent collide. The productive force of ideology may reaffirm the solidity of the body, the unshakable truths of the social imaginary, and the givenness of the world as it is. Conversely, the revelatory force of heightened consciousness may yield instruction and pleasure that vivifies the sense of the historical body as subject to erasure and possession yet still capable of making a difference of its own. This moment of amplified magnitude may restore difference to what has ossified into a social imaginary of identities and oppositions, icons, stereotypes, and symbols. Heightened consciousness reaffirms the fabricated and mutable nature of a world we not only adapt to but shape.

The attempt to construct an interior meaning and subjective experience propels films like *Roses in December, Witness to War, Frank: A Vietnam Vet, Las Madres de la Plaza de Mayo, Wedding Camels, Dear America, Shoah, Daughter Rite, Consuming Hunger,* and *Hotel Terminus,* among others, toward the imaginary coherence of actual person and fictitious character in the image of an icon, and yet they also insist on the dispersal of that very coherence. The ground of documentary resides in the relation between character, icon, and *social* agent. Here the person acts as an agent in history, not narrative, no matter how persistently we give meaning to one by means of the other. The representation of this relationship is the moment of crisis in documentary. After all, on the other side of the text is that contested territory for which our ideological formations produce their endless array of maps. What a text must figure in, as subtextual acknowledgment, is that history hurts. It is not only subtext and excess, but limit and horizon, the location where utopias must finally take root.

History and our historical imagination, then, is what is at stake. History and what we make of it is the excess that we engage through the representation of bodies. The documentary film is an active reassemblage of the body as the repository of personal meaning and of a utopian unconscious of collective values. Reassembly may conform to ideological propositions about facts, practices, and ideals, but it may also qualify and contest these propositions, formally and politically. *Roses in December* demonstrates the range of issues that surround the representation of the body along the positive axes of narrative, myth, and history, and is noteworthy for its ability to suspend the three domains in relative balance. It avoids the risk of having the full, ideological coherence of narrative impose itself. (Coherence stems from a psychological realism that casts the person into the imaginary mold of narrative agent, introduces other characters in terms of their functional motivation in the story, and subordinates history to narrative structure.) At the same time, *Roses* provides sufficient narrative structure to prevent the raw, inchoate flux of history from overwhelming the film and subsuming the person into the senseless swirl of the anecdotal and eternally contingent. Finally, it utilizes the cinematic apparatus for the engenderment of the person as icon or symbol without dissolving the linkage between the person and the plane of history.[38]

When held in unstable, dispersed balance, as in *Roses in December*, representations of the human body take on the attributes of character (here clustered around the journey as spiritual odyssey and the attendant rituals of both witness and self-discovery) and icon (here associated with qualities of dedication, devotion, agape love, and grace), but the body also remains situated as social actor in history to which the stickiness of the film's indexical sounds and images continue to return us. The result undermines the imaginary solidity of the fictive and mythic and confirms the necessary alliance between contradiction and closure in narrative. A resistance occurs. Magnitudes prevail that make the stable, coherent alignment of person/character/icon into a violation of the body of the social actor. This imaginary coherence becomes all the more transgressive of a historical field that refuses all attempts to arrest it, however momentarily.

This does not remove *Roses in December* or the other films cited from the other half of the moment of crisis (the lapse into consent for ideological propositions that sustain hegemony). *Roses* is a film like any other in holding to an argumentative or persuasive purpose, an ideological propositionalism. In this case the combination of spiritual odyssey and sacrificial iconography proposes an injunction: "Go and do likewise." In this regard *Roses* does not escape some of those impediments to magnitude with which we began—of victim and charity, sympathy and sacrifice, even if the tension of upholding them is also left in evidence. The representation of Jean Donovan as an exemplary individual involves an exclusionary focus that leaves the Salvadoran people with whom she works as, once again, primarily Other, as figures not massively different in their subordinated representation to the figure of "Cathy"/Jean Donovan in *Salvador* or the native people filling the negative space of *The Mission* as backdrop for the moral struggle between Robert DeNiro and Jeremy Irons. The Salvadoran people function in the film's narrative structure as donors. These are terms of encounter with which we are abundantly familiar, in life and in representational texts, from *Lawrence of Arabia* to *The Emerald Forest* and from *The Ugly American* to *The Mosquito Coast. Roses* works well to avoid hagiography but does finally accept a form of charitable reaching out toward others whose terms and conditions are more a manifestation of personal witness than of collective *negotiation* between self and other.

At stake in the documentary representation of the body is not only the courage to be, but the courage not to be, not to be represented strictly in terms of those potentially full and positive values running along the axes of history, myth, and narrative. The concept of truth as always in relation to falsity—always a thing of indefinite approximation whose elusiveness has prompted more than one collective sigh—conjures a magnitude that many a film would prefer to avoid. Reflexive strategies turned to a political purpose recall this relationship, obliquely, in experiential terms that make it all the harder to evade, or, if understood, not to believe.

The body presented in *Speak Body* or *Our Marilyn* approximates this condition: Marilyn Bell, immersed in the waters of Lake Ontario, passing in and out of focus, and sight, bobbing up and down within the frame, grainy and ill-defined, in a near-hallucinatory state brought on by cold, exertion, sleeplessness, and spatial disorientation, moving toward the limits of any ego-enforced sense of self at the same moment as her body moves her toward extraordinary physical achievement. There is a sense of affinity between self and other, person and environment, subjectivity and experience that contrasts with the unity of opposites and any (Hegelian/Marxist) dialectic of synthesis among monads.[39] What *Our Marilyn* helps make vivid is how the body represented by a documentary film must be understood in relation to a historical context which is a referent, not an ontological ground. History is where pain and death occur but it is in representation that these facts and events gain meaning. At moments of crisis such as this (as Marilyn Bell struggles on and on across the lake; as the text devises strategies to render the body and event with magnitudes of sufficient approximation) we may discover, perhaps with the intensity of a first time, exactly what our stake is in questions of bodily representation.

In their different ways, most of the films discussed here raise the question of magnitudes that exceed any one logic or code. Among other things, these magnitudes exceed any discursive frame. They are the stuff to which only praxis can attend. If a raised political consciousness operates in these texts, it is one that evokes, through the stories they have to tell, an affirmation of the utopian impulse that, neither imaginary nor mythical, locates itself in the realm of history itself. This suggests less the need to accommodate a humanist or phenomenological impulse in the form of the mysterious and ineffable as much as the need to acknowledge the distinctive power of a heightened awareness capable of shattering frames, economies, and logics of every kind. In this act of radical defamiliarization lie magnitudes that conventional discourses of sobriety can only deny or disavow.

NOTES

Preface

1. These were Erik Barnouw's *Documentary: A History of the Non-Fiction Film* (1974), Richard Barsam's *Nonfiction Film* (1973), Louis Marcorelles's *Living Cinema* (1973), Alan Lovell and Jim Hillier's *Studies in Documentary* (1972), Elizabeth Sussex's *The Rise and Fall of British Documentary* (1975), and Stephen Mamber's *Cinema Verité in America* (1974). Since then we have only seen two single-author works: Jack Ellis's *The Documentary Idea: A Critical History of English Language Documentary and Video* (1989), an introductory textbook with two of sixteen chapters devoted to documentary since 1969 (mostly in the form of summarizing trends), and William Guynn's *A Cinema of Nonfiction* (1990), a work similar in spirit to this one in attempting to differentiate between fictional narrative and the documentary use of narrative structures, but organized more heavily around classic semiotic notions of code and segmentation.

2. See, for example, Julianne Burton, ed., *The Social Documentary in Latin America* (Pittsburgh: University of Pittsburgh Press, 1990); Stuart Cunningham, "Tense, Address, *Tendez*: Questions of the Work of Peter Watkins," *Quarterly Review of Film Studies* 5, no. 4 (Fall 1980): 501–18; E. Ann Kaplan, *Women and Film: Both Sides of the Camera* (New York: Routledge, 1982); Julia Lesage, "The Political Aesthetics of the Feminist Documentary Film," *Quarterly Review of Film Studies* 3, no. 4 (Fall 1978): 507–23; David MacDougall, "Beyond Observational Cinema," in Paul Hockings, ed., *Principles of Visual Anthropology* (The Hague: Mouton, 1975): 109–24, "Unprivileged Camera Style," *Rain*, no. 50 (June 1982): 8–10; Eileen McGarry, "Documentary, Realism and Women's Cinema," *Women & Film* 2, no. 7 (1975): 50–59; Peter Morris, "Backwards to the Future: John Grierson's Film Policy for Canada," in Gene Walz, ed., *Flashback: People and Institutions in Canadian Film History* (Montreal: Mediatexte, 1986): 17–35; Joyce Nelson, *The Colonized Eye: Rethinking the Grierson Legend* (Toronto: Between the Lines, 1988); Michael Renov, "Newsreel: Old and New—Towards an Historical Profile," *Film Quarterly* 51, no. 1 (Fall 1987): 20–33; Alan Rosenthal, ed., *New Challenges for Documentary* (Berkeley: University of California Press, 1988); Jay Ruby, Larry Gross, and John Katz, eds., *Image Ethics: The Moral and Legal Rights of Subjects in Documentary Film and Television* (Philadelphia: Annenberg Communication Series, 1985); Vivian Sobchak, "Inscribing Ethical Space: Ten Propositions on Death, Representation, and Documentary," *Quarterly Review of Film Studies* 9, no. 4 (1984): 283–300; Tom Waugh, ed., *Show Us Life: Towards a History and Aesthetics of the Committed Documentary* (Metuchen: Scarecrow, 1984); Brian Winston, "Reconsidering 'Triumph of the Will': Was Hitler There," *Sight and Sound* (Spring 1981): 102–7.

3. This standard version of film theory has been thoroughly described and criticized, with no small measure of exasperation, by David Bordwell in *Making Meaning: Inference and Rhetoric in the Interpretation of Cinema* (Cambridge: Harvard University Press, 1989). His exasperation seems to stem from a desire for something more formally challenging. My wish to reconceptualize what theory stands for stems from a desire for something more closely based on the form and structure of documentary, less to provide a renewed sense of formal challenge to the theorist than to gain increased use-value for theorist and filmmaker alike.

4. I discuss many of the benefits and drawbacks of contemporary theory and

the predominant critical methodologies at greater length in the introduction to *Movies and Methods*, vol. 2 (Berkeley: University of California Press, 1985).

1. The Domain of Documentary

1. Plato, *The Republic*, trans. Desmond Lee (Penguin Books, 1955): 308.

2. Digital sampling techniques, whereby an image is constituted by digital bits that are subject to infinite modification, renders this argument for the unique, indexical nature of the photographic image obsolete. The image becomes a series of bits, a pattern of yes/no choices registered within a computer's memory. A modified version of that pattern will be in no sense derivative from the "original": it becomes, instead, a new original. Any images that can be generated from these bits of information occupy exactly the same status. There is no original negative image as there is in photography against which all prints can be compared for accuracy and authenticity. There may not even be an external referent. Computer graphics can generate highly realistic renderings of real-life subjects from software algorithms rather than external referents. The implications of all this are only beginning to be grasped. They clearly set a historical framework around the discussion presented in this book, which continues to emphasize the qualities and properties of the photographic image.

3. An excellent example of how facts and themes are made to appear to emerge from the real-life world depicted in the documentary remains Robert Flaherty's *Nanook of the North* (1922). Flaherty's shooting and editing style (far more than his intertitles) work to convey a sense of events unfolding according to their own rhythm, revealing their own meaning, which the filmmaker strives to simply "bring out." They were there all along, not imposed or overlaid.

A more recent example that exposes the fissures Flaherty buried beneath his long takes and continuity editing is the PBS series, "Nature." A six-part series entitled *Australia: The Island Continent* concluded with an examination of the ways in which man has wrought havoc to the ecology of the land. After chronicling numerous major catastrophes (forests destroyed; marginal land reduced to salt flats; grazing land razed by rabbits, sheep, and goats; and so on, often with newsreel footage describing the force of the problem dating from as early as the 1930s), the program's narrator informs us that means are at hand to solve many of these issues. We see analysts who study satellite photographs of grazing land to identify the rate and extent of overgrazing and are told that this information can allow ranchers to shift their stock to other land or take them to market before excess damage is done.

The point of this narrative is to offer a reassurance that "out there" in the real world solutions to longstanding problems are now at hand because science can identify them and propose adjustments to minimize their impact. A contradiction between the severity of decades-old problems and the quick fix of data from a satellite looms, especially since the politics and economics behind the use of this information are not questioned, nor the long-term advisability of raising these particular forms of livestock in the first place. The sense of enthusiastic optimism is a function of the text, of tone, rhythm, and placement (the scientific data collection provides the sense of an ending). The sense of an imposed optimism is stronger than the sense of Flaherty's romanticism as a perspective on the world that does not, in fact, arise from the world, but in each case the text relies on creating the impression that not only the specific events but the tonalities surrounding them emerge from the world itself. Strategies of narrative style are used to efface themselves and propose that the optimism or romantic wonder resides in the world itself. The camera records or reports it. Optimism, romanticism, like solutions that "just happen," these sensibilities appear to emerge from the world itself, at the bidding of an Invisible Hand that harmonizes our own perceptions with these wondrous qualities. We need not debate their origins or implications. Our task is more to acknowledge the awe inspired by their presence as revealed by the film.

4. Jean Baudrillard, *The Evil Demon of Images* (Sydney: Power Institute Publications, 1988): 27, 28.

5. Plato, *The Republic*, 297.

6. Ibid., 184.

7. Ibid., 237.

8. The development of a postmodern culture of the simulation is discussed in Arthur Kroker and David Cook, *The Postmodern Scene: Excremental Culture and Hyper-Aesthetics* (Montreal: New World Perspectives, 1986), Jean Baudrillard, *L'exchange symbolique et la mort* (Paris: Editions Gallimard, 1976), Baudrillard, *Simulations* (New York: Semiotext(e), 1983), Hal Foster, ed., *The Anti-Aesthetic* (Port Townsend: Bay Press, 1983), Fredric Jameson, "Postmodernism, or the Cultural Logic of Late Capitalism," *New Left Review*, no. 146 (July–August 1984): 13–92, and my "The Work of Culture in the Age of Cybernetic Systems," *Screen* 29, no. 2 (Winter 1988): 22–46. It would be a grave error to think of the simulation as on the order of a copy, reflection, or illusion. Wars may be entertained in the living room but lives are still lost. Grenada may play across the nation as a rerun of *Sands of Iwo Jima* but we cannot get up from our television and say, "It is just a movie." Authenticity may be measured by congruence with previous representations of a "reality" now subject to seemingly infinite regress, but issues of power and desire, authority and finality (death) remain firmly in place.

9. Walter Benjamin, "The Work of Art in the Age of Mechanical Reproduction," in *Illuminations*, trans. Harry Zohn (New York: Schocken Books, 1969): 236.

10. Robert C. Allen and Douglas Gomery, *Film History: Theory and Practice* (New York: Alfred Knopf, 1984): 215–39. The usefulness of this definition to them is fairly obvious when we see that their concern is only with a small sample of American cinema verité, principally the work of Donald Pennebaker, Richard Leacock, and Robert Drew at ABC television. Their account of even this small fraction of documentary filmmaking is highly schematic; it is used to demonstrate the validity of a research methodology rather than to examine cinema verité or observational cinema in any great detail. The methodology proves more suggestive than the example proves conclusive.

11. David Bordwell and Kristen Thompson, *Film Art: An Introduction*, 3rd ed. (New York: McGraw-Hill, 1990): 23. In a later section meant to illustrate principles of film criticism they stress how Fred Wiseman exercises control over key aspects of the film's structure, but they continue to maintain the position that this documentary, like many others, "surrendered control over what happens in front of the camera" (337).

12. Leacock articulates his own principles of shooting quite clearly. On one occasion he commented, "I want to discover something about people. When you interview someone they always tell you what they want you to know about them. This may be interesting, and is what some people actually want to record. What I want to see is what happens when they are not doing this." Quoted in Louis Marcorelles, *Living Cinema* (New York: Praeger, 1973): 55.

13. Jean-François Lyotard, *The Postmodern Condition: A Report on Knowledge*, trans. Geoff Bennington and Brian Massumi (Minneapolis: University of Minnesota Press, 1984): 17.

14. Michel Foucault, *The Archaeology of Knowledge*, trans. A. M. Sheridan Smith (London: Tavistock Publications, 1972): 32–33.

15. The echo of Thomas Kuhn's *The Structure of Scientific Revolutions*, 2nd ed. (Chicago: University of Chicago Press, 1970) and his description of "normal"

science as precisely this sort of institutionally governed procedure was inadvertent. On rereading, the reference—ignored by French theorists like Foucault or Lyotard whom I have chosen to cite—seems quite important. Kuhn's work, in fact, prefigures central aspects of Foucault's. What Kuhn ignores, and what remains underdeveloped here, are questions of ideology: an innocence or "normalcy" presides over Kuhn's account that Foucault, despite his own extraordinary blindspots (such as matters of gender and the place of women in the history of sexuality), refuses to tolerate. Foucault, like Lévi-Strauss, is in search of the most basic elements of Western culture; Kuhn settles for an account of the institutional basis of Western science. Hubert L. Dreyfus and Paul Rabinow, *Michel Foucault: Beyond Structuralism and Hermeneutics,* 2d ed. (Chicago: University of Chicago Press, 1982) trace the relation of Kuhn's work to Foucault's in some detail.

16. This discussion of procedures used to comprehend a text is strongly informed by David Bordwell's discussion of schemata in *Narration in the Fiction Film* (Madison: University of Wisconsin Press, 1985): 31–39. I have chosen not to adopt the vocabulary of cognitive psychology because of its premise that such activity is a value-free mental base for more complex, socially conditioned forms of subjectivity and consciousness.

17. The four types of motivation discussed here are proposed, with somewhat different nomenclature, in Bordwell, *Narration in the Fiction Film*: 36.

18. In *The Thin Blue Line,* decontextualized shots of objects like a gun, milkshake, silhouette in a window, and letters being typed onto a sheet of paper, too abstract in their representation to be justified realistically, take on a formal motivation. They become a series of iconographic images that link up primarily to each other in order to suggest how the film, though a documentary, cannot assure us of the historical authenticity of its evidence. This reflexive move locates the text in a borderline territory between narrative fiction and documentary argument, a zone that is very familiar to those who work within a postmodernist aesthetic. We read it primarily as a documentary, but with a steady awareness of how what occurs before the camera displays an appearance tied less to the historical world than to choices made by the filmmaker.

19. André Bazin was a French critic who celebrated the ability of film to capture "the object itself, the object freed from the conditions of time and space that govern it." (Quoted from "The Ontology of the Photographic Image," *What is Cinema?* [2 vols. Berkeley: University of California Press, 1967]: I:14.) Editing and expressionist techniques obscured the thing itself and imposed new constraints of time and space that were the filmmaker's doing. Bazin's ideal, a realist style that engages us in a manner similar to how the world itself does, stands opposed to didactic commentary, reenactment, and montage effects.

2. Documentary Modes of Representation

1. The interactive mode frequently cedes considerable authority to those interviewed. These individuals may even provide the essence of the film's argument, as they do in *With Babies and Banners, Solovki Power, Union Maids, Through the Wire,* and *Who Killed Vincent Chin?* or give rise to the predominant tone or attitude of the film. *Where the Heart Roams, Wise Guys!,* and *Coming Out,* about women's romance literature, a television quiz show, and a debutante ball, respectively, all cede to the participants in these activities the opportunity to set the tone of the representation rather than use them to illustrate a dominant perspective constructed by the film.

2. Erik Barnouw, *Documentary: A History of the Non-Fiction Film* (New York: Oxford University Press, 1974): 254–55.

3. A paradigmatic instance of this form of debate centered around the film *An American Family*, a twelve-hour series on one family aired on public television in 1973. A rigorously observational work, the series prompted a great deal of journalistic attention in terms of how much Craig Gilbert, the person responsible for it, had shaped, prompted, or otherwise manipulated events in front of the camera. Some of these charges came from the film's subjects, the Loud family themselves, particularly the mother, Pat Loud. Most of them implied far more manipulation than Craig Gilbert saw at work in his or any documentary. See his "Reflections on *An American Family*, II" in Alan Rosenthal, ed., *New Challenges for Documentary* (Berkeley: University of California Press, 1988) for a useful summary of the ethical issues as seen by the filmmaker.

4. Semiotic approaches to cinema took it for granted that the images of people were signifiers with attachments, and hence meanings, that depended on their relation to other elements in the signifying chain. Useful as this approach may be to the refutation of notions of transparency between image and reality it does not quell the disturbances semiosis sets up in the bodies of those who have their image "taken." Legal principles of privacy, libel, and slander attest to some of the dimensions of conflict. The uncertainty of the effect on a situation of filming it forms part of the speculative involvement of the viewer. One dimension of this involvement hinges on this question of use. The discursive frame (morally, ethically, politically) within which we debate the issue has its own historical context. If a semiotics of signifiers and their attachments once had a historically valuable role to play in the theory of the fiction film, its applicability to documentary film was always less certain. The relation to what seems to elude the field of a *langue*-centered semiotics—the referent, the person who engages in *parole*, who speaks as well as is spoken—remains a central concern in documentary from multiple points of view.

5. See Paul Rock, *The Making of Symbolic Interactionism* (Totowa, N.J.: Rowman and Littlefield, 1979) for an excellent introduction to many of the methodological principles that were adopted, knowingly or inadvertently, by observational filmmakers. Rock notes that symbolic interactionism is the segment of sociology "which has devoted itself to the detailed ethnography of small social worlds" (92). Compare Rock's comment on participant-observation with the desire of Richard Leacock, for example, to observe what people do when they are not interviewed or otherwise addressed directly by the camera: "The business of ethnography is presented as comparatively hostile to rehearsal. Much of it is described as if it entailed the artless projection of the sociologist's self into the natural setting. Such artlessness is both the prerequisite and the unavoidable companion of effective communion. . . . Interactive fieldwork is designed to capture and foster prepredicative experience. It is axiomatic of the methodology that such experience can never be adequately described by words: it occupies realms which are *sui generis*. Full comprehension can stem only from engaging in the experience itself" (197–98).

6. Face-to-face encounter also has its nonpractical ends as phatic communication suggests. (Phatic communication involves interstitial fillers that let someone else know that we are attending to them, such as "um," "ah," or "well.") All utterances and texts, not only art, then, have a nonpractical dimension, while art, or fiction, as part of an ideological system, clearly has a practical outcome in its effects on subjectivity and sometimes on specific opinions, beliefs, attitudes, or forms of behavior.

7. The traditional accounts of documentary in the postwar years refer to the development of lightweight, portable cameras and magnetic tape sound recorders that allowed for synchronous sound recording on location as the central step in the transformation of documentary film from an expository mode (including its poetic variants) to direct cinema and cinema verité, what I have chosen to call observa-

tional and interactive modes of representation. These developments seem to have occurred more or less simultaneously and independent of one another in Canada, at the NFB, and in the United States, mainly through the efforts of Drew-Leacock, and in France with Jean Rouch. What often goes underemphasized, or neglected, are two things:

First, the NFB of Canada pioneered most of the technological innovation, introducing synchronous location sound recording in works like *Les Racquetteurs (1958), The Days before Christmas* (1959), *Blood and Fire* (1958), and *Back-Breaking Leaf* (1959) independent of and prior to developments in the United States that centered around Richard Leacock, Donald Pennebaker, and Robert Drew (Drew Associates). *Les Racquetteurs,* made by Groulx and Brault in Quebec, is often credited as the first cinema verité film in Canada. Origins and "firsts" are complex and often unrewarding matters to pursue, since what comes first chronologically may fall within the domain of a different institutional discourse and set of expectations, thereby limiting its impact elsewhere. The practice also tends to localize and restrict causation to a linear phenomenon propelled by a series of discrete events: "First this, then that," etc. Nonetheless, it should be noted that there was a great deal of foment in Canada around the possibilities of interactive filmmaking. It involved more people than in the United States (where the observational alternative gained the most attention) or France (where Jean Rouch worked largely on his own, although many of the same techniques were incorporated in the fictional frame of the French *nouvelle vague*). The Canadian developments, though, have gone relatively underreported and have failed to receive as much credit as an influence as they might. It is difficult to say if the lack of critical and historical attention has become a vicious circle, guaranteeing a lack of influence by neglect, or if the actual influence on interactive filmmakers was much greater than critical accounts allow. (Jean Rouch has always acknowledged the importance of meeting Michel Brault and seeing *Les Racquetteurs* for his own work—Brault and Raoul Coutard did the camerawork on *Chronicle of a Summer*—but whether a more elaborate French-Canadian connection can be identified remains unexamined.)

See Peter Morris's *The Film Companion* (Toronto: Irwin, 1984) for dictionary-like entries regarding these works and Bruce Elder, "On the Candid-Eye Movement," in Seth Feldman and Joyce Nelson, eds., *Canadian Film Reader* (Toronto: Peter Martin Associates, 1977) for a more extended discussion. See Stephen Mamber's *Cinema Verité in America: Studies in Uncontrolled Documentary* (Cambridge: MIT Press, 1974) for an account of the evolution of Leacock, Pennebaker, and Drew's film-making in the mid to late fifties before the first major breakthrough, *Primary.* Mamber only refers to the NFB developments to note that one of the Candid Eye filmmakers, Terence Macartney-Filgate (who shot a good deal of *Primary,* as Brault did *Chronicle*), felt that the Candid Eye series had already covered similar ground (p. 36).

Second, technological innovation is often offered as a casual explanation of why filmmaking styles changed. Though this does seem to be one instance in which transformations in film equipment resulted in a significant difference in how films could be made, there was absolutely no singular causal linkage between technology and a new mode of documentary representation. The development at about the same time of *both* observational styles that favored the invisibility of the filmmaker *and* interactive styles where the filmmaker's presence was not only acknowledged but often a decisive factor in the events presented demonstrates the lack of any one-to-one correspondence between technology and form or between technology and meaning. This radical variation among French, Canadian, and American filmmaking, not to mention British, Continental, and Third World practices, emanating from one set of technological innovations, seldom receives the attention it deserves.

8. See Arthur Koestler's *The Act of Creation* (1964; Pan Books, 1975) for an excellent discussion of the effect of suddenly juxtaposing two distinct frames of thought in the production of comedy, art, and science. Koestler carries the basic surrealist idea of juxtaposing two incommensurate realities within a single plane of reference far beyond its initial application and, in doing so, suggests one important way in which systems, codes, habits, subjectivities, discursive formations, and other regulatory structures remain vulnerable to change and subversion. Koestler's notion of collision between two frames of reference resulting in a transforming synthesis also bears close kinship with the concept of logical typing as an aspect of interpersonal communication in the work of Gregory Bateson. Here "errors" of logical typing allow incommensurate frames of reference to collapse into one another at the expense of the subject, especially in schizophrenia, but also, less pathologically perhaps, in relation to the effects of realism (where the signifier is mistaken for the referent, the image for the reality, or the actor for the character). See *Steps to an Ecology of Mind* (New York: Ballantine Books, 1972).

9. Marshall Blonsky, "Ted Koppel's Edge," *New York Times Magazine*, August 14, 1988.

10. See Rosenthal, ed. *New Challenges for Documentary*, especially part 3, "Documentary Ethics."

11. Both Marc Ferro's *Cinema and History* (Detroit: Wayne State University Press, 1988) and Kathleen Hulser's "Clio Rides the Airwaves: History on Television," *The Independent* 12, no. 2 (March 1989): 18–24 give examples of archival footage that provides overlooked or neglected historical evidence, often because it is used as a generalized illustration, of the Bolshevik revolution or the modern city, for example, rather than examined closely for such details as changing class participation during the days leading up to the revolution (signaled, for example, by clothing) or the social dynamics of neighborhoods as revealed through spatial relationships and specific types of residential and commercial building.

12. See my "The Voice of Documentary," *Film Quarterly* 36, no. 3 (Spring 1983) for an extended discussion of this difference as a matter of textual "voice" or authority (the place from which a sense of either authoritative knowledge or epistemological doubt derives). Of particular interest is the relative distribution of this authority between the filmmaker and social actors.

13. A similar sense of a participatory bond is very evident in Demott and Kreines's *Seventeen*, done for the Middletown series but banned by PBS, ostensibly because of the amount of foul language but more likely because of the interracial love affair between a black male and a white female teenager. Unlike the largely observational style of *Family Business* or *Community of Praise*, *Seventeen* displays a strong degree of spontaneous interaction between filmmakers and subjects. This, too, may have seemed somewhat outside the canon of objectivity for television journalism that observational films can more readily conform to, at least in their disavowal or suppression of the subjectivities of the filmmaker at the time of filming.

14. Michel Foucault, *The History of Sexuality*, vol. 1 (New York: Random House, 1980): 58–73.

15. Teresa de Lauretis, *Technologies of Gender* (Bloomington: Indiana University Press, 1987), especially chapter 1, "The Technology of Gender."

16. The concept of the "masked interview" is discussed at greater length in my *Ideology and the Image*, pp. 281–83 in particular.

17. "Suture" has a technical linguistic-psychoanalytic meaning that derives from

Jacques Lacan and arrived in film theory via Jacques-Alain Miller's essay, "Suture," Jean-Pierre Oudart's "Cinema and Suture," Stephen Heath's "Notes on Suture" (all in *Screen* 18, no. 4 [1977/78]), Daniel Dayan's "The Tutor-Code of Classical Cinema," in Bill Nichols, ed., *Movies and Methods*, vol. 1 (Berkeley: University of California Press, 1976), Kaja Silverman's *The Subject of Semiotics* (New York: Oxford University Press, 1983), and other essays. It involves the process whereby films establish themselves as discourse, as more than brute sound and image, and the viewer takes up a position as the subject addressed by the film. In Oudart's formulation this involves apprehending the work of an absent agent for whom the film provides a stand-in in the form of the Absent One, the Other, off screen, in the space behind the camera, who is the originating agent of the shot, frame, and point of view. (This anthropomorphic abstraction corresponds to what I have elsewhere described as "voice.") The Absent-One authorizes a reading of the image as discourse, as a thematically and affectively signifying form of address. The image no longer seems a brute object but the residue of an expressive intention; it remains haunted by this absence.

This eerie sense of a haunting absence can be read as a necessary condition of symbolic discourse, where we are always represented by what we are not (I am not "I," the signifier that stands in for me) or it can be regarded as an ideological operation that constitutes the subject of bourgeois ideology by means of a kind of ventriloquism. This can be used, in Dayan's view, to regard almost all cinema as bourgeois since it relies on continuity editing, especially shot/reverse shot cuts to mask the actual apparatus of production behind the apparent authorship of characters who share with us that which they themselves see through a relay of shots. (The voice-over commentator plays a similar role in documentary, complementing the process of evidentiary editing.) In a feminist version of this reading, the process of suture attempts to disavow absence, or lack, in a characteristically masculinist way where a preoccupation with the fear of absence, loss, deficiency, and lack is projected onto the image of women. (The general tendency to align the disembodied voice-over with the male and with authority might be taken as one sign of how questions of gender enter into questions of subject-address in documentary.)

18. A similar awareness of vested interest operates in the interviews in *Who Killed Vincent Chin?* but the film conveys the sense that these differences can be relayed from the historical world itself without further distortion, whereas Morris also draws attention to the mediations of interviews and reenactments in the viewer's process of understanding what occurred in the historical world.

19. The fiction "documents" the child's first encounters with his parents' sexuality in graphic form. Whether enacted or observed, and whether acknowledged or not, such representations continue to raise the question of the use of people in signifying systems not of their own making. Godard's indifference to the ethics of representation regarding the use of a child actor may also highlight the relativism that a reflexive position readily accommodates: Godard's self-consciousness as a male filmmaker addressing issues of sexual representation proposes a crucial agenda that later works, by women, address in quite distinct ways. There is the sense in *Numero Deux* that Godard's reflexive critique of the representation of sexual difference is, though profeminist, radically other from what a feminist filmmaker might propose. His perspective remains quite singularly male: controlling, cerebral, problematizing as a representational issue what is, for others, also a problem of lived experience. What is remarkable is that he produced this work in 1975, well ahead of most of the feminist works that take up similar issues, such as *Riddles of the Sphinx*, *Born in Flames*, and *Thriller*, and well ahead of the widespread adoption of video as a medium worthy of extensive consideration. (The film exists as a 35mm

print but much of the "family" life was shot on video and then transferred to film, often miniaturized within the frame as though still confined to the limits of a television screen.)

20. Hayden White, *Metahistory: The Historical Imagination in Nineteenth-Century Europe* (Baltimore: The Johns Hopkins University Press, 1973): 37–38. White's comments on satire as a fictional form parallel his comments on irony, both of which figure into his elaborate taxonomy of the possible modes of historiographic narrative. His description has provided considerable stimulus for my discussion of documentary modes of representation generally, although his specific categories do not seem as useful for documentary as they do for nineteenth-century historiography.

21. Julia Lesage, "The Political Aesthetics of the Feminist Documentary Film," *Quarterly Review of Film Studies* 3, no. 4 (Fall 1978): 507–23.

22. Lesage, "Political Aesthetics," 508.

23. Lesage, "Political Aesthetics," 509.

24. Lesage, "Political Aesthetics," 515, 519.

25. Peter Wollen, "'Ontology' and 'Materialism' in Film," *Screen* 17, no. 1 (Spring 1976): 7–23. Reprinted in Peter Wollen, *Readings and Writings* (London: Verso, 1982).

26. Wollen, *Readings and Writings*, 201, 206.

27. Dana Polan, "A Brechtian Cinema? Towards a Politics of Self-Reflexive Film," in Bill Nichols, ed., *Movies and Methods*, vol. 2 (Berkeley: University of California Press, 1985).

28. Polan, "Brechtian Cinema," 668.

29. Polan, "Brechtian Cinema," 669–70. See also, Louis Althusser, "The 'Piccolo Teatro': Bertolazzi and Brecht," in *For Marx* (New York: Vintage Books, 1970) for a similar and compelling statement of the way in which a politically reflexive stage-play (*El Nost Milan*) pits the conventions of melodramatic form against the "real time" of its working-class characters.

30. The fullest discussion of this bipolar critical stance occurs in Fredric Jameson's *The Political Unconscious* (Ithaca: Cornell University Press, 1981), especially chapter 6, "Conclusion: The Dialects of Utopia and Ideology."

31. E. Ann Kaplan, *Women and Film: Both Sides of the Camera* (New York: Methuen, 1983): 127–28.

32. Kaplan, *Women and Film*, 130.

33. Kaplan, *Women and Film*, 131.

34. Kaplan, *Women and Film*, 134.

35. See Christian Metz, *Film Language* (New York: Oxford University Press, 1974): 21–22.

36. Jay Ruby, in "The Image Mirrored: Reflexivity and the Documentary Film," *Journal of the University Film Association* 29, no. 1 (Fall 1977); reprinted in Rosenthal, ed., *New Challenges for Documentary*, identifies another form of reflexivity: metaphysical disclosure. As he puts it, "being reflexive means that the producer deliberately and intentionally reveals to his audience the underlying epistemological assumptions that caused him [*sic*] to formulate a set of questions in a particular way, to seek answers to those questions in a particular way, and finally to present his findings in a particular way" (65, Rosenthal).

The basis for this definition in the discourses of sobriety (normative science in particular) is clear, but its efficacy is less so. Few of us, including reflexive filmmakers, are fully aware of the underlying (unconscious, ideological) assumptions we have. What we can be aware of, and strive to achieve intentionally, is our effect on an audience, but announcing this intention may undercut the effect or merely repeat it in a less memorable, more didactic fashion. (As Isadora Duncan is reputed to have said, "If I could say it in words, I wouldn't have to dance it.") Any announcement or metastatement about intentions is also subject to the Cretan's paradox, the very form of uncertainty that Ruby's reflexivity seeks to dispel. (The Cretan explained that all Cretans are liars. Was he telling the truth?) There are certainly times when the reflexivity Ruby calls for will be helpful, but I regard this act of disclosure as a form of attempted honesty rather than reflexivity. My primary reservation has to do with the experiential impact of such disclosures compared to formal/political modes of reflexivity as I attempt to demonstrate in chapter 8, "Representing the Body: Questions of Meaning and Magnitude."

37. See Basil Wright, "*Land without Bread* and *Spanish Earth*," in Lewis Jacobs, ed., *The Documentary Tradition* (New York: W. W. Norton, 1979): 146–47.

38. A useful overview of the contemporary debate on truth and its claims with helpful attention to Michel Foucault, Fredric Jameson, Jürgen Habermas, Richard Rorty, Ian Hacking, and others , is Paul Rabinow's "Representations Are Social Facts: Modernity and Post-Modernity in Anthropology," in James Clifford and George E. Marcus, eds., *Writing Culture: The Poetics and Politics of Ethnography* (Berkeley: University of California Press, 1986): 234–61.

39. See Clifford and Marcus, eds., *Writing Culture* in general, but also James Clifford, "On Ethnographic Allegory," particularly and also Clifford's "On Ethnographic Authority," *Representations* 1, no. 2 (1983): 118–46.

40. Interactivity is seldom a reflexive operation in network newscasting, where it serves to authenticate the newsgathering process and legitimate the presence of the reporter in the field. Moments of social crisis, though, such as the air attacks on Iraq and Kuwait that began on Jan. 16, 1991 or the pro-democracy demonstrations and military repression in China in May-June, 1989 with their attendant prohibition of live news coverage by foreign agencies, can reflexively heighten our awareness of how much such newscasts depend on interactivity for their effect. A limited repertoire of images is recirculated on different programs, images are subjected to freeze-framing or enlargement, or to transformations between color and black-and-white. These "unnatural" devices (on network news) foreground the absence of the usual interactivity. The news apparatus collapses on itself, in a latent hysteria, when the naturalizing effect of interactivity can no longer be achieved.

41. The arrangement of these four modes into a cycle is first proposed by Northrup Frye, *Anatomy of Criticism* (New York: Atheneum, 1968): 158–239. It is also taken up by Hayden White in his *Metahistory: The Historical Imagination in Nineteenth-Century Europe*. Both authors tend toward a formalist use of the concept, granting a high degree of autonomy to this succession of forms but seeing the rhythm of succession itself as tied to a changing historical order.

42. The concept of "structuring absences" comes from Louis Althusser. It addresses how the unsaid functions when it is not a case of the irrelevant but the repressed or the structural. In these cases the unsaid is visible only as a trace or pressure, a constraint or effect, rather than as a positive (and positivist) entity. Althusser develops the concept in an essay on the painter Leonardo Cremonini. He writes, "The structure which controls the *concrete* existence of men, i.e., which *informs the lived ideology* of the relations between men and objects and between objects and men, this structure, *as a structure*, can never be depicted by its presence, *in person*, positively, in relief, but only by traces and effects, negatively, by indices of absence, *in intaglio (en creux)*" (237). Louis Althusser, "Cremonini, Painter of the Abstract," in *Lenin and Philosophy and Other Essays* (London: New Left Books, 1971).

43. A great deal of the work of Unit B at the National Film Board of Canada in the 1960s, in fact, embodies a detached view of its working-class subjects. It should, however, be more strictly labeled as satire or even class bias than irony in the sense of a discursive stance that questions the efficacy of discourse itself.

44. This commentary is a transcription of the English subtitles in the print available from the British Film Institute.

45. See Fredric Jameson, "Postmodernism and Consumer Society," Hal Foster, ed., *The Anti-Aesthetic: Essays on Postmodern Culture* (Port Townsend: Bay Press, 1983).

3. Axiographics

1. Laura Mulvey, "Visual Pleasure and Narrative Cinema," in Bill Nichols, ed., *Movies and Methods*, vol. 2 (Berkeley: University of California Press, 1985): 308.

2. Mulvey, "Visual Pleasure," 314.

3. The signal importance of space and the filmmaker's relation to it is far from lost in most documentary criticism. Whereas a definition in relation to a relative lack of control would suggest that the shooting of documentaries would be the least creative or important aspect of them, the bulk of commentary and discussion dwells precisely on this aspect with relatively little attention to pre- and postproduction. Discussion of *An American Family* (in *New Challenges for Documentary*), as just one example, bears this out. The lack of "control" is a false issue when the presence of the camera marks space with ethical dimensions.

4. For a discussion of the prefiguration of moral perspective in historical writing, see Hayden White, *Metahistory* (Baltimore: The Johns Hopkins University Press, 1973), especially 1–43.

5. Vivian Sobchack, "Inscribing Ethical Space: Ten Propositions on Death, Representation, and Documentary," *Quarterly Review of Film Studies* 9, no. 4 (1984): 283–300. I am extremely indebted to this essay for the following discussion of ethical space in relation to the camera's gaze. Though I have modified her categories, I retain the basic notion that space in documentary bears an ethical dimension distinct from that of fiction.

6. Sobchack, "Ethical Space," 287.

7. The following account of a professional photographer's response to the fact and threat of death during the suppression of riots in Soweto captures the full ambivalence described here:

> Suddenly a small boy dropped to the ground next to me. I realized then that the police were not firing warning shots. They were shooting into the crowd. More children fell. . . . I began taking pictures of the little boy who was dying next to me. Blood poured from his mouth and some children knelt next to him and tried to stop the flow of blood. Then some children shouted they were going to kill me. . . . I begged them to leave me alone. I said I was a reporter and was there to record what happened. A young girl hit me on the head with a rock. I was dazed, but still on my feet. Then they saw reason and some led me away. All the time helicopters circled overhead and there was the sound of shooting. It was like a dream. A dream I will never forget.

Quoted from an account by Alf Khumalo, a black reporter on the *Johannesburg Sunday Times*, in Susan Sontag, *On Photography* (New York: Farrar, Straus and Giroux, 1973): 191–92.

8. See Julia Kristeva, *The Powers of Horror: An Essay on Abjection* (New York: Columbia University Press, 1982) for an extended discussion of the abject.

9. A privileged position for the visible is particularly evident in observational documentary, although here, too, I would argue that there is little fetishization of the visible without the audible. Films like *Primary, High School,* and *Salesman,* or *Sherman's March,* an interactive, reflexive offshoot of this mode of representation, are close to incomprehensible without their synchronous sound tracks. The fetish is of the quotidian, the experience of the everyday without the conceptual and

generalizing frames around it that direct commentary would provide. Arguments for a fetishization of the visible such as Annette Kuhn offers in her extremely useful article, "The Camera I: Observations on Documentary" or Noel Burch makes in "*Hogarth, England Home and Beauty*: Two Recent British Films and the Documentary Ideology, " assault the "hegemony of the visible" or the "bourgeois fascination with the replica as a means of symbolically extending property" within the terms of the 1970s project to displace readerly, classical texts with writerly, radical ones. Both essays appear in *Screen* 19, no. 2 (1978). This project claimed that to observe but not confront, to represent but not explain, allowed the dominant ideology of documentary to march hand in hand with dominant bourgeois ideology. The only politically correct strategy was one that challenged convention and code in the text itself and by that means made the viewer aware of the text not only in terms of what it represented about the world but also what it represented as a text. This encourages a politics of form that tends toward the reductive in its generalizations about bourgeois ideology, the fetishization of the visible, and the work of the cinematic apparatus as a means of social control. It is no coincidence that Noel Burch has subsequently had a greater influence on formalist critics like David Bordwell and Kristin Thompson than political ones like Robert Stam or Tania Modleski.

10. Brian Winston, "The Tradition of the Victim," Alan Rosenthal, ed., *New Challenges for Documentary*, 274. The tension between subject as victim and filmmaker as artist can be profitably explored in regard to *The Thin Blue Line*, where Errol Morris's desire to make a good movie had the happy effect of helping to free a wrongfully accused Randall Adams. Adams gets to tell his story but he is less empowered than showcased. The film is less an acknowledgment of Adams's dignity or honesty than of his ability to play a key role in the orchestration of a taut drama of injustice and victimization, including the victimization Brian Winston attributes to filmmakers who present their subjects as either social victims or the stock characters required by their own dramatic treatment of reality.

11. If this strategy of disenfranchisement and mythologization does not represent control in relation to the "uncontrolled" practice of documentary filmmaking, what does? In a world of images and discourses, of languages that we speak but that also constitute us, the question of "control" returns as an issue for the viewer and social actor as much or more than for the filmmaker and his or her art. Central to any progressive political stance, this particular aspect of the question of control receives no consideration in the works by Gomery and Allen or Bordwell and Thompson discussed in chapter 1.

12. Nick Browne, "The Spectator-in-the-Text: The Rhetoric of *Stagecoach*," *Movies and Methods*, vol. 2.

13. Ibid., 468–69.

14. This concern is the reason Ed Pincus gives for holding his extraordinary documentary, *Panola*, about an unemployed alcoholic black father in Natchez, Mississippi, out of general circulation: it might simply reinforce preexisting stereotypes about Southern blacks if no further context is provided.

15. I discuss the idea of the "masked interview" in *Ideology and the Image*, 279–83. It is also explored further in chapter 2 in relation to the interactive mode of documentary representation.

16. Nick Browne, "The Spectator," 472.

17. The prime counterpoint to this position, and one that is implicitly criticized by the entirety of Nick Browne's essay, is Jean-Louis Baudry, "Ideological Effects of the Basic Cinematographic Apparatus," *Movies and Methods*, vol. 2.

18. Bill Nichols, *Ideology and the Image*, chapter 7.

19. Roland Barthes, *S/Z* (New York: Hill and Wang, 1974): 188.

20. Fredric Jameson puts it well when he writes that "ethical thought projects as

permanent features of 'human experience,' and thus as a kind of 'wisdom' about personal life and interpersonal relations, what are in reality the historical and institutional specifics of a determinate type of group solidarity or class cohesion. . . . What is really meant by 'the good' is simply my own position as an unassailable power center, in terms of which the position of the other, or of the weak, is repudiated and marginalized in practices which are then ultimately themselves formalized in the concept of evil." See *The Political Unconscious: Narrative as a Socially Symbolic Act* (Ithaca: Cornell University Press, 1981): 59, 117.

This function of ethical discourse in relation to the responsibility of the documentary filmmaker emerged in the rejection of *The Thin Blue Line* by the Academy of Motion Picture Arts and Sciences for an Oscar nomination. The film's ironic, reflexive mode seemed to fall outside the bounds of "responsible" reporting. The possibility that the film might be attempting to challenge prevailing conventions, and the ethics that underpin them, or that it might merit nomination for the quality of its accomplishment regardless of its adherence to certain canons of objectivity, fairness, and accuracy were not, apparently, entertained. See "How Oscar Shoo-In Got Dumped by Academy," *San Francisco Chronicle*, March 22, 1989, E3.

4. Telling Stories with Evidence and Arguments

1. Dziga Vertov, "From a Stenograph," in P. Adams Sitney, ed., *Film Culture Reader* (New York: Praeger, 1970): 354–55.

2. Paul Rotha, *The Film Till Now* (1930; reprint, London: Spring Books, 1967), 34.

3. For an elaborate and thorough discussion of how viewers may process narrative information cognitively, see David Bordwell, *Narration in the Fiction Film* (Madison: University of Wisconsin Press, 1985). For a critique of Bordwell's approach see Barry King, "The Classical Hollywood Cinema," and "The Story Continues . . . ," *Screen* 27, no. 6 (1986): 74–88 and 28, no. 3 (1987): 56–82. A debate between King and Bordwell, Janet Staiger, and Kristin Thompson occurs in *Screen* 29, no. 1 (1988). Also see my "Form Wars: The Political Unconscious of Formalist Theory," *South Atlantic Quarterly* 88, no. 2 (Spring 1989): 487–515.

4. André Bazin, "The Ontology of the Photographic Image," in Hugh Gray, ed., *What Is Cinema?*, vol. 1 (Berkeley: University of California Press, 1967). A typical comment by Bazin on the cinema as an "embalming" medium is, "The photographic image is the object itself, the object freed from the conditions of time and space that governs it. . . . Hence the charm of family albums. Those grey or sepia shadows, phantomlike and almost undecipherable, are no longer traditional family portraits but rather the disturbing presence of lives halted at a set moment in their duration, freed from their destiny; not, however, by the prestige of art but by the power of an impassive mechanical process: for photography does not create eternity, as art does, it embalms time, rescuing it simply from its proper corruption" (14).

5. I am indebted for this formulation to Giles Gunn, "The Semiotics of Culture and the Interpretation of Literature: Clifford Geertz and the Moral Imagination," *Studies in the Literary Imagination* 12, no. 1 (1979): 120. He writes that we must balance the mimetic and creative dimensions of art. "For if art forms refract and express certain meanings, they also help shape and sustain them. Art not only imitates life but equally influences it, and it does so by providing, often for the first time, a significant form for those very aspects of subjective human experience it purports only to reflect." This comment is itself an acknowledged paraphrase of Fredric Jameson who first formulates the idea that a text appears to refer us to a

context that is itself the invention of the text, even if this context enjoys all the illusionistic vividness provided by realism. See "The Symbolic Inference; or, Kenneth Burke and Ideological Analysis," *Critical Inquiry* 4 (1978): 507–23.

6. Prime examples include *Operation Abolition* (1960), made for the House Un-American Activities Committee to document their investigation of subversives in the San Francisco Bay Area, and *Operation Correction* (1961), made in response to the film's rhetorical manipulations; Emile de Antonio's *Point of Order* (1963) and the original live television broadcast of the United States Senate's investigation of Eugene McCarthy's dealings with the Army; *Triumph of the Will* and the Why We Fight series, which both use the same images of marching Nazi soldiers to opposite effect. Pat Aufderheide discusses several recent examples involving El Salvador in "Left, Right and Center: El Salvador on Film," in Julianne Burton, ed. *The Social Documentary in Latin America* (Pittsburgh: University of Pittsburgh Press, 1990): 151–71.

7. See Louis Althusser, "Ideology and Ideological State Apparatuses," in *Lenin and Philosophy* (London: NLB, 1971), where he writes that "the category of the subject is only constitutive of all ideology insofar as all ideology has the function (which defines it) of 'constituting' concrete individuals as subjects" (171) and "the individual is interpellated as a (free) subject in order that he shall submit freely to the commandments of the Subject, i.e., in order that he shall (freely) accept his subjection, i.e., in order that he shall make the gestures and actions of his subjection 'all by himself' (182)." This may be so, but my point is that our constitution as subjects is for naught until we are directed toward the world around us by means of propositions, protocols, procedures, and practices. Without its "This is so," ideology's "Hey there!" operates in a vacuum.

8. Jerry Kuehl, "Truth Claims," in Alan Rosenthal, ed., *New Challenges for Documentary,* 109. Kuehl's somewhat flip tone glosses over a sharp distinction between argument and evidence. A documentary may present convincing evidence that Khrushchev pounded his shoe; the image may even enter into popular memory and become an evocative icon with strong symbolic value, but this evidence is of a completely different order from the argument that accompanies it. Arguments are representations whether they occur in documentary or fiction. That documentary argument is linked to evidence from the historical world may give it considerable power to convince, but this linkage does not itself certify the argument's validity.

9. An eloquent example of how facts can be fit to more than one argumentative frame—to say nothing of a multiplicity of fictional possibilities—occurs in an essay by Gregory Bateson:

> I began to doubt the validity of my own categories, and performed an experiment. I chose three bits of culture: (a) a *wau* (mother's brother) giving food to a *laua* (sister's son); a pragmatic bit, (b) a man scolding his wife; an ethological bit, and (c) a man marrying his father's sister's daughter; a structural bit. Then I drew a lattice of nine squares on a large piece of paper, three rows of squares with three squares in each row. I labelled the horizontal rows with my bits of culture and the vertical columns with my categories. Then I forced myself to see each bit as conceivably belonging to each category. I found that it could be done.
>   . . . In fact, "ethos" and the rest were finally reduced to abstractions . . . ; they were labels for points of view voluntarily adopted by the investigator.

Gregory Bateson, "Experiments in Thinking About Observed Ethnological Material," *Steps to an Ecology of Mind* (New York: Ballantine, 1972): 85–86.

10. These categories are proposed and described in Bordwell, *Narration in the Fiction Film*, 57–61. They are also useful within a broader perspective and in relation to documentary as well as fiction.

11. David MacDougall, "Experiments in Interior Commentary," typescript.

12. Roland Barthes, *S/Z*, 76.

13. Christian Metz, "On the Impression of Reality in the Cinema," in *Film Language: A Semiotics of the Cinema* (New York: Oxford University Press, 1974): 9.

14. Roland Barthes, *S/Z*, 9.

15. See chapter 7, "Frederick Wiseman's Documentaries: Theory and Structure," in my *Ideology and the Image* for a detailed discussion of this aspect of Wiseman's work.

16. One example occurred on "Nightline," an ABC current events talk show hosted by Ted Koppel. On July 15, 1988 the guest was Jesse Jackson. After pursuing one line of questioning, Ted Koppel told Jesse Jackson that his next question, after the station break, would be about his role at the Democratic National Convention now that the presidential candidate, Michael Dukakis, had selected someone else as vice-presidential candidate. The Reverend Jackson began to reply when Ted Koppel cut him off, saying, in effect, "Not now, *after* the break." The segment ended with a close-up shot of the effectively gagged, and stymied, Reverend Jackson. The purpose of posing a question only to delay the answer was clearly to create suspense rather than sustain a dialogue. That it would be tolerated was quiet testimony to the power of the institutional apparatus. The sense of objectivity becomes a pose of innocence behind which stands hierarchy, control, and, in this case, arrogance.

17. In a previous essay, "The Voice of Documentary," *Film Quarterly* 36, no. 3 (Spring 1983), I used the term "voice" to refer to what I here call "argument." Argument (carried by commentary and perspective) allows for a wider range of strategies than voice and retains the basic idea that argumentation is a property of the documentary text regardless of its own claims of objectivity, neutrality, or deference. What I there referred to as a loss of voice in films that ceded authority to the commentary of witnesses recruited to them is what I would consider here as a deferential perspective, one that chooses to present evidence of the world as witnesses describe it rather than add a contrapuntal argument or voice of its own.

18. A more extended discussion of *The Battle of San Pietro* occurs in my *Ideology and the Image*.

19. Bordwell, *Narration in the Fiction Film*, 239.

20. Walter Benjamin, "The Work of Art in the Age of Mechanical Reproduction," in *Illuminations* (New York: Schocken Books, 1969): 236.

21. William Alexander, in *Film on the Left: American Documentary Film from 1931 to 1942* (Princeton: Princeton University Press, 1981), writes that the American political filmmakers paid little heed to the political throttling of experimentation that took place in the Soviet Union in the mid-thirties. Instead, Ralph Steiner, Paul Strand, Leo Hurwitz, and others found a valuable lesson in the move to socialist realism: "What engaged them was the fact that, in order to reach a wider audience, Soviet film had moved beyond formalism and a merely external naturalism to an exploration of individual psychology, a representation of rounded character. *Chapayev* was hailed on all sides as a peak example of this, and it reinforced the Nykino incentive to move in such a direction" (90).

22. Some recent work revives an interest in alternative ways to represent situations and subjective experience. I explore several examples, such as Marlon Rigg's *Tongues Untied*, Brenda Longfellow's *Our Marilyn*, Marilu Mallet's *Unfinished Diary* in chapter 8, and in "Getting to Know You: Knowledge, Power, and the Body," in Michael Renov, ed., *Documentary Film* (New York: Routledge, forthcoming).

5. Sticking to Reality

1. See my *Ideology and the Image* (Bloomington: Indiana University Press, 1981): 93–103 for a discussion of pragmatics and paradox in narrative.

2. Jean-Louis Comolli and Jean Narboni, "Cinema/Ideology/Criticism" in *Movies and Methods*, vol. 1 (Berkeley: University of California Press, 1976): 27. They also go on to identify a sixth category, documentary, divided according to whether the filmmaker actively engages with his/her material or thinks that by eliminating some of the trappings of narrative, reality can be allowed to speak for itself. This latter choice, which they identify with an observational style, is the target of derision since it fails to distinguish between appearances and reality (or deep structure) and does not *produce* knowledge but relays existing (ideologically permeated) knowledge (*méconnaissance*).

3. The concept of the double hermeneutic derives from work by Fredric Jameson on the representation of ideology and utopia in texts, especially in *The Political Unconscious* (Ithaca: Cornell University Press, 1981) and "Reification and Utopia in Mass Culture," *Social Text* 1 (1979): 130–48.

4. Examples are Murrow's reports on the bombing of London (9/22/40), the bombing of Germany (12/3/43), and the discovery of Buchenwald concentration camp (4/15/45). All are found on *An Ear to the Sound of Our History*, CBS Records, 1974.

5. See Nick Browne, "The Spectator-in-the-Text: The Rhetoric of *Stagecoach*," in Bill Nichols, ed., *Movies and Methods*, vol. 2 (Berkeley: University of California Press, 1985) where he argues that rhetoric represents the moral viewpoint of the author in fiction. His use of rhetoric is close to my use of style in this context in terms of an implicit system of representation, but shares with my use of rhetoric the notion of perspective as argument. Browne shows that we share the optical point of view of the upright Lucy in a scene in *Stagecoach* but identify more strongly with the "fallen woman," Dallas. A similar analysis of *Thy Kingdom Come* might show how we come to position ourselves with Kevin and against Anthony Thomas even though we share Thomas's point of view during the interview scene. Similar forms of empathetic alignment that go against the grain of the text at one level occur often in documentary. Whether they reveal the author's true sympathies or underlying fissures and contradictions has to be resolved case by case.

6. I discuss Wiseman's gaze as tactless in *Ideology and the Image* but place it more within the tradition of a radical empiricism that eschews etiquette and taboos to examine what others would prefer to overlook or ignore. In this discussion I stress the ethical ambivalence of this position toward those whom he films. Greater sensitivity toward subjects need not necessarily be an argument for more timid empiricism.

7. Eileen McGarry, "Documentary, Realism, and Women's Cinema," *Women and Film* 2, no. 7: 56.

8. Bordwell, *Narration in the Fiction Film*, 53.

9. Charles Altman, "Dickens, Griffith, and Film Theory Today," *South Atlantic Quarterly* 88, no. 2 (Spring 1989): 345, 346–7.

10. Dana Polan, "Film Theory Re-assessed," *Continuum* 1, no. 2 (1988): 15–30.

11. Richard Dyer, "Entertainment and Utopia," in *Movies and Methods*, vol. 2, 220–232.

12. Altman, "Dickens, Griffith, and Film Theory Today."

13. Fredric Jameson, *The Political Unconscious* (Ithaca: Cornell University Press, 1981): 35.

14. Hayden White, *Metahistory*, 2.

15. Clifford Geertz, "Thick Description: Toward an Interpretative Theory of Culture," in *The Interpretation of Cultures* (New York: Basic Books, 1973): 7.

16. Geertz, "Thick Description," 27.

17. Geertz, "Thick Description," 29.

18. Quoted by Peter Wollen, *Signs and Meaning in the Cinema* (Bloomington: Indiana University Press, 1972): 123–24.

19. Christian Metz, *Film Language: A Semiotics of the Cinema* (New York: Oxford University Press, 1974): 9. Digital sampling destroys the concept of the original. Altered images have identical ontological status as what was altered. The evidentiary value of the photograph (in legal cases, for example) is utterly destroyed, but, ironically, the *impression* of authenticity remains.

20. André Bazin, "The Ontology of the Photographic Image," *What Is Cinema?*, vol. 1 (Berkeley: University of California Press, 1967): 14.

21. A classic existential paradox requires the individual caught within it to act, but acting requires him or her to act in a self-contradictory fashion, one that sets up a perpetual oscillation, an on/off, yes/no form of schizophrenic response until the context or frame that created the double bind in the first place is broken. An example is the "barber's paradox," where a soldier is given the order to shave all the men who do not shave themselves. The dilemma arises when the soldier must decide whether to shave himself. If he does shave himself he has disobeyed the order (he must only shave men who do *not* shave themselves), but if he does not shave himself he also disobeys the order (he *must* shave men who do not shave themselves).

The indexical image says, in a similar fashion, "Regard this image as you would regard that which it represents." How, then, do we regard the image? If we decide that the image is what it represents, we disregard its status as image and act as though what it represents were before us (although it is not). If we decide that the image is not what it represents, we disregard its claim and act as though the image were only an image (although it also represents something else). This oscillation is akin to the "suspension of disbelief" requested by fiction generally where we retain an awareness that it is only a fiction but make believe that it is more than a fiction.

22. André Bazin, "Cinema and Exploration," *What Is Cinema?*, vol. 1, 159.

23. Gregory Bateson, *Steps to an Ecology of Mind* (New York: Ballantine, 1972): 86.

24. Bordwell, *Narration in the Fiction Film*, 322.

25. Walter Benjamin, "The Work of Art in the Age of Mechanical Reproduction," in *Illuminations*, 221. Benjamin saw aura as a quality of original objects and things that was lost when they were replicated mechanically. Photography stripped things of their aura. My point here is that subjectivity in documentary adds to the ability of a representation to convey something of the specificity and uniqueness of a historical moment. It remains, of course, a representation, devoid, perhaps, of aura in Benjamin's precise use of the term.

26. A full description of the historical overlay to *Patriamada* can be found in Julianne Burton, "Sing, the Beloved Country: An Interview with Tisuka Tamasaki on *Patriamada*," *Film Quarterly* 41, no. 1 (Fall 1987): 2–9.

6. The Fact of Realism and the Fiction of Objectivity

1. I am indebted to David Bordwell's *Narration in the Fiction Film* for initially suggesting that art cinema overcomes a possible tension between an objective view of an imaginary world (a view not that of any one character) and the personal, even idiosyncratic view of an overt author by stressing ambiguity. Although this insight does not do justice to the forms of ambiguity found in such films—ranging from a

thoroughgoing moral relativism to a Marxist modernism that distrusts appearances—it poses a very neat contrast to the documentary where authorial overtness coexists prominently alongside objective views (ones not relayed through a character) but ambiguity is an extremely rare result (reflexive documentaries may prove the principal exception).

2. André Bazin, *What Is Cinema?*, vol. 2 (Berkeley: University of California Press, 1971): 35.

3. Roland Barthes, *S/Z*, 217.

4. Robert Kolker, *The Altering Eye* (New York: Oxford University Press, 1983): 25–26.

5. A paraphrase of André Bazin, "An Aesthetic of Reality: Neorealism," in *What Is Cinema?*, vol. 2, 21.

6. Kolker, *Altering Eye*, 53.

7. Quoted in Kolker, *Altering Eye*, 54.

8. Bazin, "An Aesthetic of Reality," 36.

9. Brian Winston, "The Tradition of the Victim in Griersonian Documentary," in *New Challenges for Documentary* (Berkeley: University of California Press, 1988): 272.

10. See also Kolker, *Altering Eye*, 66–68 for a similar assessment.

11. Michael Schudson, *Discovering the News* (New York: Basic Books, 1978): 5–7.

12. Ien Ang, *Watching Dallas* (New York: Methuen, 1985).

13. The relations of the visible and the empirical and of observation, description, and explanation are discussed in my *Ideology and the Image*, 262–67.

14. Part of the new jingle ran:

> Reach out, reach out and touch someone,
> Someone whose only hope is you.
> Reach out and give a helping hand.
> Wherever you are, you're never too far
> From someone you can reach out to. . . .

A spokesman for the Live-Aid production describes their rationale for omitting the causal factors of famine this way:

> We did not address some of the causes of hunger because there are so many different causes of hunger and you get into a philosophical debate with people. What we tried to do with the editorial segments was present a point of view that was really undebatable in terms of "Hunger is ending." So we never saw this as a real political event. . . . Our feeling is that if there is popular will, the gears of politics start to move in that direction. When people say, "Let's send some money and aid to Africa," that the politicians listen, that the lawmakers listen. . . . We felt that the politics would follow along [from a grassroots level of awareness]. (Quotations extracted from the sound track of *Consuming Hunger*, Part 2)

15. Quoted from a fan letter to the author in Ang, *Watching Dallas*, 43. Numerous other letters reinforce the mix of recognition and exaggeration that attracts the viewer.

16. See my *Ideology and the Image*, 196–205, for additional discussion of the differences between fictional and documentary continuity.

17. Some of the major book-length critiques of narrative, realism, and, by implication, documentary, include: Christian Metz, *The Imaginary Signifier* (Bloomington: Indiana University Press, 1982); Stephen Heath, *Questions of Cinema* (Bloomington: Indiana University Press, 1981); Kaja Silverman, *The Subject of*

Semiotics (New York: Oxford University Press, 1983); Teresa de Lauretis, *Alice Doesn't: Feminism, Semiotics, Cinema* (Bloomington: Indiana University Press, 1984).

Some of the work that has suggested a more complex, open-minded, or ambivalent view of narrative, realism, and documentary includes: Tania Modleski, *Loving with a Vengeance* (New York: Methuen, 1982); Ang, *Watching Dallas*; E. Ann Kaplan, *Women and Film: From Both Sides of the Camera* (New York: Methuen, 1983); Terry Lovell, *Pictures of Reality* (London: British Film Institute, 1980); Christopher Williams, ed., *Realism and the Cinema* (London: Routledge and Kegan Paul, 1980); Julianne Burton, ed., *The Social Documentary in Latin America* (Pittsburgh: University of Pittsburgh Press, 1990).

18. Laura Mulvey, "Visual Pleasure and Narrative Cinema," in Nichols, ed., *Movies and Methods*, vol. 2, 315.

19. Among these qualifications is the important distinction between male and masculine. Voyeuristic structures such as point-of-view editing which focus on the woman as "to-be-looked-at" encourage a masculinist viewing position that can be taken up or refused by men as well as women. Freud, who never eluded the sexism of his own times entirely, did take pains to distinguish between masculine and feminine sex roles, or subjectivities, which every person possesses in some proportion, and the male and female sexes of which every person is necessarily one or the other. Confusion of this distinction in essays like Laura Mulvey's "Visual Pleasure and Narrative Cinema" has contributed to an unnecessary and false polarization.

20. The idea of social subjectivity relates to the call made by Terry Lovell at the end of her book, *Pictures of Reality*. She argues that cognitive rationalism is an inadequate model for a Marxist perspective on art and culture. The reliance on rationalism leads to an over-dependence on realism, or, in poststructuralism, on conventionalism, on rational arguments against the lure of direct access to the real or even of the autonomous existence of the real itself. Lovell calls for a reexamination of pleasure as a political category, not only the pleasures that circulate around individuals and all the issues of scopophilia that are so crucial to a sexual politics of the cinema, but also to social pleasures, the forms of pleasure that can come from a shared experience such as attending the cinema and seeing a film in the company of others. Although she does not take the point much further, it is a crucial one and corresponds to the construction of a social subjectivity that undercuts, even if only in some small way, the organization of representational space around the destiny of highly individuated characters or social actors.

21. An illuminating and contrasting form of social subjectivity arose in the television news footage of famine in Ethiopia. The victims of starvation frequently look directly at the camera, which stands as a surrogate but unmoved audience. The camera impassively relays its gaze to the viewer, "professionally." The cry for help written across the anonymous faces of these exemplary victims invokes a social subjectivity for the viewer unaligned with a participatory position. The viewer may care, express concern, feel the tug of pathos and charity but not in terms that place him or her within the same spatial and historical field or on the same moral and emotional plane as the victims to whom attention goes.

The news coverage of the Loma Prieta earthquake of October 17, 1989 in California confirms this perspective on the domestic front. The news places the earthquake victims "out there," apart from those who watch the news. Those who suffered injury or damage in the event cannot recognize themselves in the reporting because they have been victimized, they are denied status as subjects, denied dignity and identity. News is about them, not for them. Information that would be of genuine use to a disaster victim—how to purify water when there is no way to boil it, for example—is left for the Red Cross or others to disseminate. What roads to take to work for those who have to circumvent the trauma, as though it were the body of a fallen derelict, takes precedence. This is a social subjectivity very distinct from its representation in Humphrey Jennings. Rather than bringing viewer and representation together into a shared collectivity, news coverage insists on linkage through radical separation between them and us, epitomized, perhaps, in the news anchors like Dan Rather who arrive on the scene of disaster in limousines and trench coats only to depart before the prolonged process of recovery even begins.

22. Quoted in Christopher Williams, ed., *Realism and the Cinema* (London: Routledge and Kegan Paul, 1980): 97.

23. Ibid., 99.

24. Paul Rotha coined this term to describe Flaherty's reliance on a narrative structure that held characters and their actions in balance with an emphasis on location photography, the documentation of everyday life and established ritual, and an epistephilic emphasis on informing the viewer of historically relevant detail as much as psychologically pertinent subjectivities.

25. Michael Snow's "documentary" of the Laurentian Mountains near Montreal, *La region centrale*, demonstrates the physical presence of a recording camera that can turn in any direction and yet never reveal any human presence. Operated entirely by remote control, the film exorcises human agency from the impression of physical presence: no human was there; what we see is solely what a mechanical eye recorded. It offers an impression of objectivity for the camera as machine when it is freed of any anthropomorphic burden (representing the point of view, for example, of characters).

26. This issue runs through a great deal of left political filmmaking in the United States. Both the Film and Photo League and Newsreel, some thirty-odd years later, fractured around the question of whether members owed primary allegiance to the political causes they filmed or to the act of filming political causes. The latter was regarded as opportunistic and the former as an amateur leftism. Some individuals came to believe that a political party could provide the impetus and direction for filmmaking efforts while others argued that formal, aesthetic issues vital to political success could only come from a permanent, professional commitment to filmmaking. On the broader front of a politics of progressive representation, the appearance of a poststructural critique of realism in the 1970s tipped the scale in favor of formal, aesthetic innovation, but the debate continues as one of the most problematic questions in documentary film practice. See my *Newsreel: Political Filmmaking and the American Left* (New York: Arno Press, 1980) for a discussion of this issue in relation to Newsreel.

27. When asked after a screening if she would enter the film for an Oscar nomination, she replied, "No, maybe next time, but this film was made to serve a more immediate purpose—helping these kids, not me."

28. Cited in Michael Schudson, *Discovering the News* (New York: Basic Books, 1978): 147.

29. Hayden White, "The Value of Narrativity in the Representation of Reality," in W. J. T. Mitchell, ed., *On Narrative* (Chicago: University of Chicago Press, 1980): 13.

30. White, "The Value of Narrativity," 18.

31. Cited in Barnouw, *Documentary*, 91.

32. Forsyth Hardy, ed., *Grierson on Grierson* (New York: Praeger, 1966): 165.

33. Peter Morris, "Re-Thinking Grierson: The Ideology of John Grierson," *Dialogue: Canadian and Quebec Cinema* 3 (1987): 21–56.

34. Georg Lukacs, *History and Class Consciousness* (Cambridge: MIT Press, 1968): 100.

35. See "Narrate or Describe?" in *Writer and Critic* (New York: Grosset and Dunlap, 1970).

36. Lukacs, *Writer and Critic*, 116.

37. For a discussion of the narrative and mythic elements of news, see my *Ideology and the Image*, 174–79 and Robert Stam, "Television News and Its Spectator," in E. Ann Kaplan, ed., *Regarding Television* (Frederick, Md.: University Publications, 1983): 23–43.

38. See Teresa de Lauretis, *Alice Doesn't*, 158–86 for an excellent account of how experience can provide the ground for knowledge as political consciousness.

39. Schudson, *Discovering the News*, 186.

40. Paul Feyerabend, *Against Method* (London: New Left Books, 1975): 153–54.

41. Thomas Kuhn, "Logic of Discovery or Psychology of Research," in *The Essential Tension* (Chicago: University of Chicago Press, 1977): 292.

42. Barthes, *S/Z*, 9.

7. Pornography, Ethnography, and the Discourses of Power

1. An extended discussion of ethnographic film occurs in my *Ideology and the Image*. My intention there was to bring ethnographic filmmaking into the arena of contemporary debate on language and its effects since so much ethnographic work continues to endorse a naive empiricism and idealism regarding the objective, data-collecting capacities of the cinema. The intention here is to carry the discussion further in order to raise more basic questions about the ethnographic practice of social representation.

2. It must be added that this Other does not exist in the real. Like the Orient to Said's Orientalist, it is an imaginary construct, a Freudian displacement that is written over a real being or group. The Other is pure representation and, in this context, it is the representation of the non-white, non-male, non-heterosexual, non-Western, non-capitalist as everything we, who are everything the Other cannot be, need. The Other is also a representation of power, of that raw desire for power which power may be loath to admit in its quest for legitimacy and assent. Other terms, like "difference," "socio-sexual difference" or "subaltern," represent efforts to confront and change the dynamics of Otherness. This chapter refers to the Other since so little mainstream pornography or ethnography participates in this confrontation.

3. Jean-Paul Sartre, *Anti-Semite and Jew*, trans. George Becker (New York: Schocken Books, 1965), 149.

4. Michel Foucault, *The History of Sexuality*, vol. 1 (New York: Random House, 1980): 45. Foucault's catalogue of games occurs within specific limits. They are the limits describing what Thomas Kuhn called "normal science," a set of practices governed by a widely accepted and largely unquestioned paradigm, or ideology, and are also in accord with the dynamics of self and other described by Sartre in *Anti-Semite and Jew* as the necessary terms and conditions that bind together the anti-Semite, racist, sexist, jingoist, or homophobe and the Other without which identity collapses. Foucault captures will the *delirium* that can circulate beneath the apparent order of discourse, but he fares less well in describing how this fever can be broken, how his last term for a power that asserts itself with pleasure, "resisting," may not only sustain the prevailing discursive economy but also rupture it. What is called a political unconscious on the horizon of ideology in other chapters may eventuate in counterclaims to the dominant ideology, in radically disparate proposals regarding the facts of existence, legitimate social practices, and cultural ideals. The impact of the feminist movement has been precisely at this point, and the absence of any sustained reference to feminism in Foucault's text is a blind spot of monumental proportions.

5. Cited in Stephan Neale, *Genre* (London: British Film Institute, 1980): 38.

6. John Berger et al., *Ways of Seeing* (London: Penguin Books, 1972): 45–64.

7. Craig Owens, "The Discourse of Others: Feminists and Postmodernism," in Hal Foster, ed., *The Anti-Aesthetic* (Port Townsend, Washington: Bay Press, 1983): 65–66.

8. The argument summarized here regarding the camera gaze can be extended to take up the function of sound, especially speech. Kaja Silverman does precisely this in her *The Acoustic Mirror* (Bloomington: Indiana University Press, 1988).

9. Laura Mulvey, "Visual Pleasure and Narrative Cinema," in Nichols, ed., *Movies and Methods*, vol. 2.

10. A suggestive account of the racial stereotype as a fetish occurs in Homi K. Bhabha,"The Other Question—The Stereotype and Colonial Discourse," *Screen* 24, no. 6 (1983): 18–36.

11. Bernardino de Sahagun, *Historia general de las cosas de Nueva España*, 1565; 4th ed., ed. Angel Maria Garibay K. (Mexico: Editorial Porrua, 1979).

12. Referred to in *The History of Sexuality*, vol. 1, the distinction receives full elaboration in volume 2, *The Uses of Pleasure*, where Foucault examines Greco-Roman practice, organized around an "aesthetics of experience" or an *ars erotica*, in considerable detail.

13. See Michel Foucault's *The History of Sexuality*, vol. 1, especially part 3, "Scientia Sexualis," where he discusses the central place of the confession in the organization of knowledge and pleasure and the discursive regulation of sexuality.

14. "Thick description" is a term of Clifford Geertz's that represents an ethnographic ideal of adequacy to the complex of contextual meanings and values surrounding human encounters. A factual accounting would be skimpy compared to a description that attempts to indicate what the encounter might mean and how it might be interpreted by each of its participants. As such it relies heavily upon a largely unexamined theory of realism and unquestioned assumptions about anthropology's rights and responsibilities of cultural representation. Within its own terms it stands as an excellent articulation of a discursive model or ideal. See Geertz, "Thick Description: Toward an Interpretative Theory of Culture," *The Interpretation of Cultures* (New York: Basic Books, 1973).

15. Linda Williams, *Hard Core: Power, Pleasure, and "The Frenzy of the Visible"* (Berkeley: University of California Press, 1989) argues that late seventies to early eighties porn begins to add a convention of sexual bliss that precludes or omits the problematic "cum shot" in favor of less visible but conceivably more authentic signifiers of the inner experience of orgasm (i.e., a shift from documentary-like proof of orgasm, for men, to more subjective evocations of both male and female orgasmic experience.) This may parallel the increased representation of subjective experience in documentary generally, but more recent developments in pornography, such as mail-order videotapes, suggest that the cum shot remains a staple element of generic convention. One mail-order firm, for example, features thirty-minute tapes of sexual highlights instead of feature narratives that are the primary focus here. Typical, and self-explanatory, titles include: *Anal Cumshots*, *Slurp!*, *Spewing Black Cocks*, *Cum Bath*, and *Oral and Facial Cumshots*, among others (Leisure Concepts catalogue).

16. Tom Gunning, "The Cinema of Attractions: Early Film, Its Spectator and the Avant-Garde," in Thomas Elsaesser, *Early Cinema* (London: British Film Institute, 1990): 58, 59.

17. Kuleshov and Vertov, along with other Soviet directors like Eisenstein, saw this process of recombination more in the spirit of a social transformation of the material world. It celebrated a newly forged collectivity and the dissolution of the

bourgeois boundaries of the solitary self. The pornographic tradition discussed here knows nothing of this alternative.

18. Berger et al., *Ways of Seeing*, 62.

19. Berger et al., *Ways of Seeing*, 62.

20. In pornography, the sex act is clearly "unnatural," though also concrete. It is performed and orchestrated for the camera, not the participants, leading both to postures and positions that would not occur otherwise and to perspectives to which no participant could be privy. But it remains an authentic sexual encounter. The performers may act as characters in terms of their emotional relationship but they perform as social actors in terms of their sexual engagement: they (most unquestionably men) achieve orgasm and there is no falsification or simulation of the physical acts themselves. (Female orgasm, as a subjective experience for which an unmistakable visible correlate or convention has failed to establish itself in pornography, poses a distinct problem.) Though radically different in these ways from what it represents, the intent is to comply with the conceit that the differences should facilitate making the typical, if not ideal, visible for the observer instead of foregrounding how radically different, and dystopian, this sex truly is.

21. I use the term "postfeminist" in the sense meant by Trinh T. Minh-ha for issues of women's liberation recast to include others besides the predominantly white, middle-class, heterosexual women's liberation movement in industrial countries. Her own *Reassemblage, Naked Spaces*, and *Surname Viet Given Name Nam* approximate a postfeminist discourse on masculinist ethnography and representation. Like lesbian or experimental pornography, her films operate beyond the reach of this chapter's focus on the dominant forms of ethnography and pornography. If nothing else, though, it should be noted that these films, however problematic in other regards, do contest the forms and systems of representation characterized here. They do more than shift the subject for consideration. They suggest, as works by Chantal Akerman, Yvonne Rainer, and Lizzie Borden have also done, ways in which the question of the representation of women can itself become the point of departure for a feminist aesthetic.

22. During the process of revising the collaboratively written article into a chapter for this book, I came to agree with Linda Williams's argument in *Hard Core* that a pornotopia can be represented by women, for women, even if this representation is far from a feminist critique of gender hierarchy or oppression. (Our article was written before the book was available.) Marilyn Chambers, in *Insatiable*, discovers her sexual appetite demands more and more sex but it is *gratifying* sex. As in the musical, this image of utopian gratification wishes away real contradiction rather than undercutting its material base. Identification and pleasure may be available here for women as for men, along the lines suggested in Ien Ang's reading of Dallas (in *Watching Dallas*): the frustration and desires represented are *real*, their resolution, however fanciful or impractical, can afford pleasure, however limited it may be by some criteria.

My own sense is that the female protagonists of *Insatiable, Taboo* (1–4), or *Debbie Does Dallas* are primarily pretexts or surrogates for a masculinist perspective that remains dominant. Their discovery of sexual fulfillment revolves around a generalized eroticism (same-sex encounters, orgies, masturbation, fellatio, cunnilingus, etc.) but also tends to grant pride of place in this sexual pantheon to the phallus. Still, this reading may be a preferred reading, the one the text itself appears to support most strongly. It is important to acknowledge that equally affective, equally legitimate readings that qualify or contest this phallocentrism may simultaneously occur among viewers.

23. Roland Barthes, *Mythologies* (St. Albans: Paladin, 1973): 100–102.

24. See Stephan Mamber, *Cinema Verité in America* (Cambridge: MIT Press, 1974), especially 115–40.

25. Karl Heider, *Ethnographic Film* (Austin: University of Texas Press, 1976): 125.

26. Both Mary Louise Pratt, "Fieldwork in Common Places," and James Clifford, "On Ethnographic Allegory," in James Clifford and George E. Marcus, eds., *Writing Culture* (Berkeley: University of California Press, 1986) make reference to the function of arrival scenes and other literary devices to invoke the authority of a science and the detachment of an observer.

27. James Clifford points out that the arrival scene fits within the methodology of modern fieldwork as a certification based on the premise of "You are there because I was there." "On Ethnographic Authority," *Representations* 1, no. 2 (1983): 118.

28. I discuss possible interpretations of *The Nuer*, including its validity as an ethnographic document, in *Ideology and the Image*, 250–60.

29. This discussion treats pornographic and ethnographic authority in terms of its evidentiary claims about the authenticity or validity of what we see and hear. Argumentative claims are a separate matter. For pornography, argumentation is a matter of a narrative moral or lesson, usually involving the virtues of a liberated sexuality. For ethnography, argumentation is a matter of what counts as authoritative interpretation within the anthropological community (and only rarely within the represented society). (What counts changes with time and place in a manner similar to the changes in documentary modes of representation as strategies for conveying a persuasive impression of the historically real.) These issues are usefully analyzed in Clifford's "On Ethnographic Authority" and Paul Rabinow's "Representations Are Social Facts: Modernity and Post-Modernity in Anthropology," in Clifford and Marcus, eds., *Writing Culture*: 234–61.

30. See André Bazin, "The Myth of Total Cinema," in *What Is Cinema?*, vol. 1. For example, "The guiding myth, then, inspiring the invention of cinema, is the accomplishment of that which dominated in a more or less vague fashion all the techniques of the mechanical reproduction of reality in the nineteenth century, from photography to the phonograph, namely an integral realism, a recreation of the world in its own image" (21).

31. For further discussion of these three realisms see Ang, *Watching Dallas*.

32. Gloria Steinem, "Erotica or Pornography: A Clear and Present Difference," in Laura Lederer, ed., *Take Back the Night* (New York: William Morrow, 1980): 37.

33. Jonathan Culler, *Structuralist Poetics* (Ithaca: Cornell University Press, 1975): 132.

34. Kaja Silverman, *The Subject of Semiotics*, 158.

35. In an article, "Getting to Know You: Knowledge, Power, and the Body," in Michael Renov, ed., *Documentary Film* (New York: Routledge, forthcoming) I discuss evocation as an alternative to representation, particularly in relation to the work of exiled filmmakers like Marilu Mallet and Raul Ruiz. This concept prompts a number of provocative shifts in basic assumptions about the ethnographic enterprise particularly. It also slides inevitably toward an expository poetics that will inevitably seem beyond the pale to those who seek to uphold the disciplinary boundaries of ethnography as it currently exists.

36. Linda Williams, *Hard Core*, 276, 279.

37. See Donna Harraway, "Teddy Bear Patriarchy: Taxidermy in the Garden of Eden, New York City, 1908–36," in *Primate Visions: Race, Gender and Nature in the World of Modern Science* (New York: Routledge, 1989): 26–58 for an excellent analysis of these dioramas and their creator, Carl Akeley.

38. Trinh T. Minh-ha, *Woman, Narrative, Other: Writing Postcoloniality and Feminism* (Bloomington: Indiana University Press, 1989): 67, 68.

8. Representing the Body

1. In writing of the miniature as a special form of representation, Susan Stewart identifies a problem that clearly pertains to documentary film as a "miniaturization" of the historical world: "we find that when language attempts to describe the concrete, it is caught in an infinitely self-effacing gesture of inadequacy, a gesture which speaks to the gaps between our modes of cognition—those gaps between the sensual, the visual, and the linguistic." Susan Stewart, *On Longing: Narratives of the Miniature, the Gigantic, the Souvenir, the Collection* (Baltimore: The Johns Hopkins University Press, 1984): 52.

2. Jameson, *The Political Unconscious*, 35, 102.

3. Even some presemiotic critiques of Bazin and Eisenstein's theories, such as Brian Henderson's, fault them for relating cinema to an antecedent reality rather than elaborating its internal, more formal properties.

> It is difficult for us to find any value in this approach [of Bazin or Eisenstein] whatever. Such theories would keep cinema in a state of infancy, dependent upon an order anterior to itself, one to which it can stand in no meaningful relation because of this dependence. We no longer relate a painting by Picasso to the objects he used as models or even a painting by Constable to its original landscape. Why is the art of cinema different? (Brian Henderson, *A Critique of Film Theory* [New York: Dutton, 1980]: 31)

In Henderson's terms, documentary would be condemned to perpetual swaddling clothes since its effect and value are inextricable from "an order anterior to itself," an infantile state, perhaps, but one which is absolutely fundamental. This relation of dependence, lamented by some, is also what renders documentary so intractable or uninteresting to theories and methods whose underpinning is primarily formalist. Henderson's goal, in 1971, was to address the fiction film and to encourage more formally rigorous examinations of the text itself. This has come to pass. There is no question here of turning back this advance, but of demonstrating the differences required for an examination of documentary film.

4. This difference is sharply illustrated by fiction films that implant or incorporate historical moments in a documentary fashion. *Medium Cool* and *Patriamada*, for example, record, respectively, the historical events that occurred at the Democratic National Convention of 1968 and the return to democracy in Brazil in 1984. The viewer who lacks prior or contextual knowledge of these events and has not seen other visual evidence of the demonstrations, speeches, and police actions may have little reason to extend distinctive status to the representations of such events in the films. These moments may seem as fully fictional as any others, displaying the same metaphorical relation to the historical as the burning of Atlanta in *Gone with the Wind* or the murder of the civil rights workers in *Mississippi Burning*.

5. Questions of magnitude are precisely what are missing from work such as David Bordwell's *Narration in the Fiction Film*. Though of considerable value in other regards, Bordwell's reference to the viewer as a "hypothetical entity" rather than a historically situated person is emblematic of the limitations of his approach.

6. Films that fail or refuse to show their central subject such as *Hotel Terminus: The Life and Times of Klaus Barbie*; *Roger and Me*; *He's Like*, which features gay men describing their lovers whom we never see; *Waiting for Fidel*, about an attempt by two Canadians to meet with Fidel Castro, whom we never see; *Writing in Water*, where a Kentucky farm family recounts the effect of a visit by a stranger whom we never see; and *Shoah*, which never shows us the historic footage of the concentration camps of which its witnesses speak—such films leave a hollow at their center

that becomes filled by those who speak about that absence; it is their perceptions and values, their attitudes and assumptions that become the subject of our scrutiny. A fascinating variation on this approach is *Dear America: Letters Home from Vietnam*, where we briefly see still photographs of the soldiers who wrote the letters while they are read by professional actors over newsreel footage of the war. The individual letter writers are essentially displaced by their letters, the professional readings, and the accompanying footage. The filmmaker's perspective on the writers and the war becomes the central focus of the film, as the interviewee's own perceptions and values do in the other films cited here. *Roger and Me* belongs to this category in relation to the elusive Roger Smith, CEO of General Motors, but the film might also be excluded from this category if we consider it to be about either Flint, Michigan itself or about the response of disparate individuals to auto plant shut-downs. The latter focus is the one I find most productive in assessing the film.

7. In speaking of praxis informed by a text, I want to distinguish this notion sharply from Edward Said's quite telling criticism of Orientalist literature that serves as a guidebook for conduct. Said speaks of two cases where a "textual attitude" gains reinforcement: confrontation with the unknown and gaining the impression that it works. If a ritual appears to have the desired effect, it will very likely be repeated. (See Edward Said, *Orientalism* [New York: Vintage Books, 1979]: 93–100.) The concept of magnitude leaves the text behind as an entity experienced as profoundly inadequate and yet instructive, pleasing, and instigational. A textual attitude never leaves the text behind but clings to it as a formulaic escape from encounter and risk. The fact that a textual handbook works may say less about the nature of (Oriental) reality than about relations of power. "Orientalism" [the sum of such texts] gave Westerners like Napoleon and Mathieu de Lesseps their success—"at least from their point of view, which had nothing to do with that of the Oriental. Success, in other words, had all the actual human interchange between Oriental and Westerner of the Judge's 'said I to myself, said I' in *Trial by Jury*" (95). Action informed by a text is contingent: the text can never be a handbook nor can the text seal itself off as a discrete, consumable, and disposable experience. Questions of magnitude impel us toward dialogue. They are the antithesis of the textual attitude.

8. Vivian Sobchack in "Inscribing Ethical Space: Ten Propositions on Death, Representation and Documentary," *Quarterly Review of Film Studies* (Fall 1984) describes six different visual forms in which the encounter of filmmaker and death or dying can be registered. The "professional gaze" is one of these. These gazes are discussed in greater detail in chapter 3.

9. Anthony Wilden defines existential paradox as "the conscious or unconscious intentionalization by a subject of something about life which denies the usually accepted categories of truth and falsity about 'reality'—something 'inexplicable.' The existential paradox differs from the purely logical paradox in that it involves subjects and is primarily dependent on communication" (*System and Structure: Essays in Communication and Exchange*, 2nd. ed. [London: Tavistock, 1980]: 103). The statement "I am lying," for example, is a logical paradox but not an existential one since time and context, speaker and listener can pursue and negotiate validation for what remains a paradox in the more abstract realms of pure logic. What does loom as an existential paradox are commands that can be neither obeyed nor disobeyed. "Disregard this sentence," is an example. In the present context, questions of magnitude engender a paradox something like "Disregard this text," that we cannot entirely obey or ignore.

This paradox propels us beyond the text as a closed system and beyond those critiques of classic fiction that regard distance and separation as a necessary adjunct to an imaginary sense of unity and control. (See, for example, Stephen Heath, "Lessons from Brecht," *Screen* 15, no. 4 [1970].) As Kaja Silverman puts it in her book, *The Acoustic Mirror*, "Like the little boy who sees the female genitals for the first time and who disavows the absence of the penis, this viewer [what Metz refers to as "any spectator"] refuses to acknowledge what he or she knows full well—that cinema is founded on the lack of the object" (*The Acoustic Mirror*, 4). This refusal is precisely what the documentary viewer confronted with magnitudes that exceed the text cannot do. Classic fiction *may* suture us into a position of disavowal, a position from which a male subjectivity denies its own deficiency and lack, projecting it onto women, but documentary *identifies* this lack, this absence of the real, of history, to which we are compelled to attend. The gender-based spectatorial pleasures that arise from disavowal and the fantasy of imaginary coherence and control are far less operative in documentary than fiction. The discourses of sobriety earn their name partly for this reason. The difference, though, is not absolute but a matter of degree.

10. Roland Barthes, *Image-Music-Text*, trans. Stephen Heath (New York: Hill and Wang, 1977): 52–68.

11. See Walter Benjamin, "The Work of Art in the Age of Mechanical Reproduction." Benjamin retains an ambivalent attitude toward this loss of aura: although everything is up for grabs, the risk that those with power will use it hegemonically exerts a severe constraint. The difference between the liberating potential of the cinema ("in the midst of its far-flung ruins and debris, we calmly and adventurously go traveling," 236) and the spectacles that are actually produced provides one point of justification for Benjamin's ambivalence.

12. Fredric Jameson, "Symbolic Inference: or, Kenneth Burke and Ideological Analysis," *The Ideologies of Theory*, vol. 1 (Minneapolis: University of Minnesota Press, 1988): 141. Jameson takes this question up in his book *The Political Unconscious* (81–82) and uses the same words to describe it, this time in a somewhat broader frame of reference but with a similar distrust of the text for its potential to deceive us into believing that this reality it brings into being has no existence apart from its textual identity, a distrust that seems fueled by Jameson's own subtext of disagreement with formalist, psychoanalytic, and some poststructural readings of texts.

13. Jameson, "Symbolic Inference," 141.

14. An excellent consideration of the issues involved in the fictional and documentary representation of the Holocaust occurs in Ilan Avisar, *Screening the Holocaust: Cinema's Images of the Unimaginable* (Bloomington: Indiana University Press, 1988). Avisar details the problems inherent in narrative representation and indicates how certain filmmakers and films have successfully addressed them. He is particularly instructive in his discussion of the deformative tendencies within narrative that reduce the magnitude of historical events by constraining time and place, action and event, to those terms capable of resolution in relation to individuated characters. (See chapter 2, "The Discontents of Film Narrative," in particular.)

15. Sartre, *Anti-Semite and Jew*, 18–19.

16. The distinction between transcendent and immanent spiritual systems is well made in Gregory Bateson, *Steps to an Ecology of Mind* (New York: Ballantine, 1972), especially parts 5 and 6.

17. A fundamental, if somewhat schematic statement of this proposition occurs in Jean-Louis Comolli and Jean Narboni, "Cinema, Ideology, Criticism" in Nichols, ed., *Movies and Methods*, vol. 2. More recent explorations of troubled texts include Robin Wood, "An Introduction to the American Horror Film," also in *Movies and Methods*, vol. 2, Tania Modleski, *Loving with a Vengeance* (New York: Methuen, 1982),

Dudley Andrew, *Concepts in Film Theory* (New York: Oxford University Press, 1984),
David Bordwell, Janet Staiger, and Kristen Thompson, *The Classical Hollywood
Cinema* (New York: Columbia University Press, 1985).

18. Dudley Andrew, *Concepts in Film Theory* (Oxford and New York: Oxford
University Press, 1984): 151–52.

19. In Louis Althusser, "The 'Piccolo Teatro': Bertolazzi and Brecht," *For Marx*
(New York: Vintage Books, 1970) 131–51.

20. Althusser, "The 'Piccolo Teatro,'" 143.

21. Althusser, "The 'Piccolo Teatro,'" 143.

22. Althusser, "The 'Piccolo Teatro,'" 145–46.

23. After beginning to conceptualize these three axes, their parallelism with
Hayden White's notion of prefiguration in historical writing became more clear,
less in terms of the specific categories, which differ in accordance with the difference between nineteenth-century historiography and documentary filmmaking
today, but more in terms of the notion of the realm of prefiguration as such.
Matters of style and form remain to be decided after a text's placement in relation
to the axes has been considered. No conscious act is implied on the part of the
filmmaker, but rather the same kind of "poetic act" that White attributes to
historians when they position themselves, prefiguratively, within the possibilities of
a linguistic field. His definition of written history requires only slight modification
to be brought to bear on documentary: "a verbal structure in the form of narrative
prose discourse that purports to be a model, or icon, of past structures and
processes in the interest of *explaining what they were by representing them*" (*Metahistory*,
2, italics his). This last phrase also leads White to add a footnote over a page long
in which he takes up the vexing issue of realism. White's emphasis on the artistic
elements of realist historiography also parallels my concern here with the narrative
and mythic elements of documentary over the indexical or historical elements of
fiction.

24. Hayden White, "The Value of Narrativity," 14–15.

25. See Georg Lukacs, "Narrate or Describe?" Arthur Kahn, trans. and ed.,
Writer and Critic and Other Essays (New York: Grosset and Dunlop, 1970). Lukacs
favored "to narrate" as a way of drawing character and event into a more integral
alliance. "To narrate" approximates the introduction of subjective elements in
documentary by bringing the consciousness of characters into direct relationship
with their social milieu. Lukacs writes,

> In Scott, Balzac or Tolstoy we experience events which are inherently
> significant because of the direct involvement of the characters in the events
> and because of the general social significance emerging in the unfolding of
> characters' lives. We are the audience to events in which the characters take
> active part. We ourselves experience these events.
>
> In Flaubert and Zola the characters are merely spectators, more or less
> interested in the events. As a result, the events themselves become only a
> tableau for the reader, or, at best, a series of tableaux. We are merely
> observers. (116)

The infusion of this subjectivity into documentary strikes me as extremely welcome,
but I should note that it is precisely this sense of "experiencing" events through the
involvement of characters that was severely attacked in film theory and criticism
during the 1970s under the banners of semiology, psychoanalysis, poststructuralism, and feminism. The cinematic apparatus produced the impression of experience, masking its own work, constituting a transcendental subject (who was male
and patriarchal), and perpetuating bourgeois relations of production. Though

persuasive as a characterization of the dominant or hegemonic tendency in cinema, many critics have disputed the infallibility of its effects and the pervasiveness of its domain. We are now closer to a point in film theory where the value of this ideological critique of the apparatus may be lost in the desire to regain a finer sense of the specificities of structure, reading, and response. Its applicability to documentary has never been fully explored or demonstrated in any case.

26. Vivian Sobchack makes a similar distinction in her own description of the representation of death in cinema: "Thus, when death is represented as fictive rather than real, when its signs are structured and stressed so as to function iconically and symbolically, it is understood that only the *simulacrum* of a visual taboo is being violated. However, when death is represented as real, when its signs are structured and inflected so as to function indexically, a visual taboo is violated and the representation must find ways to justify the violation" ("Inscribing Ethical Space," 291). This is precisely the strategy of many films dealing with the Holocaust, with torture and murder by government agents in Latin America generally, and the strategy of *Roses* in particular: to offer meaningful justification for presenting images of the remains of those who were once living.

27. Barry King, "Articulating Stardom," *Screen* 26, no. 5 (Sept.-Oct. 1985): 27–50.

28. See André Bazin, "The Stalin Myth in Soviet Cinema," in Nichols, ed., *Movies and Methods*, vol. 2, 29–40.

29. Walter Benjamin, "The Work of Art in the Age of Mechanical Reproduction," 247.

30. Peter Wollen, "Godard and Counter Cinema: *Vent d'est*," in Nichols, ed., *Movies and Methods*, vol. 2, 500–509.

31. Wollen, "Counter Cinema," 502.

32. Wollen, "Counter Cinema," 503.

33. Wollen, "Counter Cinema," 505.

34. Wollen, "Counter Cinema," 506.

35. Wollen, "Counter Cinema," 507–8.

36. Frank Lentricchia, *Criticism and Social Change* (Chicago and London: University of Chicago Press, 1983): 104.

37. Jameson, *The Political Unconscious*, 82–83.

38. As noted earlier, these strategies contrast radically with the response to the explosion of the Challenger space shuttle. Part of the hysteria prompted by the Challenger disaster arose from the apparently total vaporization of the astronauts' bodies. This sudden and total disappearance of already mythologized heroes called forth prodigious acts of commemoration. Once accomplished, the physical body could once more be passed over en route to its ahistorical idealization. Myths have little need of flesh and blood that is limited by time and place, character and subjectivity. They prefer to provide the body and propose the subjectivity that suits their ends. Whereas it was the return of the historical body of Jesus of Nazareth that signaled his status as the Son of God, the Christ of legend, the recovery of these seven bodies signaled their status as all-too-human flesh, limited by the vicissitudes of time rather than transcendent to it. (In contrast to the front-page headlines of the disaster itself, for example, the shipment of the recovered remains to Dover Air Force Base in Delaware for "final treatment in accordance with the families' wishes" became a small, back-page item in the April 25, 1986 *New York Times*.)

39. Regarding the individual as monad: The crisis moment seems to address the problem of bodily representation summarized by Fredric Jameson: "The rhetoric of the body [in Kenneth Burke's theory of symbolic action], however, remains ambiguous: it can inaugurate the celebration of a kind of private materialism, from Bataille and "desire" all the way to certain readings of Bakhtin; or it can lead us dialectically beyond these individualizing and organic limits into some more prop-

erly collective apprehension of space and spatiality itself." See "The Symbolic Inference: or, Kenneth Burke and Ideological Analysis," in *The Ideologies of Theory*, vol. 1 (Minneapolis: University of Minnesota Press, 1988): 148.

The issue of historical materialism, the individual as monad, and feminism in a postmodernist age of cybernetics and simulations receives exemplary treatment in Donna Harraway's "A Manifesto for Cyborgs," *Socialist Review*, no. 80 (1985): 65–107. She particularly stresses a politics of affinity that reconceptualizes the classic categories of class, sex, race, and nationality and the various notions of unity and dialectical synthesis that derive from them. Championing the idea of an imperfect utopia with considerable eloquence and imagination, the main unresolved question, which must be put ironically, is whether an affinity-based politics would be more imperfect than utopian, postponing the resolution of contradiction until that famous "last instance" whose arrival remains as indefinite as truth is approximate.

FILMOGRAPHY

The filmography lists all documentaries mentioned in the book and any other films discussed at length; it lists films under their most commonly used English-language title but cross-references this to their original title in the case of foreign language films. The producing agency is identified when it is a significant creative or institutional force in its own right. The country of origin is provided if it is a country other than the United States. For films set in one country by filmmakers from a second country, the country or region in which the film has its focus is given first, followed by the nationality of the filmmaker(s). Release dates and running times have been cross-checked where possible, but sources are often inconsistent or unreliable. This information should be considered approximate.

Abortion Stories: North and South, Gail Singer, National Film Board of Canada: Ireland, Japan, Thailand, Peru, Colombia/Canada, 55 min., 1984

The Act of Seeing with one's own eyes, Stan Brakhage, 32 min., 1971

Action: The October Crisis of 1970, Robin Spry, National Film Board of Canada, 87 min., 1974

All My Babies, George Stoney, 55 min., 1952

An American Family, Craig Gilbert, NET, 12 one-hour episodes, 1972

Antonia: A Portrait of a Woman, Judy Collins and Jill Godmilow, 58 min., 1973

Are We Winning the Cold War, Mommy? America and the Cold War, Barbara Margolus, 85 min., 1986

The Atomic Cafe, Kevin Rafferty, Jayne Loader, Pierce Rafferty, 92 min., 1982

Australia: The Island Continent, the Nature Series, Public Broadcasting System, 1988

The Ax Fight, Timothy Asch and Napoleon Chagnon, the Yanomamö series, 30 min., Venezuela/United States, 1971

The Back-Breaking Leaf, Terence Macartney-Filgate, National Film Board of Canada, 28 min., 1959

The Battle of Chile (La batalla de Chile), Patricio Guzmán, Chile, 4 hours 30 min. in 3 parts, 1974, 1977, 1979

The Battle of China, Frank Capra and Anatole Litvak, the Why We Fight series, 67 min., 1944

The Battle of San Pietro, John Huston, 33 min., 1945

Before Stonewall, Greta Shiller, 87 min., 1984

Before We Knew Nothing, Diane Kitchen, Peru/United States, 62 min., 1988

Berlin: Symphony of a Great City, Walter Ruttman, Germany, 53 min., 1927

Bitter Melons, John Marshall, The Bushman series, Kalahari Desert (Namibia)/ United States, 30 min., 1968

Black Panther, San Francisco Newsreel, 12 min., 1968; originally known as *Off the Pig*

Blood and Fire, Terence Macartney-Filgate, National Film Board of Canada, 27 min., 1958

Blood of the Beasts (Le sang des bêtes), Georges Franju, France, 22 min., 1949

The Bridge (De brug), Joris Ivens, Netherlands, 12 min., 1928.

British Sounds, Jean-Luc Godard and Jean-Pierre Gorin, France/Great Britain, 52 min., 1967; also known as *See You at Mao*

Cabra marcado para morer: Vinte años depois. See *A Man Marked to Die*

Cane Toads: An Unnatural History, Mark Lewis, Australia, 46 min., 1987

Cannibal Tours, Dennis O'Rourke, Papua New Guinea/Australia, 70 min., 1988
Carved in Silence, Felicia Lowe, 45 min., 1987
La chagrin et la pitié. See *The Sorrow and the Pity*
Character Formation in Different Cultures series, Margaret Mead and Gregory Bateson, New Guinea, Bali/United States, shot 1936–38, released 1952. Includes *Balinese Family, Bathing Babies in Three Cultures, Childhood Rivalry in Bali and New Guinea, First Days in the Life of a New Guinea Baby, Karba's First Years, Trance and Dance in Bali*
Childhood Rivalry in Bali and New Guinea, Gregory Bateson and Margaret Mead, Character Formation in Different Cultures series, Bali, New Guinea/United States, 20 min., 1952
China Strikes Back, Harry Dunham, Frontier Films, China/United States, 30 min., 1937
Chris and Bernie, Deborah Shaffer and Bonnie Friedman, 25 min., 1975
Chronicle of a Summer (*Chronique d'un été*), Jean Rouch and Edgar Morin, France, 90 min., 1960
Chronique d'un été. See *Chronicle of a Summer*
The City, Williard Van Dyke and Ralph Steiner, 58 min., 1939
The Civil War, Ken Burns, Public Broadcasting System, 12 hours approx., 1990
The Color of Honor, Loni Ding, 101 min., 1987
Comic Book Confidential, Ron Mann, United States/Canada, 90 min., 1988
Coming Out, Ted Reed and Susan Bell, 25 min., 1989
Community of Praise, Richard Leacock and Marisa Silver, the Middletown series for PBS, Peter Davis, Producer, 60 min., 1982
Consuming Hunger, parts 1–3, Ilan Ziv, Maryknoll World Video and Channel Four, Ethiopia/Israel, 30 min. each, 1987
Cree Hunters of the Mistassini, Tony Ianzielo and Boyce Richardson, National Film Board of Canada, 59 min., 1974
Culloden, Peter Watkins, Great Britain, 72 min., 1964
A Curing Ceremony, John Marshall, The Bushman series, Kalahari Desert (Namibia)/United States, 8 min., 1966
Dani Sweet Potatoes, Karl Heider, West New Guinea/United States, 19 min., 1974
Daughter Rite, Michelle Citron, 55 min., 1978
David Holzman's Diary, Jim McBride and L. M. Kit Carson, 71 min., 1968
The Day after Trinity: J. Robert Oppenheimer and the Atomic Bomb, Jon Else, 88 min., 1981
The Day of the Dead, George Romero, 103 min., 1985
The Days before Christmas, Stanley Jackson, Wolf Koenig, Terence Macartney-Filgate, National Film Board of Canada, 29 min., 1959
Dead Birds, Robert Gardner, West New Guinea/United States, 83 min., 1963
Dear America: Letters Home from Vietnam, Bill Couturié, Home Box Office (HBO), 86 min., 1987
De grands événements et des gens ordinaires. See *Of Great Events and Ordinary People*
Demon Lover Diary, Joel DeMott, 90 min., 1980
A Divided World, Arne Sucksdorff, Sweden, 10 min., 1948
The Divine Horsemen, Maya Deren, Haiti/United States, 54 min., 1977
Don't Look Back, D. A. Pennebaker, 90 min., 1966
Downwind, Downstream: Threats to the Mountains and Waters of the American West, Christopher McLeod, 58 min., 1988
Drifters, John Grierson, Great Britain, 58 min., 1929
The Emperor's Naked Army Marches On (*Juki jukite shingun*), Hara Kazuo, Japan, 123 min., 1987
Erika: Not in Vain, Barry Spinello, 44 min., 1984

Eternal Frame, T. R. Uthco, Ant Farm Collective, 24 min., 1976
Ethnic Notions, Marlon Riggs, 58 min., 1987
Family Business, Tom Cohen, the Middletown series, Public Broadcasting System, Peter Davis, Producer, 90 min., 1982
Family Gathering, Lise Yasui, 30 min., 1988
Far from Poland, Jill Godmilow, 106 min., 1984
Final Offer, Sturla Gunnarson, Canada, 79 min., 1986
Fire from the Mountain, Deborah Shaffer, Nicaragua/United States, 58 min., 1987
First Contact, Robin Anderson and Bob Connelly, Papua New Guinea/Australia, 54 min., 1984
Forest of Bliss, Robert Gardner, India/United States, 1985
For the First Time (*Por primera vez*), Octavio Cortázar, ICAIC, Cuba, 12 min., 1967
For Your Life, Sigve Endreson, Norway, 95 min., 1989
Four Families, Ian MacNeill and Guy Glover, with Margaret Mead, National Film Board of Canada, 60 min., 1960
Frank: A Vietnam Veteran, Fred Simon and Vince Canzoneri, 52 min., 1984
Gimme Shelter, David and Albert Maysles, Charlotte Zwerin, 80 min., 1970
Glass, Bert Hanstra, Holland, 15 min., 1959
Growing up Female: As Six Becomes One, Julia Reichert and Jim Klein, 60 min., 1970
Hablando del punto cubano. See *Talking about Punto Cubano*
Handsworth Songs, John Akomfrah, Black Audio Collective, Great Britain, 52 min., 1986
Happy Mother's Day, Richard Leacock, 30 min., 1963
Hard Metal's Disease, Jon Alpert, Downtown Community TV, 30 min., 1985; with follow-up, 60 min., 1987
Harlan County, U.S.A., Barbara Kopple, 103 min., 1976
Harvest of Shame, Edward R. Murrow, CBS News, 60 min., 1960
Heart of Spain, Herbert Kline and Geza Karpathi, Frontier Films, Spain/United States, 30 min., 1937
He's Like, John Goss, 24 min., 1986
High School, Frederick Wiseman, 75 min., 1968
Un hombre cuanto es un hombre. See *A Man When He Is a Man*
Hospital, Frederick Wiseman, 84 min., 1970
Hotel Terminus: The Life and Times of Klaus Barbie, Marcel Ophuls, France, 267 min., 1988
Housing Problems, Arthur Elton and Edgar Anstey, 17 min., 1935
Hunger in America, Peter Davis, CBS Reports, 40 min., 1969
The Hunters, John Marshall, Kalahari Desert (Namibia, Angola)/United States, 73 min., 1956
Las hurdas. See *Land without Bread*
I Am Somebody, Madeline Anderson, 28 min., 1970
If You Love This Planet, Terri Nash, 26 min., National Film Board of Canada, Canada, 1982
Industrial Britain, Robert Flaherty and John Grierson, Great Britain, 21 min., 1933
In the Year of the Pig, Emile de Antonio, Vietnam/United States, 101 min., 1969
I Was a Ninety Pound Weakling, Wolf Koenig and Georges Dufaux, 28 min., 1959
Jaguar, Jean Rouch, Ghana/France, 110 min., 1971
Jane, D. A. Pennebaker, Richard Leacock, Hope Ryden, George Shuker, Abbot Mils, Time-Life and Drew Associates, 30 min., 1962
Janie's Janie, Geri Ashur and Peter Barton, 25 min., 1971
Joan Does Dynasty, Joan Braderman, Paper Tiger TV, 35 min., 1986
Joe Leahy's Neighbors, Robin Anderson and Bob Connelly, Papua New Guinea/Australia, 90 min., 1988

John F. Kennedy: Years of Lightning, Day of Drums, Bruce Herschensohn, United States Information Agency, 80 min., 1964; U.S. domestic release, 1966

Le joli mai, Chris Marker, France, 124 min., 1962

Journal Inachève. See *Unfinished Diary*

Joyce at Thirty-Four, Joyce Chopra and Claudia Weill, 28 min., 1972

Juki jukite shingun. See *The Emperor's Naked Army Marches On*

Kenya Boran, parts 1 and 2, David MacDougall and James Blue, Faces of Change series, 33 min. each, 1974

The King of Colma, Barry Brann, 26 min., 1988

The Koumiko Mystery, Chris Marker, Japan/France, 47 min., 1965

Kudzu, Marjie Short, 16 min., 1976

Land without Bread (*Terre sans pain* or *Las hurdas*), Luis Buñuel, 27 min., Spain, 1932

Letter from Siberia, Chris Marker, U.S.S.R./France, 60 min., 1957

Let There Be Light, John Huston, 58 min., 1946

The Life and Times of Rosie the Riveter, Connie Field, 60 min., 1980

Lightning over Braddock: A Rust Bowl Fantasy, Tony Bubba, 80 min., 1988

Like a Rose, Sally Barrett-Page, 23 min., 1975

The Lion Hunters, Jean Rouch, Niger and Mali/France, 68 min., 1967

Listen to Britain, Humphrey Jennings, Great Britain, 21 min., 1942

Lodz Ghetto, Kathryn Taverna and Alan Adelson, Poland/United States, 103 min., 1988

Lonely Boy, Roman Kroitir and Wolf Koenig, National Film Board of Canada, 27 min., 1962

Lorang's Way, Turkana Conversations Trilogy, David and Judith MacDougall, Kenya/Australia, 70 min., 1980

Louisiana Story, Robert Flaherty, 77 min., 1948

Love, Women and Flowers (*Amor, mujeres y flores*), Jorge Silva and Marta Rodriguez, Colombia, 54 min., 1988

Las Madres de la Plaza de Mayo, Susana Muñoz and Lourdes Portillo, Argentina/United States, 64 min., 1985

Magical Death, the Yanomamö series, Napoleon Chagnon and Timothy Asch, Venezuela/United States, 28 min., 1974

Les maîtres fous, Jean Rouch, Ghana (Gold Coast)/France, 35 min., 1957

The Making of a Legend: Gone with the Wind, David Hinten, 124 min., 1988

A Man Marked to Die: Twenty Years After (*Cabra marcado para morer: Vinte años depois*), Eduardo Coutinho, Brazil, 120 min., 1985

A Man When He Is a Man (*Un hombre cuanto es un hombre*), Valeria Sarmiento, Costa Rica/France, 60 min., 1985

The Man with a Movie Camera, Dziga Vertov, U.S.S.R., 103 min., 1929

Margaret Mead's New Guinea Journal, Craig Gilbert, NET, 90 min., 1969

Marjoe, Howard Smith and Sarah Kernochan, 88 min., 1972

A Married Couple, Allan King, Canada, 90 min., 1970

Memorandum, Donald Brittain and John Spotton, National Film Board of Canada, Canada, 58 min., 1966

Memorias del subdesarrollo. See *Memories of Underdevelopment*

Memories of Underdevelopment (*Memorias del subdesarrollo*), Tomas Gutierrez Alea, ICAIC, Cuba, 97 min., 1973

A Message from Our Sponsor, Al Razutis, Canada, 9 min., 1979

Microcultural Incidents in Ten Zoos, Raymond Birdwhistle and J. D. Van Vlack, 34 min., 1971

Millhouse: A White Comedy, Emile de Antonio, 93 min., 1971

Model, Frederick Wiseman, 129 min., 1980

Monterey Pop, D. A. Pennebaker, 88 min., 1968

The Most, Gordon Sheppard, United States/Canada, 28 min., 1963

A Movie, Bruce Conner, 12 min., 1958

The Museum and the Fury, Leo Hurwitz, Poland/United States, 60 min., 1956

N!ai: Story of a !Kung Woman, John Marshall, the Odyssey series on PBS, Kalahari Desert (Namibia, Angola)/United States, 58 min., 1980

Naked Spaces: Living is Round, Trinh T. Minh-ha, West Africa/United States, 135 min., 1985

Nanook of the North, Robert Flaherty, 55 min., 1922

Native Land, Leo Hurwitz and Paul Strand, Frontier Films, 88 min., 1942

The Netsilik Eskimo series, Asen Balikci and Guy Mary-Rousseliere, Education Development Corporation and National Film Board of Canada, Canada, 18 episodes, approximately 10 hours total running time, 1967–68

Nicaragua: No Pasarán, David Bradbury, Nicaragua/United States, 74 min., 1984

Night and Fog (Nuit et brouillard), Alain Resnais, Poland/France, 31 min., 1955

Night Mail, Harry Watt and Basil Wright, 30 min., 1936

No Lies, Mitchell Block, 25 min., 1973

Not a Love Story: A Film about Pornography, Bonnie Klein, National Film Board of Canada, Canada, 68 min., 1981

The Nuer, Hilary Harris, George Breidenbach, and Robert Gardner, Ethiopia/United States, 75 min., 1970

Nuit et brouillard. See *Night and Fog.*

Numero Deux, Jean-Luc Godard, France, 88 min., 1975

N/um Tchai, John Marshall, Kalahari Desert (Namibia)/United States, The Bushman series, 20 min., 1966

N.Y., N.Y., Francis Thompson, 15 min., 1957

Obedience, Stanley Milgram, 45 min., 1965

Ocamo Is My Town, Napoleon Chagnon and Timothy Asch, the Yanomamö series, Venezuela/United States, 23 min., 1972 approx.

Off the Pig. See *Black Panther*

Of Great Events and Ordinary People (De grands événements et des gens ordinaires), Raul Ruiz, France, 65 min., 1979

One Man's Fight for Life, Richard Scott and Robert Niemac, 56 min., 1984

Operation Abolition, House Committee on Un-American Activities with Washington Video Productions, 45 min., 1960

Operation Correction, American Civil Liberties Union, 47 min., 1961

Les ordres, Michel Brault, Canada, 107 min., 1974

Our Marilyn, Brenda Longfellow, Canada, 22 min., 1988

Passion of Remembrance, Isaac Julien, Sankofa Film Collective, 82 min., 1986

Patriamada, Tisuka Tamasaki, Brazil, 103 min., 1984

People of the Cumberland, Jay Leyda and Sidney Meyers, Frontier Films, 21 min., 1938

The Plow That Broke the Plains, Pare Lorentz, U.S. Resettlement Administration, 25 min., 1936

Point of Order, Emile de Antonio and Dan Talbot, 97 min., 1963

Por primera vez. See *For the First Time.*

Portrait of Jason, Shirley Clarke, 105 min., 1967

Poto and Cabengo, Jean-Pierre Gorin, 77 min., 1979

Powers of Ten, Charles Eames, 8 min., 1968

Prelude to War, Frank Capra, the Why We Fight series, 54 min., 1942

Primary, D. A. Pennebaker and Richard Leacock, with Terence Macartney-Filgate and Albert Maysles, Drew Associates, 60 min., 1960

Punishment Park, Peter Watkins, United States/Great Britain, 89 min., 1971

Quebec, USA ou L'invasion pacifique, Michel Brault and Claude Jutra, Temps Présent Series, National Film Board of Canada, 27 min., 1962

Les Racquetteurs, Gilles Groulx and Michel Brault, National Film Board of Canada, 15 min., 1958
Rain, Joris Ivens, Holland, 14 min., 1929; with music, 1931
Rape, JoAnn Elam, 35 min., 1975
Rear Window, Alfred Hitchcock, 112 min., 1954
Reassemblage, Trinh T. Minh-ha, Senegal/United States, 40 min., 1982
La région centrale, Michael Snow, Canada, 180 min., 1971
Remedial Reading Comprehension, Owen Land (a.k.a. George Landow), 5 min., 1970
Report, Bruce Conner, 13 min., 1967
Riddles of the Sphinx, Laura Mulvey and Peter Wollen, Great Britain, 92 min., 1977
Roger and Me, Michael Moore, 87 min., 1989
Roses in December, Ana Carringan and Bernard Stone, El Salvador/United States, 56 min., 1982
Rosie the Riveter. See *The Life and Times of Rosie the Riveter*
Rouli-roulant, Claude Jutra, National Film Board of Canada, 30 min., 1966
Sadobabies: Runaways in San Francisco, May Petersen, 30 min., 1988
Sad Song of Yellow Skin, Michael Rubbo, National Film Board of Canada, South Vietnam/Canada, 58 min., 1970
Salesman, Albert and David Maysles and Charlotte Zwerin, 90 min., 1969
Salvador, Oliver Stone, 123 min., 1986
Le sang des bêtes. See *Blood of the Beasts*
Sans Soleil, Chris Marker, France, 100 min., 1982
Scott of the Antarctic, Charles Frend, Great Britain, 110 min., 1948
Seeing Red, Jim Klein and Julia Reichert, 100 min., 1984
Self-Health, San Francisco Women's Health Collective and Lighthouse Films (Catherine Allen, Judy Irola, Allie Light, Joan Musante), 23 min., 1974
The Selling of the Pentagon, Peter Davis, CBS News, 52 min., 1971
Seventeen, Joel DeMott and Jeff Kreines, the Middletown series, Peter Davis, Producer, Public Broadcasting System, 120 min., 1982 (PBS refused to air this episode in the series; First Run Films currently distributes it)
Sherman's March, Ross McElwee, 155 min., 1985
Shoah, Claude Lanzman, Poland/France, part 1, 273 min.; part 2, 290 min., 1985
Showman, Albert and David Maysles, 52 min., 1963
Sixteen in Webster Groves, Arthur Barron, CBS Television Network, 47 min., 1968
Sky, (Uaka), Paula Gaitan, Brazil, 90 min., 1989
Smoke Menace, John Taylor, 14 min., 1937
Soldier Girls, Joan Churchill and Nicholas Broomfield, 87 min., 1980
Solovetsky vlast. See *Solovki Power*
Solovki Power, (Solovetsky vlast), Marina Goldovskaya, U.S.S.R., 90 min., 1988
Some of These Stories Are True, Peter Adair, 27 min., 1982
A Song of Air, Merilee Bennett, Australia, 26 min., 1988
Song of Ceylon, Basil Wright, Ceylon/Great Britain, 40 min., 1934
The Sorrow and the Pity (La chagrin et la pitié), Marcel Ophuls, France 260 min., 1970
Speak Body, Kay Armatage, Canada, 20 min., 1987
Stagecoach, John Ford, 99 min., 1939
Streetwise, Martin Bell, Mary Ellen Mark, and Cheryl McCall, 92 min., 1985
Sundays in Peking, Chris Marker, China/France, 19 min., 1955
Surname Viet Given Name Nam, Trinh T. Minh-ha, 108 min., 1989
Talking about Punto Cubano (Hablando del punto cubano), Octavio Cortázar, ICAIC (Instituto Cubano de Arte e Industria Cinematográficas), Cuba, 40 min., 1972
Terre sans pain. See *Land without Bread*
The Thin Blue Line, Errol Morris, American Playhouse, PBS, 115 min., 1987

The Things I Cannot Change, Tanya Ballantyne, National Film Board of Canada, 58 min., 1966

Three Lives, Kate Millet, 75 min., 1971

Thriller, Sally Potter, Great Britain, 34 min., 1980

Through the Wire, Nina Rosenblum, 85 min., 1989

Thy Kingdom Come, Anthony Thomas, United States/Great Britain, 107 min., 1987

Time Is, Don Levy, 30 min., 1964

The Times of Harvey Milk, Robert Epstein and Richard Schmiechen, 87 min., 1984

Titicut Follies, Frederick Wiseman, 89 min., 1967

Tongues Untied, Marlon Riggs, 45 min., 1989

T,O,U,C,H,I,N,G, Paul Sharits, 12 min., 1968

Touch of Evil, Orson Welles, 108 min., 1958

Tourou et Bitti, Jean Rouch, Niger/France, 8 min., 1971

Trance and Dance in Bali, Gregory Bateson and Margaret Mead, Character Formation in Different Cultures series, Bali/United States, 20 min., 1952

A Trial for Rape, Maria Belmonti, Anna Carini, Rony Daupou, Paola DeMartiis, Annabella Miscuglio, Loredana Rotundo, R.A.I., Italy, 60 min., 1979

Triumph of the Will, Leni Riefenstahl, Germany, 107 min., 1934

Trobriand Cricket: An Ingenious Response to Colonialism, Jerry Leach, Trobriand Islands/Australia, 54 min., 1976

Turkana Conversations trilogy. See *Lorang's Way, A Wife among Wives, The Wedding Camels.*

28 Up, Michael Apted, Great Britain, 133 min., 1984

Uaka. See *Sky*

Underground, Emile de Antonio, 88 min., 1976

Unfinished Diary (Journal inachève), Marilu Mallet, Canada, 55 min., 1983

Union Maids, Jim Klein, Miles Mogulescu, and Julia Reichert, 51 min., 1976

The Universe, Roman Kroitor and Colin Low, National Film Board of Canada, 26 min., 1960

The Unknown Chaplin, parts 1–3, Kevin Bronlow and David Gill, United States/Great Britain, 60 min., each, 1983

Variations on a Cellophane Wrapper, David Rimmer, Canada, 12 min., 1971

Vent d'est (Wind from the East), Jean-Luc Godard, France, 95 min., 1970

Victory at Sea, Henry Salomon and Isaac Kleinerman, NBC Television, 26 30-minute episodes, 1952–53

Waiting for Fidel, Michael Rubbo, National Film Board of Canada, Cuba/Canada, 50 min., 1974

The War Game, Peter Watkins, Great Britain, 45 min., 1966

Watsonville on Strike, Jon Silver, 70 min., 1989

Ways of Seeing, parts 1–4, with John Berger, 4 30-minute episodes, 1974

The Wedding Camels, David and Judith MacDougall, the Turkana Conversations Trilogy, Kenya/Australia, 108 min., 1980

Welfare, Frederick Wiseman, 167 min., 1975

We're Alive, Joint Productions, 50 min., 1975

Wet Earth, Warm People, Michael Rubbo, National Film Board of Canada, Indonesia/Canada, 59 min., 1971

Where the Heart Roams, George Csicery, 50 min., 1989

Who Killed Vincent Chin?, Renee Tajima and Christine Choy, 87 min., 1988

Why Vietnam, U.S. Department of Defense, Vietnam/United States, 32 min., 1965

Why We Fight Series, Frank Capra and Anatole Litvak, U.S. War Dept., 7 films of varying length, 1942–45. See *Battle of China, Prelude to War*

A Wife Among Wives, David and Judith MacDougall, the Turkana Conversations Trilogy, Kenya/Australia, 70 min., 1982

Wind from the East. See *Vent d'est*

Window Water Baby Moving, Stan Brakhage, 12 min., 1959

Wise Guys!, David Hartwell, 25 min., 1984

With Babies and Banners: The Story of the Women's Emergency Brigade, Lorraine Gray, produced with Anne Bohlen and Lynn Goldfard, 45 min., 1977

Witness to War, Deborah Shaffer, El Salvador/United States, 29 min., 1984

The Wobblies, Deborah Shaffer and Stuart Bird, 89 min., 1979

The Woman's Film, The Women's Caucus, San Francisco Newsreel, 40 min., 1971

Woman to Woman, Donna Deitch, 48 min., 1975

The Women's Olamal: The Organization of a Masai Fertility Ceremony, Melissa Llewelyn-Davies, Kenya/Great Britain, BBC 110 min., 1985

Word is Out, Peter Adair, Nancy Adair, Andrew Brown, Robert Epstein, Lucy Massie Phenix, and Veronica Silver (Mariposa Collective), 130 min., 1977

Writing in Water, Stephen Rozell, 24 min., 1984

Yanomamö series. See *Magical Death, Ocamo is my Town, The Ax Fight*

DISTRIBUTORS

The following distributors carry a significant number of documentary films. Some specialize in documentary or even a specific area within documentary. When rights to distribute a film lapse, the film may be placed with another distributor or withdrawn from circulation; some films are available in one country but not another or in one market but not another (educational but not theatrical, theatrical but not video, etc.); some films are carried by more than one distributor; distributors themselves may change their names, move, amalgamate, or go out of business. For these reasons, the following information should be regarded as a starting point in locating a particular title but not as a definitive, up-to-date listing of print source availability.

California Newsreel, 149 Ninth Street, San Francisco, CA 94103 (415) 621-6196.
> Carries some of the classic Newsreel titles such as *Black Panther*, many more recent films on Africa, and both fiction and documentary, such as *James Baldwin, Price of a Ticket.*

Cambridge Documentary, Box 385, Cambridge, MA 02139.
> This distributor specializes in social issue documentary and carries titles such as *Killing Us Softly, Rape Culture*, and *Pink Triangles.*

Canadian Film Distribution Center, Canadian Studies Resources Specialist, Feinberg Library, SUNY at Plattsburgh, Plattsburgh, NY 12901-2697 (518) 564-2396.
> The Center distributes many National Film Board of Canada titles but also other Canadian films such as *Acid Rain: Requiem or Recovery.*

Canyon Cinema, 2325 Third Street, Suite 338, San Francisco, CA 94107 (415) 626-2255.
> Canyon Cinema began as a filmmaker's co-op to distribute the work of West Coast experimental filmmakers. It is still the best source for such work but it also represents filmmakers from around the world. The emphasis is on experimental film but many of these films have a documentary import. Canyon Cinema's list runs from the complete works of Kenneth Anger to early Newsreel titles like *Off the Pig* and *People's Park*, as well as newer work by independent filmmakers.

Churchill Films, 12210 Nebraska Avenue, Los Angeles, CA 90025-9816 (213) 207-6602.
> Churchill is a well-established distributor with a strong documentary library, many directed toward school use. Titles include *Why Vietnam, AIDS*, and films by Jacques Cousteau.

Cinema Guild, 1697 Broadway, Suite 802, New York, NY 10019 (212) 246-5522.
> Carries a wide array of documentaries, particularly films of social change such as *Finally Got the News, The History Book, Miss . . . or Myth*, and *Witness to the Holocaust.* Their collection includes many Latin American titles such as *For the First Time, Hablando del punto cubano, Now, Seventy-nine Springtimes, El Salvador: The People Will Win* and *Brickmakers.*

CineWest, 655 Fourth Avenue, San Diego, CA 92101 (619) 238-0066.
> CineWest has a modest but important list of special issue documentaries dealing with the Americas such as *In the Name of the People* and *Grenada: Portrait of a Revolution.*

DEC Films, 394 Euclid Avenue, Toronto, Ontario, Canada M6G 2S9 (416) 925-9338.
> DEC is a major distributor of Canadian short films and video with particular strength in social issue films such as *Speak Body* and *Our Marilyn*.

Documentary Educational Resources, 101 Morse Street, Watertown, MA 02172 (617) 926-0491.
> DER specializes in ethnographic films. The Yanomamö and Bushman series are represented as well as work such as *First Contact, Joe Leahy's Neighbors*, and the Pittsburgh Police series.

Downtown Community Television Center, 87 Lafayette Street, New York, NY 10013 (212) 966-4510.
> DCTV distributes *Hard Metal's Disease, Housing in America, Invisible Citizens: Japanese-Americans* and other social issue documentaries.

Drift Distribution, 83 Warren Street #5, New York, NY 10007-1057 (212) 766-3713.
> Drift carries independent film and video titles such as *Counterterror, The Amazing Voyage of Gustave Flaubert and Raymond Roussel*, and *Selections for the Lesbian and Gay Experimental Film Festival.*

Em Gee, 6924 Canby Avenue, Suite 103, Reseda, CA 91335 (818) 981-5506.
> Specializes in early cinema and includes some titles of interest such as *Rescued by Rover* and *La jetée.*

Facets Video, 1517 W. Fullerton Avenue, Chicago, IL 60614 (800) 331-6192.
> Facets carries an unusually diverse array of quality films on tape that can be purchased or rented by mail, including documentaries such as *Gates of Heaven*; *Harlan County, U.S.A.*; *Marjoe*; *Louisiana Story*; *Rate It X*; *Shoah*; and *The Battle of San Pietro.*

Fanlight Productions, 47 Halifax Street, Boston, MA 02130 (617) 524-0980.
> Fanlight specializes in medical issues and carries titles such as *Code Gray: Ethical Dilemmas in Nursing*; *I Don't Have to Hide: A Film about Anorexia and Bulimia*, and *Abortion Clinic.*

Film Lending Library, National Library of Australia, Canberra, 2600, A.C.T.
> The Lending Library has an extremely comprehensive collection of films that covers the span of international cinema and includes most of the documentaries discussed in this book.

Filmmakers Library, 124 East 40th Street, New York, NY 10016 (212) 808-4980.
> A very strong selection of documentary titles on topics such as race relations (*Who Killed Vincent Chin?*), women's studies (*India Cabaret, Out in Suburbia*), environment (*Contact: The Yanomami Indians of Brazil*) and AIDS (*AIDS in Africa, This is my Garden*).

First Run/Icarus Films, 153 Waverly Place, 6th Floor, New York, NY 10014 (212) 727-1711 or (800) 876-1710.
> A fairly selective but generally high-quality range of films including a number of important documentaries such as *Making "Do the Right Thing," Celso and Cora, Kim Phuc, Born in Flames, Roses in December*, and *The Man Who Envied Women.*

Flower Films, 10341 San Pablo Avenue, El Cerrito, CA 94530 (415) 525-0942.
> Les Blank's distribution company for all his own films and some others; includes *Garlic Is as Good as Ten Mothers, Burden of Dreams*, etc.

Frameline, 347 Dolores Street, Suite 205, San Francisco, CA 94110 (415) 861-5245.
> Frameline specializes in films and video on gay/lesbian themes. They have titles such as *Mala noche, This Is Not an AIDS Advertisement, Ecce Homo, Tongues Untied*, and *The Days of Greek Gods.*

Ideara Films, 2524 Cypress Street, Vancouver, British Columbia, Canada V6J 3N2 (604) 738-8815.

Carries a very substantial number of documentaries including many on Latin American and other international areas and issues.

Maysles Films, 250 West 54th Street, New York, NY 10019 (212) 582-6050.

They carry the works of the Maysles brothers such as *Salesman, Running Fence,* and *Grey Gardens.*

Movies Unlimited, 6736 Castor Avenue, Philadelphia, PA 19149 (215) 722-8398.

This company sells videotapes of films for the home video market. Its catalogue is enormous and includes documentaries such as the Jacques Cousteau Series, the National Geographic Series, the March of Time Series, *The Thin Blue Line, Heaven, The California Reich, What Sex Am I,* and *The Times of Harvey Milk.*

The Museum of Modern Art, Circulating Film Library, 11 West 53rd Street, New York, NY 10019 (212) 708-9530.

MOMA has a selective repertoire of classic documentary titles including many Lumière films, 1930s British documentaries, National Film Board of Canada films, the Why We Fight series, both Film and Photo League and Frontier Films productions, and the Navajo Film Themselves Series.

National AudioVisual Center, 8700 Edgeworth DF, Capitol Heights, MD 20743 (301) 763-1896.

The center is a clearinghouse for all federal audiovisual materials, including films made under the auspices of government agencies, from *The Plow That Broke the Plains* and the Why We Fight series to *Red Nightmare* and *Why Vietnam.*

National Film Board of Canada (NFB), 3155 Côte de Liesse, Montreal, Quebec, Canada H4N 2N4 (514) 283-9000. In the United States: National Film Board of Canada, Karol Media, 350 N. Pennsylvania Avenue, Box 7600, Wilkes-Barre, PA 18773 (717) 822-8899.

Carries most of the well-known NFB titles such as *City of Gold, Lonely Body,* and *Sad Song of Yellow Skin.*

New Day Films, 853 Broadway, Suite 1210, New York, NY 10003 (212) 477-4604.

New Day is a documentary filmmaker's cooperative with a diverse range of social issue titles such as *Family Gathering, Growing up Female, The Last Pullman Car, Men's Lives, Small Happiness: Women of a Chinese Village, Seeing Red, Quilts in Women's Lives, Union Maids, With Babies and Banners,* and *Style Wars.*

New Dimensions Media, 85895 Lorane Highway, Eugene, OR 97405 (503) 484-7125.

Carries *Radio Bikini* and *AIDS,* among others.

New Time Films, Center for Documentary Media, PO Box 315, Franklin Lakes, NJ 07417 (212) 206-8607.

This company distributes the films of Saul Landau and other titles such as *Hard Times in the Country, El Salvador: Revolution or Death,* and *Portrait of Nelson Mandela.*

New Yorker Films, 16 West 61st Street, New York, NY 10023 (212) 247-6110.

New Yorker distributes a number of important foreign feature films and also documentaries such as *Poto and Cabengo, When the Mountains Tremble, Nicaragua: No Pasarán,* and *Point of Order.*

Paper Tiger Television, 339 Lafayette Street, New York, NY 10012 (212) 420-9045.

Paper Tiger is the maverick of satellite transmission, airing material that community access channels and educational institutions can receive. The programs are also available as video tapes and include the "Read" series (*Herb Schiller Reads the New York Times, Varda Burstyn Reads Playboy,* etc.), and *Joan Does Dynasty.*

PBS Video, 1320 Braddock Place, Alexandria, VA 22314-1698 (800) 424-7963.

PBS carries material produced for the Public Broadcasting System such as *Eyes on the Prize, parts 1–2*; *Bill Moyer's World of Ideas*, and the Frontline series.

Third World Newsreel, 335 West 38th Street, New York, NY 10018 (212) 947-9277.
Carries many of the classic Newsreel titles such as *People's War, Columbia Strike*, etc. as well as more recent work addressing issues for people of color in the United States such as *From Spikes to Spindles* and *Mississippi Delta*. Also carries Black-British work.

University of California Extension Media Center, 2176 Shattuck Avenue, Berkeley, CA 94704.
This Center, like most university media centers, specializes in films that can be used in support of instructional courses of all kinds. Like other centers, there is a generous collection of works that are of specific value in film courses and many titles primarily intended for other courses that are of special interest to the documentarian. Titles held include The Turkana Conversations Trilogy, *Kenya Boran*, parts 1–2; *You Are on Indian Land* (National Film Board of Canada); *Who Are the De Bolts*; *Downwind, Downstream: Threats to the Mountains and Waters of the American West*, and *Before We Knew Nothing*.

Video Out, Satellite Video Exchange Society, 1102 Homer Street, Vancouver, British Columbia, Canada V6B 2X6 (604) 688-4336.
Video Out distributes independent video from around the world with a good range of documentary titles such as *Binge*; *Cuba: The People*; *The Jungle Boy*, and *White Dawn*.

Viewfinders, Box 1665, Evanston, IL 60204.
Viewfinders sells videotapes by mail, including a number of documentary classics such as *Victory at Sea*, *The Sorrow and the Pity*, and *Shoah*.

Women Make Movies, 225 Lafayette Street, New York, NY 10012 (212) 925-0606.
Distributes work by women filmmakers including many important documentaries such as *A Man When He Is a Man, Unfinished Diary, Surname Viet Given Name Nam, Far from Poland, A Song of Ceylon*, and *A Kiss on the Mouth*.

Zipporah Films, One Richdale Avenue, Unit #4, Cambridge, MA 02140 (617) 576-3103.
Zipporah is the distributor for all of Frederick Wiseman's films.

In the United Kingdom:
British Film Institute, 21 Stephen Street, London, England W1P 1PL
The Other Cinema, 79 Wardour Street, London, England W1V 3TH

In Australia:
Ronin Films, P.O. Box 1005 Civic Square, Canberra, A.C.T. 2608, (06) 248-0851
Australian Film Commission, GPO Box 3984, Sydney 2001, (02) 925-7333
AIATSIS Film Unit, Australian Institute of Aboriginal and Torres Straits Islander Studies, GPO Box 553, Canberra A.C.T. 2601, (06) 246-1111
For additional distributors in Great Britain and in other countries, see Peter Cowie, ed., *The Variety International Film Guide*, 34-35 Newman Street, London, England, W1P 3PD or *Kemp's International Film and Television Yearbook*, 1-5 Bath Street, London, England EC1V 9OA.

INDEX

BILL NICHOLS, Professor of Cinema at San Francisco State University, has published extensively on issues in film and contemporary culture. His two-volume anthology *Movies and Methods* helped define the field of film studies. His books *Newsreel: Documentary Filmmaking on the American Left* and *Ideology and the Image* concern issues of documentary film theory and practice.